William Nassau Molesworth

**The History of England from the Year 1830 to 1874**

Vol. 2

William Nassau Molesworth

**The History of England from the Year 1830 to 1874**
*Vol. 2*

ISBN/EAN: 9783337328245

Printed in Europe, USA, Canada, Australia, Japan

Cover: Foto ©ninafisch / pixelio.de

More available books at **www.hansebooks.com**

## From the Right Hon. JOHN BRIGHT'S SPEECH at Birmingham:

"It is a great misfortune that the history of our country that is nearest our own times young men are least acquainted with. It is not written in histories that were read at school, and they are not old enough, as I am old enough, to remember almost every political fact since the great Reform Bill of 1832. I wish young men would read some history of this period. A neighbour and a friend of mine, a most intelligent and accomplished clergyman—Mr. Molesworth—has published a work, being a political history of England from the year 1830—that is, from the first Reform Bill—until within the last two or three years: a book honestly written, in which facts are plainly—and I believe truly—stated, and a work which would give great information to all the young men of the country, if they could be prevailed upon to read it."

# CONTENTS OF VOLUME II.

## CHAPTER I.

### VICTORIA REGINA.

| | PAGE | | PAGE |
|---|---|---|---|
| Introductory and Recapitulary | 1 | The Penny Postage | 32 |
| The Accession of Queen Victoria | 3 | Meeting of Parliament | 34 |
| | | Stockdale v. Hansard | 35 |
| The Speech and Address | 4 | A Compromise | 37 |
| Affairs of Canada | 5 | Farther Legislation | 38 |
| Election Petitions | 10 | The Queen's Marriage | 39 |
| Lord Glenelg | 12 | The Trial of Courvoisier | 40 |
| Slavery | 13 | The Eastern Question | 41 |
| Banquet of the Conservative Party | 14 | The Session of 1841 | 42 |
| | | Irish Registration | 43 |
| The Coronation | 16 | Abortive Measures | 45 |
| Miscellaneous Legislation | 18 | Fixed Duties on Corn, Sugar, and Timber | 46 |
| Complaints against the new Poor-law | 18 | Defeat of the Government | 50 |
| The Courtenay Delusion | 19 | The General Election | 53 |
| The Session of 1839 | 22 | The Result of the Election | 55 |
| The Bedchamber Question | 24 | The Meeting of the new Parliament | 56 |
| Grants for Education | 26 | | |
| The Second Jamaica Bill | 29 | Speeches of Sir R. Peel and Lord J. Russell | 57 |
| Slavery and the Slave-trade | 30 | | |

## CHAPTER II.

### THE INCOME AND PROPERTY TAX.

| | PAGE | | PAGE |
|---|---|---|---|
| Ministerial Announcements | 62 | The Income-tax | 78 |
| Resignation of the Duke of Buckingham | 63 | Its reception | 80 |
| | | The Copyright Question | 81 |
| The Corn-laws | 63 | The Petition of Thomas Carlyle | 82 |
| Fixed Duty or Sliding Scale | 68 | | |
| Incidents of the Debate | 71 | The Employment of Women and Children in Mines and Collieries | 83 |
| Strength of the Protectionist Party | 74 | | |
| The Deficiency | 75 | Corrupt Practices | 85 |

CONTENTS OF VOLUME II.

| | PAGE | | PAGE |
|---|---|---|---|
| Legal Reform | 87 | Lord Ashley's Motion on Education | 99 |
| Attacks on the Queen | 87 | The Government Plan of Education | 101 |
| Disaster in Affghanistan | 88 | | |
| Bravery of General Sale | 93 | | |
| The Pass of Tezeen | 94 | Ireland | 104 |
| The Day of Vengeance | 94 | Visit to the King of the French | 104 |
| March of General Nott | 95 | Visit to Sir R. Peel at Tamworth | 105 |
| Lord Ellenborough's Proclamation | 96 | The Braintree Case | 106 |
| The Commencement of 1843 | 97 | The *Tracts for the Times* | 107 |
| Debate on the Address | 98 | Death of Dr. Arnold | 112 |

## CHAPTER III.

### THE SLIDING SCALE.

| | | | |
|---|---|---|---|
| Opening of the Year 1844 | 113 | Imperial, Royal, and Princely Visits | 142 |
| The War in Scinde | 113 | | |
| The Factory Question | 114 | Other Occurrences of the Year 1844 | 144 |
| Financial Operations of the Government | 116 | | |
| The Budget | 116 | Opening of the Session of 1845, and Resignation of Mr. Gladstone | 145 |
| Speech of Mr. Goulburn | 116 | | |
| Speech of Sir R. Peel | 120 | Financial Reform | 146 |
| The Bank Charter | 123 | Sir R. Peel's Financial Statement | 147 |
| Lady Hewley's Charities | 127 | | |
| Railway Legislation | 130 | Debate on the Budget | 153 |
| Modifications of the Bastardy Clauses of the new Poor-law | 130 | The Sugar Duties | 157 |
| | | Agricultural Distress | 163 |
| The Children of Rebecca | 131 | Free-trade | 166 |
| Opening of Letters at the Post-office | 133 | The Maynooth Bill | 167 |
| | | The Godless Colleges | 170 |
| Monster Meetings in Ireland | 136 | New Zealand | 170 |
| Indictment of O'Connell and his Associates | 137 | The Oregon Question | 171 |
| | | Conclusion of the Session | 172 |
| Appeal to the House of Lords | 137 | The Potato Disease | 174 |
| The Judgment reversed | 139 | Resignation and Resumption of Office by the Ministry | 176 |
| The Tahiti Affair | 141 | | |

## CHAPTER IV.

### THE ANTI-CORN-LAW LEAGUE.

| | | | |
|---|---|---|---|
| Manchester | 178 | More vigorous Efforts | 183 |
| The Anti-corn-law Association | 180 | Recommendations of the Delegates | 185 |
| Mr. Paulton | 182 | | |

## CONTENTS OF VOLUME II.

|  | PAGE |
|---|---|
| The League | 186 |
| Progress | 190 |
| A new Phase of the Agitation | 193 |
| The 100,000*l.* Fund | 194 |
| The League a great Fact | 195 |
| The Register revised | 199 |
| Mr. Cobden advises Free-traders to qualify | 201 |
| Subscriptions to the League | 203 |
| The Potato-rot | 205 |
| Fresh Accessions | 206 |
| The close of the Year 1845 | 206 |
| Death of Sydney Smith | 207 |
| Commencement of the Session of 1846 | 209 |
| Sir R. Peel makes his Recantation | 210 |
| Mr. Disraeli rallies the Protectionists | 215 |
| The Prime Minister explains his Financial Plans | 218 |
| Measures of Compensation to the Landed Interest | 219 |
| The Question of Reciprocity | 220 |
| Mr. Villiers' Amendment | 223 |
| Sir R. Peel's Conduct | 225 |
| The Irish Arms Bill | 226 |
| The Government defeated | 228 |
| Resignation of the Ministry | 229 |
| Formation of a new Cabinet | 231 |
| The Sugar Duties | 232 |
| Distress and Crime in Ireland | 233 |
| Anæsthetics | 234 |
| Secularism | 235 |
| Legislation for Ireland | 237 |
| Finances | 238 |
| Mr. Fielden's Factory Bill | 240 |
| The Educational Vote | 246 |
| O'Connell's last Speech | 247 |
| Dissolution of the Anti-corn-law League | 250 |
| Discovery of the Planet Neptune | 251 |

# CHAPTER V.

### THE PEOPLE'S CHARTER.

|  | PAGE |
|---|---|
| The General Election | 252 |
| The November Session | 253 |
| Baron Rothschild | 255 |
| Opposition to the Appointment of two Bishops | 256 |
| Resumption of the Sittings of Parliament | 259 |
| Financial Statement | 260 |
| Proposed Increase of the Income-tax | 263 |
| The Government yields | 263 |
| Suspension of the Habeas-corpus Act in Ireland | 268 |
| The Encumbered-Estates Bill | 270 |
| Effects of the French Revolution in England | 270 |
| Views of the Radical Party | 271 |
| Chartists | 273 |
| Mr. Duncombe's Amendment and its Results | 274 |
| The Charter formally adopted | 275 |
| Moral and Physical Force Chartists | 277 |
| O'Connor and Stephens | 279 |
| The Sacred Month proposed | 281 |
| Insurrection at Newport | 283 |
| Subsidence and Revival of the Agitation | 286 |
| Cessation of Labour in the Manufacturing Districts | 288 |
| The Land Scheme | 290 |
| Chartism and Free-trade | 291 |
| General Election | 293 |
| The Kennington Common Meeting | 294 |
| Downfall of Chartism | 296 |
| Mr. Hume's Resolution | 297 |
| Precautionary Measures | 303 |
| Diplomatic Relations with the Pope | 303 |

## CONTENTS OF VOLUME II.

|  | PAGE |  | PAGE |
|---|---|---|---|
| The Sanitary Legislation | 306 | Mr. Cobden's Motion for a Reduction of Expenditure | 320 |
| Death of Lord G. Bentinck | 309 | | |
| The Navigation Laws | 311 | The Budget of 1849 | 321 |
| Mr. Disraeli's Resolution | 313 | Various Bills | 322 |
| Irish Legislation | 314 | The State of the Nation | 323 |
| Colonial Questions | 315 | Death of the Queen Dowager | 325 |

# CHAPTER VI.

### THE GREAT EXHIBITION.

| | | | |
|---|---|---|---|
| Agricultural Distress | 326 | Mr. Paxton | 365 |
| Colonial and Irish Questions | 329 | Erection of the Crystal Palace | 366 |
| The Budget of 1850 | 330 | Opening of the Great Exhibition | 367 |
| Proposed Reductions of Official Salaries | 332 | Foundation of Owen's College, Manchester | 369 |
| The Window-tax | 333 | A Reform Bill | 371 |
| The Gorham Case | 333 | Dismissal of Lord Palmerston | 372 |
| The Judicial Committee of the Privy Council | 337 | The Derby Administration | 379 |
| University Reform | 338 | The Aberdeen Administration | 382 |
| The Sunday Delivery of Letters | 341 | Events of 1853 | 383 |
| Sir R. Peel's last Speech | 343 | Death and Funeral of the Duke of Wellington | 385 |
| Death of Sir R. Peel | 345 | | |
| The Papal Aggression | 348 | The Session of 1853 | 386 |
| The Durham Letter | 350 | Mr. Gladstone's Financial Measures | 387 |
| Mr. Disraeli's Resolution | 353 | | |
| Lord J. Russell resigns | 355 | Other Legislation | 392 |
| Lord J. Russell consents to retain Office | 355 | Prosperous Condition of the Country | 393 |
| The Ecclesiastical Titles Bill | 355 | The Eastern Question | 393 |
| Reintroduction of the Budget | 357 | Destruction of the Turkish Fleet at Sinope | 403 |
| Parliamentary Reform | 360 | | |
| Alderman Salomons | 361 | Drifting into War | 404 |
| The Great Exhibition | 363 | | |

# A HISTORY OF ENGLAND,

ETC.

## CHAPTER I.

#### VICTORIA REGINA.

WE now enter on the history of a reign the events of which are equal in importance to those of any that has preceded it, and which has as good a title as any to be denominated the Augustan period of English literature; a reign which has been illustrated not only by the events which it is the more especial business of the historian to record, but also by the poetical genius of Tennyson and Browning; by the historical and other works of Carlyle, Macaulay, and Buckle; by the ingenious and thought-suggestive speculations of Darwin and of the anonymous author of the *Vestiges of Creation;* by the scientific researches of Faraday, Owen, and Huxley; by the geological investigations of Buckland, Murchison, and Lyell; by the romances of Bulwer Lytton, Dickens, and Thackeray; by the invention of the electric and magnetic telegraphs; by works of unsurpassed excellence in science and philosophy, in sculpture, painting, architecture, and music; as well as by important social, political, moral, and religious progress.

The farther I proceed with the work I have undertaken, the more difficult do I find it to avoid being drawn into details which are not likely to be either interesting or instructive to the reader. This difficulty arises from the fact, that in each successive year the history of England becomes more closely identified with the history of the British Parliament, which as it more and more fully reflects the public opinion of the country, also becomes more completely the instrument by which that opinion is carried out. From the passing of the Reform Bill, the history of England is the history of the gradual prevalence of truth and justice by means of free discussion, which that measure rendered more searching, more impartial, more comprehensive, and based on a larger and more accurate knowledge of the facts with which it deals. Thus the existence of a reactionary party in the state, or of some such body as the House of Peers, need not be a subject of unmixed regret even to the most ardent advocate of progress and reform: no, not even when those bodies prove to be, as they sometimes have been, needlessly and unwisely obstructive. For they afford guarantees for the fullest and most jealous examination of every measure submitted to the consideration of the legislature from its central principle to its outermost detail. If they render the march of improvement less rapid, they render it more safe. But these things enormously increase the difficulty of the historian's task, and tend to detract from the interest of his narrative. How far I have succeeded in coping with these difficulties the reader must determine.

In our preceding volume we have seen the great measure of parliamentary reform, introduced by the Whig ministry, and carried by the persistence of Earl Grey, and the determination of the great mass of the people, in spite of the reluctance of the king, and the desperate resistance of a powerful and strongly-entrenched oligarchy. We have seen this popular victory closely followed by such measures of political progress as the Corporation-Reform Bill, by such exhibitions of national virtue as were afforded by the emancipation of the slave, and the shortening of the hours of labour of the factory operative; by such social and economical progress as the new poor-law, the registration act, and the lowering of the stamp-duty on newspapers; by such indications of religious vitality as the proposals for Church reform, and the formation of the Tractarian party; and we have traced a connection more or less distinct between these events and the passing of the great bill. We have now reached a period when the impulse which this important political change had given to every description of progress had, to a certain extent, spent its force, and our attention will be occupied by changes of a less organic and a less striking character. And we shall therefore be able to carry forward our narrative more rapidly, and to pass more lightly over the events of the period on which we are now entering.

William IV. died at two o'clock in the morning of the 20th of June. The Archbishop of Canterbury and the Lord Chamberlain immediately left Windsor for Kensington, where the young Queen was roused from her sleep by them to receive the tidings of her uncle's death, and of her own accession to the throne. The same evening the privy council was assembled at the palace of Kensington to give directions for her proclamation, and to go through the other formalities usual at the commencement of a new reign. The connection between the two kingdoms of England and Hanover, which had subsisted since the accession of George I., was now severed by the succession of a female sovereign to the throne of Great Britain; and the English people witnessed without a struggle and without a sigh the dissolution of a connection, the cost and peril of which greatly outbalanced its advantages. The first signature attached to the act of allegiance that was presented to the Queen, when she mounted the throne of these realms, was that of her eldest surviving uncle, Ernest Duke of Cumberland, King of Hanover.

The Queen, who at this time was only eighteen years of age, read with a dignified composure and a firm voice the declaration which her ministers had prepared. This first public appearance of the new sovereign made a very favourable impression, and she speedily acquired an unbounded popularity. The change in the person of the sovereign was a great advantage for the Melbourne administration; for they had no longer occasion to fear such summary dismissals as they had suffered during the last reign, and they were not likely to encounter from a young queen, who had been taught to regard their principles with favour, that resistance of their recommendations which they had experienced from her predecessor. The Tories were in despair. The old Duke regarded the accession of a female sovereign as a bar to the return of his party to power. 'I,' said he to a friend, 'have no small-talk, and Peel has no manners.' The accession of a new sovereign of course rendered necessary a dissolution of Parliament; and in the general election that ensued, great advantage was taken of the supposed partiality of the Queen for her present advisers by the ministerial candidates. The electors were conjured to support by their votes the friends of the young and popular sovereign, and not to force on her a government that would be unacceptable to her at the very commencement of her reign. These appeals were not without their effect, for there was a very strong disposition to make things pleasant for the new monarch; but notwithstanding the efforts made by ministers and their adherents, and a very free use of the Queen's name, the proportion of the two parties in the House of Commons was not seriously altered by the general election. The Conservatives carried many English counties and some boroughs, which had previously returned Whig or Radical members. But this English Conservative gain was counterbalanced by Irish and Scotch Conservative losses; and the only party which could be said to have decidedly profited by the election was the party that so obediently followed the lead of Mr. O'Connell. The new Parliament met on the 30th of November, and was opened by the Queen in person. The address in reply to the speech was moved by her uncle, the Duke of Sussex, who, with great good taste, avoided all expressions calculated to excite the dissent or wound the susceptibilities of any party. He was seconded by Lord Portman, and supported by the Duke of Wellington, and the address was unanimously adopted in the upper House. The ministry were not so fortunate in their efforts to secure unanimity in the House of Commons. There three amendments, embodying the principles of the radical party, were moved by Mr. Wakley; and the first of these, after long discussion, having been rejected by a majority of 509 to 20, the two others were not pressed to a division. Other amendments were moved by Mr. Harvey, having for their object to bring the hereditary revenues of the crown more directly under the control of Parliament, and to procure a revision of the pension-list. In the course of the debate on these motions, Lord J. Russell distinctly declared his entire dissent from the views and doctrines of the radical party, and his determination to resist their application. Eventually the address, as originally proposed by the government, was adopted by the House.

In spite of the completeness of his defeat on his amendment relating to the pension-list, Mr. Harvey returned to the charge on that question; and eventually the government took it out of his hands, by bringing forward a motion for the appointment of a committee of inquiry into the subject, couched in Mr. Harvey's own words, but with the following proviso attached to them: 'due regard being had to the rights of parties.' A committee of twelve was appointed, but Mr. Harvey himself was excluded from it, because he refused to promise that he would abstain from publishing a report of the proceedings, as he had already done when sitting on the poor-law committee.

The remainder of this preliminary session was taken up with the settlement of the amount of the civil-list, of the payment that should be made to the Duchess of Kent, the Queen's mother, and with other pecuniary arrangements rendered necessary by the demise of the crown. The government had intended to have adjourned Parliament to the 1st of February as soon as the arrangements were completed; but they were compelled to change their plans by the arrival of news from Canada of so serious a nature as to require prompt consideration. It was therefore decided that the vacation should be shortened by a fortnight, and that Parliament should reassemble on the 16th of January.

The intelligence that had caused this change of plan was indeed alarming. The discontent that had long been smouldering in that colony had at length burst forth into open revolt. In Lower Canada, the military, under the command of Sir John Colborne, had received a slight check, but had succeeded in suppressing the insurrection without much difficulty, though serious apprehensions were entertained that it would be followed by another outbreak, aided by a formidable body of marauders from the United States. In the upper province the administration had at this critical moment been intrusted to Major Head, who had been almost dragged from his bed while acting as assistant poor-law commissioner, that he might be sent to govern this great colony, at one of the most important crises of its history. This modern Cincinnatus acted more like a hero of romance or a knight errant than a sober statesman. Knowing that a revolt was impending, his first care was to send every soldier out of the province. He allowed the rebels to make all their preparations without the slightest hindrance. When at length they advanced, he summoned the militia and the loyal inhabitants to his aid. The call was obeyed with enthusiastic unanimity; and with the assistance thus obtained he completely suppressed the insurrection. This spirited way of dealing with the rebellion was highly applauded by many, both at home and in the colony; but in the opinion of the colonial secretary, the success which attended it did not atone for the imprudence of which he considered the governor had been guilty, in sending away the troops on the eve of a revolt, which might very probably have been supported by a large force of United States sympathisers, in which case the result would perhaps have been very calamitous. Farther differences of opinion between Major Head and the home authorities caused him to send in his resignation, which was accepted, much to the regret of the colonists. The services he had rendered were acknowledged by his being raised to a baronetcy; and he was succeeded in the government of Upper Canada by Colonel Arthur, whose administration of the province was more cautious, and more in harmony with the views and traditions of the Colonial Office.

When Parliament reassembled after the Christmas vacation, the attention of its members was directed to those Canadian affairs which had caused them to be called together before their usual time of meeting. It was announced that ministers had resolved to suspend for a time the constitution of Canada, and to send out the Earl of Durham as governor-general of that colony, with extraordinary and dictatorial powers, to remodel its constitution. This announcement was, on the whole, well received. He was a man of a really noble nature, modest, earnest, and courageous, but withal impetuous and irascible. His political opinions were strongly and decidedly liberal, and he was looked to by the radical party as the prime minister of a future administration, which it was hoped would at some no very distant period be called on by the voice of the country to undertake the settlement of these organic changes—such as secret voting, the shortening of the duration of parliaments, the extension of the suffrage, and the other measures which they advocated as the necessary and logical supplements of the Reform Bill. The approval of the appointment was, however, by no means confined to the party to which the earl belonged; there was a general disposition on all hands to make things smooth and pleasant for the man to whom so delicate and important a mission was intrusted. It was felt that this great crisis of imperial interest was not a time for the indulgence of the spirit of party; and the conservatives themselves acknowledged that the known liberality of Lord Durham's views, opposed though they were to their own, would in this instance be of advantage, because it was calculated to propitiate the more moderate portion of the discontented Canadians. It was felt that he would examine the grievances of the Canadians in a fair and candid spirit, and boldly apply the remedies that they appeared to him to require. He was known too to be a man of firmness as well as of liberality; one who would resolutely establish and maintain order, at the same time that he sought to remove the causes of Canadian discontent, and apply the remedies which, after due deliberation, and careful examination made on the spot, he found to be needed. Another circumstance that increased the sympathy felt for him, was the announcement that he did not intend to accept any recompense for his services. Thus Lord Durham carried with him the hopes and earnest good wishes of all reasonable men. Unfortunately these good dispositions did not last long; the spirit of party, which for a moment had slept, revived, and proved too strong for the spirit of patriotism. On his arrival in Canada, Lord Durham felt, as indeed all sensible men felt with him, that he must begin his work by establishing order, as the absolutely indispensable condition of the maintenance of liberty. One of his first acts was to issue a proclamation of amnesty from the Queen, containing, however, certain exceptions. The next was the issue of an ordinance prescribing the manner of disposing of those persons who were excepted from it. Unfortunately in doing this, he acted in a manner that his warmest admirers could not altogether justify, and which afforded his opponents a handle that they were not slow in laying hold of. He seems to have been disappointed at finding that the great and dictatorial powers which he had been led to believe that he would enjoy, had been considerably diminished before the bill which had been intended to confer them had passed through Parliament, and to have chafed under the restraints thus imposed on him. The act prescribed that he should be advised by a council, and that every ordinance he issued should be countersigned by at least five of its members. There was a council of twenty already in existence, nominated by his predecessor Sir J. Colborne, and selected with tolerable impartiality from the representatives of the various parties and nationalities that existed in Canada. This council he replaced by one composed of his secretaries, two of his military secretaries, and the commissary-general, all unacquainted with Canada, and all likely to consent to any measure the governor-general might submit to them. It was evidently a council not intended to advise him, but simply to give legality to his ordinances by complying with the letter of the act of Parliament. This first error was followed by a second still more serious. He found a large number of prisoners confined for offences committed during the late rebellion, and whom Sir J. Colborne had left to be dealt with by him. Some of these were induced to plead guilty, and Lord Durham issued an ordinance by which he transported some of them to Bermuda, and further decreed that if they returned to the province of Canada they should be deemed to be guilty of treason and put to death. This ordinance was duly countersigned by his five councillors. It was illegal, and Lord Durham stated that, when he drew it up, he was aware of its illegality; but that he trusted to the government and the Parliament to shield him from the consequences of a stretch of power which he deemed necessary to the preservation of the integrity of the empire. But he was not aware of the changed state of feeling in Parliament with regard to his mission. Everything connected with it, the character of his secretaries, the expenses he had incurred, the constitution of his council, had all been subject to searching and unfriendly criticisms. In the House of Lords, circumstances were peculiarly unfavourable to Lord Durham. The position of the ministry in that House may be fitly compared to that of a water-logged wreck into which enemies from all sides are pouring their broadsides. They were subject to the constant attacks of two men who were beyond all comparison the ablest debaters in the upper House—Lord Brougham and Lord Lyndhurst. The former of these noble lords especially had become a terrible thorn in the sides of the ministry, and the conservative peers were only too happy to support the fierce attacks he made on his former friends. Notwithstanding his exclusion from the ministry, in 1835 he had warmly supported the government; in 1836 he withdrew from Parliament; but returned to his place in 1837, and continued to support the ministry, though with less warmth. But in 1838 he had become the foremost of their assailants. In the debates on the Canada bill especially he attacked them with great acrimony, and his scalding sarcasm at length so irritated Lord Melbourne, that he made a feeble attempt to grapple with his powerful and provoking assailant. None but those who have seen Lord Brougham in one of his excited moods can picture to their minds the scene that followed. Before Lord Melbourne had finished his remarks, he sprang from his seat. 'I deny,' he exclaimed with that vehement energy that belonged to him, 'I *deny* that I have changed my principles. It is the changed conduct of others that has compelled me to oppose them. Let the ministers retract their declaration against reform delivered the first night of the session, or let them bring forward truly liberal measures, and they will have no more zealous supporter than myself. In the mean time,' he exclaimed, his voice and his wrath still rising as he proceeded, 'I hurl my defiance at the noble lord's head! I repeat it—I hurl at his head this defiance: I defy him to point out any the slightest indication in any one part of my political conduct having, even for one instant, been affected in any manner by feelings of a private or personal nature.' It was not to be expected that Lord Brougham in this mood would be likely to make things pleasant for the government when the ordinance came before the House of Lords. Over and above his general grudge against the ministry, he had a special quarrel with Lord Durham, which had broken out into bitter recriminations at a banquet given to Earl Grey in Scotland, at which the two noble lords were present. After bringing the matter twice before the House, he introduced an Indemnity bill, the terms of which the government disapproved, but which passed the second reading by a majority of eighteen. On the following day, Lord Melbourne announced that the ministers had resolved to advise the Queen to disallow the ordinance. Thus Lord

Durham was obliged to proclaim to the colony that the ordinance he had issued had been condemned by the government that had sent him out. This was the last act of an administration which had raised such lofty expectations, and had commenced with so much pomp and promise. This, then, was the end of those 'great and dictatorial powers,' of those visions of Canadian peace and prosperity in which Lord Durham had indulged. A man of a less irritable temper might naturally have deeply resented such an indignity. He expressed his indignation in a proclamation, which betrayed the mortification which the conduct of his friends and enemies at home had caused him. He quitted his government, and returned to England without waiting for his recall, a broken-hearted and dying man. By the express orders of the government, the honours usually paid to a governor of Canada were withholden from him; but he met with a hearty and sympathetic welcome from great bodies of the people. His place was filled by Sir J. Colborne; but this appointment was only temporary, and Sir John soon made room for Mr. Poulett Thompson, the intimate friend and disciple of the Earl of Durham, whose ideas he adopted, and whose policy he carried out under happier auspices, having for his superior, not Lord Glenelg, who had retired before he entered on his important mission, but Lord J. Russell, who by that time had removed to the Colonial Office, and gave Mr. Thompson, or, as he afterwards became, Lord Sydenham, his cordial and earnest coöperation.

Year by year the system adopted by the House of Commons in dealing with contested elections had been regarded with growing dissatisfaction. At the commencement of this session there were altogether sixty-seven election petitions lodged, and an association had been formed, known as the Spottiswoode Committee, which raised funds and promoted petitions against Irish returns, alleged to have been obtained by mob violence and intimidation. The operations of this committee were of course strongly objected to by all who were interested in maintaining the elections it sought to invalidate. But the most serious ground of complaint was the utter untrustworthiness of the tribunals, composed of members of the House of Commons, before which, in accordance with the provisions of the Grenville act, all these petitions had to be tried. It was found by experience that these committees almost invariably decided in favour of the claimant who belonged to the same party as the majority of its members; so that when the composition of an election committee was once known, it could be predicted with almost unerring certainty what its decision would be. At a public dinner given to Mr. O'Connell on the 21st of February, while most of the petitions were still under investigation, that gentleman, with his usual plainness of speech, denounced the Tory committees of the House as guilty of 'foul perjury.' As we have seen, there was some ground for such a charge, only it was applicable not to one party only, but to all the parties in the House of Commons, that to which Mr. O'Connell himself belonged not at all excepted. Two days after the accusation was made in the terms above mentioned, Lord Maidstone read to the House the report of the speech, and asked Mr. O'Connell whether it was substantially correct.

'Sir,' replied the learned gentleman, 'I did say every word of that, and I do repeat it, and I believe it to be perfectly true. Is there a man who will put his hand upon his heart and say, upon his honour as a gentleman, that he does not believe it to be substantially true? Such a man would be laughed to scorn.'

Three nights later, Lord Maidstone, in accordance with notice given, moved, 'That the expression of Mr. O'Connell's speech, containing charges of foul perjury against members of this House in the discharge of their official duties, is a false and scandalous imputation upon the honour of the House.' This motion, notwithstanding the opposition of ministers, who admitted that a breach of privilege had been committed, but deprecated the notice that it was proposed to take of it, was adopted by the House. It was also subsequently carried, that Mr. O'Connell should be reprimanded by the Speaker for the language he had employed. The rebuke was accordingly administered; but the honourable member, after having quietly listened to it, reasserted the truth of the charge for which he had been reproved; adding that he wished he could find language in which he could express it which would be equally significant but less offensive.

Mr. O'Connell was by no means the only person who openly complained of the unfairness of the election committees. A Mr. Poulter, who had been elected a representative of the borough of Shaftesbury, was unseated on a petition. Believing that he had been unfairly treated, he gave vent to his disappointment and indignation in a letter to his constituents, in which he stigmatised the decision of the committee before which the petition had been tried as 'flagrant and wicked;' adding that the ignorance of its members was only second to their corruption, and declaring that the seat had been as completely filched from him as ever a purse was from a person on the common highway. These denunciations of the committee were brought under the notice of the House by Mr. Blackstone, who had served on it; and Mr. Poulter was summoned to the bar of the House, and required to retract the offensive expressions he had applied to its members. Thereupon he said that he did not impute to them pecuniary or base corruption, but that he nevertheless regarded the seat as having been taken from him on political grounds alone. This explanation did not satisfy Mr. Blackstone; and on a division, it was carried by a majority of two only that Mr. Poulter should be censured. On another division it was resolved that the censure should be deferred for a week; and then the matter was allowed to drop altogether. These incidents, however, served to draw general attention to the very unsatisfactory constitution of election committees, and caused public opinion to demand such a reform of them as would procure more respect for them, and greater confidence in their decisions. Mr. O'Connell, Sir R. Peel, Mr. Slaney, and others, offered suggestions and proposed plans for their improvement; but for the present nothing was effected.

Loud complaints were made at this time of the colonial administration of Lord Glenelg. He was a man of amiable disposition and studious habits, but it was generally believed that his heart was not in his official work, and that the interests of the colonies, and especially of Canada, as well as those of the mother country, had suffered through his supineness. This opinion was very strongly held by Sir W. Molesworth, who had paid great attention to colonial affairs, and had arrived at conclusions with regard to their administration very different from those of Lord Glenelg. He accordingly proposed a vote of censure against him. The ministers, on the other hand, announced that they would regard such a vote as a condemnation of the whole government, and that if it should be carried, it would draw after it the resignation not of Lord Glenelg only, but also of all his colleagues. An amendment to Sir W. Molesworth's motion was moved by Lord Sandon, attributing the present condition of Canada to the want of foresight and energy on the part of the government, and to the ambiguous and irresolute course of her majesty's ministers.

This amendment being accepted by the mover of the original resolution, was substituted for it, but was rejected by a majority of twenty-nine. However, it was generally felt and acknowledged that Lord Glenelg had not successfully administered his department, and he soon after retired.

The decision of Parliament to purchase from the West-Indian planters the freedom of their slaves at the enormous price of 20,000,000*l.* had by no' means put an end to the questions relating to slavery. The abominable traffic was still carried on in Africa, in spite of great efforts which had been made by our government to put a stop to it by sending out cruisers to seize the ships employed in it. Nay, the attempts that were made to suppress it had actually increased the horrors with which it was attended. The unhappy Africans were packed together in the hold of the slave-ship, and were not only chained, but absolutely soldered and rivetted together in iron bands, so that they could not be separated till the ship in which they were imprisoned reached its destination. If the slaver was pursued by one of the British cruisers, numbers of these unfortunate victims were cast overboard, in order to lighten the vessel and give her a better chance of escaping her pursuer. In one case no fewer than five hundred negroes had been thrown into the sea from a slaver chased by a British ship. Nor was this the only slavery question which demanded and obtained attention during this session of Parliament. In some of our West-Indian possessions, the law by which the slaves had been emancipated was openly violated by many of the planters, who, under pretext of the apprenticeship permitted by the Emancipation

Act, kept the negroes still in a state of virtual slavery, often inflicting on them the most humiliating punishments, the most cruel tortures, and sometimes even putting them to death. The whole question, as it related to the African slave-trade and to the cruelties practised towards the negroes in the West Indies, was brought under the notice of the House of Peers by Lord Brougham. He denounced the horrors of the slave-trade with characteristic vehemence, and proposed some improvements in the regulations which had been made for its suppression, calculated to alleviate the sufferings to which the unhappy negroes were exposed. He also denounced the system of apprenticeship, of which he had been one of the chief authors, and by insisting on which he had caused Lord Howick's withdrawal from the ministry; but which now, after the experience he had of the manner in which it was abused, he candidly admitted to be a failure, and loudly demanded its discontinuance. This question of apprenticeship was also taken up by Sir G. Strickland; but the efforts he made to abolish it were opposed by the government, on the ground that the labour of the slaves during the period of apprenticeship formed a part of the compensation made to the masters by the Emancipation Act.

A banquet given to Sir R. Peel by the conservative members of the House of Commons was an event the political significance of which entitles it to a place in the history of this period. The invitation was signed by no fewer than 313 members of the lower House, and more than 300 were actually present at it. It afforded, as it was designed to do, the leader of the opposition an opportunity of explaining and defending his policy, not only before the assembly that had come together to do him honour, but also before the whole nation. It was very necessary to him to have some such means of appealing to his party and to the public opinion of the country; for he found himself occupying a position in which every leader of the conservative party is sure eventually to be placed, and which required all his great tact and skill to enable him to maintain. The difficulty arises from that which always has been, and always must be, the composition of what we may call the party of resistance to inevitable and indispensable change. There was a portion of that party which, like himself, felt the necessity of moderate reform, and, in fact, differed very little in opinion from the more moderate reformers. There were others, again, who, while they did not desire, but, on the contrary, deprecated farther reform, felt that concessions must be made to the spirit of the age, and supported Sir R. Peel because they thought that he would yield to it just as much as, and no more than, could not be withheld without danger. And lastly, there were the old-fashioned Tories, men who could not be made to perceive that any change whatever was required; who regarded Sir R. Peel with dislike and suspicion, but who, feeling that there was no choice for them but between him and the Whigs, preferred to support him rather than fall into the hands of Lord J. Russell. They would, indeed, have very much preferred to place themselves under the command of Sir R. Vyvian, or some other man whose sentiments and opinions were more in accordance with their own; and every now and then, when strongly dissatisfied with their leader, they seriously thought of doing so; but their numerical weakness, and the utter hopelessness of their being able to stand alone, compelled them to fall into the conservative army, of which they were a large and important division.

To this large and influential assemblage of his followers Sir Robert could boast that he had created a conservative party; that on the first dissolution, in 1835, when he was at the head of the government of the country, the conservative numbers were suddenly swollen from about 150 to more than double that number; that on the nomination of Speaker 306 members; that when a dissolution took place in the course of last year with every circumstance calculated to be favourable to those in power; the accession of a youthful and beloved Queen: producing one universal feeling of personal loyalty and attachment towards the sovereign ascending the throne with everything to prepossess in her favour; with a lavish use of her majesty's name for the purpose of influencing the elections; still, the result of the general election exhibited their numbers unbroken; for as they had voted 306, having had all the advantages of a dissolution during the tenure of government, the names attached to the invitation of this day, comprised 313 members of the House of Commons.

Sir Robert felt the necessity of restraining the impatience of his supporters to overthrow the present government without destroying their hopes of a speedy resumption of office. He therefore reminded his more impatient friends that they were a conservative opposition, adopting the principles which used to be said to prevail in an administration, performing many of its functions; and that they could not in conformity with their opinions, take that latitude of action which might befit an opposition which professed to think the ancient institutions of the country a grievance; and to consider English society as a mass of abuse.

He reminded them of the influence they had exercised over the government of the country, by enabling ministers to resist the attempts made by their own friends and supporters to exclude the bishops from the House of Lords, to repeal the customs duties, and to introduce the ballot— questions on which the government would have been in a minority, if the conservative party had not come to the rescue. He concluded by entreating his followers to persevere in the same course of action by which, though they rescued the present ministry from temporary embarrassments, they established for themselves new claims on public approbation.

The Queen was crowned on the 28th of June. This event awakened a feeling very different from the cold and languid indifference with which the two preceding coronations had been regarded. It was said that the people were 'coronation mad,' and this phrase conveys a scarcely-exaggerated idea of the feelings of the time. Some previous coronations had surpassed it, if not in good taste, at least in gorgeousness and lavish expenditure. The coronation of Victoria cost the nation 20,000*l.* more than that of William IV., but 173,000*l.* less than that of his magnificent predecessor. But on no previous occasion had there been so great a throng of foreign princes and ambassadors, such a display of splendid equipages, and, what was much more important, such a manifestation of national enthusiasm and loyalty. For the first time since the reign of Charles the Second, there was a public procession through some of the streets of the metropolis, thus affording to a large mass of the people an opportunity of being witnesses of the pageant, which for nearly two centuries had been reserved for a select few. Never before had London been so thronged. Besides the inhabitants, more than 400,000 visitors had flocked to the metropolis from all parts of the empire, as well as from foreign countries, to avail themselves of the opportunity afforded them of witnessing the procession. This gratification of the eyes of the multitude was cheaply purchased by the sacrifice of the banquet usually given to the sovereign in Westminster Hall. But the suppression of this part of the customary ceremonial gave no small offence to many loyal and many interested persons, who found a suitable mouthpiece for the utterance of their complaints in our old friend the Marquis of Londonderry. The general opinion, however, was that it was just and politic to afford a spectacle which could be contemplated by hundreds of thousands at the cost of a banquet which could only be enjoyed by a select few, and which would add considerably to the expense, while it greatly prolonged the duration, of the ceremony. In almost every other respect, the coronation resembled that of William the Fourth. The spectators of this procession must have been nearly half a million. Of this vast multitude, all appeared to be animated by one spirit. Not a discordant note was heard amidst the acclamations which were lavished on the Queen and on the principal personages who accompanied or followed her. Never was the spirit of loyalty more heartily or fervently displayed. At every advantageous spot from which the procession could be seen, galleries had been erected, which were thronged with spectators. Throughout the whole line the balconies, the windows, and the housetops were all crowded, and in many cases the windows had been taken out of the houses in order to afford those inside them a better view of the spectacle. The loudest acclamations were, of course, bestowed on the young Queen; acclamations scarcely less loud greeted the Duke of Wellington. Six years ago he had been the most unpopular man in the kingdom. Now he was the most popular. With the exception of these two, the personage who received the most enthusiastic greetings was Marshal Soult, the Duke of Dalmatia, the brave and skilful antagonist of Wellington in the Peninsula, but now sent as ambassador extraordinary to represent the French government and people at the coronation of Queen Victoria. The hearty welcome given to him was, no doubt, intended not only as a tribute to his personal character, but also as an expression of cordiality to the nation which he represented at the solemnity. This enthusiastic reception of the veteran warrior made a most favourable impression on the French people, and tended more than anything else that had occurred since the peace to efface the remembrance and the resentment of past defeats.

In the meantime Irish tithes, Irish corporation reform, Irish poor-laws, and other Irish questions, were occupying their usual disproportionately large share of the attention of the legislature. The poor-law was carried; the other measures had to wait for a more favourable consideration.

Several important legal reforms were adopted in the course of this year. As the business of the quarter sessions was rapidly increasing, and the responsibility of their chairmen was rendered more onerous, on account of the alteration in the law which allowed counsel to be heard for the defendant in cases of felony, it was enacted that sessions should be held every six weeks instead of quarterly, and that in future the chair should be filled by a barrister, who would receive a salary for his services. Imprisonment for debt was abolished in certain cases, and the process for the recovery of debt was simplified and rendered more effectual. Improvements were also introduced into the laws relating to the recovery of tenements from a tenant at will. A bill to allow a mother access to her children, notwithstanding the prohibition of the father, was carried through the House of Commons by Serjeant Talfourd, but, though warmly supported by the Lord Chancellor and Lord Lyndhurst, it was lost in the Upper House.

The winter of 1837-8 had been one of great and unusual severity, producing a reduplication of complaints of the hardships of the new poor-law, and of proposals for its modification. Whenever these complaints came to be closely investigated, it was found that there had been great exaggeration; and, on the other hand, when the proposed remedies were properly examined, it became evident that, so far from tending to improve the condition of the industrious labourer, they were rather calculated to make it worse. Such, for instance, was the proposal to check the emigration of labourers from the agricultural to the manufacturing districts; a practice that clearly tended to equalise wages throughout the country, and to improve the condition both of those who remained in the agricultural districts and those who found employment and higher remuneration in the manufacturing districts. In fact, the main agents in the agitation were farmers who wanted cheap labour, and idle vagabonds who did not want to labour at all, and looked back with deep regret to the time when they were maintained in luxurious indolence by the industry of others, instead of being compelled to support themselves by their own labour. A few facts were brought forward which placed in a very clear light the real character of the agitators and of those on whose behalf the agitation was carried on. In one instance it was shown that labourers who had been hired to clear away the snow refused to do so because a subscription had been raised for their relief; in another, that balls—fancy balls—masquerade balls—were not only attended, but given by some of those paupers for whom it was sought to obtain public sympathy, or by members of their families.

In the course of this year there occurred an instance of popular delusion which deserves to be recorded as a very remarkable moral and intellectual phenomenon. Shortly before the general election of 1835, an extraordinary stranger took up his abode at Canterbury. He first descended at the Fountain, the principal inn, but afterwards removed to the Rose, situated in the middle of the high-street, and nearly in the centre of the city. He was a man of lofty stature and imposing appearance. He wore a long flowing beard, at a time when all Englishmen were accustomed to shave off that natural appendage. He was arrayed in a magnificent uniform of crimson velvet bordered with gold, and wore a handsome sword by his side. The appearance of this personage in the quiet old city of Canterbury of course attracted much attention, especially when, mounting the balcony of the Rose, he addressed the crowds who assembled to hear him, in fluent, vehement, but not very intelligible harangues. Not content with thus introducing himself to the good people of Canterbury, he issued placards composed in the same style as his speeches; and at length published, in a penny paper which he called the *Lion*, statements of his political views and opinions, which, so far as they were intelligible, were evidently of an exceedingly violent character. These documents bore the signature of 'Sir William Courtenay, of Powderham Castle, Knight of Malta, King of Jerusalem, King of the Gipsies,' &c. There were then only two candidates in the field for the representation of Canterbury—the Honourable Mr. Watson and Lord Fordwich, both of whom were supporters of the Whig ministry; and they would have been returned without opposition, if the former of these gentlemen had not, in an evil hour for himself and his colleague, given vent to the exultation he felt at having escaped a contest, and indulged in some severe remarks on his political opponents, whom he described as weak in intellect and contemptible in numbers. This imprudent attack stung some of the hotter sort of Conservatives to the quick, and they determined to be revenged. In this mood they bethought them of the eccentric and extraordinary stranger who was creating such a sensation in their city. Though his political opinions were evidently entirely at variance with their own, they waited on him, and invited him to come forward as a candidate for the representation of their city. This invitation he most readily accepted, and entered into the contest with great alacrity. He addressed crowded meetings in all parts of the city, flourishing his drawn sword in his hand as he spoke. The ultra-tory mob and the ultra-radical mob coalesced in support of this extraordinary candidate. The majority of the inhabitants of the city were decidedly with him, though the majority of the electors were against him. The Whig mayor and corporation, besieged in the Guildhall by the friends and supporters of the popular candidate, were compelled to send to Dover for a troop of soldiers to protect them and the supporters of the ministerial candidates.

It is true that Sir William had no chance of success; but he polled a much larger number of votes than might have been expected, and completely fulfilled the wishes of those who had invited him to come forward, by causing the successful candidates great trouble, expense, and anxiety. His popularity, however, was by no means impaired, but, on the contrary, rather heightened by the failure of his attempt to get into Parliament. Portraits of him in different attitudes and at different prices were published. His likeness was stamped on pocket-handkerchiefs and painted on tea-trays. The vendors of lollipops profited by his popularity, and exhibited 'Courtenay balls' for sale in their shop windows. Nor were his followers exclusively of the lower orders. He rode about in his magnificent crimson velvet uniform, attended by two gentlemen of education and respectability, who had attached themselves to him, and were proud to be his aides-de-camp. A clergyman of mature age, resident in Canterbury, broke his tendo-achillis, and lamed himself for life, by indulging in the unwonted exercise of dancing at a ball given in honour of the Knight of Malta. Sir William attended all kinds of public meetings, patronised all sorts of performances, and insisted on addressing every assembly at which he was present. Nor did he confine himself to Canterbury, but visited also the neighbouring towns, and gave them the benefit of his opinion on all kinds of subjects and on all occasions. At Deal he introduced himself into a meeting of the corporation of that town, and, as usual, insisted on addressing the assembly. In the course of his rambling and incoherent speech, he said, that if any man dared to deny the doctrine of the Trinity—a doctrine he was very fond of asserting—he would inflict personal chastisement on him. Thereupon a sturdy and stalwart Unitarian, who happened to be present, exclaimed, that he for one denied it. Sir William seized him by the nose, and wrung it with such violence, that he nearly tore it from the face of the unfortunate follower of Socinus. At length it began to be whispered that the hero of these feats was not what he represented himself to be—that instead of being the Lord of Powderham Castle and the King of Jerusalem, he was an insolvent brewer of the name of Thom. These unromantic disclosures, though readily believed by the more intelligent portion of the Canterbury community, were regarded as blasphemous fables by his ignorant and besotted partisans; nor would they be convinced even when their hero was confined in a lunatic asylum. During his incarceration there, he wrote letters to his admirers from his 'retreat at Barning Heath,' which were duly published in the Canterbury papers of the time. After he had been confined for some months, his father, who believed him to be harmless, obtained his liberation from Lord J. Russell, through the intervention of Sir Hussey Vyvian. He returned at once to the scene of his former popularity; but, alas, he came back greatly changed. His beard had been shaven off, and instead of appearing in his splendid uniform, he came dressed as a dusty miller. His appearance in this guise broke the charm and dispelled the illusion of his Canterbury followers. But he still exercised an extraordinary fascination over the ignorant peasantry outside. He persuaded them that he was a second Messiah, and promised them the plunder of the city of Canterbury, against which he offered to lead them. A constable named Mears, who attempted to oppose these proceedings, was shot dead by Thom. Two companies of soldiers stationed at Canterbury marched out to put down the insurrection. They met Courtenay and his followers at a distance of about seven miles from Canterbury. Lieutenant Bennett, who commanded the party, stepped forward to parley with the rioters. Thom came out to meet him, and shot him dead with a pistol. He and the peasants who followed him then charged the soldiers, who, not anticipating any resistance, were unprepared for the conflict, and had not loaded their muskets. An officer who was present, and had served in the Indian wars, said that he had never seen a more violent charge than was made by these Kentish peasants. The first troop was broken, and would have been put to flight, but the other company had loaded, and poured in a volley on the assailants, which stretched Thom himself and several of his followers dead on the field of battle. The rest fled. Several were apprehended, tried for murder, convicted, and sentenced to be executed; but, in consideration of the delusion to which they had been a prey, the sentence was not carried into effect.

In the session of 1839 the affairs of Ireland once more engrossed an exorbitant portion of the time and attention of the legislature. Indeed, the condition of that country was such as to render it imperative on the legislature to attempt some means of alleviating its moral and social evils. Nothing contributed more to strengthen the feeling in favour of strong intervention than the assassination of

Lord Norbury, in open day, and on his own grounds, in which he was walking with his steward, when he was mortally wounded by a shot fired by an unseen hand. Mr. O'Connell, in order to turn away from his own supporters the infamy of this odious crime, broadly insinuated, with his usual recklessness, that the assassin of Lord Norbury was his own son; an accusation which rested on no other foundation than the alleged fact, that the print of the murderer's foot, which had been found near the spot at which his victim fell, showed that he did not wear the brogue of the Irish peasant, but a fashionable Dublin boot. But how this asserted fact, even if true, supported the frightful insinuation founded on it, did not appear. The utmost that could be inferred from it was, that the assassin of Lord Norbury was a person of higher position than that of a peasant, but of course could not show that he was the son of the murdered man. This foul crime excited a strong feeling of indignation on both sides of the Channel, which was intensified by the amiable character of the murdered nobleman, and found a vent in motions and debates, producing no effect, but occupying much valuable time.

The Queen was able to make the gratifying announcement, that throughout the whole of her West-Indian possessions, the period which the law had fixed for the complete emancipation of the slaves had been anticipated by acts of the colonial legislatures, and that the transition from the temporary system of apprenticeship to entire freedom had been effected without any disturbance of the public order and tranquillity. This result, however, had not been attained in Jamaica without a certain amount of pressure having been brought to bear by the home government on the legislature of that island, in consequence of the severities which the planters had exercised against the negroes. The assembly, after making this concession, became so contumacious, that the home government found or thought it necessary to suspend the constitution of the island for five years, at the end of which time a constitution was to be promulgated, adapted to the altered circumstances in which the abolition of slavery had placed the colony. The bill introduced into Parliament to carry out this intention was opposed, not only by Sir R. Peel and the Conservative opposition, but also by Mr. Hume and several other members of the Radical party, who, though they usually supported ministers, resisted an act which they regarded as a gross injustice and a flagrant violation of liberal principles. The consequence was, that the second reading of the Jamaica bill was carried in a very full house by a majority of only five, making it evident to the government that they would not be able to carry the measure through its farther stages, or to pass the somewhat similar measure that they thought it necessary to apply to Canada. They therefore resolved to resign office; and her majesty, by the advice of Lord Melbourne, sent for the Duke of Wellington, and on his recommendation intrusted to Sir R. Peel the task of forming a new administration, mentioning at the same time that she regretted that she had been forced to part with her late ministers, who had always given her perfect satisfaction. Notwithstanding this somewhat discouraging intimation, Sir Robert undertook the task confided to him, and delivered to her majesty a list of the principal members of his intended ministry; but in doing this he thought it necessary to require, as a public evidence of the Queen's confidence, the dismissal of certain ladies related to members of the late ministry, and holding high appointments in the Queen's household. On her majesty's refusal to consent to these changes, Sir Robert abandoned the attempt to construct a ministry, and Lord Melbourne and his colleagues determined that they would retain their offices, thus making themselves responsible for the Queen's refusal to comply with Sir R. Peel's demands. This affair produced a great deal of controversy, not only in Parliament, but throughout the country. The determination of the government was vehemently assailed by their opponents, and by none more vehemently than by Lord Brougham, who taunted the ministers with having lost the confidence of the House of Commons, with never having possessed that of the House of Lords, although they had not lost the confidence of the sovereign. 'But how,' asked the ex-chancellor—'how is it that that confidence seemed of so much more value on Monday the 14th of May than on Monday the 7th of May?'

'I thought,' he proceeded, 'that we belonged to a country in which the government by the crown and the wisdom of Parliament was everything, and the personal feelings of the sovereign absolutely not to be named at the same time; to be, of course, most respectfully venerated, but never to be allowed to interfere with the sober judgment of Parliament, to countervail the highest interest of the state. That is the language of the constitution. I little thought, in this advanced period of our history, to be obliged to argue this question with Whigs, the descendants of the ministers who, because they would not subscribe to this creed, refused to be ministers in 1812. I little thought to have lived to hear it said by the Whigs of 1839, " Let us rally round the Queen; never mind the House of Commons; never mind measures; throw principles to the dogs; leave pledges unredeemed; but, for God's sake, rally round the throne." Little did I think the day would come when I should hear such language, not from the unconstitutional, place-hunting, king-loving Tories, who thought the public was made for the king, not the king for the public, but from the Whigs themselves. The Jamaica bill, said to be a most important measure, has been brought forward. The government staked their existence upon it. They were not able to carry it; they therefore conceived that they had lost the confidence of the House of Commons. They thought it a measure of paramount necessity then. Is it less necessary now? O, but that is altered. The Jamaica question is to be new-fashioned, principles are to be given up, and all because of two ladies of the bedchamber.'

It cannot be denied that there was no little justice in the vehement invective of the ex-chancellor. The ministry were guilty of manifest inconsistency in resuming office after they had distinctly admitted that they had lost the confidence of the legislature, and were unable to carry measures of the highest importance, and essential, in their opinion, to the well-being of the empire. Yet, in spite of those avowals, they decided that they would retain office; and the loyal sympathy with which the young Queen was regarded caused the nation to view with indulgence a determination which at other times, and under other circumstances, would have been very damaging to those who adopted it. However, in justice to the ministers, it should be remembered, that if the Melbourne government was weak, the administration framed by Sir Robert Peel would probably have been still weaker. And putting aside altogether the bedchamber question, it is difficult to see why a government which felt that its majority was not sufficiently large should make way for a government with no majority at all, and the head of which had explicitly declared that he did not intend, at least for some time to come, to appeal to the nation. Had he gone in at this time, he would probably have been compelled by an adverse vote to resign, in the same manner as he had been when he took office before. So that, though the conduct of the government certainly laid them open to that charge of inconsistency with Whig principles that Lord Brougham so forcibly urged against them, good rather than evil resulted from the determination to which they came to remain in office. But it would have been much better for them if they had never resigned. They incurred ridicule more damaging than graver censures by sheltering themselves behind the petticoats of the ladies-in-waiting; and the shout of derision which was raised against them was soon after changed into a feeling of a more damaging character when the death of Lady Flora Hastings was supposed to have been hastened by unjust suspicions which were entertained respecting her by some of the ladies of the court. No real blame attached to any one in the matter; but the event served as a handle against the government, of which many of its opponents availed themselves without scruple and with no little success.

We have already mentioned, that in the year 1833 a grant of 20,000$l$. had been made for educational purposes. This grant had been voted annually ever since, and was dispensed by the lords of the treasury to the National Society and the British and Foreign School Society in aid of their educational operations. But as the amount of aid was proportioned to the size and cost of the school-buildings and to the number of scholars attending them, by far the larger portion of the grant went to the Church, and this gave rise to a good deal of murmuring and discontent. It was now proposed to increase the amount of the grant to 30,000$l$., and to transfer the dispensation of this sum to a committee composed of the president of the privy council and not more than five of its members. It was also enacted that this committee should establish a normal school for the training of masters; that they should appoint inspectors to visit the schools aided by the privy council and report on their condition. They were also empowered to depart from the principle of proportioning their grants to the amount of contribution raised locally, that they might establish in poor and populous neighbourhoods schools not necessarily connected with either of the two great educational societies. They were also allowed to extend their assistance to schools in which the Roman Catholic version of the Scriptures was read.

This arrangement, which has lately been so much extolled by Conservatives and churchmen, was met, when proposed to the House of Commons, with the most strenuous Church and Conservative opposition, and the whole country was strongly agitated against it. The scheme was objected to on various grounds. It was a violation of the privileges of the House of Lords, and was denounced as a device similar to that of *tacking* to a money-bill. A loud anti-popery outcry was raised against the proposed application of public money to aid schools in which the Douay Bible was used. But the feature of the plan which excited the greatest storm of objection and vituperation was that which sanctioned the inspection of schools, and especially the inspection of the religious instruction given in them; a part of the plan which every dispassionate man must see to be most reasonable, inasmuch as it was the evident duty of the dispensers of the public funds to take care that they were applied with some tolerable fidelity to the purposes for which they were granted. But the managers of schools at that time did not consider this; they suffered themselves to be persuaded that the proposed inspection would be attended with all kinds of interference in the management of the schools, and especially in the religious instruction imparted in them. The effect of the agitation that was raised, and of the prejudices and errors that prevailed on the subject, was very considerable, and it appeared in the division on the question which took place in the House of Commons. The increased grant made on the above-mentioned conditions was carried by a majority of two only; there being 275 in favour of it, and 273 against it. But notwithstanding the smallness of the majority, and in spite of an address to the Queen from the House of Lords strongly deprecating the proposed application of the public money, the plan was carried into effect by the government; and the committee of council was constituted, composed of the president of the council and five members of the government, by which the education of the country has been ever since superintended. This system, which the conservative party encountered with such determined opposition at the time of its introduction, has since found favour in the eyes of that party, and we have lived to see it fondly clinging to that denominational system and that government inspection which is so strongly denounced, and from the introduction of which it predicted the most direful disasters. Of all the long speeches that were delivered on this occasion, there is only one that we think it desirable to rescue from oblivion, and that not so much on account of the spirit of eloquent earnestness it breathed, as because of the beautiful plea for a just toleration which it put forth. We refer to the very remarkable speech of Mr. Sheil.

'Why,' he asked, addressing himself to the conservative opposition—' why are you for ever crying out, in reference to popery, that your church is in danger, and giving way to the most fantastic fears? What in the world makes you so much afraid? Your church is incorporated with the state, supported by the interests of the higher orders and by the faith of the humbler classes. " It lifts its mitred head amidst courts and parliaments;" it possesses vast revenues; it rules over the two most famous universities of the world; it presides over the great patrician seminaries of the land; it has retained all the pomp, pride, and glorious circumstance of the establishment, of which it is a perpetuation—archbishops, bishops, deans, cathedrals, golden stalls. It is distinguished by a prelacy eminent for learning, and a clergy distinguished for energy, activity, and an organised spirit of confederacy. Such is your establishment. And can you bring yourself to believe that such a fabric, based on the national belief and towering amongst aristocratic sustainment, can be prostrated on the rock of truth on which you believe it to be raised, not by foreign invasion, not by intestine commotion, not by great moral concussion, but by a discharge of Douay Testaments and popish missals from the hands of a set of shoeless, shirtless popish paupers, gathered, under the command of the privy council, from the lanes of Liverpool, the alleys of Manchester and Salford, or the receptacles of St. Giles? This ague of apprehension for your church is idle, and would be ridiculous but for the fatal results it produces, and the constant injustice it works.

'I have heard much, in the course of this discussion, of the dogmas of theology. I do not profess to be conversant with them; but I sometimes read my Bible, in every page of which lessons of mercy are so admirably inculcated; and it strikes me, if there be a passage in which the character of our Saviour is described in a peculiarly amiable light, it is that in which he is represented as desiring his disciples not to forbid little children to come to him; and I cannot help thinking, that if among that little group on whose heads he was invoked to lay his hands, there had been the child of a Sadducee or a Samaritan, the God of mercy and of love would not have put the little schismatic aside. Do not imitate the example of those by whom the children were rebuked. Suffer them to approach him; let them have access to the sources of pure morality, and of that truth which is common to all Christians. Do not close the avenues of that knowledge which leads to happiness when "time shall be no more;" and instead of engaging in acrimonious contention about ecclesiastical prerogatives and pretensions, act on the precept contained in the divine injunction, " Suffer the little children to come unto me, and forbid them not; for of such is the kingdom of heaven."'

As the government had gone out of office on the avowed ground of the necessity that existed for dealing with the affairs of Jamaica in a manner distasteful to the majority of the house, it now became a question of great importance to determine what should be done with regard to this matter. To bring in again the bill which had caused them to retire was only to expose themselves to a fresh defeat, which consistency would require to be followed by a second resignation. A new bill was therefore framed, which, it was hoped, would not provoke the combination of parties by which the previous measure had been defeated. The chief feature by which this second bill was distinguished from the first, was a proviso, directing that the assembly should once more be called together, and allowed a farther opportunity of adopting the measures to which the government attached so much importance. If they neglected to avail themselves of the opportunity thus given them, the governor was to be empowered to suspend their sittings, and to legislate without their concurrence. The opposition denounced this new bill as worse than the last. Sir R. Peel strenuously opposed it; but it was passed in the House of Commons by a majority of ten. The course which the conservative minority in the lower house had contended for was adopted by the conservative majority in the upper house, Lord Brougham leading the opposition with his accustomed vigour and eloquence. When the bill came back again to the lower house, Lord J. Russell moved that the amendments made in it by the Lords should be accepted, on the ground that it was better that the bill should go out in the form into which the Lords' amendments had brought it than that it should not go out at all.

This was not the only attempt that ministers made to promote the freedom of the negro. They also laboured hard to induce the Portuguese government to second the efforts made by Great Britain on the coast of Africa to put down the slave-trade, and even went so far as to cancel a debt of 600,000*l.* due from that government, on an express stipulation that it would cease from countenancing the abominable traffic. Hitherto, however, the Portuguese government had eluded the performance of the engagements into which they had entered. A bill brought forward by the government empowering them to deal with the matter was strongly opposed by the Duke of Wellington, and rejected by a small majority. But a motion was proposed by Lord Brougham for an address to the crown, 'praying her majesty, by all the means in her majesty's power, to negotiate with the governments of foreign nations, as well in America as in Europe, for their concurrence in effectually putting down the traffic in slaves; and also that her majesty will be graciously pleased to give such orders to her majesty's cruisers as may be most efficacious in stopping the said traffic, more especially that carried on under the Portuguese and Brazilian flag, or by Portuguese and Brazilian ships; assuring her majesty that this house will cheerfully concur with the other house of Parliament in whatever means may be rendered necessary, if her majesty shall be graciously pleased to comply with this prayer.'

The Duke of Wellington seems to have supposed that this motion implied an approval of the course recommended in the bill which had been recently rejected, and of which he had so strongly disapproved. But his objections were removed by the assurances and explanations afforded by Lord Brougham. The address was then unanimously adopted by the house; and the Queen in her reply, transmitted through the Duke of Argyll, assured the house that she would direct orders to be given to her cruisers in accordance with their wishes.

Afterwards another bill, founded on the bill which had been rejected by the House of Lords, but modified in a manner calculated to obviate the objections which had been urged against it by the Duke of Wellington and others, was brought into the House of Commons by the government. It passed through all its stages in the lower house, and was strongly supported in the House of Lords by the ministry and by Lord Brougham. But in spite of the modifications which had been introduced by the Commons, and notwithstanding some amendments made by the Lords, with a view to remove the objections which had been made against it, the Duke of Wellington still vigorously opposed it, protesting against it, and denouncing what he termed its criminal character; declaring it to be a breach of the law of nations, a violation of international treaties, and a measure rather calculated to promote than to prevent the infamous traffic against which its enactments were levelled. In spite, however, of this strong condemnation of the bill, in spite of the great influence which the Duke at this time exercised over the opinions and votes of the peers, the feeling against the slave-trade proved too strong to be resisted even by his great authority. It passed the Lords on the 20th of August, and the Lords' amendments having been accepted by the Commons, it received the royal assent.

The budget of this year was brought forward at the unusually late period of the 5th of July. Its most noticeable and interesting feature was the bold adoption by the chancellor of the exchequer of a new and uniform system of postage, the immediate effect of which must necessarily be a great loss of revenue; and this with a deficit already amounting to a million and a half. Up to this time the rates of postage on letters were very heavy, and varied according to the distance. For instance, a single letter conveyed from one part of a town to another cost 2*d*.; a letter from Reading to London, 7*d*.; from Brighton, 8*d*.; from Aberdeen, 1*s*. 3½*d*.; from Belfast, 1*s*. 4*d*. If the letter was written on more than a single sheet, the rate of postage was much higher. Early in 1837 a pamphlet was published by Mr. Rowland Hill, in which he showed that the actual cost of the conveyance of letters through the post was very trifling, and very little increased by the distance over which they had to be conveyed; and advocated with great ingenuity and a strong array of facts the substitution of one uniform postage of a penny the half-ounce, in place of the heavy and various rates of postage that then prevailed. It happened that a commission was engaged in inquiring into the management of the post-office department at the very time that his pamphlet appeared. They had indeed concluded their investigations relative to the general post, and had entered on the investigation of the twopenny post, when their attention was drawn to Mr. Hill's plan; and they determined to give it a careful consideration. The post-office authorities expressed an unfavourable opinion of the scheme, basing their objections to it on the loss of revenue, which they thought its adoption would involve. However, in spite of their dissent, the commissioners reported in favour of the plan. The attention thus gained for it, both in Parliament and throughout the country, produced a strong admiration of the boldness and excellence of Mr. Hill's ideas. When Parliament assembled in November, 1837, Mr. Wallace, a zealous advocate of the proposed scheme, obtained a committee 'to inquire into the present rates and mode of charging postage, with a view to such reduction thereof as may be made without injury to the revenue; and for this purpose to examine especially the mode recommended for charging and collecting postage in the pamphlet of Mr. Hill.' This committee, notwithstanding the strongly-expressed contrary opinion of the postmaster-general, and the greater part of the post-office officials examined by them, recommended uniform charges, and prepayment by stamps. They also expressed an opinion that the revenue would not ultimately suffer from this great change; but, as they considered themselves bound by the terms of the vote under which they were appointed to recommend a plan which would not involve even a temporary loss of revenue, they recommended that for the present a uniform rate of twopence on the half-ounce should be adopted. In 1838 and 1839 numerous and numerously-signed petitions were presented in favour of Mr. Hill's plan; and the government, greatly to its honour, notwithstanding the large deficiency that already existed, courageously resolved to adopt it, and to substitute a uniform postage and prepayment by stamps for the various rates of postage that then prevailed; a noble example to the world, and one that has been followed by every civilised state. They also abolished, except in the case of official letters on government business, the system of *franking*, or sending letters free through the post, which had hitherto been enjoyed by members of parliament to a limited, and by members of the government to an unlimited, extent. The House of Commons, by a solemn resolution, pledged itself to provide for any deficit in the revenue which this measure might produce. The proposal met with strong opposition from various quarters. The officials of the post-office, almost to a man, were hostile to it. Even the enlightened Sydney Smith stigmatised it as the 'nonsensical penny-postage scheme.' In the lower house it was strongly condemned, chiefly on financial grounds, by Sir R. Peel and Mr. Goulburn; but it passed, notwithstanding their objections. When the measure came before the upper house, the Duke of Wellington said that there was not one clause in the bill on which they could make an amendment or give a vote, except in the affirmative or negative, without committing a breach of those conventional rules which had been established for the conduct of business between them and the House of Commons. He therefore announced that, notwithstanding the strong objections he entertained against the scheme, he should feel himself obliged to vote for the bill; and he entreated the House to pass the measure, because it was one that was most anxiously expected by the country. The peers, followed this prudent recommendation; and thus another great change, then regarded by eminent statesmen as very rash and hazardous, but now acknowledged by all men to be fraught with moral, intellectual, and physical advantage to the community, was adopted by the legislature, and was soon after brought into operation. For a few weeks the postage was maintained at fourpence, in order to prevent the servants of the post-office from being overwhelmed by a sudden and enormous increase in the number of letters. Then it was reduced to a penny.

During the winter very severe distress prevailed throughout the kingdom; and the Chartist agitation, which rose and fell with the increase or diminution of the people's sufferings, was now in one of its most eruptive conditions, spreading consternation everywhere, and aggravating the distress by which its flame was fanned. We will not enter at present into the details of this agitation, reserving them for a part of this work in which we propose to trace the rise, progress, and decline of Chartism.

In consequence of this state of things, Parliament assembled under somewhat gloomy auspices. The Queen, in the speech with which she opened the session, made a formal announcement of the fact, already well known, that a marriage had been arranged between herself and Prince Albert of Saxe-Gotha. In the debate on the address in answer to this speech, the Duke of Wellington proposed the insertion into it of the word 'Protestant' before prince; and this suggestion was warmly supported by Lord Winchelsea, somewhat contemptuously treated by Lord Brougham, and assented to by Lord Melbourne. In the Commons, the first question was that of the allowance to be made to the prince on his marriage with the Queen. The government proposed that the amount of it should be 50,000$l.$, Mr. Hume 21,000$l.$, and Colonel Sibthorp 30,000$l.$ The last-mentioned proposition was supported by the leaders of the conservative party, except Sir R. Inglis, who earnestly advocated the more generous vote proposed by the government; but in the disordered state of the finances, and the distressed condition of the country, most men thought it better to adopt the more moderate allowance of 30,000$l.$; and that sum was accordingly voted by a large majority.

The Stockdale case not only occupied a large share of the attention of the House of Commons, but threatened to bring it into direct collision with the Court of Queen's Bench.

Messrs. Hansard, the printers of the House of Commons, having been condemned at Stockdale's suit for a libel contained in papers printed under its orders, and as Stockdale persisted in bringing action after action against the Hansards, they appealed to the house for protection from penalties incurred in carrying out its orders. The sheriffs, who had managed to delay the payment of the damages awarded to Stockdale till the commencement of the parliamentary session, were summoned for the 17th before the Court of Queen's Bench, to show cause why they had not paid them. On the 16th the House of Commons took into consideration the petition of Messrs. Hansard, presented by Lord J. Russell, who strongly insisted that the house was bound in honour, as well as by a regard for its own privileges, to support its printers, who had acted under its authority in the publication of the alleged libel. In this view of the matter he was supported not only by the leading members of his own party, but also by Sir R. Peel, Lord Stanley, and Sir J. Graham. Week after week, long weary discussions on this question of privilege were carried on. The attorney-general supported the view of his leader; but the great majority of the lawyers of the house, including the solicitor-general, Mr. Pemberton, Sir E. Sugden, and Sir W. Follett, took the opposite view of the question, and contended that the privilege of the house could not protect a libel, even though published under its authority. Stockdale, Stockdale's attorney, the sheriffs of London, and several other persons who were concerned, either in bringing the action or carrying out the sentence of the Court of Queen's Bench, were brought to the bar of the house. The sheriffs pleaded that they were acting under the authority of the court, and in accordance with the oath they had taken to it. But, in spite of this plea, they were incarcerated; and, on suing out a writ of habeas corpus, were sent back to prison, the serjeant-at-arms, in whose custody they had been placed, having declared that they had been committed for breach of privilege on an order of the House of Commons. Subsequently one of the sheriffs was released by order of the house, his medical attendant having certified that his life would be endangered by a more prolonged confinement. An application to obtain the release of his colleague on the same grounds was rejected by the house. Meanwhile

Stockdale continued to bring fresh actions; and actions were also brought by other parties against Messrs. Hansard on similar grounds. The position of the House of Commons became every day more and more embarrassing. It was evident that public opinion strongly condemned its proceedings. The sheriffs, when summoned to attend at the bar of the house, were enthusiastically cheered throughout their whole progress; and when they were brought up on a writ of habeas corpus, the reception given them by the citizens of London was equally enthusiastic. There can be little doubt that the majority of the House of Commons were right in asserting a privilege indispensable to the due performance of the functions of that assembly. It was necessary that they should have the power of publishing to the country the evidence taken on questions of general importance, and thus furnishing the public with the means of forming a sound opinion with regard to them. Sir R. Peel put this necessity in a very clear light, when he asked the members of the house, 'Do you believe that slavery would have been abolished unless we had published to the world the evidence of the abuses and horrors of slavery?' But if this power was necessary to the house, it was equally necessary that it should have the power of protecting those employed by it to publish its proceedings from vexatious prosecutions and ruinous damages. The privilege would have been of no use, if it could have been rendered inoperative through the impossibility of finding agents who would incur the responsibility to which the publication of the proceedings would expose them. If, therefore, the house did not enjoy the powers claimed for it, clearly it ought to possess them. But the clumsy and antiquated methods of enforcing the privileges of the house by reprimands and incarcerations of persons who were only fulfilling duties the law imposed on them, and observing oaths they had taken in obedience to its requirements, were not suited to the spirit of the age, and placed the house in a very unfortunate and undignified position. It was therefore felt and acknowledged by the strongest assertors of the privileges of the House of Commons that other methods must be resorted to. Accordingly Lord J. Russell, acting on suggestions thrown out by several members, brought in, with the concurrence and approval Sir of R. Peel, a declaratory bill, which was carried through both Houses of Parliament with a few amendments, and thus at length put an end to this troublesome and undignified contest, by which nothing could be gained, and a great deal of valuable time was wasted.

The evident and increasing weakness of the government induced their opponents to endeavour to turn them out of office by a direct vote of want of confidence. The motion for that object was proposed by Sir J. Y. Buller, seconded by our inadvertent friend Alderman Thompson, and after a very long debate was rejected by a majority of twenty-one; but another motion, brought forward by Sir J. Graham, condemning their policy towards China, was only defeated by a majority of nine. It was evident, however, that the conservative party was gaining strength, while their adversaries were every day becoming weaker; and it seemed more than probable that they would be speedily placed in a minority on some question which would render their resignation unavoidable; so that their removal from power, and the accession of Sir Robert Peel to it, appeared to be only a question of a very short time. Under such circumstances it was useless for the Whigs to continue to press the policy of the appropriation clause. They felt that in bringing forward that question in the then existing state of public feeling and opinion they had made a great mistake, which had tended perhaps more than anything else to place them in the position of weakness in which they now found themselves. On the other hand, the conservatives were anxious that a reform of the Irish corporations, which they felt could not be much longer resisted, should be carried; and thus both parties and their leaders had come to an understanding, dictated by their common interests, that a settlement of the tithe question and of the Irish corporation question should be effected by mutual concession. In accordance with this understanding the long-delayed measure of Irish municipal reform was carried through both houses, encountering many protests, but no serious opposition. In vain did stout-hearted Sir Robert Inglis denounce it as a heavy blow and great discouragement to Protestantism; in vain did the Bishop of Exeter loudly proclaim the surprise and disappointment with which he viewed the conduct of his friends in withdrawing their opposition to a measure which he deemed to be fraught with danger to the cause of Protestantism in England as well as in Ireland. His eloquent predictions of the terrible disasters which would follow from such a dereliction of principle were unheeded; and the bill, so long held in suspense, was at last allowed to pass.

A registration of voters (Ireland) bill, proposed by Lord Stanley, met with determined opposition from the ministerial party and the followers of Mr. O'Connell. The latter strongly denounced it, and gave it a factious and unscrupulous opposition. Nevertheless it was carried forward through the second reading; and in the committee, on no fewer than nine divisions, there was only one division in which a majority voted against any part of the plan. But the Fabian tactics of Mr. O'Connell prevailed, and Lord Stanley withdrew the measure; finding that in five days only five out of forty clauses which the bill contained had been passed, and knowing that it was impossible that it should be carried through during the present session. He, however, pledged himself to bring it forward again at an early period of the following session. Four other bills relating to the question of Irish registration were withdrawn by the government, on account of the lateness of the session. The same fate, and for the same reason, overtook Serjeant Talfourd's copyright bill, and Mr. Ewart's for the abolition of the punishment of death.

The financial statement of the chancellor of the exchequer, if not altogether satisfactory, was at least reassuring. Notwithstanding the great reduction of the post-office revenue, consequent on the introduction of the new penny-post system, the deficiency for the year ending April 5th, 1840, only exceeded that of the preceding year by 273*l*., which the chancellor proposed to meet by increasing the assessed taxes ten per cent.; the customs and excise, with some exceptions, five per cent.; and the duty on spirits by fourpence the gallon. These proposals were adopted.

It will be remembered by the reader that the bill which embodied the recommendations of the ecclesiastical commissioners relative to the cathedral chapters had been withdrawn by the government, from want of time to carry it. It now went through both houses with very little opposition. A bill having been passed appointing Prince Albert to be regent in case of the death of the Queen, the session was closed by her majesty in person on the 11th of August. On the 10th of February the Queen's marriage with Prince Albert was celebrated with all fitting pomp and splendour. The venerable Archbishop of Canterbury officiated with that placid and paternal dignity that was natural to him. All remarked with pleasure the clear and firm voice and modest bearing with which the Queen took the part in the service which the Book of Common Prayer assigned to her.

The credit of having brought about this marriage was mainly due to Lord Melbourne, and there can be no doubt that he deserved well of his country for the part he had taken in promoting it. It would have been impossible to have found any one who would have better discharged his duties as a husband and a father, would have more diligently devoted himself to the peculiar and delicate functions which devolved on him as consort of the Queen of England, or would have kept more completely and conscientiously within the lines of the British constitution than Prince Albert. But, notwithstanding the admirable manner in which he discharged all the duties of his exalted position, he perhaps never enjoyed during his lifetime that popularity and consideration to which he was fairly entitled. The insular prejudices against foreigners prevented his conduct from being duly appreciated; and many of the nobility and the upper classes regarded him with disfavour when they found that he preferred the society of men eminent for their attainments in science and literature to that of dukes and marquises.

On the 10th of June an insane potboy named Oxford attempted to assassinate the Queen by discharging two pistols at her, as she was driving out with Prince Albert, according to her frequent practice, unattended by any escort. The Queen and Prince Albert displayed great coolness and presence of mind. It was never ascertained, except by the untrustworthy admission of Oxford himself, whether the pistols were charged with bullets or not. On the twenty-first day of the following November her majesty gave birth to her eldest child—the present Crown Princess of Prussia.

Chartism, which we have already mentioned as being rife at the commencement of this year, and of which we shall have more to say hereafter, was very rampant during a great part of it, creating disturbances of a very serious character at Newport, Birmingham, London, and several other large towns, and exciting terrors out of all proportion to their real importance.

We must not pass without notice the trial and conviction of François Benjamin Courvoisier, valet of Lord William Russell, for the murder of his master. This trial deserves attention, not so much on account of the rank of the victim as of the peculiar code of the morality of the members of the legal profession which it brought to light. Courvoisier was defended by Mr. Charles Phillips, an advocate of high reputation, great ability, and extraordinary eloquence. Throughout his address to the jury Mr. Phillips spoke in terms which implied a strong conviction of Courvoisier's innocence, and concluded it with the following animated and impassioned appeal: 'Mine has been a painful and an awful task; but still more awful is your responsibility. To violate the living temple that the Lord has made, to quench the fire that his breath has given, is an awful, a tremendous responsibility. The word once gone forth is irrevocable. Speak not that word lightly. Speak it not on suspicion, however strong; on moral conviction, however cogent; on inference, doubt, or anything but a clear, irresistible, bright, noonday certainty. I speak to you in no spirit of hostile admonition—Heaven knows I do not. I speak to you in the spirit of a friend and a fellow Christian, and in that spirit I tell you, that if you pronounce that word lightly, the memory of it will never die within you. It will accompany you in your walks; it will follow you in your solitary retirement like a shadow; it will haunt you in your sleep, and hover round your bed; it will take the shape of an accusing spirit, and confront and condemn you before the judgment-seat of your God. Beware, then, how you act.'

The advocate who addressed to the jury this solemn adjuration knew, while he was delivering it, that the prisoner whom he defended was guilty of the crime of which he was accused, and had consulted some of the highest legal authorities in the kingdom as to the course he ought to take under such circumstances, and, acting on their opinion of an advocate's duty as well as his own, pronounced the words we have just cited! But the moral sense of the nation was revolted by this professional view of the duty of an advocate to his client; and Mr. Phillips, notwithstanding his amiable character and shining abilities, never recovered the estimation he had lost by adopting in this instance the course which his advisers had sanctioned. Courvoisier was found guilty, and made a second and very full confession of his crime and of the circumstances that suggested and accompanied it.

In the course of this year the Eastern question seemed likely to give rise to very serious complications. The Pasha of Egypt not only rejected the authority of his sovereign the Sultan, but endeavoured to persuade the other pashas of the Ottoman empire to join him in his revolt. He also attempted to make himself master of Syria, and in all probability would have completely succeeded, if foreign intervention had not defeated his designs. Everything at first seemed to favour the attempt of the rebellious pasha. He overran the country without difficulty, crushed all opposition, and governed it as it had never been governed before since the days of Soliman, bringing out its material resources, and making all the improvements that a wise and enlightened statesmanship could have suggested. The sultan, unable to subdue his rebellious vassal, had recourse to England, to France, to his old enemy Russia, which was supposed, not without good reason, to cherish the design of assuming a protectorate over Turkey, with a view to its ultimate absorption within the vast dominions of the czar. England and France, though opposed to the ambitious designs which were imputed to the Russian government with regard to Turkey, were yet unable to agree between themselves. While the English government acted on her traditionary policy of supporting the sultan, that of France seemed rather inclined to ally itself with the pasha, or, at all events, to preserve a dubious and menacing neutrality. However, as the other powers acted in concert for the maintenance of the integrity and independence of the Ottoman empire, France did not venture to interfere. The combined fleets attacked the strongly fortified town of Acre, which they speedily captured, and thus defeated the designs of the Egyptian pasha. He might have maintained his conquest against all the forces the sultan could send against him; he could not maintain it against such a combination of powerful and civilised states as that by which the sultan was supported; and so the Ottoman monarch was enabled to continue to misgovern and oppress some of the finest and most fertile provinces on the face of the globe. In France the conduct of the allies was regarded with so much dissatisfaction, that it was at one time feared that the French fleet would take part in the contest against them; and though this apprehension was not fulfilled, yet the feeling continued to rankle for some years, after producing a coolness in the intercourse between the two countries and their respective governments. The English people troubled themselves little about a contest with the merits of which most of them were imperfectly acquainted, or about a country so far removed from them; but they appreciated the skill of their commanders and the gallantry of their seamen displayed in the capture of Acre, and the speedy suppression of the Egyptian rebellion. There was a general feeling of admiration of the manner in which the negotiations had been managed by the foreign secretary, Lord Palmerston; and the popularity he thus acquired virtually extended itself to his colleagues, and helped for a moment to mitigate the feeling of disapprobation with which the legislative shortcomings of the ministry were generally regarded.

On the whole, therefore, the year 1841 opened auspiciously for the government. Abroad victory had crowned their arms, and success had attended their diplomacy. The objects for which they had contended might not be very desirable, but at all events they had been attained, and this was all that the great mass of the English people cared to know about the matter. The agricultural, manufacturing, and commercial interests were all prospering, and peace and contentment seemed everywhere to prevail. It was therefore seen with little disappointment that the Queen's speech of this year was more barren in promises of those progressive reforms which the opinion of the country demanded even than the royal speeches of previous years had been. The Whig government had evidently made up its mind to 'rest and be thankful;' and its chief was too busy in attendance at the court, and too much engrossed with its amusements, to be able, even if he had been willing, to assist in framing any great measures for the consideration of Parliament. It was evident that the government was now resting on the favour of the Queen rather than on the support of the House of Commons and the people; and though such a state of things would soon be brought to an end in a period of political earnestness, it seemed likely to endure for some time longer in a period of political apathy. The ministry was indeed almost sure to be defeated and compelled to resign, if it brought forward great and important measures; but it might avoid that danger by political inaction. Lord Brougham in the upper House, and Messrs. Grote and Hume in the lower, referred to the omission of all mention of France in the Queen's speech, and censured the manner in which that power had been treated by our government during the late complications: but no serious opposition was offered to the address in reply to the speech from the throne.

Lord Stanley lost no time in fulfilling the promise he had given, when he withdrew his registration bill at the end of the last session, and on the very first day of this session he gave notice that it was his intention again to press his plan on the attention of Parliament. Lord Morpeth also announced that the government intended to deal with the question in a bill of their own, which would include a definition of the qualification of the franchise, the want of which was one of the strongest objections that had been made to Lord Stanley's plan in the debates on it which had taken place during the last session. The discussion on the second reading of this measure was carried on for four successive nights, and terminated in a division which gave ministers a majority of five; a majority clearly insufficient to enable them to carry it through committee, much less to lead them to hope that it would pass the upper House. Lord J. Russell, however, put a good face on the matter, and at once announced that he should move the committal of the bill on the following Monday; but when that day arrived, he stated, amidst the loud laughter of the opposition, that he saw no objection to a trifling delay, which would enable him to place before the House more positive information; and he therefore moved the postponement of the committal of his bill over the Easter holidays, to the 23rd of April. Lord Stanley then postponed the second reading of his bill till the 11th of March; and on that day he gave notice of a farther postponement to the 28th of April. The course taken by ministers was generally regarded as an expedient to get rid of Lord Stanley's bill; and this accusation was strongly urged both by the conservative and repeal newspapers. But the tone of these latter was quickly changed when it was found that ministers were strenuously supported in the course they had determined to take by Mr. O'Connell. The bill not only provided a remedy for the present state of the registration laws, which all men admitted to be vicious, and which opened the door to every species of fraud, but it also lowered the franchise to 5*l*. It was manifest that this provision of the bill would greatly increase the number of Roman Catholic voters, and thus augment the following and the power of the great agitator, which the measure of Lord Stanley tended to diminish. O'Connell therefore wrote a letter to the Repeal Association of Ireland, exhorting its members to support the bill of Lord Morpeth, and to oppose with all their might that of Lord Stanley, the title of which he declared to be 'as false as the black heart of its inventor.' The Irish repeal press at once took its cue from this letter, and agitated strongly in favour of the ministerial measure, and against that of Lord Stanley. On the 23rd April Lord Morpeth announced that the government had determined to raise the rating qualification proposed in their bill from 5*l*. to 8*l*. When the first clause came under the consideration of the committee, Lord Howick moved an amendment, which was carried by a majority of twenty-one. The government, after taking time to consider the course they would adopt, decided to accept the amendment; but after a good deal of parliamentary manoeuvring, with the details of which it is not necessary to trouble the reader, they found themselves in a minority of eleven; and Lord J. Russell then withdrew the bill. This ministerial defeat on the most important question of the session was decisive of the question itself. If Lord Morpeth had not succeeded in carrying his bill, he had at least succeeded in rendering it impossible for Lord Stanley to carry his. It was too late to allow any hope of its passing; and therefore a reform, the necessity of which was admitted on all hands, was once more relegated to another session. The manner in which ministers had dealt with this matter seriously damaged them, and increased the number of defections from their ranks. Their position was one of immense difficulty and embarrassment. The exceeding smallness of their majority enabled the Lords to deal with the measures that came up to them in a way they would not have ventured to do, if the government had enjoyed the confidence of a large majority of the House of Commons, or had been supported by the public opinion of the country.

It must not, however, be supposed that these ministerial defeats were entirely due to the weakness of the liberal party. There were many votes of this session which strongly testified its real predominance. Thus the Jews' disabilities bill, introduced again, and perhaps affording as good a test as could be found of the strength of the liberal feeling that existed in the House, was read a second time by a majority of 113, and carried through the lower House, only to be once more rejected by the Lords. We pass by the non-intrusion question, of immense importance to the Scottish nation, and exercising a great influence over the history of Scotland, but not seriously affecting the course of events in this country; the affairs of Canada, now united into one dominion, and becoming gradually tranquillised; the Maynooth grant; the church-rate question, which emerged for a moment, and was soon sucked under again by the whirlpool of party struggles; the abortive attempts of the attorney-general and Sir E. Sugden to effect a reform of the Court of Chancery. One beneficial measure, however, was promoted by the ministers and carried through this session. They took out of the hands of Mr. Fitzroy Kelly a bill for the abolition of capital punishment in certain cases. Considering that the measure went too far, they brought in a bill of their own on the same subject, which was carried, and had the effect of substituting the punishment of transportation for life in the place of the penalty of death in those cases of forgery, embezzlement, and rape, which up to this time had been punished capitally.

The government made one bold effort to recover the ground it had lost, and to draw to itself once more the sympathies of the great body of the nation. If their general measures were little calculated to excite the enthusiasm of the country, this could not be said with regard to their financial plans. The statement of Mr. Baring, the chancellor of the exchequer, which had been promised for the 31st of April, was looked for with more than usual interest. It was generally expected that the budget of this year would be based on some great financial reforms, on which the government intended to make its appeal to the country. The anxiety was increased and the expectation confirmed when Lord J. Russell announced that he intended to move on the 31st of May the following resolution: 'That the House should resolve itself into a committee of the whole House, to consider the act of parliament relating to the trade in corn.' From this it was evident that the government had resolved to make the question of the corn-laws the working question of the coming election, and to stake their political existence on the alterations they had determined to make in them. The question of the corn-laws was indeed forcing itself more and more strongly every year on the attention of the government. Various circumstances had contributed to make their pressure to be more deeply felt. There had been a great increase of population; a succession of bad harvests had occurred; Russia, Sweden, America, and France, had adopted retaliatory tariffs. Scarcity thus produced had engendered discontent, which manifested itself in Chartist outbreaks and other violences. There were, too, at this particular moment special reasons in favour of a reconsideration of the corn-laws, with a view to some relaxation of their stringency. Our treaties with Brazil were on the point of expiring, and must be speedily renewed, with such modifications as might be deemed necessary. The tariff of the United States was to be revised; and the Zollverein, which had imposed very heavy duties on British manufactures, would have an opportunity of readjusting them. A diminution on our side of the duties on the admission of their corn would probably be followed by advantageous concessions on their part. But the strongest argument in favour of change was founded on the state of the finances, which had become more and more unsatisfactory, till in this year the income fell short of the expenditure by an amount of more than 2,101,370*l*. Such were the motives which determined the ministry to deal with the corn-laws, notwithstanding the hostility which they knew would be excited by any attempt to alter them; and thus commenced in good earnest the great anti-corn-law struggle, which, hitherto carried on in languid and ineffectual skirmishes, henceforward became the most important question of the time, and the cause of the rise and falling again of many parties, giving no peace to England until its final settlement had been effected. It is true that Harvey, Molesworth, Grote, Villiers, Poulett Thompson, and many others had already pointed out the mischief that these laws did, and had repeatedly urged those arguments which at length induced Parliament and the nation to sweep away the so-called protection they afforded to the agricultural interest. But the public mind was only slowly and gradually awakened to the necessity that existed for their abrogation. The announcement made by Lord J. Russell was followed by the financial statement of the chancellor of the exchequer, which inaugurated a new system of finance, and dealt the first really formidable blow against that great system of monopoly which had so long been upholden under the specious but deceptive title of protection.

'When I came forward last year,' said Mr. Baring, 'I anticipated that the expenditure would amount to 49,499,000*l.*, and the income to 48,641,000*l.*, leaving a deficiency of about 858,000*l.* Among the articles in which there has been the most marked falling-off are currants, molasses, spirits, sugar, tea, wine, and sheep's wool; but for the decline of each of these a reason will readily suggest itself to the House. The diminished revenue from sugar and molasses I attribute to the exorbitant price to which that article has risen; the anticipation of a commercial treaty with France has naturally tended to interfere with the duty arising from wine; and in the diminished consumption of spirits Ireland has borne a large share; but, however that circumstance may inconvenience my statement this evening, I should be ashamed of myself if I did not allude to it with sincere pleasure. The revenue from the post-office has fallen short of my anticipations; but that is owing, not to a deficiency in the anticipated increase of letters posted, but to the increased expenses which have become necessary in consequence of the opening of railroads and of the great augmentation in the business of the office. I calculate that the national expenditure for the ensuing year will be:

| | |
|---|---:|
| Interest on debt . . . . . . . | £29,424,000 |
| Other charges on consolidated fund . . . | 2,400,000 |
| Army . . . . . . . . . . | 6,587,000 |
| Navy . . . . . . . . . . | 6,805,000 |

| | |
|---|---:|
| Ordnance | £2,075,000 |
| Miscellaneous | 2,935,000 |
| Extraordinary expenses for Canada | 183,000 |
| Expedition to China | 400,000 |
| Making a total of | £50,731,226 |

'The items having been stated in round numbers, the total does not exactly agree with them; but it is as I have given it. The following are the items of the revenue which I anticipate for the ensuing year. I expect that the customs will produce 22,000,000*l*., the excise 14,000,000*l*., and the stamps 7,130,000*l*. I think, therefore, that the revenue will not fall short of 48,310,000*l*., leaving a deficiency of 2,421,000*l*. to be provided for; but I think I can show that the permanent deficiency which I shall have to provide for will be 1,700,000*l*., as several items of the expenditure of next year are of an extraordinary character. Under these circumstances, it becomes necessary to find some means of making up the revenue of the country to 50,000,000*l*. No taxation can be so injurious as a permanent disorder in the national finances, and the sum we have now to provide for is so large as to make it absolutely necessary that we should act with some degree of boldness.

'The question, then, is, what shall we do? Shall we fall back on the taxes that we have lately repealed—the house-tax, for instance, or the tax on coals? Shall we impose taxes on things that have hitherto been exempt—a legacy-duty on real property, or a tax on agricultural horses? Shall we lay taxes on new articles that have come into existence since the present system of taxation, as gas and steam? Ought we to adopt the once execrated but now popular plan of a property-tax? or might we not make some new arrangement of existing taxation, so as to obtain the required supplies without adding to the burdens of the people?

'The present duty on colonial timber is 10*s*. a load, and on Baltic timber 55*s*. This duty Earl Spencer proposed to modify, by raising that on colonial to 20*s*., and reducing that on Baltic timber to 50*s*. a load. I intend to adopt the plan of my noble friend. From this change Earl Spencer anticipated an increased revenue of 750,000*l*., but said that he should be content with 600,000*l*. I shall be content to take the same sum as Earl Spencer. I intend to propose an alteration in the sugar-duties, which will still leave a protection of 50 per cent. to colonial sugar. I mean to leave the duty on colonial sugar at the present amount of 24*s.* per cwt.; but that on foreign sugar, now amounting to 63*s.*, I propose to reduce to 36*s.* per cwt. From this change in the sugar-duties I expect an augmentation of 900,000*l.* to the revenue; but I will estimate it only at 700,000*l.* From sugar and timber, then, I look for an increase to the revenue of not less than 1,300,000*l.*, which will still leave a deficiency of 400,000*l.* to be provided for. My noble friend (Lord J. Russell) has this evening given notice of his intention at an early period to submit the question of the corn trade to the consideration of the House; and if the propositions of my noble friend are agreed to, it will of course become my duty to make provision by direct taxation.'

Subsequently, in answer to a demand from Lord Sandon for an explanation of the intentions of the government with regard to the corn-laws, Lord J. Russell announced that he should propose a moderate fixed duty—a principle he had already supported—and that the measure would be brought forward as the measure of a government united on the subject. On the 7th of May he made the farther announcement, that the duties he intended to propose on the importation of corn were, on wheat 8*s.* per quarter, on rye 5*s.*, on barley 4*s.* 6*d.*, and on oats 3*s.* 4*d.*

This announcement filled the liberal party with hope, and the conservatives with consternation. The two parties began to agitate the country for and against the proposed change. The party that desired a repeal or a modification of the corn-laws, formed associations, employed lecturers, and took every means in their power to awaken a strong feeling on the subject in the country.

The plan of government was now fully before the House. Important in itself, it derived still greater importance from the circumstance, that the existence of the government and the continuance of the present House of Commons depended on the decision. It therefore gave rise to one of the longest debates that has ever been carried on in either House of Parliament, extending over no less than eight days. The discussion turned principally on the proposed alteration in the duties on sugar and corn. The debate was indeed nominally on the sugar-duties alone; but it was felt that the decision come to on that question involved the acceptance or rejection of the ministerial plan as a whole; and therefore the discussion turned on the question of the fixed duty on corn, and on the timber duties, as well as on the question more immediately before the House. The ministerial proposals on that subject were regarded as involving the encouragement of the produce of the sugars of Cuba and other slave states at the expense of our own colonies, in which slavery had been so recently abolished. The consequence was that many liberal members of the antislavery party opposed this part of the plan, as tending, in their opinion, to defeat the great experiment of free negro labour, which was being so successfully carried out in our West-Indian possessions. They were joined in their opposition to it by the agricultural party, many of whom were Whigs, but all of whom were greatly incensed and alarmed at the proposal of a fixed duty, which they justly regarded as a prelude to the abolition of all duties on foreign corn. But by none was the plan more decidedly condemned than by Sir R. Peel, who declared his preference for a sliding scale, and his belief that a fixed duty could not be maintained. These reasons inclined many to oppose the measures of the government, but the long debate ended with a division on the question, that the speaker do now leave the chair; which was decided against the government by a majority of 36, there being 281 in favour of the motion, and 317 against it.

There was a very general expectation that this great defeat, which destroyed the financial plans of the government, would be followed either by its resignation or an appeal to the country. And in this expectation, anxious and expectant crowds beset all the passages of the House, and every avenue by which it was approached. The House itself was densely thronged with members and such strangers as were fortunate enough to obtain admission into the galleries, all waiting in breathless suspense the communication of the course which the government had resolved to adopt.

Astonishment, therefore, was mingled with disappointment when the chancellor of the exchequer, rising in his place as if nothing extraordinary had occurred, quietly gave notice that on the following Monday he should move the usual sugar-duties; and the surprise and disappointment caused by this announcement were increased when Lord J. Russell, without giving any explanation whatever of the course he proposed to adopt, moved that the House should adjourn to the following Monday. An outburst of indignant disappointment from the Earl of Darlington was the only notice taken of the course which ministers had thought fit to pursue; and in answer to a question from him, Lord J. Russell said that he would take the discussion on the proposed alterations in the corn-laws on the 4th of June. It was now, therefore, evident that ministers intended to continue in office, and appeal to the country on the question of the alterations they proposed to make in the corn-laws. Throughout the length and breadth of the land that question had been agitated by the Anti-corn-law League, and it was hoped that, although the proposals of the government did not go the full length of what the league aimed at, yet inasmuch as they tended to remove many of the evils and grievances of which that body complained, they would be favourably received by its leaders and by those who had been influenced by the arguments and statements which the league had industriously put forth. Nor were they altogether deceived in this expectation. The opponents of the corn-laws saw clearly that a fixed duty was preferable to a sliding scale, and was besides a step towards that total abolition of duties on corn for which they contended, and with which alone they would be satisfied. But in thus procuring the support of the league they incurred the bitter hostility of the agricultural party; and the Whig government, in passing the Reform Bill, had deliberately and intentionally maintained to a great extent the preponderance which the landed interest had always enjoyed, by giving so many additional members to the counties, and by consenting to allow so many insignificant boroughs in the agricultural districts to be represented in the House of Commons. In acquiring the confidence and support of the weaker party in the House and in the electoral body of the nation they incurred the strong displeasure and fierce opposition of the dominant party; and the consequence was, that their defeat in the coming elections had already become almost a matter of certainty. Sir Robert Peel saw at once, that in consequence of the feeling they had raised against them, he might now take a bolder step. The reader will remember, that at an early period of the last session a vote of want of confidence in the government, proposed by Sir J. Y. Buller, and seconded by Alderman Thompson, had been lost by a majority of twenty-one. But the government was now so much weaker than it was then, that Sir Robert felt he should now probably be able to carry the resolution which had then been rejected. Therefore, on the day on which the House met again, he announced, amidst the tumultuous cheering of his followers, that it was his intention to move a direct vote of want of confidence in the ministry—a vote which, if carried, would force them either to resign or dissolve, without allowing an opportunity for the discussion of the corn-laws. The motion was accordingly brought forward, and carried by a majority of one; there being 312 votes in favour of it, and 311 against it. This was of course a condemnation which no government could brook. Lord J. Russell announced that he would state on the following Monday the course which the government would adopt. Accordingly on that evening there was the same anxious and excited curiosity which had been displayed on the occasion of the last ministerial defeat. The House and all the avenues leading to it were once more gorged with an anxious and impatient multitude. This time they were not disappointed. Ministers, after maturely weighing the two alternatives of resignation and dissolution, had determined to adopt the latter. Lord J. Russell announced that the government intended to advise the crown to dissolve the present Parliament as soon as possible, and to summon another without delay; and Sir R. Peel stated that he was perfectly satisfied with this declaration.

The moribund Parliament sat for about a fortnight longer, engaged in winding up the business of the session, and passing as quickly as possible through their various stages the measures which needed to be carried before the prorogation could take place. But most of the members of the House of Commons were already in the provinces, busily engaged in canvassing and in making preparations for the approaching electoral struggle, which promised to be one of no ordinary severity; while many of those who still remained, in order to transact the indispensable business of the session, were casting anxious glances towards the places they represented, and were feverishly hoping for the moment which would release them from their senatorial duties, and enable them to go down to the constituencies which they had hitherto represented, or to those which they hoped to represent in the new Parliament. A session in which more was said or less effected has seldom occurred. From its commencement to its close it was one prolonged party struggle, brought at length to a crisis by the vote of want of confidence.

Every nerve was strained by both parties to gain a majority in this election. The conservatives appealed to every class of persons who had been injured, or could be made to imagine that they had been injured, by the measures of the Whig ministry, and called upon them now to avenge themselves by their votes. The friends of the Church were reminded of the attempts that had been made to carry the appropriation clause, and her enemies of its abandonment. The army and the navy were conjured to exert all the influence they possessed to throw out a ministry which was likely to make great reductions in both services. The moneyed interest was called on to use its influence against a government which had increased the national debt, and caused a deficit of seven millions. The colonial and shipping interests were incited to resist the losses with which they were threatened by the measures of the Whig administration. The manufacturers were exhorted to withdraw their support from a government which would render their situation even more precarious than it was already. The landed interest and the British farmers were plied with predictions of utter ruin, which would follow the withdrawal of protection, to which they listened with almost implicit faith. The working classes were assured that the delusive promise of cheap bread would be followed by the stern reality of low wages. Loyal subjects and Chartists were exhorted to remember that the ministry had first encouraged public meetings, and then violently suppressed them; first made Frost a magistrate, and then, without any change of opinion on his part, caused him to be sentenced to death for high treason. The sticklers for the constitution were called on not to forget how ministers had regained office through the influence of the ladies of the bedchamber, after having admitted that they no longer possessed the confidence of the legislature. The friends of religion and morality were implored to vote against the minister who had presented Robert Owen, the socialist, to our young and innocent Queen; and every lover of his country was invoked to use his vote and influence against the patrons, or rather the slaves, of O'Connell and the Irish repealers. It was true that the other side met these election cries with others of a like character. For instance, at the London election shilling and twopenny loaves were placed on the top of poles, and were respectively ticketed as the Russell loaf and the Peel loaf. But these cries were less effective than those raised by the opponents of the government, for the simple reason that, with one short exception, the Whigs had enjoyed ten years of power, and had therefore incurred those enmities which are sure to overtake every government that remains many years in office. There can be no doubt, too, that the Whigs had made a great mistake in the choice of the question on which they appealed to the country—the question of a fixed duty. By making their stand on it they obtained the cold and languid preference of the radical and free-trade parties. The latter was indeed rising daily in influence and importance, but had not as yet attained that numerical force which it subsequently acquired. Thus the government failed to evoke that popular zeal and enthusiasm which alone could have enabled it to withstand the combination of parties, whose interests, or supposed interests, it either touched or menaced. It was true that in the instance of the Reform Bill the Whig party had succeeded in defeating a much more formidable union of powerful interests than that which was now banded together against them; but their success on that occasion was due to their having proposed a thorough-going measure, one that strongly stirred the passions of the multitude, whereas they now appealed to the people to come and help them to carry a half measure, coldly supported and vehemently resisted. The result was, that the conservatives gained largely on the appeal that the Whigs made to the country, thereby showing that the latter had committed a great mistake in dissolving as they did. In the English counties, where the voters had been led to believe that free trade was agricultural ruin, and that the farmers would be completely undersold by the foreigner, the conservatives gained twenty-two seats, and in the boroughs seven. In Scotland they gained two, and in Ireland eight. They therefore reckoned that in the new Parliament Sir R. Peel would be able to command a majority of about seventy-six. In the course of this election the conservatives won some very signal victories, which gave great encouragement to the party everywhere. The city of London, which had returned four Whigs to the last Parliament, sent two conservatives and two Whigs to the new House of Commons. A conservative headed the poll; and Lord J. Russell, who was one of the candidates, was at the bottom of it, only escaping defeat by a few votes. In the West Riding of Yorkshire two conservatives, the Hon. S. Wortley and Mr. Denison, defeated Lords Morpeth and Milton. Two conservatives represented the Irish metropolis, though Mr. O'Connell was again a candidate for that city.

The result was hailed by the Tories as a great party triumph, and pointed at as a proof of a national conservative reaction. This, however, was far from being its real import. It was rather, on the one hand, a condemnation of the financial policy of the Melbourne administration, and especially of the fault they had committed in allowing so enormous a deficiency to grow up; and, on the other, a vote of personal confidence in Sir R. Peel, as being the man best qualified to deal with the great fiscal and financial difficulties which had accumulated under his opponents. This opinion was perhaps unjust to the party which had certainly produced a large deficit, but which, it should be remembered, had done so by carrying on wars in India, China, and Syria, in which any government in office at the same time would probably have been forced to engage, and by adopting such salutary changes as the reduction of the stamp-duties on newspapers, and the penny postage—bold and important changes, which Sir R. Peel had all along condemned and opposed, and for the sake of which it was well worth while to incur some temporary embarrassment. It is also to be remembered, that it is by no means certain that Lord J. Russell's fiscal scheme would not have filled up, to a very considerable extent, the financial chasm which he had undertaken to deal with. Mr. M'Culloch, the highest authority on such a question, calculated that the sliding scale produced an average duty of 5s. 9d. on each quarter of wheat, while Lord J. Russell's fixed duty would have produced 8s. Thus the revenue arising from the duty on corn would have been increased about forty per cent. But this was not all. There can be no doubt that the greater certainty which a fixed duty would have given to the movements of commerce would have produced a largely increased importation of wheat, and thus have doubled, or more than doubled, the revenue arising from this source alone, not to mention the result which would have been obtained by the changes which Lord J. Russell proposed to make in the sugar and the timber duties. The misfortune was, that the Whig proposition came too late; and then, instead of obtaining the consideration to which its merits entitled it, was universally, though unjustly, regarded as a makeshift, adopted on the spur of the moment to prop up a falling ministry. In estimating these measures too, it should not be forgotten that though the Whig government on this occasion took its stand resolutely, and we may almost say obstinately, on the plan of a fixed duty, for which, in the state of the finances, much might be plausibly advanced, yet they were so closely connected with and so dependent on the free-trade party, their own sympathies were so altogether with that party, and the fixed duty had so much less power of resistance than the sliding scale, that it is probable that if the Whigs had obtained a majority at this election, they would have been led to adopt the policy of free trade at an earlier period than that at which Sir R. Peel found himself compelled to become the patron of the system of which he had all along been the leading opponent.

On the reassembling of the House of Commons, in accordance with the pledge given by ministers, the Queen's speech, which was delivered by commission, contained the following clauses, showing that ministers intended to submit their measures to the legislature before they retired from office.

'It has appeared to her majesty, after full deliberation, that you may at this juncture properly direct your attention to the revision of duties affecting the productions of foreign countries. It will be for you to consider whether some of those duties are not so trifling in amount as to be unproductive to the revenue, while they are vexatious to commerce. You may farther examine whether the principles of protection, upon which other of these duties are founded, be not carried to an extent injurious alike to the income of the state and the interests of the people.

'Her majesty is desirous that you should consider the laws which regulate the trade in corn. It will be for you to determine whether these laws do not aggravate the natural fluctuations of supply; whether they do not embarrass trade, derange the currency, and by their operation diminish the comfort and increase the privations of the great body of the community.'

In the upper House, an amendment to the address, in answer to the speech, proposed by the Earl of Ripon, was carried against the government by a majority of 72. In the lower House, Mr. Shaw Lefevre was reëlected speaker without opposition. Then commenced the decisive struggle, the issue of which, after the late general election, could no longer be doubtful, which was to determine whether the country should be governed by the Whigs or the conservatives. The question to be decided was the maintenance of a sliding scale, or the substitution for it of a fixed duty. We place before the reader, with our usual condensation, the speeches of the leaders of the two parties on this important question, rendered the more interesting by the change of opinion which both of them afterwards underwent.

'I adhere,' said Sir R. Peel, 'to my determination not prematurely to develop my plans for remedying the financial embarrassments of the country; a determination which has been sanctioned by the late elections. I protest, however, against the assertion that I am adverse to the removal of restrictions on commerce, or hostile to the principles of free trade, because I oppose the measures of the government. I protest against the principles of free trade being tried by any such test. I have formed an opinion which intervening consideration has not induced me to alter, that the principle of a graduated scale is preferable to that of a fixed and irrevocable duty; but I said then, and I say now—and in doing so I repeat the language I used in 1839 —that I will not bind myself to the details of the existing law, but will reserve to myself the unfettered discretion of considering and amending that law. I hold the same language now; but if you ask me whether I bind myself to the maintenance of the existing law in its details, or if you say that it is the condition on which the agricultural interest give me their support, I say that on that condition I will not accept it.

'I have been taunted with not declaring my plans; but had I explained in May what could not possibly be carried into effect before October, my opponents through the country would have reproached me, if I had deviated from it in the slightest degree, with the difference between my promise and my performance. What is the question between me and the government? We both start from the principle of protection; but the arguments against the sliding duty as a tax on the income of the poor man are equally applicable to the 8s. fixed duty. And what would be the satisfaction of an intermediate settlement of the corn-law question? I doubt, to borrow Lord J. Russell's phrase, the finality of such a settlement. If a bad harvest took place, would you rigorously exact the 8s. fixed duty in September or October? (An honourable member called out, "Yes.") You would! Then I publicly notify to the country, upon the authority of a great manufacturer and a stern free-trader, that, if corn is at the price of 80s., or 90s., or 100s., his rigid adherence to the principles and doctrines of free trade will compel him to exact the duty of 8s.! No matter what may be the distress that prevails, no matter what may be the extent of privation, no matter what the amount of suffering, yet still the 8s. duty must be exacted; there is no power to remit it. In vain would it be to show, that under the existing scale it would have been admitted for 1s. But, notwithstanding all that parade of principle, in point of fact the duty could not be maintained under such circumstances.

'I have great doubts, too, whether the fixed duty would cause the expected fixity of price. In those countries in which there is no corn-law in operation the price fluctuates. Take the state of New York as an example. In November, 1834, the price of the Winchester quarter of eight bushels was 33*s*. 4*d*. In October, 1836, it was 54*s*. In January, 1837, it was 63*s*. In June, 1839, it was 67*s*. 4*d*.; and in October, 1839—mark, in the same year—it was 39*s*. 6*d*. Thus, in the state of New York alone, in the course of six months the price of corn varied from 67*s*. 4*d*. to 39*s*. 6*d*. Whence arose that fluctuation? How was it to be accounted for, unless by the nature of the intervening harvest producing an immense variation? In January, 1837, when corn was 63*s*. a quarter in New York, it was only 55*s*. 6*d*. in England; and in October, when it was 64*s*. in New York, it was only 45*s*. 9*d*. here.

'If I thought that the repeal of the corn-laws could be an effectual remedy for the distress of the manufacturing districts—the recital of which has caused me much pain—I should recommend it as essential to the welfare of the agriculturists themselves; but I cannot come to that conclusion.'

It will be noticed that this speech contains indications that Sir R. Peel's mind was already, though perhaps unconsciously, biassed towards that free-trade policy which he afterwards so boldly carried out. To these statements and arguments Lord J. Russell thus replied:

'I am convinced that the sliding scale is at the root of all the evil that has been referred to. Lord Ripon, in defending the corn-laws, showed that in 1834-5-6 the duty was 47*s*., neither more nor less than a prohibitory duty; in 1837 the duty was 1*s*. 7*d*., and then 1,718,000 quarters of wheat were admitted, 1740 times as much as in 1835-6. It is impossible that there can be any steadiness of trade while the averages are tampered with by corn-jobbers under a sliding scale. I admit that in my opinion the 8*s*. duty could not be maintained in a time of scarcity; but then, with a fixed duty and the consequent regular trade, there very seldom would be any actual scarcity. The present system is so essentially vicious in its nature that it ought to be abandoned, and we ought to go to a fixed duty. I do not so much expect lower prices as additional employment for the people. I have no reason to suppose that Sir R. Peel will refuse to put in practice those principles of free trade of which he is the declared advocate. I am sure, if he does, it will be from the want of inclination, not from the want of power; for, as for any imputation of his wanting any power to deal with the corn-laws as we proposed to deal with them, I think we may despise it. I know not what course he may pursue, but the full responsibility remains with him. He has no right to say that he is shackled and thwarted by party trammels, because it appears that the party to which he belongs could not resist liberal measures if he were to propose them.

The House divided at the conclusion of Lord J. Russell's speech with the following result:

For the address proposed on behalf of the ministers .. .. 296
For Sir R. Peel's amendment .. .. .. .. .. 360

Majority against the government .. .. .. 64

This division, which showed the party of Sir R. Peel in the House to be even stronger than had been anticipated, was followed by the resignation of the government.

The formation of a new ministry to replace that of Lord Melbourne was of course entrusted to Sir R. Peel, who succeeded without much difficulty in fulfilling the task. The duty of leading the upper House was confided to the Duke of Wellington, who occupied a seat in the cabinet, without holding any office in the new administration.*

* The following are the names and offices of the new ministers:

THE CABINET.

| | |
|---|---|
| Sir R. Peel | First Lord of the Treasury. |
| Lord Lyndhurst | Lord-chancellor. |
| Lord Wharncliffe | President of the Council. |
| Earl of Haddington | First Lord of the Admiralty. |
| Duke of Buckingham | Lord Privy-seal. |
| Sir James Graham | Home Secretary. |
| Earl of Aberdeen | Foreign Secretary. |
| Lord Stanley | Colonial Secretary. |
| Lord Ellenborough | President of the Board of Control. |
| Sir Henry Hardinge | Secretary at War. |
| Earl of Ripon | President of the Board of Trade. |
| Mr. Goulburn | Chancellor of the Exchequer. |
| Sir E. Knatchbull | Paymaster-general. |
| Lord Eliot | Chief Secretary for Ireland. |
| Duke of Wellington | Without office. |

NOT OF THE CABINET.

| | |
|---|---|
| Lord Lowther | Postmaster-general. |
| Lord Grenville Somerset | Chancellor of the Duchy of Lancaster. |
| Mr. W. E. Gladstone | Vice-president of the Board of Trade. |
| Sir F. Pollock | Attorney-general. |
| Sir W. W. Follett | Solicitor-general. |
| Earl de Grey | Lord-lieutenant of Ireland. |
| Sir E. Sugden | Lord-chancellor of Ireland. |
| &c. | &c. &c. |

The year 1841 was marked by a great increase of distress, factory short-time, and crime; of abstinence from intoxicating liquors, and indulgence in the use of opium; of church-building, chapel-building, and establishment of new colonial bishoprics, causing Sidney Smith to say that soon there would not be a rock in the ocean without a bishop and an archdeacon. The dangers to which the corn-laws were exposed by the agitation carried on against them caused the agriculturists to bestir themselves in defence of a protection which they had been taught to believe to be essential to their interests, and in the formation of agricultural societies, having for their object the introduction into general use of better and more scientific modes of cultivating the ground and breeding cattle; thus enabling them to produce more abundantly, and preparing them to compete with the foreigner, even if the protection they enjoyed should be withdrawn from them.

# CHAPTER II.

### THE INCOME AND PROPERTY TAX.

THE members of the new government whose seats had been vacated by their acceptance of office were all reëlected, and Parliament met again on the 16th of September. The new premier announced that he intended to adopt without alteration the estimates framed by the late government, to renew the new poor-law provisionally, and to make such other arrangements as were absolutely required; but to defer to the next session the development of those financial measures which he deemed it necessary to bring forward. He promised, however, that they should have the effect of equalising the revenue and expenditure of the country, either by increasing the former or diminishing the latter. Lord J. Russell and his adherents strongly remonstrated against this arrangement; they reminded the House of the distress that prevailed in the manufacturing districts, and bitterly complained that, after a plan which they believed would have the effect of restoring the revenue and filling up the deficiency had been rejected without discussion, another five months should be wasted. To these representations Sir Robert Peel replied by urging the necessity of proceeding with caution and deliberation in a matter of so much importance, and by declaring that he should only be countenancing a fatal delusion if he were to encourage the belief that it was possible for Parliament to adopt any measures by which the prevailing distress could be immediately relieved. The majority which the new minister commanded rendered opposition hopeless. The necessary business was therefore pushed forward as rapidly as possible, and on the 7th of October Parliament was prorogued by commission. The vacation was employed by the government, and especially by its chief, in diligently studying the financial position of the country, and preparing the measures which seemed to be required in order to place the revenue and expenditure of the country on a satisfactory footing.

The decennial census showed that the population of England and Wales amounted to 15,906,829; giving an increase during the decade of no less than 2,009,642.

Before Parliament reassembled it was announced that the Duke of Buckingham, who held the office of privy-seal in the new cabinet, had withdrawn from the ministry. This event, unimportant in itself, derived a certain significance from the fact, that the duke represented that party which was most resolutely opposed to any alteration whatever in the existing corn-laws; and therefore his resignation was regarded on all hands as an indication that his colleagues had resolved to make concessions on the subject of the corn-laws to which the high protectionist party was likely to object, and that ministers might therefore find themselves abandoned by a large number of their supporters, at the very commencement of the parliamentary campaign, on this question. This expectation was strengthened by certain expressions contained in the Queen's speech, delivered at the opening of the session on the 3rd of February, 1842; in which, after referring to the deficiency of the revenue, her majesty recommended the legislature to consider 'the state of the laws affecting the importation of corn and other articles the produce of foreign countries.' The presence of the King of Prussia, who had visited England for the purpose of standing as godfather to the newly-born Prince of Wales, caused the opening of this Parliament to be attended with more than usual pomp and circumstance.

The new minister did not leave Parliament or the country long in suspense with regard to the manner in which he proposed to deal with the corn-laws. Parliament, as we have seen, was formally opened on the 3rd of February, and on the 9th of that month Sir Robert brought the question of the corn-laws before the House. The ominous resignation of the Duke of Buckingham had greatly enhanced the impatience with which both sides of the House, and the parties they represented in the country, waited for the explanation of the ministerial measure. The House itself, and all its purlieus, afforded unmistakable indications of the interest it excited. There was a great scramble for seats in the gallery; every avenue leading to the House was crowded; the delegates of the Anti-corn-law League had filled the lobby, but having been ejected from it by the police, they stationed themselves outside the House, and greeted the members as they came down to it with cries of 'No sliding scale,' 'Total repeal,' &c. The opening statement of Sir R. Peel was listened to with an anxious curiosity and breathless expectation such as few speeches ever delivered in the House of Commons have commanded. After some preliminary observations he endeavoured to show, by a reference to a large number of returns, that the prevailing distress and depression could not fairly be ascribed to the corn-laws. In answer to the objection, that the price of food was higher in England than in any other European country, he brought forward evidence to prove that the average quantity of meal consumed by each Englishman was much larger than that consumed by each inhabitant of those states to which reference has been made; and he showed that this was also the case with regard to the consumption of tea, salt, and woollen cloth. After considering the objections that had been made to the corn-laws, he came to the conclusion that the repeal of those laws would have the effect of adding agricultural distress to manufacturing distress. At the same time he admitted the force of the objections which had been made to the existing law, based on the system of averages that it had established and of which a fraudulent use had been made by speculators. This evil he proposed to remedy by transferring the duty of ascertaining the averages to the excise, by widening the range from which the returns were to be made; but mainly and chiefly by making such alterations in the duties at present levied as would greatly diminish the temptation to be guilty of such tampering with the averages as had been complained of.

'I now approach,' he said, 'the most important part of the subject: the amount of protection to be given to the produce of the country. At the present time, as the House is aware, the duty varies in this way: when the price is 59s. and under 60s. the duty is 27s.; it then diminishes 1s. in duty with every 1s. increase in price, until corn reaches the price of between 66s. and 67s.; when the duty is 20s. 8d.; it then falls 2s. in duty with the increase of price;

so that when the price is between 68s. and 69s. the duty is 16s. 8d.; at 70s. the duty is 14s. 8d., and at 71s., 10s. 8d.; it then falls 4s. with each increase of price, so that at 73s. it is 2s. 8d.; and at 75s. and upwards, 1s. and no more. The main objection which has been urged to that way of levying the duty is this, that the reduction of the duty is so rapid, that it holds out temptations to fraud. For instance, at 60s. the duty is 26s. 8d., and at 73s. the duty is 1s. only; so that between 60s. and 73s. there is an increase of price of 13s. and a decrease of duty of 25s. 8d., affording a great inducement to fraud, or to combinations for the purpose of influencing the averages, giving, as it did, to parties so inclined, the advantage of the sale of one quarter of wheat of no less than 38s. 8d. At 66s. the duty is 20s. 8d.; so that even between 66s. and 73s. there is an inducement to parties to hold back corn of 7s. in the price and 19s. 8d. in the duty, making a total amount of pecuniary inducement to retain the article of 26s. 8d. At 66s. the inducement to retain corn in the hope of its rising to 70s. is 4s. in price and 10s. in duty; a total inducement of 14s. At 70s. price the inducement for retaining corn till it reaches 73s. is 3s. price and 9s. duty; together 12s. Thus the consumer is injured by the withholding of corn till it is dearer; the revenue by the forced reduction of duty; the agriculturist by the withholding of corn till it has reached the highest price, which is then snatched from him, and his protection defeated; while commerce suffers from the uncertainty.'

After going very minutely into the difficulties of fixing the price of foreign wheat, and into the details of the duties which he proposed to impose in the place of those which then existed, Sir R. Peel thus recapitulated the main features of the new scale that he proposed for adoption, and the reductions that he expected to effect by means of it:

'When corn is at 59s. and under 60s., the duty at present is 27s. 8d. The duty I propose is 13s. When the price of corn is at 50s., the existing duty is 36s. 8d., increasing as the price falls, instead of which I propose that the duty should be only 20s., and that duty shall in no case be exceeded. At 56s. the duty is 30s. 8d.; the duty I propose at that price is 16s. At 60s. the duty is 26s. 8d.; the duty I propose at that price is 12s. At 63s. the duty is 23s. 8d.

the duty I propose is 9s. At 64s. the duty is 22s. 8d.; the duty I propose is 8s. At 70s. the duty is 10s. 8d.; the duty I propose is 5s. These are reductions which, in my opinion, can be made consistently with justice to all the interests concerned.

'My belief, and the belief of my colleagues is, that it is of the highest importance to the welfare of all classes in this country that you should take care that the main sources of your supply of corn should be derived from domestic agriculture. You are entitled to place such a price on foreign corn as is equivalent to the special burdens borne by the agriculturist, and any additional protection you give them I am willing to admit can only be vindicated on the ground that it is for the interest of the country generally. I, however, certainly do consider that it is for the interest of all classes that we should be paying occasionally a small additional sum upon our own domestic produce, in order that we may thereby establish a security and assurance against those calamities that would ensue if we became altogether, or in a great part, dependent on foreign countries for our supply. That we might be, for a series of years of scarcity, dependent on foreign countries for a portion of its supply, I do not deny. But I nevertheless do not abandon the hope that this country, in the average of years, may produce a sufficiency for its own necessities. If that hope should be disappointed, if you must resort to other countries in ordinary seasons for periodical additions to your own supplies, then I draw a material distinction between the supply that is limited—the supply which is brought in for the purpose of repairing our accidental and comparatively slight deficiency—and the supply which is of a more permanent and extensive character.

'I consider the present as a not unfavourable time for the settlement of the subject. There is no great stock of corn on hand to alarm the growers. The recess, notwithstanding the distress that has existed, has been marked by an unusual calm. There is no popular violence to interrupt legislation, and there is a disposition to view any proposal for the adjustment of the question with calmness and moderation. Whether my proposition is accepted or rejected, I hope that the question will be adjusted in the way most conducive to the permanent welfare of all classes of the community.'

Thus the sliding scale was at once maintained and improved. The duties were lowered, the oscillations confined within narrower limits, the jumps and jerks which had attended its working were avoided, it was made to slide up and down more easily, and the public were protected from the frauds and artifices which had been facilitated by the old scale. The table given below will enable the reader to perceive at a glance the differences between them.*

On the day following this announcement and explanation

\* OLD SCALE: *Wheat.*

| Average price per quarter. | | | Duty per quarter. | | |
|---|---|---|---|---|---|
| s. | | s. | £ | s. | d. |
| At 36 | under | 37 | 2 | 10 | 8 |
| 37 | ,, | 38 | 2 | 9 | 8 |
| 38 | ,, | 39 | 2 | 8 | 8 |
| 39 | ,, | 40 | 2 | 7 | 8 |
| 40 | ,, | 41 | 2 | 6 | 8 |
| 41 | ,, | 42 | 2 | 5 | 8 |
| 42 | ,, | 43 | 2 | 4 | 8 |
| 43 | ,, | 44 | 2 | 3 | 8 |
| 44 | ,, | 45 | 2 | 2 | 8 |
| 45 | ,, | 46 | 2 | 1 | 8 |
| 46 | ,, | 47 | 2 | 0 | 8 |
| 47 | ,, | 48 | 1 | 19 | 8 |
| 48 | ,, | 49 | 1 | 18 | 8 |
| 49 | ,, | 50 | 1 | 17 | 8 |
| 50 | ,, | 51 | 1 | 16 | 8 |
| 51 | ,, | 52 | 1 | 15 | 8 |
| 52 | ,, | 53 | 1 | 14 | 8 |
| 53 | ,, | 54 | 1 | 13 | 8 |
| 54 | ,, | 55 | 1 | 12 | 8 |
| 55 | ,, | 56 | 1 | 11 | 8 |
| 56 | ,, | 57 | 1 | 10 | 8 |
| 57 | ,, | 58 | 1 | 9 | 8 |
| 58 | ,, | 59 | 1 | 8 | 8 |
| 59 | ,, | 60 | 1 | 7 | 8 |
| 60 | ,, | 61 | 1 | 6 | 8 |
| 61 | ,, | 62 | 1 | 5 | 8 |
| 62 | ,, | 63 | 1 | 4 | 8 |
| 63 | ,, | 64 | 1 | 3 | 8 |
| 64 | ,, | 65 | 1 | 2 | 8 |
| 65 | ,, | 66 | 1 | 1 | 8 |
| 66 | ,, | 67 | 1 | 0 | 8 |
| 67 | ,, | 68 | 0 | 18 | 8 |
| 68 | ,, | 69 | 0 | 16 | 8 |
| 69 | ,, | 70 | 0 | 13 | 8 |
| 70 | ,, | 71 | 0 | 10 | 8 |
| 71 | ,, | 72 | 0 | 6 | 8 |
| 72 | ,, | 73 | 0 | 2 | 8 |
| 73 and upwards | | | 0 | 1 | 0 |

NEW SCALE: *Wheat.*

| Average price per quarter. | | | Duty per quarter. | | |
|---|---|---|---|---|---|
| s. | | s. | £ | s. | d. |
| At 50s., and at all prices under 50s. | | | 1 | 0 | 0 |
| At 51s. | under | 52s. | 0 | 19 | 0 |
| 52 | ,, | 55 | 0 | 18 | 0 |
| 55 | ,, | 56 | 0 | 17 | 0 |
| 56 | ,, | 57 | 0 | 16 | 0 |
| 57 | ,, | 58 | 0 | 15 | 0 |
| 58 | ,, | 59 | 0 | 14 | 0 |
| 59 | ,, | 60 | 0 | 13 | 0 |
| 60 | ,, | 61 | 0 | 12 | 0 |
| 61 | ,, | 62 | 0 | 11 | 0 |
| 62 | ,, | 63 | 0 | 10 | 0 |
| 63 | ,, | 64 | 0 | 9 | 0 |
| 64 | ,, | 65 | 0 | 8 | 0 |
| 65 | ,, | 66 | 0 | 7 | 0 |
| 66 | ,, | 69 | 0 | 6 | 0 |
| 69 | ,, | 70 | 0 | 5 | 0 |
| 70 | ,, | 71 | 0 | 4 | 0 |
| 71 | ,, | 72 | 0 | 3 | 0 |
| 72 | ,, | 73 | 0 | 2 | 0 |
| 73 and upwards | | | 0 | 1 | 0 |

of the ministerial measure, Lord J. Russell gave notice that he would move an amendment, condemning the principle of a sliding scale. Mr. Villiers announced that he should like the sense of the house on the policy of imposing any duty whatever, fixed or sliding, on foreign corn or food imported into this country; and Mr. Christopher, one of the members for the county of Lincoln, declared that he should move in committee the adoption of a higher rate of wheat-duties, to be substituted for that proposed by the premier. Thus the questions of an improved sliding scale, a fixed duty, and an entire abolition of all duties on corn, were brought under discussion.

On the 14th Lord J. Russell proposed the amendment of which he had given notice. After showing that it was impossible that the nation should be wholly independent of foreign supplies of corn and other food, and reminding the house that even during the war with Napoleon 2,000,000 of the people of this country derived their supplies of food from foreign sources; and having answered the argument that the countries on which we chiefly depended for our corn supplies were situated nearly in the same latitude as ourselves, and therefore that their harvest might fail at the same time with our own, by saying that it showed how necessary it was that we should not confine ourselves for a supply to the north of Europe alone, but should take assistance also from the Black Sea and America, that we should stretch the arms of our commerce, as all our other powers are stretched, over the whole world—he thus criticised the proposed sliding scale:

'The proposal before the House is opposed to that extension. The first objection I take to a sliding scale is, that a high, I should say a prohibitory, duty always forms part of it. I could understand a scale not exceeding 10s. or 12s., and going down to 4s., to 3s., or to 1s. The first duty when the price is at 50s. and under 51s., is 20s.; and I shall now proceed to show that that is a prohibitory duty. From the information obtained by Mr. Meek, who was sent to the north of Europe expressly to collect information on the subject, it appears the original price of Dantzic wheat when brought from the interior of the country is 35s., that the charges amount in all to 10s. 6d.; thus making the price at which it could be sold in England in ordinary years 45s. 6d.

If you add to that the proposed duty of 20*s*., you make the entire price of Dantzic wheat 65*s*. 6*d*., when the price at home is 50*s*., showing of course that 20*s*. amounts to a prohibitory duty. In the same way at Odessa, as stated in the consul's returns, the price would be 26*s*., adding to which 10*s*. for freight, and some further charges which cannot be taken at less than 5*s*., and adding then the proposed duty of 20*s*., you would have the price up to 61*s*., without counting the profit of the merchant who would have to deal with this corn; and therefore, although you may say that you have reduced the duty to 20*s*., to 19*s*., and to 18*s*., yet in all three instances it can be shown that the duty is prohibitory; and that when the price is at 55*s*. or 56*s*.—the price at which the right honourable gentleman said it would please him to see it, nobody can tell why—there would then be a prohibitory duty on foreign corn. Indeed Sir R. Peel was right when he said that a duty of 20*s*. was quite sufficient, and that it would exclude foreign corn as effectually as a duty of 45*s*. At what time will the duty cease to be prohibitory? Suppose you admit foreign corn at 62*s*., and that that price would enable the merchant to pay a duty of 11*s*.; at 65*s*. he would sell it to greater advantage by getting 3*s*. additional. Not content with that, you tell him that when the price is at 65*s*., and a supply is required, you will admit his foreign corn at 8*s*. instead of 11*s*. What has been the consequence during the last year of that system of duties? It has been stated in two new pamphlets written on this subject—one by Mr. Hubbard, and the other by Mr. Gregg —in one of which it is shown that on the 5th of July last Dantzic wheat in bond was 48*s*. a quarter, and that if let out it might have been had with the duty of 8*s*. for 56*s*. On the 6th of August the price rose to 60*s*., your law affording special reasons for believing that a still better price could be obtained for it; and on the 3rd of September, only two months after it could have been sold at 48*s*., it was sold at 70*s*. in bond, thereby adding 22*s*. to the price, without the slightest benefit to the farmer or landholder, and with no advantage to any one but the foreign speculator.

'It is calculated by Mr. Gregg that the sum paid to owners and growers of foreign corn last year was 6,000,000*l*. I will assume that it was 4,000,000*l*. or 5,000,000*l*.; a loss which was entailed on this country by the sliding scale.

Another evil of that scale lies in the fact that, take the averages as fairly as you may, you cannot tell the quality of the corn: during the past year, and some of the preceding years, a great portion of the corn of the country was very much damaged, to the extent, as alleged by some persons well acquainted with agriculture, of one-fifth of the whole crop of England. The consequence was a considerable reduction in the market price. But did the people get their bread a whit cheaper? No; when corn comes to that degree of cheapness, it is not cheapness to the consumer of bread, because he is paying as much as when the averages are a good deal higher. This has been made out in figures by a gentleman who sent me a statement on the subject. He shows that in the month of January 1841 the average price of wheat was 61s. 2d., and that in the same month in 1842 the average was also 61s. 2d. You may therefore say that, the average price being the same at both periods, and the duty being also the same, the people obtained bread at the same price. But is it so? Far from it. According to the Mark-lane return, I find that the price of the best flour in the first four weeks of 1841 was 55s. per sack; while in the first four weeks of 1842 it was 61s. per sack; making a difference of no less than 6s. per sack in that description of flour from which bread is made, while no alteration took place in the averages or the amount of the duty. The sudden rise after a bad harvest, when perhaps there has been a prohibition for two or three years, causes the necessity of a sudden supply from abroad; there is no regular trade, and bullion is sent to meet the demand; the Bank of England contracts its issues, and there is a derangement of the currency. I am aware that corn must be dearer at some seasons than at others; but where nature places difficulties in your way, you should not aggravate them by bad legislation. With respect to frauds in the averages, the committee of 1820 exposed a great number; and a fraudulent rise in price to the extent of 9s. in one week was exposed in 1839."

After insisting on the importance of obtaining supplies of corn from America, Lord John proceeded to vindicate his own plan of a fixed duty on corn. In favour of this plan he cited Ricardo, M'Culloch, Huskisson, and the committee of 1821, of which Sir E. Knatchbull and other eminent men skilled in agricultural matters were members.

'I admit,' he proceeded, 'that I do not regard the corn-laws as the cause of the whole of the present distress, but I think they tend very greatly to aggravate it. Sir R. Peel says that an alteration in the corn-laws will not relieve it. I agree in the truth of that description, when it is made applicable to the measures of the government. I agree that it is impossible to hope that any material alleviation of distress should result from a measure which is only made to look apparently a little better than the former one; which keeps up all the vicious principle of the old law, which forbids the import of corn by a prohibitory duty, which encourages speculation, which cramps your commerce, and prevents you from resorting for food to the Black Sea and the United States.'

Lord J. Russell concluded his speech by moving the following amendment: 'That this house, considering the evils which have been caused by the present corn-laws, and especially by the fluctuations of a graduated or sliding scale, is not prepared to adopt the measure of her Majesty's government, which is founded on the same principles, and is likely to be attended with similar results.'

After four nights' debate, the amendment of Lord J. Russell was rejected by the large majority of 123. This was followed by another debate, extending over five evenings, on the amendment of Mr. C. Villiers for the entire abolition of all duties on corn. We cannot spare space for even a brief account of the principal speeches that were delivered on this occasion, and this is the less regrettable because we shall see the issue here raised fully argued at a subsequent period of our history. The most remarkable speech on the subject was that of Mr. Macaulay,* who advocated complete free trade, but thought that the protection given to the agricultural interest should be removed gradually. He thus characterised Sir R. Peel's plan:

'It is a measure which settles nothing; it is a measure which pleases nobody; it is a measure which nobody asks for, and which nobody thanks him for; it is a measure which will not extend trade nor relieve distress.'

There were one or two incidents which rendered this debate remarkable, and which, on account of the effect they

---

\* Afterwards Lord Macaulay.

produced at the time, ought not to be passed over. The first of these was the speech of Mr. Cobden, who now began to assume that leading position in the house and in the country to which his high character, no less than his great talents and oratorical powers, entitled him. Already possessing the confidence of the Corn-law League, which had become a great power in the state, he commanded the attention of the House of Commons by the lucid and unadorned eloquence with which he placed true and enlarged views on this subject in a light so clear, that none but those whose minds were partially blinded by a supposed interest or by party feeling could refuse to recognise their justice. In answer to the argument which had been much insisted on in these debates, that the wages of the English artisan were much higher than those of his continental confrère, he showed that, taking into consideration the worth of his labour, the English artisan was the worst remunerated of his class in all Europe.

The other event to which we have referred was the sudden and extraordinary, but very transient, notoriety which Mr. Busfield Ferrand, the member for Knaresborough, achieved for himself in the debate. He endeavoured to counteract the impression which the speech of Mr. Cobden had produced in the house and was sure also to produce throughout the country. He did not, however, attempt to reply to his arguments, but sought to obviate their effect by personal attacks on Mr. Cobden and the free-trade manufacturers generally. He was a ready, fluent, and effective speaker; and as he came from the neighbourhood of the manufacturing districts, of the condition of which most of the gentlemen who occupied the ministerial benches were profoundly ignorant, he was hailed by them as one who was able to grapple with their formidable opponent. After some personal attacks on Mr. Cobden in reference to the hours of labour at his printworks, he proceeded, amidst the cheers of his ministerial backers and the loud and indignant protests of the representatives of the manufacturing districts, to read letters stating that the signatures to the anti-corn-law petition were paid for, and that the distress that prevailed in the manufacturing districts was caused, not by the corn-laws, but by the oppression of the Anti-corn-law League manufacturers. We will give a short specimen of the manner in which, amidst the tremendous cheering of his friends, he carried the war into the enemy's camp. After reading a number of letters which mentioned masters in different districts, accusing them of evading the laws that had been passed to suppress the truck system—he thus described the manner in which that system was applied:

'On Saturday the people go into a room to receive their wages. They are paid at the time in money; but, instead of returning by the door at which they entered, they have to pass into another room, in which sits a person who keeps the books of the truck-shops, and to whom the workman has to pay every farthing that has been expended during the previous week in buying goods and clothes; and if it is proved that any one of the men has purchased one single farthing's-worth of goods from any other shop than that which belongs to the master, he is, without one word of explanation, discharged. This is your free trade system! It is a notorious fact that the masters clear twenty-five per cent. by the goods they sell to the workmen, and ten per cent. for the cottages in which they are compelled to reside.

'I charge the Anti-corn-law League with having enhanced the price of corn. Are honourable gentlemen aware that no less than 100,000 quarters of wheat are annually used by these men?' At this assertion the speaker was interrupted by loud cries of 'How?' from the free-traders. 'How?' he replied; 'why by daubing their calicoes with flour-paste.' He then read several letters which explained the manner in which the paste of flour was employed in the weaving of calicoes, and a letter from an English merchant describing the frauds alleged to be practised by some manufacturers in the weaving of cotton cloths. In this letter it was stated, that the manufacturers to whom it referred collected old and tainted rags, which they ground to dust, and mixed with the paste that was applied to the calicoes. The writer of the letter farther stated, that this dust made from diseased rags was so detested by the manufacturing operatives that they called it devil's dust, and by the name of devil's dust it is accordingly known.* It was

\* It may perhaps be necessary to inform readers unacquainted with the manufacturing districts, that the devil's dust is the dust produced in the

added, that many of the manufacturers in Huddersfield had put such a large quantity of devil's dust into their calicoes, that the foreign trade of the country had been almost ruined. The statements of Mr. Ferrand, and the motives he imputed to the leaders of the anti-corn-law agitation, were treated with contempt by Mr. Cobden, and indignantly contradicted by Mr. Villiers in his reply. But for a long time after, those statements were industriously circulated, for want of better arguments, and formed the political capital of a Tory-Chartist party which came into existence at this time, and had a considerable and very mischievous effect in delaying the final settlement of this great question, and causing increased agitation, both on the part of those who favoured and those who resisted the changes which Messrs. Cobden, Villiers, and their associates demanded. On the division there were

For Mr. Villiers' amendment . . . . . . 90
Against it . . . . . . . . 393

Majority . . . . . . . . 303

So powerful was the party that maintained the monopoly of the landed interest, and so hopeless at this time the prospect of its removal. Never, perhaps, was there a stronger exemplification of the fact that truth and right will ultimately prevail, however vehemently they may be denied, or however powerfully they may be resisted.

Mr. Christopher's motion to substitute a higher scale of duties for that proposed by Sir R. Peel was rejected on a division by 306 votes to 104.

We shall not follow farther the almost interminable discussions to which the government scheme gave rise, but will merely add that the bill was read a third time in the House of Commons, and passed on the 5th of April. In the House of Lords various amendments were moved, some by the promoters of free trade or fixed duties, and some by the advocates of higher protection. However, now, for the first time since the passing of the Reform Bill, a govern-

---

operation of cleaning the raw cotton, by means of an instrument properly called a scatcher, but vulgarly known by the name of a devil. The devil's dust, therefore, is simply the dust removed from the raw cotton by the scatcher.

ment was in office that was able to command a majority in both houses of Parliament without appealing to the forbearance or working on the fears of their opponents; and so the measure went through both houses without any hostile amendment having been introduced into it.

The greatest of all the difficulties that Sir Robert Peel had to deal with was the financial condition of the country. There was an estimated deficiency in the revenue for the ensuing year of 2,570,000*l*., and to this was to be added a considerable sum of uncertain amount on account of China and India. This deficiency Sir Robert had pledged himself to make up; and it was the confidence that was felt in his financial skill and dexterity that had contributed more than any other cause to the signal triumph of his party at the late general election. His plans were therefore looked for with an earnest expectation not inferior to that with which his alterations in the corn-laws had awakened.

The great deficiency we have just mentioned arose from a variety of causes. The revenue had been diminished by a series of bad harvests, and by some of the reforms which the Melbourne government had introduced, especially the great postal reform. On the other hand the expenditure had been increased by several trifling but costly wars in which the country had been engaged, but particularly by a war which had been carried on in China. This war had arisen out of disputes between the English and Chinese authorities respecting the introduction of opium into China. The former had supported their countrymen in carrying on an illicit trade in that pernicious drug, the introduction of which was forbidden by the laws of the Chinese empire; contempt on one side was met by insolence on the other; and thus the two countries gradually drifted into a war. Of course the miserable junks and pasteboard forts of the Chinese could not withstand the attacks of our men-of-war, nor were their troops, though they fought bravely, any match for the disciplined valour and superior weapons of the British army. The result of the contest was, that the Chinese were compelled to pay to our government the amount of 21,000,000 dols., equivalent to 4,375,000*l*., by instalments, to defray the cost of the war, in addition to 6,000,000 dols., or 1,250,000*l*., which they had already paid as a compensation to the merchants for the opium that had been destroyed. Both sides were greatly to blame; but the unfortunate Chinese, if not the chief offenders, were at all events the chief sufferers by this needless war. Sir Robert Peel had pledged himself to find the means of supplying the large deficiency which had grown up under his predecessors. The task he had thus undertaken was not an easy one, for the taxation of the country was already heavy, and as it applied to almost every article that could possibly be taxed, it did not seem to admit of much increase. But the new minister had determined to do much more than to accomplish the task he had undertaken. He would not only fill up the gulf of deficiency, but he would obtain a surplus, which he would apply to the remission of taxes that weighed heavily on the springs of industry, even though their removal would entail a great loss of revenue. The means by which he proposed to accomplish this was the imposition of an income and property tax; an impost which had been hitherto regarded as a resource on which government might fall back in case the country should be engaged in a formidable war; a most unpopular tax, and one which it was therefore believed by his opponents that Sir R. Peel would not have the moral courage to propose nor the country consent to accept. Indeed, it is probable that the country would not have submitted to it if its acquiescence had not been ingeniously purchased by the reduction or abolition of burdensome and mischievous taxes on 750 out of 1200 articles which at that time were subject to customs duties. Thus the minister rendered this unpopular tax almost popular by making it the means of the remission of a great quantity of taxation, which, though much less in amount than the tax it was proposed to impose, galled and shackled industry at every turn, and was more vexatious than the income-tax itself. He thus inaugurated a new system of finance, which he afterwards pushed to an extent that he had not originally contemplated, which has been still farther developed by his successors, and still continues to be carried forward, in the gradual substitution of direct for indirect taxation. But in doing this he did not venture to recommend that the income-tax should be saddled on the country as a permanent institution; but proposed it with the expectation that at the end of a few years, having accomplished the objects for which it was imposed, he or the minister of the day would be able to dispense with it.

We will not, however, forestall Sir Robert's statement, but allow him to speak for himself, only with the condensation which the limits of our work render necessary. On the 11th of March the statement was made in a committee of ways and means, to a house crowded in every part, and listening to the speaker with the most profound attention.

'The late chancellor of the exchequer has calculated the probable revenue for the year ending April 1842 at 48,310,000*l*., and the probable expenditure at 50,819,000*l*., and the consequent deficiency at 2,509,000*l*. A farther probable outlay must be provided for in respect of the war in China, something must be made good for Australia, and something in Canada, and a considerable addition must be made to the army estimates on account of the war in Affghanistan. The finances of India, too, require attention. If Indian credit should be shaken, the credit of England will be affected; and the present state of Indian finance is not a consolatory one. I fear that the deficit thereupon in the two years ending May next will not be less than 4,700,000*l*. How, then, are these deficiencies at home and in India to be met? Shall we persevere in the miserable system of the last five years, the system of loans and exchequer bills, the system of permanent addition to the debt? When the post-office revenue was abandoned—a surrender which I dissuaded—the Parliament which gave it up engaged to grant some other supply in its stead. Shall I impose a tax on the necessaries of life? 'I cannot consent to place burdens on the labouring classes; and if the House attempts that, recent experience proves that it will be defeated. The late government proposed an additional five per cent. on the customs and excise, and of ten per cent. on the assessed taxes. Last year the additional percentage on the customs and excise, instead of producing 5*l*. on each 100*l*., had produced only about 10*s*.; but the percentage on the assessed taxes had produced considerably more than the estimated result of 10*l*. for each 100*l*. These facts prove that the country has here arrived at the limits of taxation on articles of consumption. Setting aside, therefore, these resources, I ask, shall I revive old taxes? Shall

I resort to locomotion? I'm reluctant to tax the means of transferring from place to place the labour of those whose labour is their only capital. A question was raised by the late government, whether it would not be possible to obtain increased revenue from diminished taxation. It is quite true that a nation's revenue may be eventually increased by diminished taxation; but the first effect is a fall in the revenue, and a long interval is found necessary to restore the amount. I will now, therefore, state the measure which, under a deep conviction of its necessity, I am prepared to propose, and which I am persuaded will benefit the country, not only in her pecuniary interests, but in her security and her character.

'I shall propose, for a period to be limited, an income-tax of not more than 7*d*. in the pound, or about three per cent., from which I would exempt all incomes under 150*l*., and in which I would include not only landed but funded property, whether in the hands of British subjects, or of foreigners. I estimate the assessible yearly value of the land at 39,400,000*l*.; of houses, at 25,000,000*l*.; of tithes, shares in railways, mines, and other similar property, at 8,400,000*l*,; total, 72,800,000*l*. From this I deduct one-fourth for the exemption I propose to give to all incomes under 150*l*.; and then the tax thus far will give me 1,600,000*l*. The occupiers of land—assessed at half their rent—will yield 120,000*l*. Next comes funded property. The dividend paid in 1841 was 29,400,000*l*., from which I will deduct one million in respect of the savings-banks; but I must add on bank, foreign, and other stocks 1,500,000*l*., making a total of almost 30,000,000*l*., from which I will deduct one-fourth for incomes under 150*l*. a year, and then the proceeds of my tax will be 646,000*l*. I now arrive at the incomes of trades and professions. The produce I expect from this source is 1,250,000*l*. From the income of public offices I calculate on 150,000*l*. The total will be 3,771,000*l*. The view of the government is, that the impost will probably require to be continued for five years, unless in case of such a revival of commercial prosperity from the other measures I am about to propose as might induce parliament to take the opportunity of revising the subject; but I will, in the first instance, propose a continuance for three years only. With regard to Ireland,

I should, in the absence of all machinery for collecting, prefer to raise the quota of that country by other means. The first of these will be the duty of 1s. per gallon on spirits, from which I calculate I shall receive 250,000l.; and the other will be the equalisation of the stamp-duty with that of England, from which I expect to receive 160,000l. In Great Britain, however, as well as Ireland, I propose to reduce the stamp upon charter parties and bills of lading. With respect to regular absentees from Ireland, having no call of public duty to fix them in England, I propose to require from them the same property-tax that will be required from residents in this island. Another resource will be a tax of 4s. on coal exported in British vessels from this country. Such a tax will probably yield an income of 200,000l., and would operate, like most other taxes, as an encouragement to native industry.

'The aggregate revenue from all these sources will be 4,380,000l., constituting a considerable surplus after covering the deficiency on the votes of annual expenditure. This surplus I propose to apply in relaxing the commercial tariff. My main principle has been removal of prohibition and reduction of duties on raw materials, which should not in any case exceed five per cent. I shall also considerably diminish the duties on articles partially manufactured, the highest being twelve per cent.; and even on complete manufactures I contemplate that the maximum should not in general exceed twenty per cent. I now lay on the table this amended scale of duties, which has been distributed into twenty different heads, for it is all prepared. It will be found that in about 750 articles there has been an abatement of duty recommended, and that on about 450 the duty has been left untouched. The total diminution of revenue occasioned by all the reductions will probably be not more than about 270,000l. On sugar I regret to say that ministers cannot offer any reduction. They cannot consent to let in the sugars of Cuba and Brazil without some securities on the subject of slavery in these countries; and we think that to reduce the duties on British sugar, without a corresponding reduction on foreign sugars, would be merely to give the British planters a monopoly price, without advantage to the British consumers. The present prospects of supply of British sugar are, however, of a highly satisfactory character. On the subject of timber, my measure will be the reverse of that which was brought forward by the late ministry. I advise a great reduction of duty, which will benefit all classes, from the agriculturist to the ship-builder; but I will interpose protection to the interests of the Canadas, and admit their timber at a price little more than nominal. I will lower the duty on foreign timber to 25s. a load, and will let in the timber of Canada at a duty of 1s. I also propose to remit the duty on the export of certain British manufactures, and to diminish considerably that on stage-coaches. On the whole, these reductions, in addition to the excess of expenditure, will increase the deficit to something more, 3,700,000l.; but the estimated produce of the newly-proposed sources of income will not only cover this, but leave more than half a million sterling applicable to the contingencies of our distant wars.'

This plan was very favourably received. It was felt that in all its details it exhibited the hand of a master. It was true that its proposer was still fettered by the trammels of protection; but the tendency of his scheme was in favour of the principles of free trade, and the testimony that it gave to the soundness of these principles was all the more valuable because it was involuntary. The few hearty words in which Lord J. Russell welcomed the liberal feature of Sir R. Peel's scheme found an echo in all parts of the country. However, when the measure of the government was brought under the discussion of the House of Commons, a strong opposition, led by Lord J. Russell, was offered to the proposal of the income-tax, which was evidently the cardinal point of the whole budget, the removal of which from it would have frustrated the attempt to make those large commercial reductions which more especially recommended the scheme to the favour of the nation. Some members of the Whig party strenuously advocated a property-tax in the place of an income-tax. We will not weary the reader with a reference to the long debates on the income-tax bill, and the various amendments that were proposed to it. It is sufficient to say, that it was carried through the house with tolerable speed, and that on every division the government was signally victorious. The majority for the third reading was 130. The measure went through the upper house unaltered, and passed there by a majority of 71.

This triumph of the income-tax involved the triumph of the new tariff; for it was evident that so unpopular a tax would not have been supported by large majorities in both houses, if its supporters had not been influenced by the hope that the benefits to be obtained by the proposed changes in the duties would more than balance the incidence and the hardships of an impost so thoroughly unpopular as the income-tax. Some important alterations having been introduced, in consequence of representations made to the government by persons whose interests they affected, the house went into committee on the tariff thus amended on the 5th of May. Long discussions ensued: every detail of the measure was carefully, but not factiously, scrutinised; the strongest opposition was that made to the timber duties, the duties on importation of cattle, the refusal to lower the duties on sugar, and to the general policy of the differential duties, which were another form of protection. As the discussion proceeded, public opinion pronounced itself more and more loudly in favour of the new tariff. Particular interests might complain that they were unfairly treated, but on the whole the nation was satisfied. The measure was carried forward victoriously through both houses; and it was confidently anticipated that it would remedy the disorders of the finances, and draw after it a great revival of national prosperity. The income-tax was indeed a burden that the people bore with some impatience; but it was hoped that the new customs duties would enable the government to withdraw that unpopular impost at the end of the three years which had been fixed in the bill as the term of its duration; and in this hope the burden was borne patiently, if not cheerfully.

The copyright question had been repeatedly but vainly brought forward by Serjeant Talfourd; it was settled during this session, though he was no longer in the house to advocate it. There were many considerations which prompted the legislature to perform this long-delayed act of justice. Sir Walter Scott had lately departed amidst pecuniary difficulties which all regretted, and distresses with which the whole nation sympathised. The sale of his works was the only resource left to his family; and the copyright of the most important and profitable of them, the Waverley Novels, would shortly expire, unless the legislature interposed to prolong its duration. Wordsworth, now just beginning to obtain the tardy recognition of his genius, was likely to have the harvest which that genius was about to reap snatched from him by the same cause. Southey, who was in a similar position, had been deterred from publishing a great work by the apprehension that the fruit of his labours would be gathered by some adventurous bookseller. Charles Dickens, now at the height of his reputation, was actively pressing the measure. But perhaps there was nothing that influenced the house more powerfully than a characteristic Petition addressed to it by Thomas Carlyle, a writer of books, which, though presented in 1839, was not allowed to be forgotten by the advocates of the proposed change.

The sixty years' copyright asked for in this petition and in the bill originally presented to the House of Commons was not obtained; but the author was allowed to retain his property in his works during his life, and his family continued to possess it for seven years after his death. In any case, it was to be enjoyed for at least forty-two years by the author and his family.

The period we have now reached was honourably distinguished by disinterested efforts to benefit the most helpless and unprotected classes of society. This disposition showed itself in Parliament by factory bills, education bills, and bills designed to put an end to the over-working and ill-treatment of women and children in mines and factories. Out of Parliament it displayed itself in early-closing movements, attempts to relieve superannuated and infirm governesses, the erection of model cottages and lodging-houses, and many other benevolent and philanthropic works or designs.

The great measures, of which we have followed the progress up to their final adoption, were the chief achievements of the session of 1842, and their importance fully warranted the large share of attention that was bestowed on them. They were well calculated to alleviate the distress which prevailed at this time throughout the kingdom, but especially in the manufacturing districts. Of the cause of this distress innumerable explanations were given. By some it was ascribed to the employment of machinery; a large manufacturer at Stockport attributed it to the increased capital applied to manufacturing purposes; others, again, contended that it arose from the state of the currency. But the opinion which found the strongest expression, and which was daily and hourly spreading, was, that the corn-laws, by interfering with our trade with other countries, and by causing many branches of industry, which would otherwise have been carried on in England, to be transferred to the Continent, were the principal cause of the prevailing distress, and that nothing short of their repeal would effectually relieve it. The discontent of the working classes found a vent, amongst other ways, in the presentation to the House of Commons of a monster Chartist petition, of which we shall have more to say hereafter.

Another highly important question, which, as has already been mentioned, during this session occupied the attention of Parliament, was that of the employment of women and children in mines and collieries. The bill intended to deal with this question was introduced by Lord Ashley (now the Earl of Shaftesbury). The way for legislation on the subject had been prepared by long and careful inquiry. A commission, moved for by Lord Ashley, had inquired into the subject, and the result of their investigations had been embodied in a report presented to Parliament, which showed the absolute necessity that existed for the interference of the legislature. They found that children of seven, six, and even four years of age were condemned to work in those dark and noisome excavations. Females, sometimes even pregnant women, were employed in great numbers in labours utterly unsuited to their sex. In cases where the seam of coal was so narrow that it was impossible to stand up, both women and children were obliged to crawl backwards and forwards, like beasts of burden, on all fours, dragging behind them trucks loaded with coals fastened to their haunches; and all this often in water, breathing an atmosphere strongly charged with carbonic-acid gas, amidst damp, cold, and all sorts of moral and physical abominations. The regular hours of labour for these unfortunate creatures were fourteen or sixteen a day, and they were often exceeded. Women went up from the pit to be confined, and were down again at their dreadful work in less than a week. This excessive and unnatural toil produced in the bodies of those who were subjected to it the effects which might be expected: stunted growths, crooked spines, crippled gait, heart diseases, ruptures, asthma, premature old age, and early death. But if the health of those who laboured in these dens was rapidly undermined, their morals were still more speedily corrupted. The ferocity of the men was worse than that of wild beasts. The children who were employed were often maimed and even killed with impunity. The language used was shocking, the drunkenness almost universal; the natural modesty of the female sex was altogether cast away, and a frightful recklessness prevailed, which often caused accidents by which numbers of these unfortunate beings were instantaneously destroyed.

Such was the state of things which Lord Ashley brought under the notice of Parliament. The first provision of his bill was an absolute prohibition of the employment of females in mines and collieries. The next forbad the employment of children under thirteen years of age. It enacted that no person under twenty-one years of age should in any mine or colliery be allowed to act as an engineer; because it had been discovered by the investigations of the commissioners, that serious and even fatal accidents had often occurred in consequence of the management of steam-engines being intrusted to mere children. The bill provided for the entire abolition of the system of apprenticeship, by which the children of paupers were often bound apprentices to the owners of coal-mines, and compelled to work without any remuneration till the age of twenty-one, when their labour was worth from 20*s.* to 25*s.* a week. The motion to bring in this bill was carried without any expression of dissent, and the measure went through its farther stages without encountering serious opposition. In the upper house Lord Londonderry, who was a large coal-owner, and therefore had a strong pecuniary interest in the question, moved that the bill should be read a second time that day six months; but the motion fell to the ground for want of a seconder. Amendments proposed by the government, and designed to defer the period at which the prohibition of the labour of women would be brought into operation, to regulate the hours during which children should be employed underground, and to allow apprenticeship for a period not exceeding eight years and not commencing till after ten years of age, were adopted; other amendments were rejected. When the bill returned to the House of Commons, Lord Ashley agreed to accept the amendments rather than risk the loss of the many valuable provisions that it still retained; and so it passed.

We have seen already that the changes which had been made in the mode of electing members of the House of Commons had not by any means put an end to the corrupt practices that had long prevailed at elections, and that the remedies which had been devised for them had been almost ineffectual. The recent election had been attended by more corruption than ever. Great efforts had been made by the Carlton Club and the Conservatives generally to raise a large sum to 'fight the battle of the constitution,' as it was termed; and the Reformers and the Reform Club, though less wealthy, had done what they could. The money expended by the candidates themselves had been greater than at any election which had taken place since the passing of the Reform Bill. New forms of bribery and corruption had been introduced, and a very large number of election petitions had been lodged. On the other hand, new devices had been employed to defeat the inquiries that were made before the election committees. To one of these especially Mr. Roebuck drew the attention of the house. He stated to it, that he had strong reasons for believing that several election petitions had been corruptly compromised. In these cases it had happened, that when a member was charged with bribery before the committee, and it became evident that the proceedings would end in the declaration that the seat was void, the petition was suddenly withdrawn, apparently without any motive, but really on the strength of a secret engagement entered into by the sitting member and his principal friends to use their best efforts to procure the unopposed return of the petitioner. Mr. Roebuck, in bringing the matter under the notice of the house, named several boroughs which had been the subject of these corrupt bargains, and interrogated the members of those boroughs with regard to them. As the replies they made to his questions were unsatisfactory, he proposed and carried the appointment of a committee to inquire into the matter. The report of this committee, founded on careful and secret examination of a great number of witnesses, fully confirmed Mr. Roebuck's statements. It denounced the practices which he had unmasked as violations of the liberties of the people, and breaches of the privileges of the House of Commons, and recommended that the house should inquire into all cases in which there were good grounds for suspecting that such practices had been resorted to, and severely punish those who were proved to be guilty of them. The committee also recommended that no new writs should be issued for Harwich, Nottingham, Lewes, Reading, Falmouth, and Penrhyn, till farther measures had been taken by the house to protect the purity of election in those boroughs.

Corrupt practices like those which Mr. Roebuck's committee had exposed were so common, and the number of members interested in preventing farther proceedings in the matter so numerous, that the first resolution proposed by Mr. Roebuck was rejected by a majority sufficiently large to render it useless to press the others, and they were accordingly withdrawn. The government, however, determined to show their disapproval of such practices by refusing to grant the stewardship of the Chiltern Hundreds to members whom they had reason to believe to have entered into these objectionable compromises; and thus the object for which they were made was defeated. After long discussions the writs to boroughs in which bribery had been shown to prevail were at last allowed to be issued, except that of Sudbury, in which gross and systematic corruption had been shown to have been carried to an extent which seemed to mark it out for disfranchisement.

Although the majority of the House of Commons had refused to carry into effect the recommendations of Mr. Roebuck's committee, the facts which it had elicited were not wholly disregarded. Lord J. Russell introduced a bill intended to diminish bribery, check corrupt practices, and facilitate the punishment of boroughs in which corruption could be proved to have generally prevailed. This measure was tolerably well calculated to effect the objects it had in view, and was favourably received by members on both sides of the house, who promised their coöperation to Lord

J. Russell in his endeavours to put an end to practices which brought discredit on our institutions. The bill accordingly passed the lower house with a few modifications, and was adopted by the House of Lords without any change.

While the House of Commons was busied with those great financial reforms which were the most conspicuous features in the legislation of the session, Lord Lyndhurst was engaged in the other house in proposing to it measures of legal reform which were no less imperatively required. Bills were introduced by him designed to improve the bankruptcy and lunacy courts, and to facilitate the recovery of small debts by establishing county courts, or rather by improving the character and extending the jurisdiction of courts which already existed under that name to very little purpose, because, as then constituted, they afforded few guarantees of the impartiality or correctness of their decisions. The two first of these bills were passed; the third was withdrawn at a late period of the session for want of time to carry it through. Attempts made by Lord Campbell to transfer the jurisdiction of the Privy Council to the House of Lords, and by Lord Francis Egerton to amend the marriage laws, were defeated.

Before the prorogation of Parliament, Lord Palmerston made a motion for a return of the bills that had been introduced during the session, in order to gain an opportunity of criticising the conduct and measures of the government, which he accused them of borrowing from the party they had turned out of office. Sir R. Peel, in resisting the motion, raised a laugh at the expense of the late foreign secretary by observing, that the motion he now brought forward was copied word for word from a motion made by Colonel Sibthorpe on the 25th of May, 1841. He then replied at length to Lord Palmerston's strictures, dealing with his attacks point by point in a light jocular style, fairly laying himself open to the criticism of Mr. Cobden, who seriously asked, when Sir Robert sat down, whether the leaders of the two great parties had nothing better to do than to revive the old quarrels between Whig and Tory. The session was brought to a close on the 12th of August.

In the course of this year two attacks were made on the Queen, which, though more ludicrous than dangerous, deserved serious attention on account of the alarm they might have caused to her Majesty, and the example they afforded to more dangerous assailants. On the 30th of May a pistol was fired at the Queen by a man named John Francis; and as this was the second attempt that had been made on her Majesty's life, an Act of Parliament was passed authorising the courts to sentence persons guilty of such attempts to imprisonment for a time not exceeding seven years, and to periodical personal chastisement during their confinement. By this act the process of conviction was rendered more easy than in cases of high treason, and the morbid sympathy which was sometimes evoked by the formalities of a trial and the severity of the penalties for that offence, and which for some diseased minds is not without its attractions, was not likely to be excited in cases where the punishment was rather ignominious than severe. As this act passed after the attempt made by Francis, it could not of course be applied to his case. He was therefore tried under the old law of high treason, and being found guilty by the jury, was condemned to be hung and quartered. This sentence was commuted into transportation for life. On the 3rd of July a deformed dwarf named Bean levelled an old rusty pistol at the Queen as she passed him in her carriage, and attempted to fire it at her; but it did not explode. It appeared that the object of this outrage was rather to alarm than injure the Queen, or to secure a share of that notoriety which had been obtained by Oxford and Francis; for the pistol was found on examination to be only loaded with powder and wadding. Bean was therefore sentenced to be confined in the Millbank penitentiary for eighteen calendar months.

We must now turn to India, where a great and awful disaster, shaking our empire there to its very foundations, had been gallantly and terribly redeemed. The country of Affghanistan, situated at the north-western extremity of our Indian possessions, inhabited by a brave, warlike, but barbarous race of men, and defended by formidable natural barriers, had been occupied by a British force, the greater part of which was stationed at Cabul. The communication with these troops was carried on through the Koord Cabul pass, a long defile which a small body of determined men might defend against an army. The custody of this pass was claimed by an Affghan tribe, who called themselves

Ghilzies, and the Indian government thought it better to pay them to keep the pass open for our troops and convoys than to be obliged to force it every time that it was necessary to communicate with Cabul. The Ghilzies seem to have acted with good faith, and as long as our part of the bargain was carried out, the passage of our troops backward and forward was undisputed, although the Ghilzies had been much irritated by the wanton and unnecessary storming of a fort held by some of their tribe, in which several of its defenders were killed. Notwithstanding this provocation, they continued to fulfil their part of the agreement, until it was unfortunately violated on our side by the negligent withholding of a portion of the sum we had stipulated to pay them. Indignant at what appeared to be a breach of faith, they at once rose in arms, stopped the pass, cut off all communication between Cabul and British India, and seized a Kafila valued at 20,000 rupees. General Elphinstone, who commanded the English troops at Cabul, finding himself thus isolated, at once dispatched General Sale with a brigade of light infantry and sepoys, to clear the pass and restore the communication. The general encountered a brave resistance from the Ghilzies, and received a severe wound in his leg; but the defiles, though defended with great courage and obstinacy, were successively forced; and the troops reached Gundamuck on the 30th of October, 1841, and then fought their way to Jellalabad, where they arrived on the 12th of November.

While General Sale was still struggling through the defiles which led to British India, General Elphinstone was displaying an infatuated contempt of the prowess of the barbarians whose country he occupied. He neglected to take the most ordinary precautions against an attack from them. His troops occupied a cantonment commanded on all sides by the forts and artillery of the Affghans; and, by a greater and more irretrievable blunder, the provisions for the force under his command were placed in an old fort at some distance from the cantonment, and still less defensible than that which the troops occupied. One or two Affghan chiefs appear to have seen how seriously the safety of the troops was compromised by the blundering dispositions of the English commander, and to have determined to take advantage of them. They acted with consummate.

treachery and cunning. The following memorandum, written by the late Sir William Macnaughten, the unfortunate envoy of the British government, whose tragical fate we shall presently have occasion to relate, shows the artifices to which they had recourse, and the success that attended the efforts they made to induce their countrymen to co-operate with them.

'The immediate cause of this outbreak in the capital was a seditious letter addressed by Abdoolah Khan to several chiefs of influence at Cabul, stating that it was the design of the envoy to seize and send them all to London. The principal rebels met on the previous night, and relying on the inflammable feelings of the people of Cabul, they pretended that the king had issued an order to put all infidels to death, having previously forged an order from him for our destruction, by the common process of washing out the contents of a genuine paper with the exception of the seal, and substituting their own wicked inventions.'

The outbreak to which the Affghans had thus been instigated commenced with an attack on the house of Sir Alexander Burnes, who was murdered, together with his brother, Lieutenant Burnes, and Lieutenant W. Broadfoot. General Elphinstone now prepared for defence. He brought the forces under his command into the cantonment, and recalled a portion of the force he had sent with General Sale to assist in forcing the passes, and which had been left to guard them. He had then under his command in the cantonment the 5th, the 37th, and a portion of the 5th sepoy regiments, the envoy's body-guard, her Majesty's 44th foot, two troops of cavalry, three companies of the Shah's sappers and a body of the Company's sappers, five six-pounder field-guns, and two horse-artillery guns. In all the general had under his command 4500 fighting men, attended by 12,000 camp-followers, besides women and children. A vigorous and well-directed attack was made by the Affghans on the cantonment, and the old fort in which the provisions were stored. The garrison were soon compelled to evacuate it, and to retire into the cantonment, leaving the provisions it contained in the hands of the enemy. A supply was obtained from a neighbouring chief; but this was soon cut off, and famine stared the little army in the face. Under such circumstances, a Wellington or a Napier would probably have struck some sudden and decisive blow; but General Elphinstone and Sir William Macnaughten seem to have thought only of negotiating; they therefore welcomed an offer to treat made by the Affghan chiefs. But the terms proposed were so hard, that the envoy, even in this extremity, refused to listen to them; and the attack was consequently carried on. The rapid diminution of the small stock of provisions compelled him to reopen the negotiations, and a convention was made, the principal conditions of which were, that the British should at once evacuate the whole of Affghanistan, and that the force under General Elphinstone should be protected and supplied with food by the Affghan chiefs during their journey to India. It soon became evident, however, that these negotiations had been carried on with a view to compel the British to surrender unconditionally. Sir William Macnaughten was entrapped into an interview with some of the Affghan leaders, and foully murdered. General Elphinstone, compelled by his necessities to negotiate, in spite of this proof of the treachery of the Affghans, found his position becoming every moment worse. At length, on the 6th of January, 1842, he commenced one of the most disastrous and humiliating retreats that has ever been recorded. Akbar Khan, who conducted the negotiations, and who, while professing to wish to carry out the stipulations he had made in favour of the British, was really directing the operations against them, proposed new and harder terms, and required several officers to be given up to him as hostages for their fulfilment. Nevertheless, the food promised to the retreating force was not given, and the attacks on them were redoubled. Yet, notwithstanding their sufferings and privations, they gallantly fought their way through the Koord Cabul pass, though assailed with great fury by the Ghilzies, who defended it step by step. Here Akbar Khan offered to protect the ladies if they should be intrusted to him; and as there seemed to be no other chance of preserving their lives, it was thought better to take advantage of the offer, in accordance with which Lady Sale, Lady Macnaughten, and six other ladies, with their husbands, were placed under his protection. The sepoys, overcome by fatigue and benumbed by cold, were unable to go on, and were massacred without mercy and without resistance.

The British troops, however, still held together, and fought their way forward. Of the 16,500 men who left Cabul, only 300 reached Jugdulluk, after a march of thirty-five miles, in a miserable plight. General Elphinstone, having agreed to confer with Akbar Khan, in the hope of securing a peaceable retreat for the small remnant of his troops, was seized and made prisoner. The survivors, warned by a note from him of his fate, resumed their march the same night, through snow and intense cold. In the Jugdulluk pass the attack was renewed; and as the little troop could no longer be kept together, the greater part of them were put to death. A few of the officers, having the advantage of being mounted, made their way to Gundermuck. Here they separated, in order to avoid observation, and took different roads to Jellalabad, but were murdered by the inhabitants of the villages through which they passed. One only escaped. Dr. Brydon, a medical man, faint and wounded, on the 13th of January reached Jellalabad, still occupied by the force that had been sent thither under the command of General Sale.

While one part of the British army by which Affghanistan had been occupied was thus being destroyed, the other portions of it were placed in a very perilous position, in the midst of a hostile population no longer restrained by the prestige of the British arms. The Indian government was not inactive. Lord Auckland, the governor-general, who was on the point of returning to England, lost not a moment in sending forward to Jellalabad all the troops he could collect. Reiterated orders were dispatched to Sir Jasper Nichols, the commander-in-chief in India, to push forward to Peshawur as many troops as could be spared. But before Jellalabad could be reached, the Khyber pass, a long and dangerous defile, must be traversed; and the Khyberees, instigated partly by the exhortations of Akbar Khan, and partly by their own hatred of the British, resolved to defend it with all their might. A first attempt to penetrate it, made under the command of Brigadier Wild, was repulsed. General Pollock came up with large reinforcements, and took the direction of the army, which now amounted to 8000 men. Knowing that everything depended on dispatch, he endeavoured to purchase from the Khyberees permission to go through the pass without molestation, and the agreement was so nearly completed that a small instalment was actually paid to them; but finding that they were not to be depended on, and determined to lose no time, he pressed on without waiting for the reinforcements, amounting to 4000 soldiers, that were hastening forward to join him. He forced his way through defiles which had hitherto presented an impassable barrier to every army that had attempted to traverse them, in the face of a resolute enemy. He was speedily followed by the 4000 who had been left behind, and the pass was held for the British army by a body of Sikh troops.

It was on the 16th of April when the army of General Pollock approached Jellalabad, and saw the English flag flying over the fortress. General Sale, who marched into the town on the 14th of November, found the fortifications in a very dilapidated condition, and far too extensive to be properly defended by the small force under his command. There were provisions for only a few days; and the whole population, both inside and outside the town, was savagely hostile. Here, however, he resolved to make a stand, and to be ready to afford shelter, and coöperation to the army of General Elphinstone, in case, as seemed highly probable, it should be compelled to evacuate Cabul, and retreat through the Koord Cabul pass. But no messenger and no intelligence reached him from the army from which he had been detached. At length, on the 8th of January, five days before the arrival of Dr. Brydon, the general received a summons to evacuate Jellalabad in accordance with the terms of the convention which had been extorted from General Elphinstone and Sir W. Macnaughten, and which had since been so treacherously violated. General Sale, though of course ignorant of what had occurred, refused to comply. It is said that a letter from his brave wife reached him, urging him to take this resolution, and declaring that the writer preferred death to his dishonour. His troops, though sadly disheartened, and exposed to terrible privations and hardships, laboured incessantly to raise and strengthen the ruinous defences of the town. But a tremendous earthquake shook down the parapets built up with so much labour, injured several of the bastions, cast to the ground all the guard-houses, demolished a third of the town, made a considerable breach in the rampart of a curtain in the Peshawur face, and reduced the Cabul gate to a shapeless mass of ruins. 'It savours of romance,' wrote the general, 'but it is a sober fact that the city was thrown into alarm, within the space of a little more than one month, by the repetition of full one hundred shocks of this terrific phenomenon of nature.' The mischief thus done was assiduously repaired. Akbar Khan, accompanied by a large force, and flushed with the success that had thus far crowned his enterprise, appeared before the town, and at once began to cut off foraging parties, blockade the town, and compel the little garrison to fight for forage under every disadvantage. Profiting by his great superiority in cavalry, he kept them closely shut up within the walls, hoping that the want of supplies would speedily compel them to surrender. On the 7th of April, the British sallied out in force, attacked the camp of the besiegers, completely defeated them, and compelled them to retire towards Cabul. On the way Akbar Khan's barbarous followers gradually fell away from him, and returned to their homes; so that at length he was left almost without attendants.

General Pollock was in no haste to follow him. The enterprise before him was both difficult and dangerous, and required ample preparations to be made for it. It was not therefore till the 20th of August that he began to advance towards those fatal passes which General Sale had forced with so much difficulty, and in which the army of General Elphinstone had perished. The Ghilzies were again on the alert to resist the British invasion. Every height was crowned with large bodies of them, very advantageously posted, and protected by such defences as they had been able to erect. These obstacles to the march of our troops through the defiles were removed one after another in spite of the stubborn resistance made to the British attacks. At length in the valley of Tezeen, a very narrow and difficult pass, the Affghans made their last stand, and our troops won a great and decisive victory, which put an end to all farther resistance and opened the way to Cabul.

The Koord Cabul pass, the scene of so much slaughter, was traversed without resistance, and the British flag once more waved over the citadel of Cabul. The prisoners were recovered, but not without some difficulty; and now came the day of vengeance. The town of Istalif, to which a great number of the Affghan chiefs had retired with their wives and children because it was supposed to be almost impregnable, was stormed by a force composed of British and Indian soldiers, who in their rage gave no quarter, putting every male in the place to death, and pillaging in a manner disgraceful to the character of the British arms. In Cabul too a signal and memorable example was made. The body of Sir W. Macnaughten, after his assassination, had been exposed to the insults of the populace in the great bazaar of Cabul. This building, the pride and chief ornament of the city, the emporium of that part of Asia, renowned at once for the antiquity of its associations and the majesty of its architecture, was completely destroyed. The greater part of the city was also levelled, except those quarters whose inhabitants throughout these troubles had adhered to our cause. Having struck this blow, having signally punished as far as possible the authors of the late disasters, having made themselves masters of the government of Affghanistan, the Indian government wisely determined to withdraw our armies from a country they never ought to have entered, and to leave the inhabitants to settle their own form of government as best they could.

But there was yet another body of troops which had been placed in a very critical position through the events we have narrated. General Nott, with a body of 10,000 men, was stationed near Cundahar. The Affghans, emboldened by the destruction of General Elphinstone's army, ventured to attack him; but he marched out to meet them with four regiments and a thousand horse, and completely defeated them. He was then summoned, as General Sale had been, to fulfil the convention which General Elphinstone had signed, and to withdraw his troops from Affghanistan. This summons he peremptorily refused to obey. Meanwhile General England, who commanded in the part of India which was next to the position occupied by General Nott, vainly attempted to force his way through the Bolar Pass, which leads to Cundahar, to effect a junction with him. Having learned the true state of affairs at Cabul, General Nott resolved to coöperate with General Pollock, who was then making his way through the long series of defiles which intervened between Jellalabad and Cabul. On his way he encountered an Affghan army twice as numerous as that under his own command, well disciplined and full of resolution, but which he nevertheless completely routed. He then took Ghuznee, and destroyed its fortifications. In his advance from this place he drove another body of 12,000 Affghans from strong positions which they occupied. He then pursued his onward march without meeting any resistance, and effected a junction with General Pollock without farther molestation. The two armies marched together down those disastrous passes, which had been the scenes of so much slaughter; the sight of the unburied skeletons of their comrades maddened the soldiers, and they took a terrible vengeance on the unfortunate inhabitants, without attempting to discriminate between the innocent and the guilty. These great achievements, important not so much in themselves as on account of the effect they had in restoring the prestige of the British arms, not in India only, but throughout the whole world, were officially communicated to the different governments and to the people of India in a proclamation issued by Lord Ellenborough, the new governor-general of India, which contained the following passage:—

'My Brothers and my Friends,—Our victorious army nears the gates of the temple of Somnauth in triumph from Affghanistan, and the despoiled tomb of Sultan Mahmoud looks upon the ruins of Ghuznee. The insult of eight hundred years is at last avenged; the gates of the temple of Somnauth, so long the memorial of your humiliation, are become the proudest record of your national glory, the proof of your superiority in arms over the nations of the Indus. To you, princes and chiefs of Sirhind, of Rajwanah, of Malwa, and Ghuzerat, I shall commit this glorious trophy of successful war. You will yourselves, with all honour, transmit the gates of sandal wood through your respective territories to the restored\* temple of Somnauth. The chiefs of Sirhind shall be informed at what time our victorious army will first deliver the gates of the temple into their guardianship at the foot of the Sutlej.'

It does not fall within the province of this History to

---

\* This expression was suggested by an unfortunate error into which Lord Ellenborough had fallen: he was not aware that the temple to which he referred no longer existed; and it was at first supposed that he intended to rebuild it at the expense of the Indian government. The gates were carried into Delhi, with much ceremony, under a canopy of crimson and gold.

refer to the reception given to this extraordinary state paper in the country to which it was addressed; but in England it met with a degree of reprobation perhaps more severe than it deserved. Many regarded what was really an attempt made by Lord Ellenborough to accommodate his language to the opinions and feelings of the majority of the people which he was appointed to govern as a positive homage to their idolatry, and a virtual denial of Christianity. Others derided the style and censured the taste of the luckless document. All sides of the House of Commons condemned it; even the ministers by whom Lord Ellenborough had been sent out did not venture to defend it. The spirit of party laid hold of it. The successes that had been achieved in India tended to strengthen the administration under whose auspices they had been gained, and to throw discredit on that which was in power when the disasters which preceded them had occurred. The consequence was a strong manifestation of that party spirit which seems to be the almost necessary alloy of the many advantages of a free government, leading public men too often to regard almost every question with a view to the party purposes to which it may be turned; accordingly, when the events we have thus succinctly related came under the consideration of the legislature, much more was said about the gates of Somnauth and the supposed idolatrous tendencies of the governor-general than about the infinitely more important military and political questions that these momentous events ought to have suggested.

The year 1843 commenced ominously. The distress which had hitherto prevailed was still increasing, and the revenue still diminishing. Some ascribed this unfortunate state of things to the insurrection, some to the corn-laws, some to the Chartist agitation; but the real explanation was to be found in a series of deficient harvests, the calamitous effects of which would have been diminished by a free importation of corn. Parliament was opened by commission on the 2nd of February. The announcements made in the Queen's speech of the measures to be brought before Parliament were more than usually vague, except with regard to law-reform; a subject which, as we have already seen, had been left over from the last session. The address in answer to the speech, after having been subjected to a large amount of criticism, and having given rise to long discussions on the conduct of the governor-general, as well as on the merits of the corn-laws and of the income tax, was adopted unanimously by both houses.

The long debate on the address was followed by another long debate on a motion brought forward by Lord Howick for the appointment of a committee to inquire into the causes of the distress, the severity of which was acknowledged on all hands. The discussion turned chiefly on the question of free trade; and was remarkable for the frankness with which Sir R. Peel, Mr. Gladstone, and Sir James Graham admitted the general soundness of the principles of free trade, while pleading for the continuance of protection to agriculture, on the ground of the interests which had grown up under it. The only difference between them and the most advanced free-traders was as to the time when free-trade principles should be carried out. They could not but feel that the necessity for a repeal or a modification of the taxes on food was daily and hourly growing more imperative,—as, with a population increasing every year at the rate of 200,000 persons, the burden of the corn-laws must needs become progressively more heavy, and they were gradually and cautiously paving the way for the repeal of duties which the others wished to abolish without delay. At the commencement of the century England was perhaps capable of producing corn sufficient, or nearly sufficient, for all her inhabitants; but as her population increased, the home-supply fell more and more short of its requirements, and importation from other countries became more and more needful. All who thought on the subject felt that the impost could not be maintained much longer, especially in seasons of commercial and agricultural depression. The discussion showed that the House instinctively anticipated the result of such an inquiry as Lord Howick asked for; but the division proved that this was a result which the majority was not yet prepared to accept. The numbers were:

    Against the motion . . . . . . . . . 306
    For it . . . . . . . . . . . 191
        Majority against the motion . . . . 115

An incident that occurred in this debate elicited at the

time a very strong feeling, and no doubt helped to swell the majority by which the motion was refused. On the 21st of January, Mr. Drummond, the private secretary and confidential friend of Sir Robert Peel, was fired at and mortally wounded in the open day, as he was walking from Charing-cross towards Whitehall, by a man named M'Naughten, who appeared to be insane. There was no doubt that the assassin had mistaken Mr. Drummond for Sir Robert Peel, and had intended to murder the premier. This event produced a very strong impression on the public mind, and was felt by no one more acutely than by Sir Robert himself. When therefore, in the course of the debate on Lord Howick's motion, Mr. Cobden, repeating an expression he had already employed elsewhere, declared that he held the prime minister as 'individually responsible' for what might happen, Sir Robert Peel, who was suffering at the time from nervous depression, intensified by the feeling that he was overmatched in argument, passionately laid hold of the phrase, as if it had been designed to menace him with the fate that had befallen his unfortunate friend, and, amidst the loud cheers of his followers, indignantly stigmatised it as intended to hold him up as a mark for the pistol of the assassin. In vain did Mr. Cobden attempt to disavow a design so foreign to his character. The majority clamorously refused to listen to him. However, before the conclusion of the debate, he succeeded in giving an explanation, in which he strongly, and, as Sir R. Peel subsequently admitted, truly, repudiated the interpretation that had been put upon his words.

A motion on the subject of education, brought forward by Lord Ashley, afforded the House of Commons an opportunity of discussing that important question. In bringing his motion forward, Lord Ashley stated facts which have a permanent interest, because they indicate the position which the question of education then occupied. After a carefully-conducted calculation of the number of children who at that time were being educated at the expense of private individuals or at the cost of the nation; of those educated by daily schools in connection either with the established church or the various dissenting communions; he stated that there remained no fewer that 1,014,193 children capable of education, but receiving no instruction whatever in any daily school. He followed this statement with details of the condition of vice, crime, depravity, and ignorance, in which a large proportion of the population was sunk, chiefly through the want of education; and he dwelt on the mischief and danger to the country with which such a state of things was fraught. The details he laid before the House were too voluminous to be given even in a compressed form; and therefore we will content ourselves with citing, as a specimen of them, the statements which he made with regard to the educational, moral, and religious condition of the 'dangerous classes' residing at Manchester.

'By the police-returns for Manchester, made up to December, 1841, it appears that 13,345 persons were taken into custody, of whom 10,208 were discharged by the magistrates without any punishment. Of these 3069 were under twenty years of age, and 745 were females. The return for the next six months—namely, to July, 1842—of persons taken into custody was 8341; and if the whole year bears a like proportion, the number will be 16,682. Of the 8341, there were 5810 males and 2531 females. Of the persons so committed the number who only read or who read or wrote imperfectly was males 1999, females 863; of those who neither read nor wrote, males 3098, females 1519, making a total of 4617. The number of those from fifteen years and under twenty was 2360, and of these 1639 were males and 721 females. Take what may be called the *curable* portion at ten years and under fifteen at 665; of these 547 were males and 118 females. The magistrates discharged without punishment about 12,614 in a year. Is it to be wondered at that crime should so abound when there is every incentive to its committal? In Manchester there are 129 pawnbrokers, 769 beerhouses, 498 public-houses, 309 brothels (119 brothels have been lately suppressed), 163 houses where prostitutes are kept, 223 houses where they resort, and 763 street-walkers in the borough. The thieves known to reside in the borough and do nothing but steal are 212. The persons following some lawful occupation, but who augment their gains by habitual violations of the law, are 160. There are 63 houses for receiving stolen goods, and 32 others have been lately suppressed. Of lodging-houses where the sexes indiscriminately sleep together there are 109. Another cause which tends to increase the amount of juvenile crime is, that a vast number of children of tender years are allowed by their parents to roam through the streets, where they necessarily contract the most idle and dissolute habits. The number of children found wandering about the streets and restored to their parents by the police in 1836 was 8500, and in 1840 the number so restored was 5500. It is calculated that in the borough of Manchester 1500 children are annually added to *les classes dangereuses*.'

After remarking that the total annual expenditure for the punishment of crime was 604,965*l*., in the county of Lancaster alone, while the annual vote for education for all England was only 30,000*l*., he urged the expediency of gradually diminishing the criminal expenditure, and applying the funds thus saved to the extension of education. He concluded by moving, 'That a humble address be presented to her Majesty, praying that her Majesty will be graciously pleased to take into her instant and serious consideration the best means of diffusing the benefits and blessings of a moral and religious education among the working classes of the people.' The motion was received on all sides of the house in a manner that seemed to show a general feeling that this was a question into which the spirit of party ought not to be allowed to enter, but that all should unite, as far as possible, in an effort to remedy the evils which had been so vividly depicted, and to place England in this respect on a footing of equality with the other countries of Europe, most of which had already adopted a national system of education, and almost all of which were educationally very far in advance of us. Sir J. Graham met this general desire by giving the house an outline of the plan which the government intended to bring forward. It did not propose for the present, to do more than attempt to promote the compulsory education of two classes of children to whom it was thought that compulsion might properly be applied in this matter—the children of paupers, and the children who were employed in factories. It was intended that district schools, placed under the superintendence of the clergy of the Church, should be established in the metropolis and the larger towns of the kingdom for the children of paupers and of such other persons as might wish to send their children to them, provision being made for the religious instruction of children of dissenting parents by ministers of their own persuasion. The buildings were to be erected by a rate not exceeding one-fifth the annual amount of the poor-rate for the last three years. The legislation for the education of factory children had, from various causes, hitherto proved ineffectual. It was now proposed that children between the ages of eight and thirteen should not be allowed to be employed in factories for more than six and a half hours a day, the whole work to be done either in the forenoon or the afternoon, nor without having certificates of attendance during the other half of the day at some school in connection with the National Society or the British and Foreign Society, or, in the case of Roman Catholics, at some Roman Catholic school. It was also intended that the authorised version of the Scriptures, and some portion of the liturgy, should be used in those schools which were to be placed under the care of the clergy.

Such was the general outline of the plan which the government of Sir R. Peel had determined to place before the House of Commons. And when we consider the obstacles with which that government had to contend from its own extreme supporters, and the difficulty with which a measure of national education was at length, in the year 1870, forced through the two branches of the legislature, it must be admitted that such a proposal in the year 1843, avowedly as a first step towards a more extended plan, was a bold and praiseworthy attempt. The reception which this scheme met with in the House of Commons was very encouraging. Lord J. Russell, with a warmth that did him great honour, expressed his approval of the plan; though he very properly objected to its being limited to the manufacturing districts, when, as he truly remarked, the agricultural districts were in this respect certainly not better off than the towns. He reserved his opinion with regard to the details of the measure, but added, with characteristic frankness, that if the plan should be found to answer to the view that Sir J. Graham had given of it, it would not only be folly but wickedness to oppose it. Several other members also spoke approvingly of the proposed measure. It was true that Sir R. Inglis, always zealous for what he conceived to be the interests of the church; Mr. Hawes, no less zealous for the dissenters; and Mr. O'Brien, who expressed the sentiments of a large number of his Roman Catholic co-religionists, raised objections to parts of the scheme which trenched on their opinions; but these objections were made in a manner so temperate as scarcely to interrupt the general desire that seemed to be felt to settle this important question, and to put aside all party feeling in approaching the consideration of the ministerial measure. The address proposed by Lord Ashley was accepted, and on the 8th of March a favourable answer to it was delivered at the bar of the house by the Earl of Jermyn. On the same evening the factory bill, containing the educational provisions already mentioned, was brought in and explained to the house by Sir J. Graham. The measure was readily accepted by those members who were supposed to represent the church; but it was vehemently condemned and strenuously opposed by the dissenters, who complained that it was not based on principles of fair and equal justice. The consequence of this outcry was that, though the government carried the second reading by a considerable majority, they abandoned the educational clauses.

This year was marked by the existence of an amount of distress which, though it was cast into the shade by that which prevailed in some subsequent years, was sufficiently severe to demand the serious consideration of the legislature, and the best endeavours of all its members to devise some remedy for it. As the corn-laws, which were jealously upheld by the great majority of both houses, prevented food from coming freely to the people, Mr. Buller suggested that the people should be taken to the food. This object he proposed to effect by encouraging emigration on a large scale to our colonies, where the labour of those who could find no employment at home was greatly needed and would be largely recompensed. Mr. Villiers, speaking as the representative of the free-traders, proposed to allow the food to be brought more freely to the people by the entire and immediate repeal of all duties on the absolute necessaries of life. It is a curious fact, that the first inroad made on the policy of agricultural protection, the first opening for the inlet of foreign corn, was afforded by Lord Stanley himself; who, in his capacity of colonial minister, brought in a bill to carry into effect an arrangement that had been entered into with the Canadian government for the admission of corn and wheaten meal at diminished fixed duties. The bill was strongly opposed by a combination of free-traders, who thought it did not go far enough, and of ultra-protectionists, who feared—and as the event proved not without reason—that it would open the door to farther relaxations of protection. However, in spite of the opposition offered to it, the bill passed through both houses by considerable majorities.

In the course of this year the chronic disorders of Ireland broke out into a paroxysm of unusual violence, producing murders, agrarian outrages, monster meetings, a sudden rise of the repeal rent from 500*l.* to 3000*l.* a week, and a general and vehement revival of the agitation for the repeal of the Union. These things made it imperative on the ministry to have recourse to measures of coercion; and unfortunately these measures were neither accompanied nor followed by measures calculated to remove the political maladies of which the crimes and violences that prevailed were the natural outcome. Nor, indeed, were ministers either able or willing to deal with those maladies in an effectual manner; for they were doubly and trebly pledged to the upholding of that which lay at the root of the evils and discontents of that unfortunate country—the existence of a richly-endowed established church, which was not only entirely at variance with the religious belief of the vast majority of the Irish people—was not only officered by ministers, many of whom were in the constant habit of denouncing the religion of their more numerous fellow-countrymen as an idolatrous and anti-christian superstition —but was regarded by the Irish Catholics as a badge of conquest, and was upheld against their wishes by the power of the English government and the English Parliament.

In narrating the events of the year 1843 we must not omit to mention the visit paid by the Queen and Prince Albert to the King and Queen of the French. It is true that the visit was of a private nature, and that a mere exchange of civilities between monarchs has not, as a general rule, much political importance in modern times; but a visit made at a time when the alliance between the two countries had been nearly broken—a visit which called forth the most cordial expression of good feeling, not only on the part of the French sovereign, but also of the French nation—which brought together not only Victoria, Louis Philippe, and Prince Albert, but also Guizot, Aberdeen, and other French and English statesmen of high character and great abilities, possessing considerable influence over the opinions of their respective countrymen—which evoked on both sides of the Channel feelings which were the best guarantees for the continuance of peace between the two nations—such a visit, however private in its character, was an event of no ordinary political importance, and the English History of this year would be imperfectly narrated without some reference to it. After graciously receiving the addresses of the mayors of Falmouth and Penrhyn, and no less graciously receiving the apologies made for the mayor of Truro, who, having fallen into the water in full municipal costume, had been fished out with his address, both too wet for presentation, her Majesty sailed from Plymouth Sound at 3 o'clock on the afternoon of the 1st of September, and being joined by the fleet which had been appointed to escort her on this occasion, she proceeded to Treport, a small French harbour situated near to the Château d'Eu, at which the French royal family was prepared to receive her visit. Here the royal party were welcomed and entertained in the most hospitable manner from the time of their arrival to the 7th of September, when they quitted the port at which they had been received, after having contributed greatly by this intercourse with the royal family and principal statesmen of France, if not to strengthen the diplomatic ties that bound the two countries together, at all events to do that which was much more important—to remove many of those prejudices and hostile feelings which, even more than the seas that roll between them, have served to separate two countries which have the strongest motives for maintaining peace and friendly intercourse, and to lead two nations, who had so long regarded one another as 'natural enemies,' to feel more and more strongly that they were natural allies.

A visit paid by the Queen, Prince Albert, and the Duchess of Kent to Sir Robert Peel showed that the prime minister enjoyed, not only the confidence of the country and of the two houses of Parliament, but that he stood high in the favour of his sovereign, and that she no longer regarded the leaders of the opposite party with that partiality which, at the commencement of her reign, she had so frankly avowed. This circumstance no doubt tended to strengthen Sir Robert's position, and seemed to indicate that, possessing as he now did the confidence of the Sovereign, the Lords, and the Commons, he might hope for an undisturbed tenure of power and office for many coming years. There was indeed a cloud, at present no bigger than a man's hand, just appearing above the horizon, in the umbrage which the enlightened financial policy of the premier was giving to some of the more extreme members of the party of which he was the leader. Little was it then expected that this speck in the political firmament would become a great cloud—the precursor of a violent storm, which would shipwreck a ministry now apparently so secure, and led by a premier of such remarkable tact and ability.

In the course of this year the old contest about church-rates entered on a new phase. The parishioners of the small parish of Braintree in Essex had for some time past refused, by a considerable majority, to make a rate for the repair of their church, which was almost in ruins. Under these circumstances, the churchwardens were advised that it was their duty to lay a rate on their own authority, and that the law would support them in collecting it. On this advice they acted; the matter was then brought before the Court of Queen's Bench, and Lord Denman gave judgment against the legality of a rate so laid. From this decision an appeal was made to the judges sitting in Exchequer, by whom the decision of Lord Denman was confirmed; but in delivering the judgment of the court, Lord Chief Justice Tindal remarked, that there was a wide and substantial difference between a rate laid by the churchwardens alone after the meeting had taken place, and one laid at the meeting with the concurrence of the minority. The churchwardens at once acted on this hint; another meeting was called, at which it was proposed that a rate of two shillings in the pound should be laid; and as the majority passed a resolution tantamount to the rejection of the rate, the churchwardens proceeded, with the concurrence of a minority of the ratepayers present at the meeting, to levy the rate which had been virtually refused. It became evident that Braintree was the field on which the church-rate battle for the whole kingdom was to be fought. Large contributions were raised both by the opponents and the supporters of the rates throughout the kingdom. The case was carried by appeal before the Court of Arches; and the judge of that Court, Sir H. J. Fust, gave judgment in favour of the validity of the rate; thus deciding that the liability to support the fabric of their parish church, and to provide the things needful for the services carried on in it, was a burden from which the parishioners could not exonerate themselves, however large might be the majority in favour of such a course, as long as any ratepayers could be found who were in favour of levying the rate. In spite, however, of this decision, the rate continued to be refused in a great number of large and populous parishes; but it had the effect of giving a new direction to the anti-church-rate agitation. Hitherto it had been carried on at meetings of parish-vestries throughout the kingdom; henceforth it was conducted with a more distinct aim at the entire abolition of the impost by Act of Parliament. In the manufacturing districts and in many other parts of the kingdom it had almost ceased to be levied, owing to the stubbornness with which it was resisted.

The publication of the *Tracts for the Times*, of the origin and commencement of which a brief account was given in the first volume of this work, had been carried on up to the 25th of January, 1841, the date of the publication of the ninetieth of the series. During the period that had elapsed since their commencement, they had leavened to a considerable extent the minds of the young men who were educated at Oxford, and especially of those who, being designed for the clerical profession, naturally gave greater heed than the generality of the students to publications on religious questions such as those that were treated in these tracts. But in proportion to the success which attended the movement was the hostility which it roused in the minds of those who viewed with jealousy and alarm the progress that these opinions were making, not only in Oxford but throughout the kingdom, and not only among the clergy and students of divinity but also among the laity.

This feeling of hostility was strongly brought out by the publication of Tract No. 80, the title of which was on 'Reserve in communicating Religious Knowledge.' The tract was written with great ability, in a very moderate tone, and contained many plain but neglected truths, expressed in beautiful and sometimes highly poetical language. It was designed to inculcate the obvious though often neglected lesson, that great care should be used in the conveyance of religious teaching, and to contend against the practice of throwing down the highest mysteries of Christianity before the careless and indifferent: in a word it was a lengthened comment on the text, 'Cast not your pearls before swine.' If the writer had shown as much good sense in the choice of a title as he displayed ability in the treatment of his subject—had he, for instance, employed the word *caution* instead of *reserve*—it is likely that much of the prejudice and obloquy brought by him on the cause he advocated would have been avoided. But the truth was that he and they who were associated with him in this work were too firm and sincere in their convictions, had too strong a faith in the system they upheld, to listen to the dictates of prudence. Believing what they taught to be the truth, they scorned all management, and delighted in putting forward their views in the form most calculated to rouse and shock their opponents, thinking that the more they were discussed and decried, the more rapid and complete would their triumph be. Accordingly the use of the unfortunate word 'reserve' revived the ecclesiastical panic which had well-nigh subsided. Men who had never read a line of the tracts jumped at the conclusion, that the object at which the writer aimed was to keep back the most unpopular doctrines of Romanism till the way had been prepared for them by the teachings of the tractarian party. This feeling was greatly increased when the 90th tract appeared, the avowed object of which was to show that a person might honestly subscribe all the articles and formularies of the church of England, and yet hold almost all those doctrines of the Romish church against which the articles had been always regarded as a protest. The feeling which the publication of these arguments excited was increased when it came to be understood that the tract was written for the purpose of retaining in the English communion many who, under the teaching of the tracts, had embraced the doctrines of the Roman Church, and were preparing to join it. Now that the outburst of party feeling to which the appearance of this tract gave rise has almost entirely subsided, no one will accuse Dr. Newman, the author of it, of deliberate disingenuousness; but it cannot be denied that he laboured to persuade his followers that they might honestly sign the articles while holding doctrines which the framers of these articles intended to condemn; and that if the interpretations which he advocated were sound, it is scarcely possible to conceive how any one could have scruples about subscribing those articles, whatever his opinions might be. The general feeling was well expressed by the following resolution, adopted in reference to it at a meeting of the vice-chancellor, heads of houses, and proctors of the University of Oxford, held in the delegates' room on the 15th of March 1841, that is to say, about six weeks after the appearance of the obnoxious tract:

'Resolved, that modes of interpretation such as are suggested in the same tract, evading rather than explaining the sense of the thirty-nine articles, and reconciling subscription to them with the adoption of errors which they were designed to counteract, defeat the object and are inconsistent with the due observance of the above-mentioned statutes,' *i.e.* the statutes requiring every student of the university to be instructed in and subscribe the thirty-nine articles. This condemnation was met on the part of the authors of the tracts and their disciples by the assertion, which to a certain extent was well founded, that the assembly which passed this resolution did not authoritatively represent the university, and therefore the censure of Tract 90 conveyed by it was nothing more than an expression of the opinion of the individuals who attended the meeting at which it was passed. But this condemnation of the unpopular tract was followed by one to which its authors acknowledged that more deference was due. As we have seen, they had always strongly upheld the divine institution and authority of bishops; when therefore the Bishop of Oxford desired that the publication of the tracts should be discontinued, his request was at once complied with. The tractarian party received another blow in the suspension of Dr. Pusey, in the year 1843, an event which marked the transfer of the real as well as the nominal leadership of the party which the tracts had created from Mr. Newman to the professor of Hebrew. On the fourth Sunday after Easter that divine preached before the university in the cathedral church; the subject of his sermon was 'The holy eucharist a comfort to the penitent.' This discourse, which was soon after published, attracted much attention by the bold and distinct assertion of doctrines with regard to the eucharist, which, if not absolutely identical with those of the Church of Rome, on that subject, were hardly distinguishable from them. In consequence of the complaints made to him respecting the sermon, the vice-chancellor, acting in accordance with the statutes of the university, appointed five doctors of divinity to examine the sermon, and report to him on it. Dr. Pusey strongly and justly complained that the vice-chancellor, whose theological views were diametrically opposed to his own, had refused to adopt an alternative allowed him by the statutes, which would have given the accused party an opportunity of defending himself, and that no definite proposition had been extracted from the sermon, which in the opinion of the judges, was at variance with the teaching of the Church of England on the subject. However, the five doctors condemned the sermon; and the vice-chancellor sentenced Dr. Pusey to be suspended for two years from preaching before the university. The following passage is probably the one on which the condemnation was based, and will afford the reader a good specimen of the style and teaching of one who has powerfully influenced the opinions of a large portion of his fellow countrymen:

'Would that, instead of vain and profane disputings, we could but catch the echoes of those hallowed sounds, and, forgetting the jarrings of our earthly discords, live in this harmony and unity of heaven, where, through, and in our Lord, we are all one in God! Would that, borne above ourselves, we could be caught up within the influence of the mystery of that ineffable love whereby the Father would draw us to that oneness with him in his Son, which is the perfection of eternal bliss, where will, thought, affections shall be one, because we shall be by communication of his divine nature one! Yet such is undoubted Catholic teaching, and the most literal import of holy Scripture and the mystery of the sacrament, that the eternal Word who is God, having taken to him our flesh, and joined it indissolubly with himself, and so where his flesh is there he is, and we receiving it receive him, and receiving him are joined on to him through his flesh to the Father, and he dwelling in us we dwell in him and with him in God. "I," he saith, "in the Father, and ye in me, and I in you." This is the perfection after which all the rational creation groans. . . . The same reality of the divine gift makes it angels' food to the saint, the ransom to the sinner. And both because it is the body and blood of Christ. Were it *only* a thankful commemoration of his redeeming love or *only* a showing forth of his death, or a strengthening *only* and refreshing of the soul, it were indeed a reasonable service, but it would have no direct healing for the sinner. To him its special joy is that it is his Redeemer's very broken body, it is his blood which was shed for the remission of his sins. In the words of the ancient Church, he "drinks his ransom, he eateth that very body and blood of the Lord, the only sacrifice for sin;" God "poureth out" for him yet "the most precious blood of his Only begotten."'

Amidst all these adverse circumstances the movement was still carried forward with no abatement of zeal, with little diminution of success, and with greater boldness—we may almost say intemperance—than ever. After the suppression of the tracts, the views of their authors were still advocated and developed in a publication called the *British Critic*, edited by Mr. Newman. The miracles of the middle ages were narrated and defended; the doctrine of transubstantiation was promulgated and elaborately justified by numerous quotations from the ancient fathers and Anglican divines; the Church of Rome and the Greek Church, which in the earlier numbers of the *Tracts for the Times* had been acrimoniously condemned as full of corruptions, were now referred to with respect and admiration, while the Anglican Church was mentioned in cold and contemptuous terms. These significant indications called forth the warm and ever warmer applauses of the Roman Catholic periodicals, while they excited the serious alarm of many who had hitherto sympathised with or aided the tractarian party. Mr. Palmer and Dr. Hook in particular strongly protested against these later developments, while they still adhered to the principles that had been promulgated in the earlier tracts. The cry thus swelled waxed louder and louder, the *British Critic* was discontinued, many of its supporters joined the Church of Rome; and at length Mr. Newman himself followed them, and published his celebrated work on the development of religious doctrine, in which he recanted many of the opinions he had previously maintained, and justified the step he had taken in abandoning the church of his youth for that which he had once regarded as the congregation of Antichrist and mother of harlots. But notwithstanding the heavy blows and serious discouragements it had received; notwithstanding the apostacy of many of its members; notwithstanding the vehemence with which it was assailed by Tories, Conservatives and Liberals; in spite of episcopal censures and academic protests,—the party still survived, and under the leadership of Dr. Pusey continued to preach and promulgate the principles which had been abandoned by most of those who had originated the movement.

While the real leader of the party deserted his friends in the manner most calculated to damage the movement of which he had been the head and the soul, its ablest and most uncompromising antagonist was removed by the hand of death,—Dr. Arnold, head master of Rugby; a great educationist, and the man who had done more to elevate the character of our public schools than any other man who had ever lived—a really great and good man—a vehement political and religious Liberal; the violence of whose partizanship prevented him from doing justice to the motives and the characters of men like Pusey, Newman, and Keble. He may be regarded as the founder of the Broad Church party, not only because he strenuously urged the views it holds, but also because by his letters, his publications, his conversation, and his influence on the minds of his pupils, he trained most of those who now are or who formerly were promulgators of those opinions which that party upholds.

# CHAPTER III.

#### THE SLIDING SCALE.

The year 1844 opened under the happiest auspices. England was at peace with all the world. A war commenced last year against Scinde had ended in the signal triumph of our troops, and the annexation of that province to our Indian possessions. The financial measures of the government had in every way answered the expectations that had been formed respecting them, and had changed a growing deficiency into an increasing surplus. Great improvements had manifested themselves in many branches of trade and manufacture. The Chartist and anti-corn-law agitations, so formidable and threatening during the distresses of the last few years, were now languishing. Ireland alone presented an exception to the general contentment, and still continued to be, as she had been all along, Sir Robert Peel's chief difficulty. Under these circumstances, the Queen's speech consisted chiefly of congratulations on the happy state of the country, and of the announcement that a commission had been appointed to inquire into the law and practice with regard to the occupation of land in Ireland; indicating an intention on the part of the government to bring before Parliament some farther measures for the pacification of that country. Amendments on the address moved by Mr. Sharman Crawford and Mr. Hume, as well as a motion made by the former for stopping the supplies till grievances had been redressed, were rejected by very large majorities.

Although the war in Scinde had terminated in a manner so satisfactory, the affairs of India continued to occupy a large share of the attention of the legislature and the country. The war originated in a dispute that had arisen between the Ameer of Scinde and the East Indian government, which charged the Ameer with being guilty of secret, treacherous, and systematic violations of the engagements into which he had entered. The dispute ended in a war. Sir Charles Napier, with a force of only about 2000 soldiers, stormed a strong position in which 22,000 Belochee troops were intrenched, completely defeated and dispersed them, with very small loss, and made the Ameer of Scinde a prisoner of war. While Parliament was engaged in voting thanks to Sir Charles Napier for this brilliant and almost unparalleled achievement, and discussing the manner in which the captive and dethroned Ameer should be treated, the nation was startled by the intelligence that the directors of the East India Company had recalled the Earl of Ellenborough; and before the astonishment created by this news had subsided, it transpired that this extraordinary step had been taken in spite of the strong remonstrances of the government; and the amazement was still farther increased when the Duke of Wellington, speaking in his place in the House of Lords, declared that he regarded the step which the directors had taken as the indiscreetest exercise of power that he had ever known during the whole of his long period of public service. Sir Henry Hardinge was appointed, with the full approbation both of the government and the directors of the Company, to succeed the viceroy who had been thus unceremoniously recalled.

In this session the factory question occupied a large share of the attention of Parliament. Lord Ashley earnestly contended for a limitation of the time of labour for women and children to ten hours, and twice obtained a majority in spite of the opposition of the government. Ministers, on the other hand, insisted on twelve hours, and declared themselves determined to stake their existence as an administration on that point. The result was, that the clauses of the measure on which ministers had been in a minority were now amended to meet their views; and the measure thus altered was carried through both Houses by considerable majorities. It changed the age of children admitted to work in factories from nine to eight, diminished the working hours of children under thirteen years of age to six and a half hours, extended the time during which they were to be under daily instruction in schools from two to two and a half hours in winter, and three hours in summer; continued the limitation of the labour of persons between thirteen and eighteen to twelve hours a day, and applied the same limitation to the labour of women; required the production of a certificate of baptism, if demanded, to prove that the child was really of the age required by the law; lowered the amount of the fines imposed for the violation of the law, but inflicted them for each person improperly worked, instead of for each offence, which might include several persons; it required that the machinery should be guarded, to prevent accidents. Such were the principal provisions of a measure which the government carried not without difficulty, and which Parliament would have rendered much more efficient, if the government had not met the attempt with so determined a resistance. It was evident, however, from the manner in which the measure had been received in the House of Commons and in the country, that the bill would not be accepted as a final settlement of the factory question, and would not put an end to the agitation which had been set on foot in the manufacturing districts for a limitation of the hours of labour going considerably beyond the provisions of the measure to which the government had assented.

Lord Ashley took the lead in this agitation. In doing so, he laid himself open to the application of the old maxim, 'Physician, heal thyself,' and his opponents did not hesitate to apply it to him. They pointed out, that while he was exerting himself on behalf of that portion of the labouring class which was of all others the best instructed, the most intelligent, the best able to support its own interests and to resist oppression, the labourers on the Dorsetshire estates of his father, among whom he himself lived, were sunk in ignorance and vice, and needed his assistance at least as much as the Lancashire operative.

The public confidence in the government showed itself in various ways; amongst others, in a very considerable rise of the public securities. The $3\frac{1}{2}$ per cent. consols were now at $102\frac{1}{2}$. This naturally suggested the expediency and propriety of making a better bargain with the public creditors, and of relieving the nation of some portion of that load of debt which pressed so heavily on it. It had therefore been announced at an early period of the session, that the government intended to lay before Parliament a plan for effecting this object. Accordingly, on the 8th of March, Mr. Goulburn, the chancellor of the exchequer, explained the government scheme. He announced that he intended to deal with public stocks amounting to the vast sum of 250,000,000*l*., bearing $3\frac{1}{2}$ per cent. interest. He proposed that the amount of this interest should be reduced to $3\frac{1}{4}$ per cent. until the year 1894, and that it should then undergo a farther reduction to 3 per cent., after which it was to continue unchanged. A certain time was to be allowed to the holders of these stocks, to decide whether they would accept the offer made by the government, or be paid off. It was calculated that the adoption of this scheme would save the nation the annual sum of 625,000*l*. from 1844 to 1894, and that after that period the annual saving would amount to 1,250,000*l*.

This plan met with a most frank and favourable reception from all parties in the House. Mr. Francis Baring at once rose to express his hearty approval of it. He characterised it as a very honest scheme, and warmly praised the chancellor of the exchequer for having resisted the temptation to gain a great immediate relief by an increase of the national debt, and for having broken the fall of the fund-holder by a gradual rather than an immediate reduction of the interest. He applauded the proposed measure as one worthy of the country, and calculated to impart to foreign governments a useful lesson of the economical advantages of keeping good faith with public creditors. This testimony, equally honourable to the government to which it was given, and to the opponent of the government by whom it was offered, was followed by a general chorus of approval from men of all parties. The bill in which the plan of the chancellor of the exchequer was embodied went rapidly through all its stages in both Houses, without a single dissentient voice.

Seldom has a budget been brought forward under circumstances more favourable than those which attended that of the present year. The great and evident improvement which the trade and commerce of the country had undergone, the signal success which had attended the financial measures of the government, encouraged ministers to carry farther a policy, the soundness of which had been proved by an experience which, though short, was ample and manifold. The confidence which had originally been reposed in Sir Robert Peel's financial skill, and which gave him so large a majority at the last general election, had been strengthened by the results of his administration. The budget of this year was therefore looked for with a stronger expectation and a warmer interest even than his first had commanded. The importance of the proposals it contained, and the liveliness of the interest it inspired, make it necessary to give an account of the financial statement, and of the debate to which it gave rise. Seldom had it been the good fortune of a chancellor of the exchequer to lay before the House of Commons so favourable a representation of improvement, not only in the amount of the revenue, but also in the trade and prosperity of the country, or to be able to point at so speedy and manifest a success in the financial measures of the government.

The revival of industry and commerce had produced a favourable change in the condition of the public finances. The estimate of the income formed last year had been greatly exceeded by the actual receipts. The customs, estimated at 19,000,000*l.*, amounted to 21,426,000*l.* A considerable importation of foreign corn took place, and produced a revenue of 800,000*l.* not included in the estimate. Great improvement had also taken place in the wine duties on the cessation of the negociations, which paralysed the trade while they lasted, producing 350,000*l.* above the estimate. The duties on sugar had produced 200,000*l.* in excess; the duties on tea 300,000*l.*, indicating revived power of consumption on the part of the labouring population; the duty on cotton wool 300,000*l.*, denoting increased activity in that department of industry. In almost every minor article there had been a uniform augmentation. There was an increase in some of the chief articles of excise, which, if it did not begin quite so soon in the year as the advance in the customs, was nevertheless surely indicative of an improved state of the country. The other estimates were generally correct. There was an impression that the imposition of the property-tax would cause a considerable diminution in the produce of other direct taxes, and especially of the assessed taxes. But this had not been the result. The estimate of the total revenue was 50,150,000*l.*; the sum received 52,835,134*l.*; showing an excess above the estimate of about 2,700,000*l.* The actual expenditure of the country had been less than the estimate by 650,000*l.* The total result was, that instead of the estimated surplus of 700,000*l.*, the gross surplus actually amounted to 4,165,000*l.* There was, however, last year a deficiency of 2,400,000*l.* That deficiency, including some additional items, which raised the amount to 2,749,000*l.*, had been cleared off and discharged out of the present year's revenue, leaving a net surplus of 1,400,000*l.* above the expenditure for the year ending the 5th of April last. The estimate for the revenue of the ensuing year was 51,790,000*l.* Of the estimated expenditure, that on account of the debt was 27,697,000*l.*, the charges for the year on the consolidated fund were expected to amount to 3,097,000*l.*, including the deficiency exchequer bills and the interest on them. The estimate for the army was 6,616,000*l.*; navy, 6,250,000*l.*; ordnance, 1,840,000*l.* The extraordinary expenses on account of the late war in China; the payment of the dissentients in the reduction of the 3½ per cents., to complete the sums which it was agreed to pay to the South Sea company for the surrender of their privileges, and payment of interest, amounted altogether to 239,000*l.* The total expenditure of the year was estimated at 48,643,170*l.*, the income at 51,790,000*l.*; leaving an apparent surplus of 3,146,000*l.* or, making a deduction for a portion of the debt to be discharged next year, 2,376,000*l.*

The source of the surplus was mainly the income-tax, and the House would have to consider next year whether it should be prolonged, as was originally proposed, for two years beyond the first three. For if other taxes were now to be hastily reduced, before the operation of the tariff could be thoroughly known, the House might be left next year without an option as to the continuation of the income tax. There are, however, some articles upon which remission might be afforded with a fair prospect of making up revenue by increased consumption, and with a probability of increasing the consumption of other articles. The articles selected for such remission were glass, vinegar, currants, coffee, marine assurance, and wool, on the aggregate of which the amount of duty remitted would be 387,000*l.* a year. With regard to the sugar duties, as the Brazilian treaty would expire in November, it was proposed to recommend that England should admit at a differential duty of 10*s.* per cwt. the sugar of those states which did not cultivate that commodity by slave labour.

This statement was followed by the running fire of comment and criticism which every budget has to undergo. Mr. Hume recommended a reduction of the army and navy, in order to relieve the country from the burden of the income tax. Mr. Williams approved the suggestion, and wished he could compliment Mr. Goulburn as much on his scheme as he justly could do on the manner in which he had brought it forward. Mr. Bell, member for Northumberland, regretted that the chancellor of the exchequer had not done something for his constituents by a reduction of the coal duty. Mr. F. Baring entered into a more serious and detailed consideration of the ministerial scheme of finance. 'If,' said he, 'Sir Robert Peel had not made his reductions in the revenue, it is clear that the revenue would have recovered itself without resort to the income tax. I want to know what is the effect of these reductions, for I have not been able to ascertain it—especially of the alterations in the timber duties. In 1841 the amount paid for timber was 1,566,000*l.* The amount received last year was but 688,000*l.*, showing a loss of 878,000*l.* It would have been more manly if Mr. Goulburn had declared whether or not the income tax is to be continued beyond the three years. As, however, the surplus is only about 3,000,000*l.*, and the income tax produces 5,000,000*l.*, it must be feared that there is but little chance of its being taken off. I approve of the proposed reductions as far as they go, but would push some of them farther; and I object to the enhancement of the duty on chicory, denying that its admixture injures coffee. As to the sugar duties, I am quite sure that sooner or later they must be dealt with as timber and corn have already been dealt with; and I am curious to know how Sir R. Peel will get over the difficulty placed in his way by the resolution that threw out the late administration. It is clear that ultimately the plan of the late ministry will swallow up that of Sir R.

Peel. I much fear that Brazil will retort the differential duty against slave-grown sugar by making a difference between our cotton goods and those of other countries; and I doubt whether existing treaties with Denmark and Sweden will not enable those countries to claim admission for their sugar on lower terms. After having been told, as I was when I made my proposal for a shilling duty, that the introduction of one ounce of slave-grown sugar is contrary to the gospel, it is odd to be told now that very little is to be imported.'

*Sir R. Peel:* 'I am sure that if the government had not availed themselves of the earliest opportunity afforded by the expiration of the Brazilian treaty to admit free-grown sugar, they would have been accused of an indirect effort to keep up the West Indian monopoly. Mr. Hume and Mr. Williams have called on ministers to get rid of the income tax by reducing the estimates. I say, as loudly and as heartily as they do, by all means reduce the estimates—reduce them to the lowest point that is at all consistent with the interests of the country. No matter what taxes may be affected by the change—no matter what surplus revenue we may have—no matter what may be our commercial condition—let us on no account have anything like needless estimates. But I must confess that I am unable to discover how it would have been possible for us to have fixed our estimates at a lower amount. Mr. Hume has compared the military and naval estimates with those of the year 1835 when I was first lord of the treasury; but no inconsiderable part of the increase was to be applied to the improvement of prisons, and to other purposes of a judicial nature. I must also request hon. members to recollect what has occurred to us since the year 1835. There has been a rebellion in Canada, there have been hostilities in Syria, and a war in China. It is true that these events did not take place during our administration; but it is nevertheless our duty to provide for them. It is very easy to talk of making reductions; but the difficulty is, to show that in the end these reductions will consist with true economy. What interest can we have in maintaining a system of extravagant expenditure? There is a vulgar notion prevalent in some quarters that we have a motive for proposing excessive estimates, on account of the patronage they are supposed to yield; but a more unfounded and erroneous impression it is hardly possible to imagine. It would be far more agreeable to us to show to the nation a surplus revenue than to press upon their resources with superfluous expenses. Mr. Williams has spoken of the estimates of 1790, as if it would be possible to go back to them, with our great colonial establishments needing defence, and foreign nations accumulating steam-vessels and munitions of war. Mr. Bell has spoken of the duty on coals, but has made no distinct proposal. With respect to the income tax, Mr. Baring has complained that it has not been distinctly stated whether or no it is to be continued. He has no right to expect any such statement until next year. We shall then be enabled to take an enlarged and comprehensive view of the financial condition of the country; and I must say, that I think it is too much to ask the House of Commons to determine at this moment whether or not they will continue the income tax. We shall be in a much better condition to do so when we reach another session. We may or we may not be in a more favourable condition at the end of the present year. The estimated amount of the revenue last year was 50,100,000*l*.; but it yielded 52,835,000*l*. How do we know that our calculations may not be equally fallacious in the present year? We may have a farther surplus of 2,600,000*l*., or we may have a greater or a less surplus Should we, then, be justified in saying now that we might venture positively to diminish the amount of our taxation? In proposing the income tax for three years, I distinctly stated that I contemplated its continuance for five. To consent to any large reduction of taxes would virtually decide the continuation of the income tax; and I contend, that with only about 400,000*l*. to dispose of, a better selection of taxes to be reduced could not have been made, or one more in accordance with the principles on which the new tariff is based. The articles whose price is now to be lowered are especially those which are extensively consumed by the labouring classes.'

To the greater part of this budget no serious opposition or even objection was made. The chief struggle was over the sugar duties, the government contending that some advantage ought to be given to the sugar produced by our West Indian colonies, which were now, with great difficulty and danger, passing through a period of transition from slave labour to free labour, and therefore, having a strong claim to be protected by a moderate differential duty, which was, as the government believed, a real boon and advantage to them. On the other hand, the opposition, led by Lord John Russell, insisted that the attempt to protect free-grown against slave-grown sugar was utterly absurd. They maintained that we had nothing to do with the social institutions of the nations that were willing to trade with us; that the principle of determining the amount of the duties we thought fit to impose on the products of foreign countries, by our approval or disapproval of slavery, was one which would lead us, if we were consistent, to mark in the same way our disapproval of other institutions of the nations with which we traded, many of which were quite as objectionable as the institution of slavery; and that the question we ought to consider with reference to the duty on sugar was, how we could best adapt it to increase the revenue of the country, and cheapen the article on which the duty was imposed. Notwithstanding this opposition, the resolutions proposed by Mr. Goulburn were carried by a majority of sixty-nine, and the bill founded on them was introduced and read a first and second time without discussion. It was committed on the 14th of June. In committee the ministerial plan encountered a most formidable opposition from the ultra-protectionists, who took up a line of argument exactly opposite to that which had been urged by Lord J. Russell and the Whigs. They contended that ministers ought to give a larger amount of protection to our own colonies. This opposition is the more deserving of notice, not only because it proceeded from some of the most thorough-going supporters of the government, but also because it indicated a growing and not altogether groundless suspicion on the part of the country party, that the tendency of the measures which ministers were bringing forward was to strengthen the hands and to secure the ultimate triumph of the free-traders. The leader of this opposition, and the mover of the resolution which embodied its views, was Mr. P. Miles. He dwelt on the ruin and desolation that were overspreading our West Indian colonies, and loudly accused ministers of bringing in a measure which afforded no adequate protection to the planters, and had not even the merit of finally settling the question with which it dealt. He insisted that the interests of the British and the West Indian farmer were identical, the only difference between them being, that the one produced wheat and the other sugar; and he predicted, that if the protection which was given to one description of agriculture should be withdrawn, that which was afforded to the other would speedily be abandoned. Mr. Baillie, who seconded the motion, maintained that the ministerial plan would encourage the foreign slave-trade, and yet afford only a very partial advantage to the British people. Common sense, he urged, dictated that we should raise our revenue from foreign sugar rather than from that which was produced by our own colonies. This resolution was supported by Lord J. Russell and several members and followers of the late administration, and was carried against ministers by a majority of twenty. But after they had distinctly intimated, that if the vote was not reversed, they should regard it as a vote of want of confidence, and act accordingly, another division on the question was taken, and the ministerial plan was sustained by a majority of twenty-two, whereupon Mr. Miles withdrew from farther opposition to it.

The time had now arrived when Parliament was required to deliberate on the renewal of the Bank charter, involving a reconsideration of the whole banking system of England. It had been provided, by the act passed in 1833, that the government might give notice to the Bank before August 1844, that Parliament intended to deal again with the question of the Bank charter. The government was thus called on to decide, in the course of this session, whether it would take advantage of this provision of the last Bank charter act. They resolved to do so—indeed they could hardly do otherwise; and the high financial reputation enjoyed by Sir R. Peel caused the announcement of their determination to be received by the country with great satisfaction, and the ministerial plan to be anticipated with a confidence which was strengthened by the fact that the present minister enjoyed the advantage of considering the elaborate report of the committee which had been appointed in 1833 to inquire into the whole banking question.

The measure was submitted to the House of Commons on the 6th of May by the prime minister himself; and the full explanation he gave of it was listened to throughout with the most profound and sustained attention. But we are persuaded that we shall best meet the wishes of our readers by allowing the author of the scheme to speak for himself, with that abridgement and condensation which alone our limits admit.

Sir Robert Peel, in his opening remarks, referred to a manifesto which had been put forth against the scheme by the country bankers, and entreated the house to address itself to the consideration of this question without party bias or predetermined hostility. He then proceeded to enunciate his views on the currency and the standard of value. Having laid down his principles, he then explained his plan.

'I propose,' he said, 'with respect to the Bank of England, that there should be an actual reformation of the two departments of issue and banking; that there should be different officers to each, and a different system of account. I likewise propose that to the issue department should be transferred the whole amount of the bullion now in the possession of the Bank, and that the issue of bank notes should hereafter take place on two foundations only; first, on a definite amount of securities, and after that exclusively upon bullion; so that the action of the public should in this latter respect govern the amount of the circulation. There will be no power in the Bank to issue notes on deposits and discount of bills, and the issue department will have to place to the credit of the banking department the amount of notes which the issue department will by law be entitled to issue. With respect to the banking business of the Bank, I propose that it should be governed on precisely the same principles as would regulate any other body dealing with Bank of England notes. The fixed amount of securities on which I propose that the Bank of England should issue notes is 14,000,000*l.*, and the whole of the remainder of the circulation is to be issued exclusively on the foundation of bullion. I propose that there should be a complete and periodical publication of the accounts of the Bank of England, both of the banking and issue department, as tending to increase the credit of the Bank, and to prevent panic and needless alarm. I would therefore enact, that there should be returned to the government a weekly account of the issue of notes by the Bank of England, of the amount of bullion, of the fluctuations of the bullion, of the amount of deposits; in short, an account of every transaction, both in the issue department and the banking department of the Bank of England, and that government should forthwith publish unreservedly and weekly a full account of the circulation of the Bank.

'With regard to private banks, the general rule will be to draw a distinction between the privilege of issue, and the conduct of banking business; the object being to limit competition, but to make the great change with as little detriment as possible to private interests. From this time no new bank of issue will be constituted; but all the existing banks of issue will be allowed to retain the privilege, on condition that they do not exceed the present amount, to be calculated on the average of a term of years. This is necessary to enable the Bank of England to know the extent of issue with which it will have to compete. But while the issues will be restricted, banking business will be facilitated; the privilege of suing and being sued, at present withheld from joint-stock banks, will be accorded; the law of partnership will be so altered, that while the acts of an individual director or other authorised partner will bind the whole, the acts of an unauthorised partner will not do so. Joint-stock banks in London, which at present are forbidden to accept bills for a date of less than six months, will be placed on an equality with other banks, and allowed to accept bills of any amount or date. If the last privilege should be abused by the circulation of small bills, I shall at once appeal to Parliament to correct the evil. Joint-stock banks will be required to publish a full and complete periodical list of all partners and directors, and banks of issue to publish an account of their issues; a much better security for the public than many delusive checks to which my attention has been invited. Joint-stock banks will be prohibited from having shares less than some fixed amount, and no new joint-stock bank shall be constituted except on application to a government department.

'I now revert to my propositions respecting the Bank

of England. It is to be allowed issues to the extent of a fixed amount of securities, 14,000,000*l*. The existing loan of 11,000,000*l*. to the government will be continued, the remaining 3,000,000*l*. will be based on exchequer bills and other securities over which the Bank will have entire control. It will also be allowed to extend its issues beyond the 14,000,000*l*. on emergency, but only with the consent of three members of the government; and in such a case the whole of the nett profit on any amount beyond 14,000,000*l*. will revert to the government. It is proposed to continue the legal-tender clause, in order to facilitate the circulation of Bank paper. I must now explain the pecuniary arrangements between the Bank and the Government. The Bank retains the privilege of issuing notes on securities to the amount of 14,000,000*l*. at 3 per cent., which would yield 420,000*l*. From this there are deductions to be made. The total cost to the Bank on an issue of 20,000,000*l*. was estimated by the committee of 1833 at 117,000*l*.; but take it at about 113,000*l*., which, subtracted from 420,000*l*., leaves 307,000*l*. There is then to be deducted about 60,000*l*. composition with the stamp-office for the privilege of issuing notes. Then there is about 24,000*l*. paid by the Bank to those bankers who undertake to issue Bank of England notes. This leaves 220,000*l*. derived from the issue of notes. Hitherto the Bank has paid 120,000*l*. to Government for its privileges: they are now to be affected, but, on the other hand, increased stability is given to its banking business; and I propose that in future the Bank shall pay that sum, besides the 60,000*l*. for the composition with the stamp-office, making in all about 180,000*l*. Government pay to the Bank 248,000*l*. for the management of the public debt, and the difference between the two last sums will be the balance that the Government will have to pay over to the Bank. This measure applies only to England; the subject of Scotch and Irish banks being reserved for future consideration.'

Eleven resolutions, carrying out the plan indicated by Sir R. Peel, were then read from the chair, and in compliance with a request conveyed in his speech, the discussion of the plan he had so lucidly enunciated was deferred until after the resolutions had been printed, and had been given to the members of the House. On the 20th of May they went into committee on the resolutions proposed by the prime minister; and then he entered into some farther explanations of his scheme, and defended it from some criticisms to which it had been subjected, especially with regard to the bearing and operation of foreign exchanges on home issues, and on the restriction placed on the issue of notes by country banks. At the conclusion of these remarks a general discussion on the plan took place.

Mr. C. Wood, Sir W. Clay, Mr. Stuart Wortley, Mr. P. Stewart, Mr. Montague Gore, Mr. Gisborne, Mr. F. Baring, expressed in terms more or less strong their approbation of the measure. It was mildly criticised by Mr. Newdegate, Mr. Plumtre, Mr. Muntz, and Mr. Charles Buller; and the resolutions were passed without any dissent. When, however, the bill founded on them was proposed to be read a second time on the 13th of June, the following amendment was proposed by Mr. Hawes: 'That no sufficient evidence has been laid before this house to justify the proposed interference with banks of issue in the management of their circulation.' This amendment only obtained 30 supporters, while 185 voted against it. The bill was then read a second time, and Sir Robert Peel was sustained by large majorities in upholding its provisions against all opposition. He agreed to admit a few modifications of no great importance, pressed on him by high banking authorities, and the bill, thus slightly amended, went through the House of Commons. In the House of Lords it was read a first and second time without remark, and passed through the committee without a single division.

Another subject which occupied a considerable share of the attention of Parliament during the session of 1844, was the consideration of the ownership of certain chapels, which had originally been founded by Trinitarian nonconformists, but had gradually passed into the hands of Unitarians. Many of these had been built by a Lady Hewley, and she had directed that they should be held by 'godly preachers of Christ's holy gospel;' and other cases had occurred in which chapels founded by persons who undoubtedly were Trinitarians, but had used terms equally vague in stating their intentions with regard to the doctrines they wished to be taught in them. Actions had in some cases been brought, in order to deprive the Unitarians of these chapels, and to hand them over to ministers whose opinions on the nature of the godhead were more in accordance with those of their founders. It was indeed admitted that they had failed to specify their intentions with regard to the doctrines they intended to have taught; but that failure was accounted for by the objections which they were known to have entertained to creeds as being mere human inventions, and that this scruple had prevented them from giving any distinct statement of the doctrines they wished to have taught, which, in fact, could not be done without enunciating a creed. Thus they had been led to express their intentions in terms the letter of which did not absolutely prohibit the introduction of doctrines which they abhorred, and certainly would have precluded if they could have foreseen that their introduction would have been attempted. On the other hand, it was argued, on behalf of the present holders of the chapels, that the vagueness with which the doctrines to be taught in these chapels were described by their founders was purposely adopted, in order to evade the law, which, at the time of their foundation, did not extend to Unitarians the toleration it afforded to every other denomination of nonconformists, and thereby prevented the erection of chapels in which the teaching of Unitarianism was avowed; so that the vagueness of the description was rather to be taken as a proof that the use now made of these chapels was in accordance with the intentions of their founders. It was farther argued, that, even admitting their intentions to have been such as they were represented to be by those who sought to dispossess their present occupants, yet it was quite certain that they had for a long course of years been in the hands of the Unitarians, who, in the expectation that they would continue to retain them, had expended considerable sums on their enlargement and improvement, as well as in making additions to the burial-grounds that in some instances were attached to them. The question had been tried in the case of some chapels founded, as we have already mentioned, by Lady Hewley. They were built for the Calvinistic Methodists, and therefore there could be no doubt that they were intended by their founder to be places in which Trinitarian doctrines should be taught; but in the absence of any distinct statement of her wishes in this respect, they had come into the hands of Unitarians, who for many years had held undisturbed possession of them. Their right to them had, however, been called in question, and on trial the decision had been against their present holders. It was feared that this decision would give rise to much litigation, and would probably cause the Unitarians to be deprived of many other chapels. The government therefore adopted a course which did them great honour. They were all decided Trinitarians; their followers, almost without a single exception, were zealous on the same side. They knew that by interfering with the regular course of the law in this matter, in order to do justice to a sect everywhere spoken against, they would give offence to large numbers of their supporters both in and out of Parliament. But they felt that a great wrong would be done if they allowed the law to take its course, and to eject the Unitarians from chapels which they claimed by a prescription more than sufficient to make good the title to any other description of property. They therefore framed a bill securing to Unitarians the possession of chapels of which they had held the unquestioned possession for a period of more than twenty years; thus putting a stop to farther litigation on the question. The measure was brought into the House of Lords by Lord Lyndhurst. It was strenuously opposed in the upper house by the Bishop of London, and in the House of Commons by Sir R. Inglis, Mr. Plumptre, and the party with which they usually acted. Great efforts were made to agitate the country, and deter the legislature from passing the measure, not only by churchmen, but also by many Protestant dissenters. The ministers, warmly supported in the course they had determined to take by Lord J. Russell and the majority of the Whig party, carried their measure triumphantly though its various stages, and thus prevented much vexatious litigation and shameful injustice, though in doing so they widened still farther the breach which already separated Sir R. Peel and most of those who comprised his cabinet from the more extreme section of their followers, and was soon destined to change a hesitating and suspicious support into an open and uncompromising opposition.

An attempt which Lord Powis had made last year to

repeal that portion of the bishops' bill, passed in accordance with the recommendations of the ecclesiastical commissioners, which had enacted that the sees of St. Asaph and Bangor should be united, was renewed this year, and met with a considerable amount of support in the upper house. It was got rid of for the present on the technical ground, that, as it affected the rights of the Crown, it was necessary for the consent of the Queen to be signified before it could be proceeded with.

A measure which attracted little public attention, and went through without much discussion, but was nevertheless a measure of great practical utility, was introduced by Mr. Gladstone—a bill for the regulation of railways, founded on the report of a committee that had been appointed to inquire into the subject. Up to that time the accommodation which had been provided for the working classes by the railway companies had been of a very inferior description. The third-class passengers were conveyed in carriages without seats, and without any covering to protect their occupants from the rain, in which they stood crowded together like cattle. Moreover, most of the trains to which these carriages were attached travelled very slowly, stopped at every station, were shunted aside to make way for other trains, and ran over distances much shorter than those now traversed by third-class trains; so that persons who wished to go considerable distances were compelled either to travel in other classes at a heavier expense, or to be subject to frequent delays, and to find themselves lodgings for the night, even in cases where the distance was such as might have been travelled over in a few hours. Mr. Gladstone's bill dealt with these and other evils attendant on the railway system as then carried out. The measure was strongly opposed at its first introduction by the representatives of the railway interest in the House of Commons; but after some concessions had been made to them by alterations in the details of the bill, which, without impairing its efficiency, interfered less than was originally contemplated with the discretion of the directors of the different railway companies, the bill was carried through both houses without much farther opposition.

Some modifications were introduced in the course of this session into the bastardy clauses of the new poor law, which had imposed on the mother the burden of supporting an illegitimate child. The opposition which these clauses had originally excited had been rather confirmed than removed by the experience of their practical working, and therefore the law was now so far altered as to enable the mother, under certain circumstances, to recover from the putative father a portion of the cost of the maintenance of an illegitimate child.

Another subject that forced itself on the attention of the legislature was the state of the turnpike-laws in the principality of Wales. That country has generally been remarkable in modern times for the peaceable and orderly conduct of its inhabitants; but at the period we have now reached they exhibited a turbulence like that for which they had been notorious under the Plantagenets. A feeling of discontent had been for some time growing up on account of the exorbitant and increasing tolls exacted for the support of the turnpike roads. New toll-bars were being continually erected, and the tolls had been greatly and, as the people generally believed, illegally raised. These exactions roused in the minds of that proverbially fiery people some sparks of that spirit which Edward I. had found it so difficult to quell. Accustomed to regard every question from a religious point of view, and to express their thoughts and feelings in scriptural phraseology, the simple inhabitants of these secluded and mountainous districts applied to the turnpike-gates the promise which the Bible records to have been given to the descendants of the wife of Isaac, that they should possess the *gate* of their enemies, and thus they were led to connect their hostility to the turnpikes with the name of Rebecca. Finding that peaceful agitation was of no avail, they determined on violent measures. They resolved to destroy the obnoxious turnpikes by force; and carried out their intentions in a manner suggested by the scriptural notions they had adopted. A number of them dressed themselves up in women's clothing; the leader of the party was known by the name of Rebecca, and those who executed his orders were called daughters of Rebecca. They began their operations in the year 1839, when a party of them assembled in the disguise we have mentioned, and levelled to the ground in open day a turnpike-gate and the hut of the toll-keeper. The gate was, however, reinstated, and no farther proceedings of the kind took place till the year 1843, in the beginning of which more serious and systematic attacks were made on the turnpike-gates. They were carried out in the night. The toll-keeper was warned off; he was allowed a short time to convey away his furniture and effects; and then the gate-posts were sawn across close to the ground, and the gate and toll-house destroyed. As the perpetrators of these lawless acts could not be discovered, their impunity encouraged them to do farther mischief, and procured them many imitators in other parts of the country; and soon the example was followed in almost every part of South Wales except the county of Brecknock. No fewer than eighty gates had been destroyed in the county of Carmarthen alone, and almost every turnpike-gate had disappeared from the counties of Pembroke and Cardigan. The mischief did not stop here. The rioters, emboldened by success and impunity, began to turn their attention to other real or imaginary grievances, which they thought might be redressed in the same violent manner. And soon the whole of that usually tranquil district was in so disturbed a condition that the government found it necessary to adopt vigorous measures. The upper classes, who had witnessed without much concern or disapproval the destruction of the turnpikes, became seriously alarmed at the course that things were now taking. Threatening letters were sent to magistrates, clergymen, and others who attempted to put a stop to the proceedings of the Rebeccaites. Shots were fired into many houses; the town of Carmarthen was tumultuously attacked by large bodies of rioters, who held possession of it for several hours, and were only dislodged by the arrival of a troop of light dragoons, who were compelled to use their swords, in order to overcome the resistance offered to them. The government therefore sent down a considerable military force, as well as a large body of London police. They also appointed a special commission for the trial of persons accused of complicity with these disturbances, and who, even when captured, and proved by the clearest evidence to have been guilty, were almost sure to escape the due punishment of their offences, in consequence of the sympathy with which their proceedings were regarded throughout the principality. But the government felt that, while it was necessary that the majesty of the law should be maintained, and such riotous proceedings as had been carried on sternly repressed, still the Rebecca riots had their origin in real grievances, which it was the duty of the legislature to redress; and therefore they determined to remove the abuses of which the inhabitants had just reason to complain. A commission was appointed to inquire into the causes from which these disturbances had arisen; and in conformity with their recommendations a bill was framed by the government to remodel the whole system of turnpike trusts in Wales, which became law with little remark or opposition, and the disturbed districts resumed their habitual tranquillity. A few years before this time the government would have thought it had done its duty by simply sending down troops and police, suppressing the riots by main force, severely punishing the Rebeccaites who could be detected, and reinstating the turnpikes. Had it taken any other course, it would have been accused of feebleness and want of vigour, and would have been taunted for proposing to make concessions to violence. But since the passing of the Reform Bill a new spirit had been infused into the administration; even a Tory government had learnt to regard wide-spread disorder as a symptom of political malady, and instead of being reproached with not asserting the majesty of the law, they obtained universal support and complete success in the wiser course they adopted.

But while important measures were thus passing through the legislature almost unnoticed, it was intensely occupied and almost convulsed by a matter of inferior importance, which involved party considerations, and therefore excited strong feelings. On the 11th of June a petition was presented by Mr. T. Duncombe, member for Finsbury, from Mr. Joseph Mazzini and others, complaining that their letters had been opened in the post-office. To this complaint the home secretary, Sir J. Graham, replied that the power of opening and examining letters transmitted through the post had been given to the home secretary by an act passed in 1837, which consolidated previous laws, and authorised the post-office authorities to open and examine letters; that, under the powers conferred by that act, he had issued a warrant, which had since been destroyed, ordering that the letters of one of the petitioners should be opened and their contents examined. Efforts were made by several members of the house to extract from the home secretary a more explicit explanation, but without success. These revelations, however, drew forth some very strong expressions of opinion both in favour of the right which had been exercised by the secretary and in opposition to it. Some maintained that it was a state necessity, while others denounced it as a shameful violation of the confidence reposed in the post-office; and the manner in which it was exercised, so as to prevent the sender or the receiver of the letter from discovering that the communication had been thus tampered with, was still more strongly condemned than the act of opening itself. Mr. Duncombe and his supporters urged that if the writer of the letter had supposed it would be opened, he would no doubt have transmitted it through another channel; and that by ordering it to be opened, the minister had taken an advantage of the confidence reposed by a foreigner in British honour, which would tend to lower the character of this country in the eyes of all civilised peoples. It appeared, however, that the practice of opening letters had been frequently exercised by previous governments, as well as by that which was now in office. But this explanation did not satisfy Mr. Duncombe, who followed up the question which had elicited these statements by moving, a few nights after, for the appointment of a select committee to inquire into a department of the post-office called the 'secret' or 'inner' office, to ascertain the duties of the persons employed in it, and the authority under which their functions were discharged. Government did not resist the motion; but, as the investigation was of great importance, and involved the highest interests of the state, they stipulated that it should be conducted secretly. A committee was accordingly nominated, but Mr. Duncombe himself was not placed on it; and a motion made by Mr. V. Smith, that his name should be added to it, was rejected after a long and somewhat acrimonious discussion. On the motion of Lord Radnor a similar committee was appointed by the House of Lords. The reports made by these committees to the houses to which they respectively belonged showed that the power to which public attention had been drawn had been in existence for a very long period, and had been exercised by all administrations, and consequently by different parties; that it had only been used when some great emergency seemed to require its employment; that, on the whole, it had been employed less frequently of late years than formerly; and that there was no reason to apprehend that ordinary private correspondence would ever be in any way interfered with, but that, on the contrary, there was every reason to believe that the power would be exercised with great discretion, and only when some state emergency required that recourse should be had to it. These reports abated considerably the excitement which the revelation of the inculpated practice had at first produced. A bill introduced into the House of Lords by Lord Radnor, and designed to put a stop to the practice, never got beyond the first reading, and the matter was allowed quietly to drop into oblivion.

The business of the session of 1844 had been completed in sufficient time to have allowed the prorogation of Parliament to take place on the 9th of August; but a weighty matter of a very exceptional character remained to be determined. Ireland was still Sir R. Peel's chief difficulty. He was deeply and sincerely anxious to tranquillise it. He had hoped that the Catholic emancipation act, which he had made such sacrifices to carry, would have been the harbinger of peace and prosperity to that unhappy and distracted country; but measure after measure had been since passed for its pacification, concession after concession had been made, but all had been in vain. In 1843 a new agitation for the repeal of the union between the two countries had been set on foot by Mr. O'Connell, and had assumed very alarming dimensions. The demands of the Irish agitator were at bottom not unreasonable. What he required was the substitution of imperial legislation for merely local legislation. He insisted that if the union continued to exist, it should be an identification of the two islands of Great Britain and Ireland; that both should have the same rights, the same privileges, the same immunities; that the electoral franchise should be the same, the organization of the municipal corporations alike—in fact, that there should be one law throughout the British Islands. If this were conceded, he was willing to accept the legislative union between the two countries; if this were denied, he was determined to go on agitating for its repeal. Accordingly he did agitate most vigorously. The people were diligently drilled, monster meetings were held, which were formidable, not only on account of the multitudes by which they were attended, but on account of the semi-military organisation which was exhibited, and the spirit of bitter hostility to England and England's government that was ostentatiously displayed. On the 15th of August, 1843, one of these assemblages was held at Tara, the place at which the old kings of Ireland had been elected, and at which in the great Irish rebellion the insurgents had suffered a signal defeat. At this meeting O'Connell, encouraged by the vast numbers and the frantic applauses of those by whom he was surrounded, rashly promised that within a year from that time a parliament should be sitting in College Green at Dublin; a prediction which evidently could only be accomplished by a general and successful rising against the English government. Another meeting, which was expected to surpass that at Tara in numbers and in violence, was convoked for the 8th of October, at Clontarf, near Dublin, celebrated on account of a victory gained there by the Irish over their invaders. A regular programme was published of the whole of the intended proceedings of this meeting, in which the order of march, the place of arrival, the position to be occupied on the ground, and the dress to be worn by the different detachments were all regulated with a degree of military precision, which gave to the whole the air rather of an army to be reviewed by its general than of a meeting to be addressed by the leader of a great agitation.

No government could allow proceedings such as these to be carried on without interference, and it was felt both at Dublin and London that a decided step must be taken. On the 7th of October a proclamation appeared on the walls of Dublin prohibiting the Clontarf meeting, and threatening with punishment all who disobeyed the prohibition. O'Connell at once countermanded the meeting, though not without difficulty, on account of the extreme shortness of the notice given. The agitator himself, his son John, and his principal adherents, were prosecuted for a conspiracy to raise and excite disaffection among her Majesty's subjects, and for exciting them to hatred and contempt of the government and constitution of the realm as by law established, &c. After many delays and much legal skirmishing, the prisoners were produced before the court of Queen's Bench and a jury in Dublin on the 15th of January. But even then every obstacle that legal ingenuity could devise was interposed, and new delays caused by lengthened discussions raised on them.

It was an unfortunate, though perhaps an unavoidable, circumstance that all those who tried the prisoners, both judges and jurymen, were, without a single exception, Protestants. The advocates of the crown, knowing that almost every Roman Catholic was sure also to be favourable to the cause of repeal, and would, in all human probability, give a verdict in favour of the prisoners, however strong the evidence and the law might be against them, felt it to be their duty to strike off the name of every Roman Catholic that appeared on the panel. But though this proceeding probably promoted the cause of substantial justice, it deprived the finding of the jury of that moral weight which attaches to a verdict that is felt to have been fairly obtained, especially in the eyes of the great majority of the Irish people, who saw with indignation their co-religionists all struck off the jury list by the crown lawyers. The trial extended over twenty-four days. In the course of it the Irish attorney-general so far lost his temper, and forgot what he owed to the office he filled, as to challenge one of the opposing counsel to a duel, and to persist in his challenge in spite of all the remonstrances that were offered to him, until the matter had become a public scandal. O'Connell spoke at great length in his own defence; but the judges charged against him and his fellow-prisoners, and the jury, after long deliberation, returned a verdict of guilty against all the prisoners on some counts of the indictment, while they acquitted them on others. O'Connell was condemned to be imprisoned for twelve calendar months, and to be fined the sum of 2,000*l*. The other prisoners received sentences proportioned to the degree of their guilt, with the exception of the Rev. Thomas Tierney a Roman Catholic priest, in whose case the crown lawyers did not press for judgment. Against the decision thus given an appeal was made to the House of Lords, resting chiefly on technical grounds; but before it could be heard the period had arrived at which, under ordinary circumstances, the session would have closed. As, however, the judges, whose opinions it was thought necessary to take on some points of law raised in the appeal, were engaged in the summer circuits, Parliament, instead of being prorogued, was only adjourned—the House of Lords to the 2d of September, when the appeal would be heard, and the House of Commons to the 5th of that month, by which time it was expected that the hearing would be concluded, and the decision given. After the hearing of counsel, the judges gave their opinions on the points submitted to them. They all thought that the indictment contained both good and bad matter. Lord Chief-Justice Tindal and six other judges very confidently maintained that the good matter did away with the bad, and that the judgment of the court below should be affirmed. On the other hand, Baron Parke and Judge Coltman gave a somewhat hesitating opinion that the bad matter in the indictment destroyed the good, and that the judgment ought to be reversed.

Then came the turn of the peers to deliver their decision. The usual practice in such cases is for the law lords only who have been present at the whole of the hearing to speak and vote. But on this occasion a large number of lay lords attended, who had not been present throughout the proceedings. The lord chancellor (Lord Lyndhurst) gave his judgment at length in accordance with the opinion which had been given by the majority of the judges, and concluded his address by moving that the judgment of the court below should be affirmed. Lord Brougham followed him, and came to a similar conclusion. Lord Denman, Lord Cottenham, and Lord Campbell in turn delivered their opinions on the opposite side, and the last-mentioned lord moved that the judgment of the court below should be reversed.

Then followed a curious scene. The majority of the lay lords present, who were warm supporters of the government, considered that the judgment of the court below was about to be reversed, and a damaging blow inflicted not on the present administration only but on the authority of the English government in Ireland, by three strong Whig partisans, in the teeth of the distinctly expressed opinion of a large majority of the judges, and of two such high authoritics as Lords Lyndhurst and Brougham. When, therefore, the question was put by the lord chancellor, several of them called out, 'Aye.' The chancellor was embarrassed, and seemed at a loss to determine what course he ought to take. Lord Brougham lamented the decision to which the majority of the law lords had come, declaring that it would 'go out without authority, and come back without respect;' but deprecated the contemplated interference of the lay lords. Lord Campbell observed that the constitution knew no distinction between law lords and lay lords; all had a right to vote; but it was improper that those who had not been present throughout the whole hearing should exercise that right. In spite of these dissuasions the Earl of Effingham announced that he was determined to vote; but as the lord chancellor and other peers remonstrated against this course, the lay peers retired from the House, leaving the five law lords to decide the question before them, without extraneous interference; and so the judgment was reversed. The consequence was that O'Connell, who had been already detained some weeks, was set at liberty. The news of this decision was received in Ireland with ecstatic delight. O'Connell was conducted to his house in Merrion-square, Dublin, by an innumerable multitude, amidst the most triumphant demonstrations of enthusiasm and affection, and addressed them in his usual style. Similar demonstrations were made in all parts of Ireland. But the object of all this demonstration was now nearly at the end of his career. He was not far from seventy years of age, and the fatigues and excitements of the long agitation he had carried on had begun to tell on his iron constitution. Rivals too were now springing up, who seemed likely to outbid him, and thus deprive him of that popular adoration in which he so greatly rejoiced. His condemnation too and imprisonment had told on him, and taught him a lesson of caution, which prevented him from indulging in those denunciations of the English authority with which he had been accustomed to delight his hearers. Henceforth he felt that he had to do with a government that was not to be trifled with, and he spoke and acted accordingly.

By many persons the decision which thus set O'Connell at liberty was deeply regretted. It was felt that a violation of the law had been committed, and that the persons who had been guilty of it had escaped through a mere technical quibble; that the impunity which had attended those who had roused the passions of an ignorant and impulsive peasantry was likely to encourage the spirit of lawlessness, which was doing so much mischief in Ireland, and rendering its pacification so extremely difficult. It cannot be denied that there was much reason in these regrets, or that a miscarriage of justice had occurred. But when we remember the strong and bitter feelings of hostility which prevailed between the Protestant and Catholic inhabitants of Ireland, and that the decision which had been given in Dublin was given by judges and jurymen who were all Protestants, we cannot be surprised that it should have been regarded by the Irish people as a gross and glaring injustice. It therefore produced the happiest effect in that country, and afforded the best possible reply to the assertions of those who so loudly complained that justice could not be obtained from Englishmen for Irishmen, when it came to be known that the final court of appeal in the empire, composed on that occasion entirely of Englishmen and Protestants, after a careful hearing of the arguments on both sides, had reversed the decision of the Irish court, and set the prisoners free. Thus this judgment, which many bewailed as calculated to weaken the authority of the law in Ireland, probably contributed even more than the determined attitude of the government to strengthen and uphold it. Certain it is that it was very speedily followed by a complete collapse of the repeal agitation. For, though a new race of agitators arose, surpassing O'Connell in the extravagance of their demands, and though agrarian and other outrages continued to be perpetrated to a very lamentable extent, yet the agitation never recovered the formidable character it had assumed before the liberation of O'Connell and his associates. Few legal victories have ever done so much to strengthen the Irish government as did this legal defeat of Sir Robert Peel's administration.

The decision having been given, Parliament was prorogued by commission. The Queen's speech, read, as usual on such occasions, by the lord chancellor, referred to discussions in which the government had recently been engaged with the King of the French on events calculated to disturb the good understanding and friendly relations which had so long subsisted between the two countries, and it announced that, by the spirit of justice and moderation which had animated the two governments, the danger had been happily averted. The events thus referred to were the assumption of sovereignty over the island of Tahiti by Admiral Dupetit Thouars, and the insult offered to the British nation by the violent removal of its flag, and by what Sir R. Peel, who was generally so measured in his language, justly described as a 'gross outrage' inflicted on Mr. Pritchard, the English consul at Tahiti. The question itself might have been settled without much difficulty, as there could be no doubt that the French admiral had acted in a very improper manner, by such a moderate apology as the English government had a right to demand, and the French government could hardly refuse. Unfortunately, however, there existed in France at the moment when these events occurred a bitter hostility against this country, which the French government found it very difficult to control. Indeed, the war spirit on both sides was strongly roused; and thus, though the governments of both countries were animated by pacific sentiments, they found it no easy matter to resist the warlike pressure that was brought to bear on them. It was a fortunate circumstance for the peace of Europe that the men who had the chief share in these negotiations on the part of France were Louis Philippe, Guizot, and Soult; men who regarded peace and a cordial understanding with England as the corner-stone of their policy. Soult especially could not but remember the enthusiastic welcome he had received from all classes in England, when he represented his own country at the coronation of Queen Victoria. By the resolute determination of these three men to resist the impulse which urged them towards a war with England, that terrible calamity was avoided, and a great hindrance to the progress and civilisation of the world was averted. And thus, at the late conclusion of this session, the English government was able, in the terms we have quoted, to announce that war between the two countries had been avoided, and that the good understanding which had so long existed between the two governments was fully maintained. Still the incident had left behind it a very unpleasant feeling on both sides of the Channel. It was therefore a bold, and well-timed act on the part of the French king to choose this period as the one for returning the visit he had received from our Queen and Prince Albert. The anxiety he had displayed to maintain peaceful and cordial relations with our government secured him a most hearty and enthusiastic welcome from all classes of Englishmen. That reception completely effaced the unpleasant feelings which the Pritchard affair had left behind it, and placed the two nations on a more friendly footing with each other than before the occurrence of this untoward event.

The satisfactory state of our relations, not only with France, but also with another great European power, with which it was of the utmost importance that this country should maintain a friendly intercourse, was attested by a visit paid to this country by the Emperor of Russia. This visit, like that of the French King, was not a mere interchange of personal civilities between crowned heads. Both of these visits were the means of drawing closer the ties of amity between this country and the great nations over which these potentates reigned, and which, to a certain extent, they represented. The inhabitants of Russia and France justly regarded the cordial reception given to their respective sovereigns as the manifestation of a desire on our part to maintain a good understanding with themselves. They also brought together some of the chief statesmen of Russia, France, and England, enabling them to become better acquainted with one another's views and characters, and to discuss questions which had arisen, or were likely to arise, between their respective countries much more fully in free and friendly conversation than in communications carried on through diplomatic agents and in formal state papers. Unhappily these visits did not last long enough, and the ties that were formed were not sufficiently strong to bear the strain which unfortunate and then unforeseen circumstances put on them. However, during the visit of the Russian Emperor 'all went merry as a marriage-bell.' He had much free and friendly intercourse with the Queen, Prince Albert, the Duke of Wellington, Sir R. Peel, Lord Aberdeen, and many of the most distinguished personages of the English government and legislature. He was entertained with splendid hospitality at Buckingham Palace and Windsor Castle, and with a magnificence scarcely less than regal at Chiswick by the Duke of Devonshire, and by others of the English nobility at their princely mansions. He assisted at a review held specially in honour of him at Hyde Park, at which every branch of the service was represented. This review was the occasion of a very pleasing and characteristic display of the Duke of Wellington's right feeling. Finding that the spectators were bestowing their acclamations on himself rather than on the imperial visitor, he rode along the front of the people, saying to them as he passed, in tones of earnest entreaty, 'Please don't cheer for me; cheer for the Emperor.' The czar, after spending more than a week in England, and receiving the hospitable attentions of the crown and nobility, and a very cordial welcome from all classes of our countrymen, embarked on board the Black Eagle, the steamer which had conveyed him to our shores, and was waiting to convey him back to his own capital. It was noticed by some of the on-lookers, that one of the sailors conveyed a large bundle of straw on board the vessel, and it was explained to them that this was the bed on which the Emperor of All the Russias preferred to sleep, leaving the members of his suite to occupy the magnificent and luxurious couches with which the steamer was fitted.

We must not altogether pass over the visits paid to this country in the course of the year by the King of Saxony and Prince William of Prussia, now the Emperor William. They represented the feelings and interests of Germany; divided indeed at that time, and very far from possessing the almost paramount influence in the affairs of Europe which she has lately acquired, but even then having interests in common with us, which rendered it very desirable that the two nationalities should cultivate each other's friendship. Thus, though these visits had not the political importance that belonged to those of the two greatest potentates of Europe, they were not without value and significance, as testifying to, and, to a certain extent, promoting a good understanding between England and Germany.

A select committee, which had been appointed to inquire into the rapidly extending railway system of this country, made a report which conveyed some interesting information with regard to the cost of the construction of the principal lines of railway, and of the legal and parliamentary expenses. The following table, compiled from those drawn up under the direction of the committee and appended to their report, contains the charges per mile under these heads for the principal lines of railway which had been laid down up to the time at which the committee was appointed:

| Name of Railway. | Parliamentary expenses. | Law charges, Engineering, and Directors. | Land and Compensation. | Works and Stations. | Rolling-stock &c. establishment. |
|---|---|---|---|---|---|
| London and Birmingham | £650 | £1500 | £6300 | £38,280 | £3000 |
| London and South-western | 650 | 900 | 4000 | 18,450 | 2850 |
| Great Western | 1000 | 2500 | 6300 | 40,000 | 4800 |
| Manchester and Leeds | 1000 | 1600 | 6150 | 41,400 | 3000 |
| London and Brighton | 3000 | 1800 | 8000 | 38,000 | 3000 |

A bill for the abolition of imprisonment for debts under the amount of 20*l*. had received the royal assent by commission on the 9th of August, and came into operation the day following, on which several persons who had been confined in prison for debts below that amount were set at liberty.

The parliamentary session of 1845 began under peculiarly favourable auspices. The harvest of the preceding year had been unusually abundant; and trade and commerce had thoroughly revived from their long-continued depression. The fiscal measures of the government had answered, and more than answered, the anticipations of their framers. The income tax, which at first had caused great discontent and loud complaints, was endured with patience when the advantages of the remission of taxation that it had enabled ministers to make began to be felt, and the burden was the more cheerfully borne because it was hoped that in no long time it would be removed. The agitation for repeal in Ireland had almost entirely subsided, while the disputes between O'Connell and some of his principal followers indicated the completeness of the success which attended the measures of government notwithstanding, or rather to a great extent on account of, the defeat they had sustained in the late prosecutions. The great difficulty of the government was the question of the corn-laws, which was still kept open by the vigorous and persistent efforts of the anti-corn-law league. But the return of plenty and prosperity, the success that had attended the measures of the government, and the confidence which the financial ability of the prime minister inspired, enabled the government to resist every effort it made to compel them to change their policy of protection.

The session was opened on the 4th of February by the Queen in person. Her speech indicated that it was the intention of the government to propose measures for improving the sanitary condition of the houses of the poor in large towns, and the continuance of the income tax for a farther period. During the recess the government had lost one of its ablest and most useful members. It was generally understood that Mr. Gladstone, as president of the board of trade, had taken at least as large a share as the prime minister himself in the financial reforms which had so greatly increased the reputation of the present administration, and he had displayed no less tact and eloquence in explaining and defending those measures than skill and diligence in preparing them. Parliament and the country naturally expected to know the reasons which had caused him to secede from a cabinet of which he was so conspicuous and so serviceable a member. In the course of the debate on the address, Lord John Russell made some remarks on his resignation, which drew from him an explanation of the cause of his withdrawal from the ministry. Some years before this time he had published a volume on the relations between the church and the state. In this work he had advanced opinions at variance with the course which the government had determined to take in reference to the endowment of Maynooth College. It was true that he no longer held those opinions, and was prepared to support the provisions of the bill which the government intended to bring forward, so far as they had been imparted to him; but he feared that if in office he should advocate a measure that he had previously condemned in a work prepared with much care and reflection, it might be supposed that his change of opinion was dictated by interested motives; he therefore determined to retire from the ministry, and thus place himself in a position to take a free and independent course with regard to the proposed measure. At the same time he expressed great regret at having to withdraw from the cabinet, and respect for the colleagues from whom he had felt obliged to separate himself. This explanation caused a strong feeling of regret that a scrupulousness, generally regarded as over-sensitive, should have deprived the government and the country of the services of an able and upright minister. The statement made by Mr. Gladstone called up Sir Robert Peel, who, after expressing the high value he attached to the services of his late colleague, announced that he intended to propose to the House 'a liberal increase of the vote for the college of Maynooth,' and that he did 'not propose to accompany that increased vote by any regulation with respect to the doctrine, discipline, and management of the college, which can diminish the grace and favour of the grant.' Mr. Sheil amused the House and excited its 'loud laughter' by regretting that the statesman should have been sacrificed to the author, and that Sir Robert Peel should have reason to say, 'O that my friend had not written a book!'

The reader of this History can hardly fail to have perceived that, in the period we have now reached, the question of financial reform had acquired the place of paramount importance which in preceding parliaments had been occupied by questions of parliamentary, municipal, and administrative reform. It was because Sir R. Peel was generally regarded as the ablest financier of his day that he had been called to the first place in the government. It was this, more than the conservative reaction, more than the activity that had been displayed in the registration of voters, and the money that had been expended in the elections, that had enabled him to defeat the late government, and had given him the large majority on the dissolution to which he had forced them to resort. And the favourable expectations that had been formed respecting his fiscal measures had been more than fulfilled. The whole country, we may almost say the whole civilised world, was watching with intense interest the bold but wary advances he was making in the path of financial reform, guided by the experience gained in carefully watching the operation of the changes he had succeeded in introducing. The interest taken in them was, indeed, greater on the part of many of his enlightened opponents than on the part of many of his followers. The former could not but feel that, though he was not prepared to carry his principles to their logical conclusions, yet that his principles were identical with their own, while the applications he made of them were bolder and happier than they could have devised. These circumstances give to the financial measures introduced by Sir R. Peel during the period of his administration an interest and an importance which do not belong to the history of any other financial measures which at any former period had been placed before the House of Commons. The parliamentary, municipal, and administrative revolutions which had already taken place, were now, in fact, being followed by a financial revolution, none the less worthy of attention because it was calmly and quietly carried out with the full assent of a large majority both in the legislature and the country. Sir Robert Peel showed his sense of the importance of his plans, and his desire that they should be submitted to the fullest and most searching investigation, by bringing forward his budget at the earliest possible period of the session. On the 14th February, in accordance with notice previously given, he thus explained and developed his financial plans in a committee of ways and means.

'Though I rise under some disadvantages as to the period of the year at which this communication is made, yet after the declaration contained in her majesty's speech, that it is the intention of ministers to propose the continuance of the income tax for a certain number of years, I feel that there is no other alternative than to submit to the House the general views which the government takes of the financial condition and the commercial policy of the country. It will be my duty to discuss the great question, Whether it is consistent with the public interest that the present amount of public expenditure should be maintained, or whether it is not right that there should be, in some important respects, an increase of expenditure beyond the precedent of former years. If the committee maintain the latter proposition, the question which I shall then have to submit will be this, Whether it is fitting that the expenditure should be met from the ordinary sources, or whether it is more advisable that the tax on income and property should be continued, for the double purpose of providing for the due execution of the public service, and of enabling Parliament to repeal other taxes pressing on the industry and commercial enterprise of the country.

'I anticipate that the surplus revenue which will be in the exchequer on the 5th of April 1845 will at the very least amount to 5,000,000*l*.; and I estimate the revenue for the year ending April 5th, 1846, on the assumption that the House will not sanction the income tax, will amount to 51,000,000*l*.; and supposing the estimates of the ensuing year to be the same as those of the last, I calculate the total amount of expenditure to be 48,557,000*l*. But if you deduct from this surplus the sums to be derived from the receipt of half a year's income tax which will become due in the interim, and from the payment of the instalment from China, there will in that case be a small deficiency in the revenue as compared with the expenditure of the year. The question then arises, Are ministers justified in demanding, under such circumstances, an increased expenditure on account of the public service? I am satisfied that they are justified. No saving can be made by the abolition of offices, or the reduction of salaries; a sufficient force of revenue officers must be kept up; no diminution of our army can be recommended; the growing necessity for a farther protection to our commerce in every part of the globe induces me to propose that we should employ 4,000 more men in the navy this year than were employed under the estimates of last year. There will also be a vote for always keeping at our command a squadron of eight or nine sail of the line, and another for the purpose of increasing and improving our steam navigation. In respect, therefore, of the vote for the navy, and the ordnance connected with the navy, there will be votes this year of an increase of nearly a million. For this increased expenditure the revenue of the year will, I think, suffice, even if the House will not consent to continue the income tax. It is quite clear, however, that if it does not continue the income tax, in the year following a deficiency of revenue will occur; and the question I must next put to the committee is, Whether they will run the risk of that deficiency by making no provision to meet it; or Whether they will postpone the consideration of that deficiency till the year 1846? Her majesty's government think that it will not be a prudent course so to disregard the future condition of the country, and ministers are therefore induced to propose the continuance of the property tax for a farther period; but before I ask the assent of the House to that proposal, I feel it necessary to explain our views as to the appropriation of the surplus revenue which will then be placed at our disposal, after all the exigencies of the public service are provided for. Assuming that the committee will sanction the continuance of the property tax, the revenue on the 5th of April 1846 will amount to 53,700,000*l*. Deducting from this the sum of 600,000*l*. from China, which will only be receivable one year more, we may take the amount of the revenue at 53,100,000*l*. The public expenditure I have already calculated at 49,000,000*l*. There will therefore be left on the 5th of April 1846 a net surplus of 3,400,000*l*., if the committee acquiesce in the demand of ministers for increased naval estimates. I now approach the most important question of all, How can this surplus be applied to the relief of taxation? I would not have proposed the continuance of the income tax if I had not felt the strongest persuasion that it is competent for the house, by means of it, to make arrangements with respect to taxation which will be the foundation of great future commercial prosperity, and which will add materially to the comforts of those who are called on to contribute to it. In determining how you will appropriate any surplus of revenue, several important considerations should always be before you. You must first consider the claims to reduction of taxation on account of the heaviness of the duties on articles which enter into general consumption; then you must also consider what are the taxes that press most heavily on those raw materials which constitute the staple manufactures of the country; then you must consider what are the taxes which require the greatest establishment of revenue officers for their collection; and then what are the taxes which, if reduced, would enable you to diminish that establishment so as to reduce your expenditure; lastly, you must consider what are the taxes which, if removed, will give a new scope to commercial enterprise, and occasion an increased demand for labour. I do not say which of these considerations ought to preponderate, but they are all important. If the property tax is continued, ministers intend to make a great experiment with respect to taxation, in the hope that the general prosperity which will result from it will fill up the void caused in future years by the cessation of taxation. We do not propose to maintain any material surplus of income over revenue, in the conviction that the house will, at all events, maintain public credit if they propose the reduction of certain taxes which are more onerous than productive. I will take first the taxes connected with the customs, and will submit to the house a proposition with respect to the reduction of the duty on sugar. I propose, with regard to all sugars but refined sugars, to make this reduction: on brown muscovado sugar, which now pays a duty of 25s. 3d., I propose to make a reduction of 11s. 3d., and to reduce the duty to 14s. That reduction will apply to all British-plantation sugar, and to sugars produced in the Mauritius; but there are certain districts in British India with regard to which a different rule now applies, and I propose they should pay the same relative proportion of duty which they pay at present, and that the duty should be 18s. 8d. On free-labour foreign sugar I propose that the protecting duty shall not exceed 9s. 4d., and therefore the duty will be 23s. 4d. Any country which has a reciprocity treaty with us cannot, of course, be deprived of any privilege that it enjoys at present. As to white or clayed sugars, or sugars equal to clayed sugars, I propose that the duty should be reduced on British plantations from 25s. 3d. to 16s. 4d.; that the duty on sugar imported from India should be 21s. 9d., and that the duty on free-labour foreign sugar should be 28s.; thus retaining the whole amount of the discriminating duty which was imposed last year, but applying that discriminating duty in a different manner, giving 9s. 4d. as a protection on muscovado sugar, and an increased protection of 11s. 4d. on the more valuable and costly article. I propose to reduce the duty on molasses in the same proportions, and to remove the prohibitory duty on refined sugar imported from those British possessions which are entitled to import muscovado sugar at 14s., and to place on such sugar a proportionate import duty, 18s. 8d. on refined sugar, and 21s. on double refined. I calculate that this reduction of duty will make a reduction of price amounting to $1\frac{1}{2}d.$ per pound, and that the loss to the revenue of next year will be 1,300,000*l*. In the tariff of 1842 I abolished the duties on exports, with the exception of some few articles; I now propose as a general rule the abolition of export duties on all articles, not excepting coal; and I hope that, after having benefited the coal-owners by the removal of this duty, we shall hear no more of their combinations to restrict supply and enhance price. I estimate the total loss from the reduction of the coal duty at 120,000*l*. I now come to the consideration of duties levied on and applicable to raw materials used in manufactures. The tariff now includes 813 such articles. I propose to remove the duties applicable to 430 of them. By abolishing these duties, we shall get rid of a number of troublesome accounts, as well as of the warehouse system. Among the articles to which this abolition of duties will apply are the fibrous materials of silk, hemp, and flax; yarns of certain materials, excepting woollen; furniture goods; animal and vegetable manures; ores and minerals, with the exception of copper ore; iron and zinc in their first stage of manufacture; dye stuffs generally, and certain drugs of a noxious character. There are some articles to which this total removal of duties will not apply. I do not propose to interfere with the general principles which the government has applied to the timber duties, with the exception of staves, of which I have determined to permit an unrestricted importation, for the benefit of the coopers, limiting, however, the length of the staves, to prevent their importation, for the benefit of other parties than the coopers. The whole loss occasioned by the omission of 430 articles from the tariff would amount to 320,000*l*. I next approach the consideration of that article of raw material which is most important to the prosperity of the country, cotton wool. As the impost presses most heavily on the coarser fabrics, I am prepared to advise the abolition of it altogether. The loss to the revenue on that article will not be less than 680,000*l*. I do not intend to propose any farther alteration in the revenue of the customs. I have reviewed the excise duties, in order to ascertain which of them pressed most grievously on the interests and industry of the country. I found first and foremost among these the uncertain duty on the transfer of property, which, in accordance with the recommendation of a commission appointed some years ago to examine into the excise duties, I propose to repeal. I likewise propose that auctioneers, instead of taking out several licenses at an expense of 5*l*. each for selling different articles, should take out one general license at an expense of 15*l*., to sell any article they please. Their licenses now often cost them 25*l*. The number of auctioneers is 4,000, and the establishment of a 15*l*. license will produce a revenue of 60,000*l*. I intend to relieve the article of glass from all excise duty. The amount of duty at present imposed on it is 200*l*. and even 300*l*. per cent. on its manufacture, and there is no duty which occasions such vexatious interference with the manufacturers. The loss arising from the remission of the glass duty will amount to 642,000*l*. The total immediate loss which the revenue will sustain from the repeal of the duty on all the articles on which I propose a remission of taxation will be 3,338,000*l*., which will nearly absorb the surplus of 3,400,000*l*. on which I have calculated. I do not deny that the financial scheme which I have just explained to the committee is a bold experiment: but, responsible as I am to Parliament for its success, I am not afraid of making it. I now propose to the committee to continue the income tax for a farther limited period of three years, because I have a confident expectation that the reduction in the price of articles of great importance which will follow this proposed remission of taxation will be, if not a complete, yet a great, compensation for its burden. I will not say that it may not be wiser to give a longer time than three years for testing this experiment. I think, however, that Parliament ought to have a control over such a tax. I hope that so great a source of revenue will not be dried up before the expiration of three years; but at the end of that time, such is my confidence in the elasticity of the country, I think you will be able to dispense with the tax if you think proper. I recommend this plan with a deliberate conviction that your sanction of it will conduce to the extension of industry and the encouragement of enterprise; so that all classes, whether agricultural, manufacturing, commercial, or parties not engaged in any particular branch of industry, will either directly or indirectly be benefited by it.'

Sir Robert sat down, after having spoken for three hours

and a quarter. His speech was not equal in length, nor perhaps in financial ability, to some of those which have been delivered within the last few years; but in both respects it surpassed all those that had ever been delivered before on similar occasions. The great and comprehensive changes which it proposed completely carried away the house, and called forth very loud cheering from all quarters of it, and not least from the benches occupied by those who differed most entirely from the general policy of the party of which he was the leader. As soon as the cheering had subsided, the prime minister again rose to express a hope that the house would be prepared to decide on the principle of his resolutions on the following Monday. The plan underwent a slight degree of criticism. Lord J. Russell and Lord Howick objected to the proposed arrangement for the sugar duties, and Messrs. Roebuck and Curtis to the renewal of the income tax, but the expressions of satisfaction greatly predominated.

On the evening of the 17th the budget came again before the house. Lord J. Russell stated his strong objection to an income tax, and predicted that it would be renewed perpetually. He denied that the burden of a permanent income tax would be sufficiently repaid to the country by the benefit to be derived from taking off certain taxes. He objected to that part of the plan which gave away 300,000*l.* of auction duties, contending that the reduction of the duty on fire-insurances and that on soap, the only tax now left on the absolute necessaries of life, would have been more expedient changes. He condemned Sir R. Peel's interference with the article of sugar as being most injudicious and impolitic, contending that if the sugar of all foreign countries were admitted on the same principle as that of our own colonies, the estimated loss of 1,300,000*l.* would be avoided, and there would be no occasion to abandon any part of our revenue. He hoped the people would resolve to set trade free, and thus get rid of the odious and inquisitorial income tax. He concluded his speech, however, without proposing any amendment on the proposition before the house. Not so Mr. Roebuck, who followed him. He concluded a long and able speech, in which he assailed with great acrimony and ingenuity the ministerial plan, by moving an amendment that the words 'professions, trades, and offices' should be omitted from the resolution moved by Sir R. Peel; and he explained that he proposed this alteration not with the view of altogether excluding them from taxation, but for the purpose of subjecting them to a discriminating scheme of taxation. It has been admitted over and over again, that the income tax has pressed most unjustly on those classes which Mr. Roebuck mentioned in his amendment: but though this injustice has been urged on the attention of successive Parliaments, and been almost universally acknowledged, no government has been bold enough to attempt to redress it. The hope that the income tax would only be continued for a few years induced the classes who felt themselves aggrieved to bear the load in the first instance with more patience than they would have displayed if they had believed that it would be permanent; and then the habit of bearing it has inured them to it.

The chancellor of the exchequer replied to Mr. Roebuck, and answered the question, What grounds have ministers for supposing that the income tax will not be permanent? by saying, 'Our expectations of the future are based on the experience of the past. The income tax was originally submitted to the consideration of the house in 1842, for the purpose of covering a large deficiency, and releasing a number of articles from restrictions which pressed heavily on industry. The amount received from the ordinary sources of revenue was 47,000,000*l*. The measures proposed to Parliament in that and in the last session for the reduction of taxation withdrew from the public income no less a sum than 1,400,000*l*.; and yet on the 10th of October 1844 the same taxes produced not 47,000,000*l*., but 47,497,000*l*.' He argued against the distinction which Mr. Roebuck proposed to make between realised and fluctuating capital, and quoted the authority of Mr. Pitt in support of his argument. He promised to give Lord J. Russell an early opportunity of fighting over again the battle of the sugar duties.

After Mr. C. Wood and Colonel Conolly had spoken—the first in condemnation, and the second in support of the income tax—Mr. Bankes, as the champion of the agriculturists, rose to complain of the manner in which his clients had been disregarded by the prime minister and the chancellor of the exchequer, though the distresses which they were enduring had been formally communicated to the house. 'By this plan,' he exclaimed, 'everything is given to the mercantile, and nothing to the agricultural interest. Why is the establishment of our army so great? To protect our colonies and our commerce. Why are the navy estimates to be increased to the amount of 1,000,000*l*.? Because both in China and the Pacific new naval stations are necessary to defend the interests of the merchants in their vicinity. Does the agricultural interest object to this? No such thing. Then let not that interest, if it is as powerful and as predominant as is stated, be taunted in future as selfish and ungenerous. As to the vote before the house, those who represent the distressed districts can only act as circumstances permit. I see that both sides of the house are prepared to vote for the continuance of the income tax; I have therefore no choice, and must accommodate my vote to the situation. The farmers are ill able to bear this or any other burden.' Mr. Warburton thought that if the income tax were made permanent, all objections to it would vanish; while Mr. Robert Palmer, on the contrary, contended that a permanent income tax would be an intolerable evil. In answer to the complaints of those who represented the agricultural interest, Sir R. Peel stated that his reason for not alluding to the distress of that interest in his speech on Friday was that he had entered on the subject at some length two or three evenings before. He expressed the firmest conviction, that if the agricultural interest would agree to the continuance of the income tax, and consent to take their share in the general prosperity, which he believed would be derived from it, they would gain more than they would if he were to relieve them from some local taxation, and burden the consolidated fund with a grant of 500,000*l*. for their advantage; and he pointed out in some detail how the agriculturist would be benefited by many of the remissions of duty he proposed to make. The debate was continued some time longer, and at the conclusion of it Mr. Roebuck's amendment was rejected by a majority of 208, there being 55 in favour of it, and 263 against it. The chief attack on the ministerial plan was made on the 5th of March, when it was moved that the house should go into committee on the income-tax bill. Mr. Bernal Osborne then moved that it should be committed that day three months. Mr. F. T. Baring took this opportunity of entering into a searching examination and carefully-prepared criticism of the financial plans of the government.

'Sir R. Peel,' he said, 'originally demanded the income-tax for three years, as a means of recovering the revenue, the income tax to be then remitted. But what is the state of the finances now? On the face of Sir R. Peel's estimate, the income for the ensuing year, without the Chinese money or the income tax, will be 47,900,000*l*., the expenditure 49,700,000*l*., leaving a deficiency of 1,800,000*l*.; therefore the income tax cannot be got rid of without imposing additional taxes to the amount of 2,000,000*l*. After completing the whole of his operations, Sir R. Peel calculates the surplus at only 90,000*l*. or 100,000*l*. Even that surplus rests on the sugar duties; they again rest on the calculation that the consumption will increase by nearly one-fifth beyond the largest consumption yet attained, and that sugar will come in at the higher rate of duties, while it is not yet certain what scale the right hon. gentleman will be obliged to fall back on. It may be admitted that the poor man will derive some benefit from the remission of duties on other articles, but these remissions will not touch his bread, cheese, butter, soap, tea, tobacco, or coffee. The right honourable gentleman says that his selection has been made with reference to one great point, that at the end of three years he may be able to take off the income tax. In his anticipations of the future the chancellor of the exchequer has borrowed the too sanguine pencil of his colleague Prosperity Robinson.\* He took off taxes to the amount of three or four millions, and expected to increase the revenue in three years by five millions. The facts did not justify that calculation. The chancellor of the exchequer forgets that in 1816 the income tax was taken off. In 1816 the ordinary revenue was 71,900,000*l*.; taxes were taken off to the amount of 17,500,000*l*. In 1819 the revenue was 52,155,000*l*., being a loss of 19,745,000*l*. In the five years ending 1826 the taxes remitted were 13,000,000*l*., and the revenue was not restored by about 4,000,000*l*. In the three years ending 1829 the taxes taken off were 9,600,000*l*.,

---

\* A nickname given to the Earl of Ripon, on account of the over-sanguine anticipations of prosperity arising from his financial measures, in which he had indulged when chancellor of the exchequer.

but by 1829 the revenue had not recovered, the loss being 4,600,000*l*. From 1815 to 1830 the taxes taken off were 33,000,000*l*., and the loss to the revenue was 22,000,000*l*.' Mr. Osborne's amendment, and another by Mr. Curtis, limiting the duration of the tax to two years instead of three, were rejected by considerable majorities. In answer to remarks made by Mr. Wakley, Sir R. Peel said that if the house was so enamoured of the income tax at the end of three years as to renew it again, they would amend it as might seem best. He did not at all despair of being able to part with it at the end of three years, but if the house would give it to him for five years, on condition of adopting alterations which would render it less onerous to the working classes, he would willingly agree to that amendment. On the whole, there was a strong expression of opinion in favour of direct taxation, and the bill passed through the committee without any material alteration, and was sent up to the House of Lords, where it was also carried. This question being disposed of, the not less interesting and important question of the sugar duties came under debate, the discussion turning almost exclusively on the merits of differential duties. The issue on this question was very distinctly raised by a resolution proposed by Mr. Milner Gibson on the 24th of February, stating that no arrangement of these duties would be satisfactory which did not involve an equalisation of duty on foreign and colonial sugars. The question then proposed was of so much importance, was so ably brought forward by Mr. Gibson, and so thoroughly discussed on his motion, that we think it desirable to give, with our usual condensation, an account of the principal arguments made use of by those who took part in the debate.

*Mr. Gibson:* 'I rise to call the attention of the house to a plain matter of justice in taxation, and to assert that it is not consistent with the fair performance of our functions when we resolve ourselves into a committee of ways and means to consider of a supply to her majesty, in order to enable her to meet the expenditure of the country, to levy another tax, which is not paid to the crown or to the exchequer, but to a class of our countrymen who have not made good their claim to any compensation for a grievance inflicted on them. I contend that to levy a discriminating duty on foreign and colonial sugar is to give the amount of that discriminating duty to the parties for whose protection it is levied. Now the difference between the duty imposed on colonial sugar and that imposed on foreign sugars is to be 10s. per cwt.; and the amount of loss which will be sustained by the exchequer, and of gain to the West and East Indian proprietors in consequence of this difference of duty, will be no less than 2,300,000l. a year. This addition to the price of sugar is an injustice to the consumer. It has been defended on two grounds: first, that there is a deficiency of labour in our colonies; and secondly, that the colonies are exposed to greater expense in the production of sugar now that slavery and the slave-trade are abolished. With regard to the first, I may quote the authority of Lord Stanley, who has stated that there is an adequate supply of labour in the West Indies, and has shown that the hill coolies are wandering about in crowds and in penury in the Mauritius because they are unemployed. With regard to the second, I may mention that the production of a cwt. of sugar in the time of slavery cost 9s. $10\frac{1}{2}d.$, and that at present it costs somewhat between 10s. 2d. and 9s. $9\frac{1}{2}d.$ It is evident, then, that the discriminating duty of 10s. a cwt. for the benefit of our colonial dependencies is more than all the cost of producing a cwt. of sugar. The colonial proprietors are very deficient in their knowledge of the cultivation of the sugar-cane, and in the application of science and machinery to it. They live far from their estates, and do not place them under proper superintendence; but they have no reason on that account to call on the people of England to give them compensation for their want of skill and necessary superintendence. They will derive no benefit from any juggling of duties in this house, or from any applications to secretaries of state for higher duties for the protection of their monopoly. They must gird up their loins, and no longer suffer themselves to be enervated by that monopoly which is as injurious to themselves as it is to the trade and manufacture of England. Besides, our merchants and manufacturers have an equal right with those who produce sugar from their own estates to supply the British community with sugar from Brazil and other countries, which they obtain in exchange for their commodities and home-made produce. Our colonies can no longer supply us with a sufficient quantity of sugar now that we have a vast increase in the number of our population, while the import remains stationary. The consequence is, that, as the affluent classes will not forego their usual supply of sugar, a less portion remains to be divided amongst the poorer classes, and that too at a higher price. Thus the monopoly diminishes the consumption of sugar, and thereby diminishes the amount of customs duties paid on it into the revenue. But if the import of sugar has diminished, perhaps the loss has been made up by our exports to the West Indies? Quite the reverse. The exports to the West Indies in 1794 were as great as they are now, and during the last twenty years they have not increased. I therefore contend that this protection is not for revenue, for it defrauds revenue; that it is not for the producer, for his produce has not increased; not for the exporter at home, for his exports to these colonies are stationary; it is not to be defended on the score of consistency, for Sir R. Peel is now going to admit cotton the produce of the East Indies, and cotton the produce of the United States of America, on the same terms. It is also at variance with the principles of the greatest practical political philosophers. It is a mere arbitrary exaction, carried by the force of numbers in this house for the benefit of a class, for which no adequate explanation has been offered. I trust that the house will desist from this unwise legislation, and no longer sanction this principle, that free labour is not able to contend with slave labour.'

Passing by the speeches of Mr. Ewart, who seconded the motion, and Mr. James, who opposed it, we come to that of Mr. Ricardo, a gentleman who enjoyed a high and deserved reputation as a political economist, and whose opinions on this question, therefore, carried great weight with them. He said:

'The government resolution contains nineteen different rates of duty to be levied on sugar. It makes distinctions for which there are no real grounds of difference; and it proposes an immense sacrifice of revenue without the least compensating advantage. Brokers and wholesale grocers have publicly declared that they cannot comprehend the distinction which Sir R. Peel has drawn between different kinds of brown muscovados and of clayed sugars, nor tell where muscovados end and clayed sugars begin. I calculate the sacrifice made by the English consumers of sugar under the present system to be 3,790,000*l*. more than under the old system, and this is paid to the West-India proprietors exclusively. To this may be added 1,300,000*l*. more which will be lost, according to Sir R. Peel, to the exchequer; so that 5,000,000*l*., or the amount of the income tax, is sacrificed by the country for these discriminating duties. I think it would be much better to equalise the sugar duties than to propose the continuance of the income tax in order to make the proposed reductions in the sugar duties.'

*Sir George Clerk:* 'Protective duties may in some cases be carried too far, but, considering the heavy burden of our national debt, it is a very serious thing to say that we are to remove all protection from native industry. I contend that the depression to which the West-India interest has been subject for some time past, owing to the abolition of slavery, affords a fair claim to legislative protection. When it is just commencing to recover from that depression, is it wise for the house to interfere, and assert that the planters are not entitled to any protection at all? If the West-India proprietors have not applied to the cultivation of sugar all the modern inventions of science and machinery, it is owing to their want of capital, occasioned by the immense depreciation of their properties; but I deny that this is the fact to anything like the extent alleged by Mr. Gibson.'

*Mr. Villiers:* 'The assertion that the West-India interest has suffered by the abolition of the slave-trade is quite contrary to the fact; the reverse was admitted by Lord Ripon twelve years ago. As for the argument, that the colonial proprietors require protection, it rests with Sir G. Clerk to show that protected interests have ever prospered. These duties cost the country 4000*l*. a week in the metropolis, and 50,000*l*. a week in the rest of the kingdom, and all for the benefit of the West-India proprietors.'

*Lord Howick:* 'I cannot call this duty, as Sir G. Clerk has done, a protection to British industry; on the contrary, I denounce it as an unjustifiable impost on the hard-earned wages of the British labourer. Brazilian sugar is now selling in bond at 18*s*. 6*d*. per cwt., and 18½ tons of colonial sugar, at 26*s*. per cwt., would cost each 481*l*. Therefore the produce of British labour to the amount of 481*l*. would exchange for sugar of Brazil in bond to the amount of 26 tons, but for sugar of the West Indies in bond to the amount of only 18½ tons. Seven and a half tons of sugar is, then, the amount of spoliation from the British labourer taken by the West-India proprietor, on so comparatively insignificant a sum as 481*l*. Again, look at the advantages which would be derived to this country from abolishing the discriminating duties in an increased trade with South America, and especially with Brazil. When the Brazilian treaty, which admitted all British produce and manufactures for consumption into Brazil at a duty of 15 per cent., expired last year, the government of Brazil informed our government that they would exclude our produce from their dominions unless we admitted their produce at reduced duties into ours; but that they would admit it on the old terms if we would relax the sternness of our tariff. The equalisation of these duties would therefore restore us to a state of commercial harmony with the Brazils, and so open to us a market which already takes annually five millions of our exports. The retention of these discriminating duties, so far from being a benefit, is absolutely a detriment to the West Indies themselves. I will not say that the equalisation of duties might not give a temporary stimulus to slavery and the slave trade, but I am persuaded that, in the end, it would enable the friends of humanity to gain a great triumph; for it would show that, on'a clear stage and without favour, free labour is more than able to compete with slave labour.'

Mr. Gladstone, who continued to give his old colleagues a warm support, rose after Lord Howick and said:

'I admit that the supporters of the resolution are bound to show cause for maintaining the existing protection; but it has been the policy of Parliament for some time past to maintain protection where capital and skill are invested in certain forms, perhaps defective, but still adopted under its sanction. Mr. Villiers has asked what claims have the West-India proprietors to this discriminating duty? I wish heartily that equalisation of duties could be adopted on native and on foreign productions; but I am convinced that if it were adopted in this case, it would bring ruin on a number of our countrymen at home, and dismay and indescribable confusion on the West-India islands. It is the dearness of production there which creates all the difficulty in this question. The scarcity of labourers is one great cause of the dearness in the West Indies; and the scarcity of resident landlords is another and a still greater cause. Now the West-India proprietors became non-resident in consequence of the protection given by Parliament to the slave-trade. If, then, the dearness of their produce was caused by acts of Parliament which they were compelled to obey, they have a right to claim that Parliament should go shares with them in bearing the mischievous effects of those acts. The House, in the practical application of the doctrines of free trade, ought to begin where there is no apprehension of mischief, where there is great capital and powerful machinery, and where there is every prospect of success; but not with the West-India proprietor, whose inability to compete with his foreign rivals is of parliamentary origin.'

Mr. Cobden and Mr. Bright, who now began to command the attention of the House, not only from the important position they occupied as leaders of a mighty party and a formidable agitation out of doors, but also on account of the clearness of their views and the lucidity with which they expressed them,—addressed the House towards the close of the debate, and therefore at a time when the arguments on both sides, as well as the attention of the House, were nearly exhausted. They, of course, both advocated the cause of free trade against that of protection. On the other hand, the ministerial scheme was supported by Messrs. Cardwell and Goulburn, the latter of whom briefly replied at the close of the debate. When he sat down, the House divided, with the following result:

| | |
|---|---:|
| For the ministerial resolution | 217 |
| For Mr. Gibson's amendment | 84 |
| Majority for ministers | 133 |

An amendment, proposed by Mr. Hawes, 'that provision should be made in the bill for the drawback of the amount of the duty reduced on such duty-paid sugar as now remains in the queen's warehouses,' was carried in spite of the opposition of the chancellor of the exchequer, and embodied in a bill which was founded on the resolution, and carried through both Houses.

The remissions of duties proposed by the government

were not agreed to without some opposition. The claims of the consumers of soap were strongly urged as being very superior to those of auctioneers. The chancellor of the exchequer was reminded of his own efforts to obtain a remission of the soap tax when it was proposed to reduce the stamp duty on newspapers. However, in spite of these arguments and appeals the government persisted in their proposals, and their bills were carried through without any material alterations.

Notwithstanding the largeness of the majorities by which the moderate protectionist policy of the government had triumphed in every division, the question of free trade occupied a much larger share in the attention of the House than had been given to it in any previous session, and out of all proportion to the number of members by which it was supported. The reason of this was, that the argument against protection had made far greater progress with the people than with their representatives, and that the steadily-growing public opinion in its favour compelled even those who were most strongly opposed to any change to give a respectful consideration to the arguments of its advocates.

We have already seen that the discussion on the budget and the sugar duties had to a great extent resolved themselves into debates on free trade; and so it was with almost every fiscal question that occupied the attention of Parliament. But in addition to the indirect attention which the question thus obtained, it was formally submitted to the House of Commons on the 18th of March by Mr. Cobden, who asked the House to 'grant a select committee to inquire into the causes and extent of the alleged existing agricultural distress, and into the effect of legislative protection upon the interests of landowners, tenant-farmers, and farm labourers.' In moving this resolution Mr. Cobden contended that the distress which had been so much and so long complained of in the agricultural districts was the inevitable consequence of that very protection which was regarded as the mainstay of agricultural prosperity. He pointed out that the system of leases and the tenure of farms then in vogue tended to hinder capital from being invested in the improvement of the land; and to prove the strength of his own convictions, he promised that, if the committee should be granted, he would place a majority of protectionists on it, feeling certain that even with a committee so constituted he would be able to explode the fallacy of agricultural protection, and put an end to the present system within two years after the publication of the report. Mr. Cobden's motion was opposed on the part of the government by Mr. Sidney Herbert, who argued, that the question of agricultural distress had already been very fully investigated by numerous committees without result, and that the granting of the committee asked for by Mr. Cobden would produce an impression that the government was prepared to depart from that policy of protection which it had hitherto maintained. These reasons were deemed unsatisfactory, not only by Mr. Cobden and his free-trade associates, but also by men like Lord Howick, who were rapidly becoming converts to free trade. However, the government triumphed by a majority of 92.

The question of agricultural distress, which Mr. Cobden had attempted to deal with on free-trade principles, was in turn taken up by Mr. Miles from the protectionist standpoint. He attributed the distress under which the agricultural interest was suffering to erroneous and mischievous legislation. He showed that under the new cornlaws the importation of wheat had been seven or eight times greater than at the period immediately subsequent to the introduction of the corn-law of 1828; and he argued that the British farmer had suffered great losses from the reduction that had taken place, not only in the price of wheat, but in that of every kind of food, through the importation of foreign cattle. He acknowledged that he had himself supported the new sliding scale, but added, that if he and his friends had entertained any idea that it would be followed by such measures as the Canada corn-law and the tariff, they would have offered it such a resistance as no minister could overcome. The farmers attributed the distress under which they were suffering chiefly to these measures; but they also complained of the poor-rate and county-rate, and insisted that in these two instances they were taxed more heavily than the rest of the community. He suggested several projects for the alleviation of agricultural distress; but that on which he chiefly insisted was the transfer of the cost of several charges connected with the administration of justice and of the registration of voters from the county-rate to the exchequer. He believed that if this suggestion were adopted, the sum transferred to the general taxation of the country would be about 300,000*l.* He declared that the agriculturists had no confidence in the ministry. They saw that the tariff which had been adopted three years ago was about to be revised again, and that the shield of protection, which had been thrown over some of the productions of their industry, was to be removed still farther from them. They could not, therefore, refrain from asking themselves what there was to prevent the corn-laws from going next. He demanded protection, not for agriculture only, but for every branch of native industry. He concluded by moving, 'that it is the opinion of this House that in the application of surplus revenue towards relieving the burden of the country by reduction or remission of taxation, due regard should be had to the necessity of affording relief to the agricultural interests.' This motion was seconded by the Earl of March, who expressed his cordial concurrence in the opinions advanced by the mover of the resolution. Proposals identical with that now presented to the House had been brought forward in 1834 and 1836, but had been rejected by the government of that day, and were still less likely to find favour now. They were, however, zealously supported by a little party of clever young men, who attracted a good deal of public attention by the extravagance of their Toryism, and were known through the country by the name of 'Young England.' The most prominent members of that party were Mr. Disraeli, Mr. Smythe, and Lord J. Manners. The first-mentioned of these gentlemen had already gained the ear of the House by extraordinary readiness in debate, and by the sarcastic severity with which he attacked the policy of the government. On this occasion he denounced them more strongly than before, and declared, that under existing circumstances, a conservative government was an organised hypocrisy. This declaration was cheered by the ultra-protectionists with a zest which showed that the breach between the government and the more extreme section of the conservative party was every day widening. The members of the government did their best to conciliate a party whose support was indispensable to their continuance in office. They took frequent opportunities of expressing their unabated confidence in that policy of moderate protection to which they had hitherto faithfully adhered. But these declarations did not allay the suspicions and jealousies of the protectionists. Meanwhile the Whigs as a party had altogether abandoned the policy of protection, and Lord J. Russell did not hesitate to denounce it as 'the bane of agriculture.' With their assistance the ministry had no difficulty in resisting the motion, which was rejected by a majority of 135.

While Mr. Miles contended that the land was subject to peculiar and excessive burdens, Mr. Ward maintained that it enjoyed peculiar exemptions and advantages. He accordingly renewed a motion, which he had been in the habit of bringing forward for some years past, for inquiring into the subject. But it was opposed now, as it had been previously, by the government, and was rejected by a majority of 71. Nine resolutions were moved by Lord J. Russell, which proposed to embody in an address to the queen a recommendation of the abolition of all protective duties, but especially of that on corn; a revision of the law of parochial settlements; a systematic plan of colonisation; and a farther extension of religious and moral education; in a word, a tolerably complete programme of the policy of the Whig party. The resolutions, nine in number, gave rise to a long debate, ending in their rejection by a majority of 78.

The free-trade question was still more distinctly brought under the notice of the House by the annual motion of Mr. Villiers for the abolition of all duties on corn, which was rejected, after a long and earnest debate, by a majority of 132. At any rate the free-traders could not complain that the House of Commons had not paid due attention to their favourite question; but the majorities against them were so large, the opposition still offered so determined, the resolution of the ministry to adhere to protection apparently so fixed, the House of Lords so dead against them, that the most ardent and sanguine felt that probably many years of struggle still awaited them before their minority could be changed into a majority, and their final triumph achieved.

The dissatisfaction and suspicion with which ministers were regarded by their more extreme followers was not diminished by the concessions they intended to make to the Roman Catholics of Ireland. The no-popery cry had not altogether lost its efficacy either in the House or outside. The opposition came, not only from many members of the church who supported the government, but also from a large number of dissenters, who feared that the measure would encourage the diffusion of Romanism, which already seemed to them to be spreading, not only in Ireland, but also in this country. But the opposition thus offered to the Maynooth bill was balanced by the support which the Whigs and Radicals gave to the ministry on the question. When, therefore, on the 3rd of April, Sir Robert Peel introduced his measure to the House, he spoke amidst the loud applause of his usual opponents, and the chilling silence or strongly-expressed dissent of the majority of his usual supporters. Before he commenced his address, a scene occurred which, though it afforded a good deal of amusement to others, must have been intensely painful and disheartening to a man so sensitive as Sir R. Peel, not only on account of the triumph it afforded to his opponents, but also because it displayed the almost mutinous disposition of the majority of his own followers. The speaker called on those who were entrusted with petitions against an increase of the amount of the Maynooth grant to present them. Instantly the occupants of the ministerial benches rose *en masse*, while the opposition retained their seats, and roared with laughter. When their merriment had subsided, and the petitions had been laid on the table, the speaker called on Sir R. Peel. The premier, after endeavouring to disarm the hostility of those who opposed him on this question by a candid appreciation of the motives by which they were actuated, demonstrated the insufficiency of the existing grant by showing that the professors were miserably paid, the students baldy lodged, and the buildings dilapidated. He then proceeded to consider the relative merits of the three courses which it was open to Parliament to take in reference to the college—to withdraw the grant now made to it, to keep it at its present amount, or to increase it; and he strongly insisted that the last of these courses was the one which both policy and justice required to be taken. He urged the wisdom and propriety of dealing with the institution in a generous rather than in a niggardly spirit. He then explained the plan which the government recommended to the House for its adoption. He proposed that the trustees of the college should be incorporated by the title of 'trustees of Maynooth College;' that they should be allowed to hold real property to the amount of 3000*l*. per annum; that they should have a sum annually paid to them, not exceeding 6000*l*., for the purpose of enabling them to pay 600*l*. or 700*l*. a year to the president of the college, 260*l*. or 270*l*. a year to the theological professor, and 220*l*. or 230*l*. a year to the other professors. To this might be added a farther sum of 14,000*l*. for the students; thus making a total annual amount of 20,000*l*. devoted to the support of the institution. He also proposed to ask for a vote of 30,000*l*. for this year only, in order to put the buildings in good repair, to provide proper accommodation for the president and professors, and to improve the appearance of the college. He proposed to limit the number of students attending the institution at one time to 500, in order that the reminiscences of the college should no longer be revolting, as they had been in times past. Future repairs were to be the subject of an annual vote, and to be included in the estimates of the Board of Works. The plan included a provision for the appointment of visitors to the college.

This proposal of course met with a loud outcry from the Inglises, the Plumptres, and the Colquhouns of the ultra-protestant party. The Roman Catholic members on the other hand expressed in warm terms the gratitude with which they hailed a measure framed in so liberal a spirit. From Lord J. Russell, and the Whig party generally, it received a cordial and generous welcome. A debate earnestly carried on, and continued by successive adjournments through six nights, was thus concluded by the prime minister:

'I freely own that every feeling with regard to imputations of inconsistency, every feeling with regard to the security of the government, is subordinate to one—do not reject the measure. As I said before, punish us; visit us with censure; let the two parties combine on the ground that this policy ought to be carried out by those who were its original projectors; take what course you please; but do not let your indignation fall upon the measure; let it be confined to those who have opposed it. We have been responsible for the peace of Ireland, and I tell you that you must in some way or other break up that formidable confederacy which exists against the British government and the British connection. I do not believe that you can break it up by force. I believe you can do much by acting in a spirit of kindness, forbearance, and generosity. There rises in the far western horizon a cloud, small indeed, but threatening future storms. Ministers were lately called upon to declare that they were prepared and determined to maintain the rights of this country. I own to you that when I was called upon to make that declaration, I did recollect with satisfaction and consolation that the day before I had sent a message of peace to Ireland. I deprecate war with earnestness; but if it should come, I pray that every pulse throughout the frame of the empire may be found beating in harmonious union, Ireland ranged firmly on our side. I doubt whether, considering what is now transpiring, the vindication of the honour and interests of the country will not be committed to other hands; but to whomsoever it may be committed, I shall take my place beside them, encouraging them by every support I can give in a just and honourable cause.'

At the conclusion of this address the House divided, when there appeared:

| | |
|---|---|
| For the second reading | 323 |
| Against it | 176 |
| Majority for the government | 147 |

Notwithstanding the largeness of this majority, and the proof it afforded that the bill would be carried without much alteration, many of its details were opposed in committee. Mr. Ward moved an amendment involving the principle of his celebrated appropriation clause, and proposing to take the grant from the funds of the established church in Ireland; but it was rejected by a majority of 174. The third reading of the bill was carried by a majority of 133. It was then sent to the upper House, where the second reading was proposed by the Duke of Wellington, and the discussion on the motion extended over three nights. It was carried through all its stages by large majorities, in spite of the strenuous opposition of many of the bishops and of those peers by whom the government was usually supported. An amendment moved by Earl Winchelsea limiting the operation of the bill to three years was negatived without a division.

Another measure of ministers gave even a greater shock to their more extreme supporters than the Maynooth bill. They proposed to establish colleges in Ireland in which no definite religious instruction should be imparted. The bill for this purpose was introduced on the 9th of May by Sir J. Graham. The plan was favourably received by the majority of the English Whigs, but was denounced by Sir R. Inglis as a gigantic scheme of godless education. In a subsequent stage of the bill Mr. O'Connell came forward on the same side, and strongly objected to the omission of all religious teaching in the colleges, and this objection was supported by Lord J. Russell. But though the scheme met with opposition from so many and such different quarters, and shocked so many prejudices, the bill went through all its stages in both houses by large majorities.

In the course of this session two events forced themselves on the serious, and we may say alarmed attention of the legislature. The first of these was an outbreak that had occurred in New Zealand, in which nine Englishmen had been put to death by the natives. The governor of the colony and the New Zealand Company mutually accused each other of being the authors of a calamity which seemed likely to lead to farther mischief and danger. And the government at home showed that it did not regard the former as altogether blameless, for he was recalled soon after the news of the outbreak reached England. The matter of course came before Parliament; but with little result except that the debate on it drew forth an announcement that the home government had succeeded in bringing about an arrangement between the New Zealand Company and the government of the colony, which it was hoped would prevent any recurrence of the terrible scenes which had been enacted in that country. The news of the pacification of the colony was soon followed by the intelligence that one M. Thierry, who had made himself king of the insurgent natives, having given umbrage to his barbarous subjects, had been killed, cooked, and eaten by them at a solemn banquet. The other event to which we have referred was of a far more serious character. A dispute had arisen between our government and that of the United States of

America on the subject of the Oregon territory, situated in North America beyond the Rocky Mountains. President Polk, in his inaugural address, insisted that this territory unquestionably belonged to the United States. 'Our title,' said he, 'to the country of Oregon is clear and unquestionable, and already are our people preparing to perfect their title by occupying it with their wives and children.'

The claim thus confidently asserted was one that the English government was by no means prepared to admit. Public men of all parties here were firmly convinced that the country belonged to England by right of discovery and by right of treaties. In both houses the representatives of the government announced its determination to maintain the title of this country to the disputed territory. In the House of Commons the prime minister thus concluded a temperate and judicious speech on this important and exciting question: 'We have a right to this territory of Oregon which is clear and unquestionable; we desire an amicable adjustment of the differences between ourselves and the United States; but if, after having exhausted every effort to obtain it, our rights are invaded, we are resolved and prepared to maintain them.'

This declaration was received with such a burst of enthusiastic cheering as has hardly ever been heard within the walls of the House of Commons, and which signified the determination of the representatives of the English people to support the government in any means they might think proper to adopt for asserting what were believed to be the just claims of the nation. Lord Clarendon in the upper House, and Lord J. Russell in the lower, warmly expressed their determination to strengthen the hands of the government in these negotiations, and in the consequences that might arise out of them. Happily, however, such a direful calamity, not to say insanity, as a war between these two nations for a territory of little value to either of them, was averted. The American government was induced to abate its pretensions, and to agree to an equitable adjustment of the claims of the two countries, which the imprudent appeal made by the newly-elected president to popular passions seemed at one time likely to render extremely difficult.

The steady progress of the principles of toleration, even

under a conservative ministry supported by a conservative majority, was marked this year by the passing of a bill for the admission of Jews to municipal offices. Up to this period the Jew, though eligible to the offices of magistrate and sheriff, nay even compellable to serve in the latter office, was yet excluded, by the form of the oath he was required to take, from the offices of mayor, alderman, or common-councilman. The words that prevented him from taking it were 'on the true faith of a Christian;' words which had been introduced into the oath by the House of Lords in the year 1828, apparently without any intention of excluding Jews. The removal of this disability was proposed by Lord Chancellor Lyndhurst, and passed through the House of Lords without a single division. Of course it was adopted by the Commons.

On August 5th, the business of the session being now nearly completed, Lord J. Russell, as leader of the opposition in the House, in accordance with a practice which had now become a custom, entered into a searching examination and criticism of the legislative performances and shortcomings of the government. We refer to his speech on account of a remarkable passage which it contains, and which forcibly exhibits the mental differences between the two rival leaders of the House of Commons. Sir R. Peel, superior to his opponent in clearness of statement and administrative ability, was far inferior to him in political foresight. This latter quality of Lord J. Russell's mind is well exemplified in the following passage, showing, as it does, a clear perception of the policy which ought to be adopted towards Ireland at a time when the avowal of that policy seemed to be calculated to damage rather than to strengthen the hands of the statesman by whom it was made;—a fact which no one knew better than Lord J. Russell himself, after the lesson he had been taught by the fate and the results of the unfortunate appropriation clause.

'As to the church of Ireland, I am convinced that government will be driven, before long, either to endow the Roman Catholic church, and to place it on the same level with the Protestant, or else to destroy the establishment of the latter, and to leave it to support itself, as the Roman Catholic church now does, on the voluntary principle.

Either one principle or the other must be the foundation of our future policy. Government therefore must be prepared to say which they will adopt, or the mind of Ireland will still remain unsatisfied. At present no party is content with the policy of the government; for while there are millions under O'Connell clamouring for repeal, there are a number of Protestants equally hostile to the government. I have formerly proposed that we should give the people of Ireland civil equality before we meddle with the religious question. The government, however, has followed a different course; and on a review of the conduct which it has recently pursued, I draw this conclusion: that it has done well in abandoning its former opinions and declarations, but that in not advocating some clear and large line of policy its course is defective.'

On the 7th of August Parliament was prorogued by the Queen in person.

Throughout the whole of the session the government had resolutely and successfully maintained that middle position of moderate protection which it had taken up at the commencement of its official existence. Standing between the two extreme parties, and receiving support from protectionists against free-traders, and from free-traders against protectionists, it had triumphed in every division by considerable majorities. Their measures had been successful; the condition of the country was prosperous; there was a general acquiescence in their policy, and great confidence in the financial and administrative qualities of their chief. It seemed likely, therefore, that they would retain office for a long time in spite of the vigour and eloquence with which they were assailed by protectionists, who thought that they did too much, and free-traders, who complained that they did too little. But an unforeseen calamity completely disappointed this expectation.

The summer of 1845 had been cold, damp, and rainy, in every part of the United Kingdom, and, for the first time since its accession to office, the Peel ministry had to contend with a bad harvest. The crops, though not very deficient, were below the average. If this had been all, their difficulties would not have been very great; but a more formidable evil than this had arisen. A rot, produced by the excessive quantity of rain that had fallen during the summer, appeared among the potatoes and spread with great rapidity. In the course of a few hours, whole crops of that plant, which had appeared perfectly healthy, were reduced to a black and fetid mass. The consequences of this disease were alarming enough even in England, but in Ireland, where a large portion of the people depended on this plant for their subsistence, they were likely to be terrible indeed. The sliding scale of the government was thus subjected to a strain to which it had not hitherto been exposed. The emergency which it was constructed to meet had now arisen, and it failed conspicuously; failed even more signally than a fixed duty could have done if exposed to a similar test. Ministers had before them the prospect of scarcity in England and famine in Ireland. The Anti-corn-law League urged that, under such circumstances, corn should be allowed to enter the United Kingdom freely; and their opinions began to be shared by men who had hitherto held aloof from their agitation. Not only Whigs like Lord John Russell and Lord Morpeth, but also Conservatives like Lord Ashley, began to press for free trade, at all events during the continuance of the potato-rot. The last-mentioned nobleman published an address to his constituents, who had sent him to Parliament to defend the corn-laws, containing the bold and honest declaration that, in his opinion, the destiny of the corn-laws was fixed. Meanwhile the prime minister was in a state of great perplexity. With this terrible scourge of famine impending over the country, what was he, as the responsible adviser of the crown, to do? One thing he certainly could not do: he could not fold his arms, sit still, and allow the people, for whose welfare he was answerable, to be starved to death. But what could he do? Should he fulfil the predictions of those who had so often accused him of intending to betray the cause he had volunteered to defend? On the other hand, should he allow the duty he owed to his party to prevent him from discharging the higher duty he owed to the crown as its principal adviser, and to the people as its chosen leader? There was one plain and obvious course before him—that of opening the ports and allowing the free entrance of foreign grain. This had already been done in Belgium, Holland, Germany, Russia, and Turkey. But if he opened the ports, could he close them again? If he allowed the people once to taste the sweets of free trade, would they be willing to return to the bitterness of monopoly; especially at a time when the Anti-corn-law League was deluging the country with tracts and lectures, and was straining every nerve to make protection impossible? With such thoughts as these continually passing through his mind, he summoned his colleagues to a cabinet council on the 1st of November, and proposed to them 'that the duties on the import of foreign grain should be suspended for a limited period, either by order in council or by legislative enactment, Parliament being summoned without delay.' At the same time he frankly told them that he considered the proceeding he recommended involved the necessity of an entire reconsideration of the corn-laws, and that the measure to be adopted must provide for their gradual reduction and final abolition. He was too wise not to see that a return to protection would be impossible, and too honest to conceal from his colleagues the conclusion to which he had been brought. Only three of them were prepared to agree with his proposal, and therefore it was for the present abandoned. Meanwhile the danger became more imminent; and surprise and indignation began to be expressed at the inaction of the government. On the 22nd of November a letter appeared from Lord J. Russell which contained the following passages:

'The imposition of any duty at present, without a provision for its extinction within a short period, would but prolong a 'contest already sufficiently fruitful of animosity and discontent. The struggle to make bread scarce and dear, when it is clear that part at least of the additional price goes to increase rent, is a struggle deeply injurious to an aristocracy which (this quarrel once removed) is strong in property, strong in the construction of our legislature, strong in opinion, strong in ancient associations and in the memory of immortal services.'

The letter from which these lines are extracted brought public opinion and public censure to bear strongly on the inaction of the ministry under the circumstances in which the country was placed. Another cabinet-council was summoned, at which Sir R. Peel renewed the recommendation he had made on the 1st of November, with the exception of that part of it relating to the order in council; and now, so rapid had been the progress of conviction among his colleagues, the whole cabinet was prepared to accept his recommendation with the exception of two of its members, of whom one was Lord Stanley, and the other soon came round to the views of the head of the government. The two dissidents were willing to consent to a suspension but not to a final withdrawal of protection. They therefore determined to resign, and their resignation drew after it the dissolution of the cabinet, the members of which were doubtless glad to escape from the necessity of being the advocates of a change they had hitherto strenuously resisted. Their resignation was accepted by the Queen on the 9th of December. The protectionists, though they had not yet formed themselves into a separate party, hailed the news of the downfall of the Peel administration with exultation, loudly proclaiming their delight at the termination of the 'organised hypocrisy' of a conservative government. Lord Stanley declined to attempt to form a ministry, and announced to the sovereign, as well as to others, his intention to promote the passing of the measures which Sir R. Peel might think it necessary to propose. Lord J. Russell, who was at Edinburgh, was sent for to form a government; Sir R. Peel promising that he would, as an independent member of the House of Commons, give him all the support in his power. After some time spent in endeavouring to make himself acquainted with the situation of affairs, Lord John with some hesitation undertook the task which had been intrusted to him; but was stopped because Lord Howick—who, by the death of his father, had become Earl Grey—had refused to join the new ministry, on the ground of the insuperable objections he entertained to the foreign policy of Lord Palmerston, who had accepted the post of foreign secretary. Lord J. Russell, feeling that under the circumstances in which he was placed by this refusal, and by his inability to count on the support of a majority in the House of Commons, he could not satisfactorily carry on the public business, felt himself obliged to desist from the attempt to construct a ministry. Sir R. Peel was thus in a manner compelled to continue in office. All of his colleagues retained their posts except Lord Stanley, who was replaced by Mr. Gladstone, who had long been inclined towards the policy now adopted by the government. Some inferior offices that had been vacated were filled without much difficulty. It had now become evident and notorious, that if nothing more was done, at least the ports would be opened; and the members of the Anti-corn-law League, who by their efforts had been the chief instruments in bringing matters to this point, were fully determined to make the most strenuous efforts to prevent them from ever being closed again. The whole nation impatiently waited for the *dénouement* which would no doubt be witnessed in the commencement of 1846. Never was the opening of Parliament expected with greater or more general impatience. The protectionists, still far from regarding themselves as beaten, and knowing that a large majority in both Houses favoured their views, were mustering their forces for the battle.

# CHAPTER IV.

### THE ANTI-CORN-LAW LEAGUE.

BEFORE we enter on our narrative of the events of the year 1846, it is necessary that we should preface it with an account of the origin and progress of the powerful organisation which had produced that great change in public opinion which forced a protectionist ministry, brought into office by a strong protectionist party, backed by a large protectionist majority in both Houses of Parliament, to propose and carry through a bill for the abolition of that very protection to which it owed its existence.

In doing this, we shall have to trace the course of an agitation without a parallel in the history of the world for the energy with which it was conducted, the rapid advances it made, and the speedy and complete success that crowned its efforts; for the great change it wrought in the public opinion and the consequent legislation of the country, overcoming prejudice and passion, dispelling ignorance and conquering powerful interests, with no other weapons than those of reason and that eloquence which great truths and strong convictions inspire.

The centre of the agitation was Manchester. No town in the kingdom had advanced more rapidly in weight and importance during the period whose events we have narrated. At the commencement of that period it was a political cipher, unrepresented in Parliament, and having the municipal institutions of a village. It had now grown to be the metropolis of a great part of the northern and midland counties, and was more especially the centre of a district which was regarded as one that was emerging from barbarism; the inhabitants of which still used an uncouth dialect which provoked the derision of their southern countrymen; and which was chiefly known by its smoking chimneys, its perpetual rains, the length and severity of its winter, its almost sunless summer, as well as by a lawless turbulence which embarrassed the government, perplexed the legislature, and dismayed the inhabitants of the more favoured parts of the kingdom. Notwithstanding all these disadvantages, notwithstanding the manner in which they were regarded by the majority of their fellow-countrymen, the inhabitants of this cheerless region were rapidly advancing in population, intelligence, wealth, and the influence they exercised over the growth and direction of the public opinion of the country. Thus the district of which Manchester was the centre, though just emerging from political nullity, and presenting an almost repulsive ruggedness, had acquired a sudden importance, and began to manifest an extraordinary energy, and to rival the metropolis itself in the influence it exercised over the progress of civilisation and the march of legislative improvement. The emancipated city seemed determined to show its appreciation of its newly-acquired privileges by the use which it made of them. From the very first moment that Manchester had been permitted to send representatives to the House of Commons, its voice had been given in favour of free trade in no indistinct tones. The two first members that it elected were Poulett Thompson, afterwards Lord Sydenham, who at that time was the most conspicuous free-trader in the kingdom, and Mr. Mark Phillips, well known as an ardent radical and a zealous free-trader. These two gentlemen represented Manchester in several successive parliaments; and the former of them, whose character and attainments gave him great influence and a commanding position in the House of Commons, seized every opportunity that presented itself of advancing the principles of free trade, and when invited to enter the Whig cabinet, accepted the invitation on the distinct understanding that he should be at liberty to support any free-trade motion that might be submitted to the consideration of the House of Commons; he also showed his fidelity to the free-trade principles of his constituents by using his position as president of the board of trade to initiate that policy which Sir R. Peel carried out so fully, of removing taxes which were unproductive of revenue, but fruitful of vexation to those who were engaged in the various branches of that manifold industry of which Manchester was the centre. In all these efforts he was zealously supported by his colleague.

It is not difficult to understand why Manchester, and the district of which Manchester was the centre, was so zealous for free trade, and so far in advance of most other parts of the country with regard to this question, and why the views taken by its inhabitants on it were so much more enlightened than those that were entertained by the inhabitants of other parts of England, who in cultivated intelligence then certainly surpassed them. The staple manufactures of these districts brought those who carried them on into communication with all parts of the world, and everywhere they found themselves fettered by the trammels which the so-called protective duties imposed on them. On the other hand, the farmers and the landowners of the manufacturing districts, who, producing for the home market only, clung to the partial monopoly of that market which protection gave them, dreaded above all things the free importation of food, the first effect of which would evidently be to bring down prices, which they complained of as being already barely remunerative. When, therefore, the question was first brought forward, it assumed the character of a struggle between the manufacturing and the agricultural districts; and Manchester, as the centre of the former, naturally took the lead in it.

Such an enterprise as that which the free-traders undertook seemed at first sight almost quixotic. Notwithstanding the increased number of representatives which the Reform Bill had given to the manufacturing districts, the landed interest still returned nine-tenths of the members of the House of Commons. The whole of the House of Lords belonged to it. Therefore it would seem that upon any question in which manufacturing and agricultural interests clashed, the latter must necessarily triumph. It therefore does no small credit to the sagacity and courage of those who first entered on this struggle, that they should have ventured on an enterprise apparently so hopeless, confiding in the goodness of their cause and in the power of free discussion to secure its eventual prevalence.

The agitation of this question commenced towards the end of the year 1836. It was a period of great depression of trade and general suffering throughout the country. An anti-corn-law association was formed in London, which displayed a list of twenty-two M.P.s at the head of its members, and enjoyed a momentary importance. It was soon found, however, that the metropolis was not the place in which the movement was likely to be vigorously worked or efficiently supported. There is in London none of that *esprit de corps*, which is often found in large provincial towns. Its enormous size prevents its citizens from acting together with effect on any great political or social question, or regarding with any other than a very limited and languid interest any struggle that may be carried on within it. The metropolis too is largely occupied by persons who are rather visitors than inhabitants, drawn to it during a part of the year by its pleasures, its dissipations, its business, or its legislative functions, but not regarding themselves as its citizens. Moreover, London was the very centre of the districts by which protection was most strongly upheld, and the overwhelming majority of its citizens who took any side were protectionists. It is no wonder, then, that the association did not thrive, and had but a brief existence. It circulated tracts, held meetings, and imparted a good deal of information; but it was soon found that, if the agitation was to go on at all, it must find for itself another centre of operations. Meanwhile, year after year, motions were brought forward in the House of Commons which aimed more or less directly at the repeal of the corn-laws; but these motions were either not carried to a division or rejected by overwhelming majorities. It was quite clear that the battle of free trade was to be fought neither in London nor yet in the Houses of Parliament. If it was ever to be won at all, it must be won by vigorous agitation; and of that agitation Manchester must be the head-quarters. Accordingly a new association was formed there, and began to raise funds, and seek to diffuse information by means of tracts and pamphlets. The plan of a fixed duty, to which the Whigs so long clung, found no favour with this body, except as a stepping-stone towards the entire removal of all duties. The steadiness with which its members pursued their aim, not allowing themselves to be diverted from it for a single instant by any compromise, however promising, was manifested by the refusal of a contribution of 100*l.* from a gentleman, who accompanied it with advice that they should be satisfied with something less than the entire removal of all duties on corn. This resolute determination to be contented with nothing short of their full demand was one of the chief causes of the success with which their efforts were at length crowned. From time to time they were encouraged by fresh adhesions and cheering indications of the progress that their doctrines were making. An incident which occurred during the year 1838 gave a new impulse to their agitation, and suggested a means of carrying it forward, which was afterwards employed with great effect. The town of Bolton-le-Moors contained at this time upwards of 50,000 inhabitants, whom the commercial crisis which then prevailed had thrown into the most cruel distress. Out of the fifty manufacturing establishments which the town at that time contained, thirty were closed, and more than 5000 workmen did not know where to find the means of subsistence. Nearly a fourth part of the houses of the town were deserted, and the prisons were literally crammed with persons whom despair and hunger had driven to commit some offence against the laws. Children died of hunger in the arms of their mothers. Fathers, unable to find food for their families, fled from the spectacle of their misery, and left them to shift for themselves. These facts were brought under the attention of the House of Commons by Dr. Bowring, one of the representatives of the town in Parliament. But nothing effectual had been done. In the midst of this frightful state of things, in the month of August 1838, Dr. Birney, an old physician of Bolton, announced that he intended to deliver a lecture on the corn-law and its effects, in the theatre of the town. A great multitude assembled to hear him, and the building was crowded in every part. But the would-be lecturer was so unnerved by finding himself in the presence of an audience so much larger, and probably so different from that he had expected to address, and by the disorderly conduct of many among them, that he was unable to proceed. A serious riot seemed inevitable. At this critical moment a Mr. Thommasson, a gentleman well known in Bolton, said to a young surgeon named Paulton, who was sitting near him, and whom he knew to be an able and ready speaker, 'Do, pray, go on the stage and say something to the meeting.' Mr. Paulton ran round to the stage, extemporised a speech against the corn-laws, and the sufferings they inflicted on the working classes, which was received with tremendous applause. Thus the meeting, which at one time seemed likely to end in serious confusion, was turned into a great success. He was asked to repeat his speech; which he accordingly did, with an array of fresh facts and arguments; and the second discourse was even more successful than the first. Dr. Bowring happened to be at Manchester at the time, and as a committee was sitting there to inquire into the causes of the prevailing distress, and to endeavour to provide a remedy for it, he induced them to engage Mr. Paulton to deliver a lecture in the Corn-Exchange of that town, which was then the largest building available for the purpose. He was as successful here as he had been in his own town; and was then regularly engaged to go through the manufacturing districts to prove to their inhabitants that the corn-laws were the cause of the evils they were suffering, and to persuade them to unite in a great effort to procure their repeal. Such was the commencement of that systematic diffusion of information on the corn-law question, by lectures and other means, which we shall presently see carried out so extensively, and on a scale never equalled in any other age or country. Another great step in the free-trade agitation was taken in the course of the same year by Mr. J. B. Smith, a gentleman who was afterwards the first chairman of the Anti-corn-law League; a post he resigned on becoming member for the borough of Walsall. He submitted to the Manchester Chamber of Commerce a petition in favour of the repeal of all duties on corn. That body, the majority of whose members were well-known opponents of free-trade principles, had up to this time evaded the consideration of this question; but it was now ably and fully discussed; Mr. Smith being supported by several speakers, among whom was Mr. Cobden, then chiefly known as a successful calico-printer, whose prints competed in markets in which Manchester designs had not hitherto been able to hold their ground. The petition was finally adopted by a majority of six to one.

These successes were followed by new and still more vigorous efforts. An Anti-corn-law Association had been started, with subscriptions of the modest amount of five shillings; but those who estimated the difficulties that the free-traders would have to surmount soon saw that much more would be required. Accordingly, at a meeting held on the 10th of January 1839, subscriptions to the amount of 50*l*. and 100*l*. were given; and one gentleman who was present at the meeting, the late Mr. J. C. Dyer, said that he was ready with 1000*l*., if it should be required. The sum of 1800*l*., considered a very large amount in that day of comparatively small subscriptions, was contributed in the room, and this amount was afterwards largely augmented. It was felt more and more strongly, that the battle that was now being waged was one on the event of which the interests, and almost the existence, of all classes connected with the manufacturing districts depended; for their trade was being rapidly transferred to foreign centres of industry under the baneful operation of the corn-laws, and was in danger of being lost to this country entirely, if other countries, guided by their observation of the pernicious consequences of protection in England, should be beforehand with her in their abandonment of it. Meanwhile they who were thus advocating the interests of all classes in the manufacturing districts sometimes found themselves exposed to an insensate opposition from some of those on whose behalf they were contending. For instance, at Leeds, the Chartists, blindly following the blind leadership of Mr. O'Connor, made an irruption into a free-trade meeting held in that town on the 15th of January, for the purpose, as they affirmed, of 'vindicating the rights of labour.' In consequence of this opposition, the attendance at the meeting was so unexpectedly large, that it was necessary to adjourn it to the Cloth Hall. An amendment proposed by Mr. O'Connor was rejected. Other meetings were held in all the principal towns of the kingdom, and the unanswered arguments of those who took part in them were not without their effect on the country. From this time forward the war was carried on, not only in the manufacturing districts, where much information on the question was still needed, but also in the towns of the agricultural districts, where the shopkeepers, the farmers, and even the landlords, were plied with arguments intended to convince them, not only that the monopoly that had been given them was no advantage to them, but that the distress and suffering of which they so bitterly complained were in a great measure produced by it. With this out-of-door agitation a strong parliamentary agitation was combined. However hopeless success might seem to be with assemblies constituted as the two Houses then were, and at a period when Whigs and Tories were almost equally hostile to free trade, the discussion did much good. Men who scorned to look at the arguments which were brought forward at meetings, and who would not on any account be present at them, would read with attention the debates that were carried on in the House of Commons, and weigh the arguments brought forward by the free-traders; and in this way parliamentary discussions ending in signal defeats promoted the cause of the Anti-corn-law Association. It could not be concealed that the advocates of free trade, though inferior in numbers, were triumphant in argument; and the arguments they employed gradually made their way from the readers of the newspapers into the minds of all classes. But the process was very slow; and the two hundred delegates who had been sent up by the association to watch the debates on the question could not help feeling that the results of the discussions on the motion presented to Parliament had not answered their too-sanguine expectations, and that, unless they could bring to bear on the legislature a force of public opinion far greater than any that had hitherto been applied to it, the struggle might be carried on for twenty years and more before redress could be obtained. It was under a gradually strengthening sense of this truth that the delegates who had come up to London to watch the proceedings of Parliament, and to promote the cause of free trade in the metropolis, before returning to their homes put forth an address to the public containing the following recommendations:

'The formation of a permanent union, to be called the Anti-corn-law League, composed of all the towns and districts represented in the delegation, and as many others as might be influenced to form anti-corn-law associations and to join the league.

'Delegates from the different local associations to meet for business from time to time in the different towns represented.

'With the view to secure unity of action, the central office of the league shall be established in Manchester, to which body shall be intrusted, among other duties, that of engaging and recommending competent lecturers, the obtaining the coöperation of the public press, and the establishing and conducting of a stamped circular for the purpose of keeping a constant correspondence with the local associations.

'That, in addition to the funds subscribed for local purposes by the several associations, at least 5000*l*. shall be raised to defray the expenses of the general league for the ensuing year; and that every sum of 50*l*. entitle the individual or association subscribing it to one vote in the appropriation of the funds of the league, and that in all other questions the votes of the persons present be equal.

'That this meeting adjourns, subject to the call of the Manchester Anti-corn-law Association; that it be left to their discretion at what time to bring forward the substantive question for the total abolition of the corn-laws before Parliament, and to adopt any other measure to secure the great object of this association which they may think fit.'

The delegates, after having adopted these resolutions, returned from the metropolis to their respective towns, determined to employ their best efforts to carry them into effect. And certainly never in the history of the world was an agitation carried on with such vigour, industry, and untiring perseverance, as that which had its origin in these resolutions. The leading spirits of the league gave themselves up to the work. Many of them almost entirely neglected their own business in order to carry it forward. Mr. Cobden, who had hitherto run a most successful career as a calico-printer, was now obliged to choose between the sacrifice of that career and the sacrifice of the great cause of free trade that he had espoused; and he determined to incur any risk and any loss rather than desert the agitation in which he had engaged. Others, more fortunate, were able, like Mr. Bright, to devolve the care of their business on relatives or partners, who cheerfully undertook the additional labour thus cast on them. During six years what may be called the inner council of the league met twice a day at Newalls-buildings, Market-street, Manchester, to decide on the steps to be taken in order to secure the final triumph of the cause they had so much at heart. It was at these meetings, often to an audience not exceeding 200, but fortunately in the presence of reporters, that Mr. Cobden delivered some of the best speeches he made on the question. It was at them also that the real business of the league was done. It was at these meetings too that Messrs. Thomas Potter, J. Brooks, Dugdale, G. Wilson, S. P. Robinson, and other free-traders, rendered quiet but real and valuable services to the movement, the importance of which, and the obstacles it had to contend with, became daily more and more evident. It was felt that the battle must be fought first by the conversion of individuals, then at the hustings, and lastly in the House of Commons. It was felt, too, that attempts must be made to convert those classes which had been led to believe that their interests were identified with protection. The league therefore sent forth by tens of thousands pamphlets and tracts specially addressed to them, such as 'Facts for the Farmers,' 'An Address to the Farmers on the way in which their families are to be provided for.' The speeches of Messrs. Villiers and Poulett Thompson in the House of Commons were also industriously circulated. The anti-corn-law circular, which had been published in accordance with the recommendations issued by the delegates, was largely distributed in the agricultural districts, and very generally read there. This great issue of tracts, pamphlets, and newspapers, was followed up by the dispatch of an army of lecturers into the agricultural districts, who exposed the fallacy of the arguments by which the system of protection was upheld, and challenged discussion on the questions they raised. Truth thus actively urged could not be hindered from prevailing. The upholders of monopoly saw with dismay that free-trade principles were beginning to spread among their own tenants and farm-labourers, and the farmers were having their eyes rapidly opened to the fact, that whoever else might be interested in maintaining the protective laws, they certainly were not. It must not, however, be supposed that the lecturers were allowed to disseminate their views without encountering any opposition. The formation of the league led to the formation of an antagonistic society, which was denominated 'The Central Agricultural Society of Great Britain and Ireland,' intended to combat the league with its own weapons. This association, however, was rather a help than a hindrance to the work of the league. By promoting discussion, it drew attention to the arguments of the free-traders, and thus hastened the spread and prevalence of the truth. But if its aims were thus advanced by its opponents, they were no less powerfully aided by the measures of the Whig government, by the reduction of the newspaper duty, and the adoption first of the fourpenny and then of the penny postage-stamp; which enabled it to carry on its proselytising efforts on a far larger scale than would otherwise have been possible. Then, again, the railway lines that had been laid down, transported the lecturers of the league from place to place with a rapidity that would have been out of the question in the old days of the stage-coaches. The great majority of the newspapers also gave it very valuable aid, though the *Times* still withheld its powerful assistance. These efforts were aided by a 'Manchester Working-man's Free-trade Association,' and thus assisted were strong enough to triumph over a very formidable Chartist opposition at a town's meeting expressly called to consider the propriety of petitioning in favour of free trade.

The success which had thus far attended the efforts of the league encouraged its leading members to renewed exertions in the year 1840. It was determined that a meeting of delegates from all parts of the kingdom should be held at Manchester; and as that town had no room large enough to contain those who were expected to be present on the occasion, it was resolved to construct a building expressly for the accommodation of the assembly, and for the general purposes of the league. Mr. Cobden, who was now just beginning to take that lead in the agitation which his talents, his eloquence, and the depth and earnestness of his convictions, were sure eventually to secure for him, happened at the time to be the owner of the field on which the 'Peterloo massacre' occurred, and he placed it at the disposal of the league for the erection of the proposed building, which was designed to be of a temporary character. A spacious wooden hall, capable of holding a larger number of persons than the grand hall of the magnificent structure which bears its name and occupies its site, was built, and named the Free-trade Hall. Its erection was accomplished in eleven days, by the labour of one hundred men; and on two successive days banquets were held in it, followed by able speeches from Daniel O'Connell and many other members of Parliament, as well as several leaders of the free-trade party. Deputations were also sent to Lord Melbourne and other members of the government, producing apparently little effect on them; but the reports of these interviews, which appeared in the newspapers, made a considerable impression on the public. They showed that the free-traders had little to expect for their principles from the Whigs, and excited a general determination among the members of the league, and free-traders generally, to support those candidates for seats in the House of Commons, whether Whig, Tory, or Radical, whose opinions on this subject were most in accordance with their own. And the time soon came for giving effect to this determination. At Sudbury the league successfully promoted the election of a Whig who was pledged to free trade; while at Walsall it compelled the retirement of Mr. Littleton, another Whig, who avowed himself favourable to protection.

The announcement made by Lord J. Russell on the 7th of May, of the intention of government to propose a fixed duty of eight shillings the quarter on corn, in lieu of the present sliding scale, was met by the league with a resolution to agitate more strongly than ever for the total and immediate repeal of the bread tax, and to accept no compromise. Measures were promptly taken to carry this resolution into effect. Communications were made to the principal associations throughout the country, recommending renewed and still more vigorous agitation. On the other hand, the Chartists, still guided by Mr. O'Connor, endeavoured to compel the league to combine with them for the attainment of their objects, and to force them to use their organisation for the double purpose of promoting the repeal of the corn-laws and carrying the five points of the Charter. The free-traders, though many of them were very favourably disposed towards the objects at which the Chartists aimed, were wisely unwilling to introduce such an apple of discord into their camp, or to consent to an alliance that was likely to alienate many who were rapidly coming round to their views. The consequence of this refusal was, that the Chartists attended the free-trade meetings, and sometimes carried amendments in accordance with their own political views. The protectionists naturally endeavoured to avail themselves of these Chartist tactics in order to defeat and embarrass the league. A meeting called in Stevenson's-square, Manchester, and presided over by Mr. Cobden, was attended, not only by a large body of Chartists, but by two conservatives—Dr. Sleigh and Mr. Wilkins—who were generally supposed to be the emissaries of the Central Agricultural Association. However, notwithstanding this coalition of Chartists and protectionists, the cause of free trade triumphed, and the meeting passed by large majorities the resolutions which the free-traders submitted to it. Another mode of carrying on the agitation was suggested, and adopted with considerable effect. A great conference of ministers of religion of all denominations was appointed to be held in Manchester, at the time fixed for the meeting of the Wesleyan Conference, in the hope that a large number of the Wesleyan ministers who were assembled in Manchester would assist at the sittings of the free-trade conference. This expectation, however, was disappointed. Only one Wesleyan minister, one clergyman of the Church of England, and two ministers of the Presbyterian Church of Scotland, accepted the invitations, which were sent, as far as could be ascertained, to every minister of every denomination of Christians in the United Kingdom. However, upwards of 700 nonconformist ministers assembled, and after listening to the statements submitted to them by some of the leading members of the league, passed resolutions strongly condemnatory of the tax on corn. This meeting had a double advantage. It procured a condemnation of the corn-tax which carried with it no inconsiderable weight, and it furnished the league with an opportunity of indoctrinating with the principles of free trade upwards of 700 men of education and intelligence from all parts of the kingdom, who would thus be enabled and stimulated after their return home to diffuse the principles which they had thus sanctioned and adopted. About the same time renewed efforts were made. Meetings were again held in all the most important towns, at which the repeal of the obnoxious impost was advocated, and resolutions condemning it adopted. The accession of Sir R. Peel to office did not discourage the free-traders. They soon saw that they had in him a minister who took very enlightened views of all financial questions. They could not help contrasting the mastery he evidently possessed of all the bearings of the question with the ignorance respecting it that had been manifested by his predecessor; and they hoped that by carrying on their agitation vigorously they would make him see the necessity of yielding on this question, as he had already yielded on that of Catholic emancipation. These hopes were not a little strengthened by the corresponding fears and jealousies of the more extreme protectionists, who, after the first burst of exultation on the overthrow of the Whig administration, began to suspect that their champion would turn out to be their betrayer. The free-traders resolved to carry on their agitation more actively than ever. More funds were required for it; and in order to obtain them, it was resolved that recourse should be had to a great anti-corn-law bazaar, which was held in due time, and not only realised a large amount of money, but also was made in various ways subservient to the great object of creating interest in the question and diffusing information respecting it. The ladies who were engaged in the work were instructed more fully than before in the various arguments which were used against the continuance of the corn-laws, and the replies made to those which had been urged against their repeal. From time to time they were addressed by the ablest advocates of free trade, and they readily adopted a suggestion made to them, that they should prepare and send up an address to the Queen, which, though it might have little effect on the opinions and counsels of her constitutional advisers, caused the question to be favourably discussed in thousands of homes, and increased the interest taken in it by the ladies themselves, as well as by those whose signatures they procured. Thus the league pursued in various ways the one object it proposed to itself — that of enlightening all kinds and classes of persons on the mischiefs which the corn-laws were doing, the suffering they were producing, and the advantages which almost every interest in the country would derive from the repeal of them. By these means they gradually formed a strong public opinion in favour of right and truth, which was certain eventually to sweep away all opposition, though it seemed likely the struggle might be still protracted for a long time.

The bazaar was held in the Theatre Royal, Manchester, at the beginning of the year 1842, and produced a clear profit of about ten thousand pounds. Meanwhile, chiefly through the influence of Mr. Cobden, an anti-corn-law conference was appointed to sit in Palace-yard through a great part of the session, watching with intense interest the proceedings of Parliament, lending its aid in every possible way in support of the various free-trade motions that were submitted to the legislature, sending deputations to those ministers whose official positions imposed on them the duty of receiving representations on the subject, and superintending the progress of the agitation both in Parliament and out of doors.

The 30th of January 1843 witnessed the opening of a new and more substantial free-trade hall in the place of the temporary building which has already been mentioned, and which had been destroyed by fire. It was the largest room available for public meetings in the kingdom, and though not intended to endure for many years, was considered sufficiently strong to serve the purposes of the league until the attainment of the objects for which it was formed should have allowed it to be dissolved; a consummation which the free-traders, confiding in the justice of their cause, in the progress which they had already made, and in their determination to put forth fresh efforts, hoped to see realised in three or four years. The new building was at once put into frequent requisition. Banquets, meetings, conferences designed to promote the cause of free trade, were held in it, and were attended by thousands, not only of the citizens of Manchester, but of the inhabitants of the towns and villages with which the district surrounding Manchester is so thickly studded, and which the railroads recently constructed were now beginning to bring into closer connection with the cotton metropolis. In London the league could not procure a room capable of containing the multitudes who flocked to their meetings, attracted chiefly by the eloquence of Mr. Cobden and Mr. Bright, who was now beginning to be actively associated with him in the direction of the movement and the advocacy of free frade. Exeter Hall was applied for, but refused. The Drury-lane Theatre was engaged for one day of each week in Lent, during which the performances at the theatres were prohibited. Crowded and most enthusiastic audiences assembled within its walls, and were addressed by Messrs. Cobden and Bright, and the other leaders of the agitation. But they were soon driven from this refuge, in consequence of the interference of the proprietors of the theatre to prevent Mr. Macready, the lessee, from allowing it to be used for political purposes.

Meanwhile the agitation was passing through a new phase. Emboldened by the success which had hitherto attended their efforts, the council of the league resolved to carry the war more vigorously into the enemy's camp. In pursuance of this resolution, they appointed meetings to be held in the very strongholds of protection, at Bedford, at Penneden Heath near Maidstone, at Carlisle, and many other places. And here, as elsewhere, they were triumphant. In vain did the champions of protection make some feeble effort to withstand them at these assemblies. Neither their clamours nor their arguments availed anything against the powerful arguments and persuasive eloquence of the free-traders, and they were compelled, time after time, to retire discomfited from the field. Mr. Cobden attended no fewer than twenty-nine great country meetings, at all of which he was triumphantly successful, notwithstanding a formidable opposition made to him at Birmingham by the Chartists, headed by O'Connor. But the protectionists, though beaten at every public meeting, and worsted in every discussion, could still boast that they possessed an overwhelming majority in the representative body, determined, come what might, to maintain protection and it seemed only too likely, considering the ascendancy enjoyed by the landlord interest, that the struggle would be maintained for many years to come. The free-trade party in the House of Commons, though reinforced by the addition to its ranks of 35 members, could still only muster about 125, against 533 on whose support their opponents could reckon. Dispassionate men could not help seeing that many efforts must still be made, and that many years would probably elapse, before such a minority could be converted into a majority. The leaders of the league were, however, by no means disheartened, and braced themselves up for renewed and still more vigorous exertions. Twelve or fourteen lecturers were now hard at work. Cobden and Bright were ubiquitous, holding meetings, and carrying all before them wherever they went. Tracts, pamphlets, placards, anti-corn-law wafers, were all diligently employed in the work of proselytism. A new paper, called the *League*, and published weekly, took the place of the fortnightly *Anti-Bread-Tax Circular*. Covent-garden Theatre was engaged for fifty nights, at an expense of three thousand pounds. Fifty thousand pounds had already been subscribed and expended, and it was resolved that an additional sum of 100,000*l.* should at once be raised, to carry on the war against protection. To prepare the way for the campaign at Covent-garden Theatre, the league published a well-considered address to the people of the United Kingdom, in which an account was given of the operations of the first year. It contained the following programme of the manner in which it was intended to carry on the agitation in future:

'1. Copies will be obtained of the registration lists of all boroughs and counties throughout the kingdom, and the collection lodged at the metropolitan office of the league, as a central place of deposit, to be consulted as occasion may require.

'2. An extensive correspondence, by means of the post and of stamped publications, will be kept up with electors in all districts, on matters connected with the progress and success of our cause.

'3. It is intended that every borough in the kingdom shall be visited by deputations of the league, and meetings held, which the electors shall be specially invited to attend.

'4. Prompt measures will be taken to ascertain the opinions of each elector in every borough, with a view of obtaining an obvious and decided majority in favour of the total and immediate repeal of the corn-laws.

'5. Every constituency, whose representatives have not hitherto supported Mr. Villiers' motion for the repeal of the corn-laws, will be invited to memorialize its members to vote for such motion when next brought forward.

'6. Whenever a vacancy occurs in the representation of any borough, the electors will be recommended to put a free-trade candidate in nomination; and the league pledges itself to give such candidate every possible support by deputations, lectures, and the distribution of publications.

'7. In the event of any borough being unable to procure a suitable candidate, the league pledges itself to bring forward candidates, so as to afford every elector an opportunity of recording his vote in favour of free trade until the question is decided.'

It was becoming every day more and more evident that this league was a body that none could afford to despise; and it was daily gaining strength, through the accession to its ranks of men occupying high positions, and remarkable for their caution. Foremost among these was Mr. S. Jones Lloyd, now Lord Overstone, who openly avowed himself a convert to free-trade principles, joined the league, and sent a contribution of 50*l.* to its funds. The Earl of Fitzwilliam attended a great free-trade meeting at Doncaster, where, standing side by side with Cobden and Bright, he spoke strongly and ably against the corn-laws. In London Mr. Baring, though supported by the whole influence of the government, was defeated in a contest for the city by the free-trade candidate, Mr. Pattison. In the old cathedral city of Durham Mr. Bright, though a Quaker, had been elected its representative, the Dean, Dr. Waddington, bravely voting for him. On the 18th of November the *Times* gave a testimony in favour of the growing weight and influence of the league, which was all the more valuable because it was reluctantly and grudgingly given by a journal which, almost up to the final triumph of the league, continued to regard it with jealousy and alarm. That testimony was an important event in the history of the agitation, producing so great an effect, and giving such an impulse to the agitation, and such encouragement to those who were carrying it on, that we ought to quote it at length.

'THE LEAGUE IS A GREAT FACT. It would be foolish, nay rash, to deny its importance. It is a great fact that there should have been created in the homestead of our manufacturers a confederacy devoted to the agitation of one political question, persevering at it year after year, shrinking from no trouble, dismayed by no danger, making light of every obstacle. It demonstrates the hardy strength of purpose, the indomitable will, by which Englishmen working together for a great object are armed and animated. It is a great fact that, at one meeting at Manchester, more than forty manufacturers should subscribe on the spot each *at least* 100*l.*, some 300*l.*, some 400*l.*, some 500*l.*, for the advancement of a measure which, right or wrong, just or unjust, expedient or injurious, they at least believe it their duty or their interest, or both, to advance in every possible way.

'These are facts important, and worthy of consideration. *No moralist can disregard them, no politician can sneer at them, no statesman can undervalue them. He who collects opinions must chronicle them; he who frames laws must to some extent consult them.*

'These things are so. It matters not that you tell us, as you may tell us with truth, that the league has another character, and other objects, than those which it now professes. The league may be a hypocrite, a great deceiver, a huge Trojan horse of sedition. Be it so. But we answer, THE LEAGUE EXISTS. You may tell us, and with truth, that there are men in the league sworn foes to church and crown, to peers and dignities, to bishops and judges; that, now speaking, and declaiming, and begging, and taxing, and, an' you like, plundering even, to resist the corn-laws, this monster being will next raise its head and subdue all laws beneath it. You may tell us that its object is not to open the ports, to facilitate commerce, to enrich England, but to ruin our aristocracy, whom leaguers envy and detest. You may tell us that no men of honesty or intelligence could, consistently with their honour and their knowledge, seek to rifle an embarrassed state of that just subsidy which all states impose upon articles of the most necessary consumption. You may tell us that, whatever may be the specious pretext which they hold out, or the disguise under which they work, they can really only look forward to that disastrous crisis in the annals of a kingdom when indiscriminate plunder consummates the work of hopeless and inextricable confusion. You may tell us that the league has whined and canted about the sufferings of the poor; that its orators wink with malicious cunning at the "point" they make about the miserable victims of landlord legislation. In all this there is doubtless much truth.

'But, we ask, tell us this: Who created the league?' Who found the ribs and the planks of this *infandum monstrum*? Who filled it with armed men, and introduced its perilous presence within the walls of the constitution? We answer, *Experience set at naught, advice derided, warnings neglected;* these brought the league into existence; these gave it power, and motion, and vital energy; these gave it an easy and unresisted ingress into the very sanctuaries of our domestic life:

> " Scandit fatalis machina muros,
> Fœta armis; pueri circum innuptæque puellæ
> Sacra canunt, funemque manu contingere gaudent:
> Illa subit, mediæque minans illabitur urbi.'

'A NEW POWER HAS ARISEN IN THE STATE; and maids and matrons flock to the theatre as though it were but a new "translation from the French."

'Let no man say that we are blind to the possible mischief of such a state of things. We acknowledge that we dislike gregarious collections of cant and cotton-men. We cannot but know that, whatever be the end of this agitation, it will expire only to bequeath its violence and its turbulence to some successor.'

It is impossible adequately to describe the effect produced by the appearance of this manifesto in the columns of the leading journal; the encouragement it afforded to the leaguers, or the dismay and consternation it spread through the protectionist ranks. It is true that it contained some very unjust imputations on the members of the league, and displayed a great dislike of their leaders; but this very circumstance increased the value of the testimony tardily and reluctantly given to the great importance which that body was assuming. The acknowledgment that the league was a great fact, and a great power in the state, was echoed from mouth to mouth, and served still farther to increase the power of the body whose importance was thus grudgingly admitted. Perhaps no royal speech, no state paper, no public document of any kind, ever caused a stronger sensation or attracted more general attention than this leading article of the *Times* newspaper. The phrase 'The league is a great fact' was in everybody's mouth. By some it was pronounced with hope and triumph, by others with disgust and apprehension. The organs of the conservative party called on the agriculturists to rouse themselves from the apathy and indolence in which they were sunk, while there was yet time, and to come forward at once in defence of the present ministry and of their own interests. But these appeals met with a very feeble response from those to whom they were addressed. The article of the *Times* was speedily followed by new adhesions, and other encouraging tokens of progress. At the commencement of the year 1844 the Marquis of Westminster, the wealthiest nobleman in England, addressed a letter to Mr. George Wilson—who had succeeded Mr. J. B. Smith in the office of chairman of the league—in which, after congratulating him on the success which had hitherto attended the effort it was making to overthrow an odious monopoly, and expressing his opinion that the country would be so greatly enriched by the removal of the duty on corn, that the revenue would suffer no loss in consequence of its repeal, he announced his intention to contribute the sum of 500*l*. to the funds of the league. Lord Morpeth, who since the fall of Lord Melbourne's administration, of which he had been a member, had lived in retirement, and who up to this time had been regarded as an opponent of the free-trade party, attended a great meeting of that party at Wakefield; where, though he did not give a full and unreserved adhesion to the policy of the league, nor entirely renounce the opinions he had formerly maintained, yet spoke in such a manner as to show that he was almost a free-trader, and to draw forth the warm and enthusiastic applause of an assembly devoted to that cause. But while the league was receiving these important accessions to its ranks, the ministry showed no disposition to yield, nor did the large party which sat behind them in the House of Commons. On the contrary, both in Parliament and elsewhere, they took every opportunity of dilating on the prosperity which the country enjoyed, as a proof that the policy they had determined to adopt was answering the expectations they had formed of it; and the prime minister could exclaim, amidst the approving shouts of his delighted followers, 'The experience we have had of the present law has not shaken my preference for a graduated duty; and although I consider it inconsistent with my duty to make engagements for adherence to existing laws, under all circumstances, in order to conciliate support, I can say that the government have never contemplated, and do not contemplate, any alterations of the existing law.' This declaration, intended to allay the suspicions and jealousies of the more ardent protectionists, also served to announce to the members of the league that they must gird themselves up for the battle, and expect nothing from the present government. They did not need this incentive to farther exertion; they were fully minded to carry forward the agitation till its object was attained. But during the latter part of the year it seemed to flag. For this there were two causes: the abundance of the harvest, which alleviated for the moment evils which the corn-laws inflicted, and assuaged the discontent which scarcity had produced; and the attention which the council of the league was giving to the state of the electoral register, which was known to contain the names of many protectionists who were not entitled to be on it, and to omit the names of many free-traders who possessed voting qualifications. The work of instructing the people on the question of free-trade had been pretty effectually carried out; but the other and not less necessary work of revising the register had been neglected. The exhortations which Peel had addressed to the conservative party, previously to the late election, to attend to the register, had not been thrown away on those to whom they were delivered; but the liberal party had been careless in this respect, and this neglect was one of the causes of the great conservative triumph that had then been achieved. But now the league had become fully alive to the necessity of paying attention to the registration, with a view to the next general election; and its ramifications, extending into all parts of the kingdom, enabled it to fulfil this task very effectively. From July to October the council of the league was almost incessantly occupied with this great and necessary work; and the results produced were very considerable, and would have brought about a very decided change in the composition of the House of Commons, if a dissolution had occurred before the question had been settled.

When this great work was nearly completed, a crowded meeting was held in the Free-trade Hall, presided over by Mr. Wilson, in which he gave an account of the diligence and success with which the league had applied itself to the revision of the register. The speech in which this account was given is valuable and interesting, as a record of the labours of the league, in this department, not only in the county of Lancaster, which of course received the largest share of its attention, but also in other parts of the kingdom, which were by no means overlooked.

'Most of you are probably aware of the result of the last election for South Lancashire. There were 14,544 votes given for the two candidates together: being for Entwisle 7571, and for Brown 6973, leaving a majority for Entwisle of 598. On the objections against those 7571 voters who polled for Entwisle, we struck off 878 at the revision (*loud and repeated rounds of applause*); and of the 6973 who voted for Brown, our opponents have struck off 422, we striking off more than two to their one; thus having a majority, or a gain on the objections over them of 456, and within 142 of the whole majority by which Mr. Brown was defeated in the late contest. (*Loud applause.*) Then the register has gained at this revision by the new claims. There were 4982 new claims. Of these the free-traders made 3141, and established 2821 (*loud applause*), being a failure of only 320 of the whole of the claims made. So much for the reports propagated week after week that the free-traders were filling the register with spurious claims. The number of claims made by the monopolists was 1841, of which they established 1357, being a failure of 484 cases, and giving us a majority on the claims of 1464 votes. (*Cheers.*) Well then there are 169 new claims, belonging to parties whose opinions we have not yet had time to ascertain; but we will give the monopolists the whole of them, and we shall still have a gain on this revision, taking claims and objections together, of 1751 votes. (*Great and prolonged cheering.*) An analysis of the new register therefore shows of old electors (free-traders) 6551, new electors (free-traders) 2821; total free-traders on the register 9372. Of the old electors being monopolists 6693, new electors 1357, neutrals 169: leaving a total of 8219, or a working majority, as already stated, of 1153. (*Applause.*) And now, gentlemen, we come to the northern division. We have not done much there, but we have done something. We have attained a gain on the revision, with comparatively little exertion, of 533. (*Applause.*) The result has been, then, to give us a gain of 533 votes for North Lancashire; to give us a seat for South Lancashire (*cheers*), and to leave the monopolists three seats in the boroughs, or five out of the whole twenty-six members for the entire county. I think, then, you will agree with me that there never was, in the history of the registration, so complete a sweep of a county as this has been. (*Hear, and loud cheers.*) I have also in my hand a list of returns for seventy out of the hundred and forty boroughs over which the league has exerted some influence; and of these there are sixty-eight in which there has been a clear gain upon the registration; in some a great gain, but less or more in all. (*Applause.*) Well, now we will leave these results to speak for themselves; they are here before the country. Our opponents may gather from them whether the league has been dead or slumbering, and they will accordingly derive what consolation they may from them. (*Applause.*) We have concentrated our energies on these points. We thought it was where, for the season, our efforts were most required; and although I may say we have done much, I believe the league is as yet in its infancy, that it is opening up new fields of labour, is occupying ground not before occupied, and that the exertions being made will afford no parallel to future efforts.'

Sir R. Peel, when out of office, had said to his party, 'Register, register, register!' and his followers, by adopting that advice, had been enabled to defeat the Whigs and force him into office; and now the league was raising the cry, and, as we have seen, with still greater effect; and Mr. Cobden added to it another, 'Qualify, qualify, qualify!' He pointed out to the free-traders that by investing their money in land, instead of putting it in the savings-bank, they would place it where it would be perfectly secure, where it might be recovered whenever wanted, where it would yield interest, and in addition to all this, would confer the franchise; and in the same way, if they wanted to give a 'nest-egg' to their children, they might, by giving it in the shape of a piece of land, confer on them a vote, which they might use to defend themselves and their children from political oppression. And referring to the objection, that it was foolish thus publicly to announce such a plan as this, when their enemies could take advantage of it as well as they, he replied, 'My first answer to that is, that our opponents the monopolists cannot take advantage of it as well as we. In the first place, very few men are, from connection or prejudice, monopolists, unless their capacity for inquiry or their sympathies have been blunted already by possessing an undue share of wealth. In the next place, if they wish to urge upon others of a rank below them to qualify for a vote, they cannot trust them with the use of the vote when they have got it. But apart from this, I would answer those people who cavil at this public appeal, and say, "You will not put salt on your enemy's tail; it is much too wise a bird,"—they have been at this work long ago, and have much the worst of it now. What has been the conduct of the landlords of this country? Why, they have been long engaged in multiplying votes upon their estates, making the farmers take their sons, brothers, nephews to the register; making them qualify as many as the rent of the land would cover; making their land a kind of political capital, ever since the passing of the Reform Bill. You have, then, a new ground opened to you, which has never yet been entered upon, and from which I expect, in the course of not more than three years from this time, that every county, if we persevere as we have in South Lancashire, possessing a large town population, may carry free-traders as their representatives in Parliament.'

At the commencement of 1845 much, as we have seen, had been already done; much also remained to be effected. When the session opened, there sat, as before, the serried ranks of the protectionists, distrusting their leader, but unable to find another; disgusted with the concessions he was continually making, yet determined to stand by him as long as he stood by protection. And with all the labours of the league, with all its diligence in instructing, in qualifying, or registering voters, it seemed as though many years must still elapse before that strong party could be broken up, and the protection it so strenuously maintained be swept away. Now too the abundant harvest of last year, and the remarkable success that had attended Sir R. Peel's financial measures, had relaxed the sinews of the opposition as much as they had nerved and strengthened those of the supporters of the ministry. Still the league showed no signs of discouragement. Before Parliament assembled, a great meeting was held at Covent-garden, for the purpose of making known to the members of the league and to the country generally the manner in which it was intended that the anti-corn-law agitation should be conducted during the year 1845. It was one striking characteristic of this agitation that there was no secrecy or concealment about it. The leaguers were no conspirators; the object at which they aimed, and the means by which they hoped to accomplish it, were both fully and publicly proclaimed. The proceedings of this formidable body were such as could only be carried on in a country which had long been habituated to freedom. But now they had begun to change their character. The meetings now held were no longer held for the diffusion of information on the advantages of free trade; they were strictly business meetings, having for their immediate and avowed object to carry into effect the plans which had been devised, and to induce those who attended them, and those who read the reports of them, to proceed at once themselves, and to urge as many of their friends as they could influence, to take steps to qualify themselves as voters by purchasing forty-shilling freeholds. The work of removing the ignorance that still remained with regard to the question, and of answering objections, was not neglected; but the principal aim of the league now was to place the largest possible number of free-traders on the electoral register.

We have already given an account of the budget of this year. It was, as we saw to a great extent based on free-trade principles, and afforded much more satisfaction to free-traders than to protectionists. Even those parts of it which the free-traders disliked, such as the retention of the duties on corn, and the differential duties on sugar, were apologised for, rather than defended, as special and temporary exceptions to the principle of free trade, rendered necessary by peculiar circumstances. At a meeting held in Covent-garden Theatre in the evening of the 19th of February, this free-trade character of the budget was dwelt on with much complacency and satisfaction, as a proof of the progress that free-trade principles were making. At this meeting also the pecuniary history of the league was thus strikingly and succinctly related by Mr. Bright:

'In the year 1839 we first asked for subscriptions, and 5,000*l.* was given. In 1840 we asked for more, and between 7,000*l.* and 8,000*l.* was subscribed. In 1841 we held the great conference at Manchester, at which upwards of 700 ministers of religion attended. In 1842 we had our great bazaar in Manchester, from which 10,000*l.* was realised. In 1843 we asked for 50,000*l.*, and got it. In 1844 we called for 100,000*l.*, and between 80,000*l.* and 90,000*l.* has been paid in, besides what will be received from the bazaar to be held in May. This year is yet young, but we have not been idle. We have asked our free-trade friends in the northern counties to convert some of their property, so as to be able to defend their right and properties at the hustings. This has been done, and it now appears that, at the recommendation of the council of the league, our friends in Lancashire, Cheshire, and Yorkshire have invested a sum of not less than 250,000*l.* in the purchase of county qualifications. Besides all this, we shall have our great bazaar in May.'

The bazaar alluded to was held in London at the appointed time. Great preparations had been made for it, sanguine expectations were entertained respecting it, and much interest was taken in it. Probably no such bazaar was ever held in the world before, or will ever be witnessed again. More than 20,000*l.* was realised in admissions and sales, besides 5000*l.* given in direct contributions. It was followed by another bazaar in Manchester later in the year. Meanwhile Parliament, as we have seen, was engaged in repeated discussions on the question of free trade in various ways, but without any definite result. The weather seemed to give promise of an abundant harvest; and Peel, suspected by the ultra-protectionists, but warmly and zealously supported by the more sensible and liberal portion of the conservative party, stood by his free-trade measures and his modified sliding scale, and seemed likely to remain at the head of affairs, carrying out this policy, for some years to come. Before the close of the year, the league succeeded in collecting not only the 100,000*l.* it had proposed to raise, but 17,000*l.* in addition to it.

And now there came heavy rains. At first it was hoped that the moisture would swell the grain, and cause the harvest to be more abundant; but they continued all through August. Nevertheless, men clung to the hope that sunshine would succeed to rain, and that an average harvest might yet be housed. But the rain continued to fall with little intermission through September. Yet still they buoyed themselves up with the belief that, after all, things were not so bad as they seemed to be, and that the harvest would not be very far below the average. It was not till the middle of October had arrived that it began to be generally admitted that there was a great failure in the wheat crops.

But the rain, which had done this direful mischief in England, had produced far more serious consequences in Ireland. We need not here repeat the tale of the rotting of the potatoes, and the consequent imminence of famine in that unhappy country. Subscriptions were promptly entered into in various parts of the kingdom to alleviate the distress caused by this terrible visitation. But what could private liberality do to relieve a starving nation? The league at once demanded the opening of the ports by an order in council for the free admission of grain. The cry thus raised was taken up by thousands who had hitherto held themselves aloof from the agitation, and by some who up to this time had been reckoned among its stanchest opponents. The cabinet, as we have seen, was deliberating, but, owing to the differences of opinion among its members, had not come to any resolution. But the course of events would not wait for their decision. While the ministry was doing nothing, famine was stalking on in Ireland. While Peel was hesitating and doubting, Lord J. Russell was acting promptly and decisively. He saw that whatever might be the merits of his favourite plan of a fixed duty, the time for bringing it forward had now passed; and on the 22nd of November he published the celebrated letter at Edinburgh, which we have already quoted. Two days after its publication, Lord Morpeth announced that he had made up his mind to cast in his lot with the free-traders. On the 4th December the *Times* announced that the cabinet had decided on proposing a measure for the repeal of the corn-laws, which would be introduced in the House of Lords by the Duke of Wellington, and by Sir R. Peel in the other House. This statement, though not altogether groundless, was premature, and was denounced by the *Standard* as an 'atrocious fabrication;' but it was so completely in accordance with the fears of one party, and the hopes of the other, that, notwithstanding all the denials of it that were published, it obtained very general credit, and was immediately followed by a great reduction in the price of corn.

While Lord J. Russell was labouring to construct his administration, the league was not idle. It was still doubtful whether, with all the assistance that Peel and Wellington were prepared to give him, he would be able to carry the repeal of the corn-laws against the large protectionist majority of the House of Commons, or to force it on the acceptance of the reluctant lords. It was quite certain that he could not succeed unless well backed out of doors. It was felt, therefore, that this was no time for the friends of free trade to put off their armour, but on the contrary that they must buckle it on more firmly than ever. All now evidently depended on the exertions put forth at this critical moment. Seventy of the largest contributors to the funds of the league on former occasions were convened in the league rooms on the 13th of December, and they resolved that an appeal should be made to the public for an additional fund of 250,000*l.*; and that a meeting for the purpose should be held in the Townhall on the 23rd. On that day Mr. Robert Hyde Gregg presided at the meeting, and put down a thousand pounds as the subscription of the firm to which he belonged. Mr. James Chadwick followed with another thousand. The subscriptions then came in so rapidly that the chairman had scarcely time to read the papers announcing the amounts as they poured in on him. Twenty-three persons or firms subscribed each a thousand pounds to the fund; twenty-five gave five hundred; fifty-one gave sums varying from two to four hundred; sixty-one sums between a hundred and a hundred and fifty; and about fifty more put down their names each for fifty pounds. In an hour and a half upwards of sixty thousand pounds were subscribed. Thus the year 1845 ended in the midst of deep distress, extending to all classes and conditions of men; in the midst of fearful forebodings of still severer calamities in the near future; but still with a full hope that before a much longer time had elapsed, the bread-tax and its baneful influence would be for ever taken out of the way, and that an unchecked admission of corn from all parts of the world would alleviate, if not altogether remove, the sufferings which were impending over great masses of the people in England, and still larger masses of them in Ireland. The league had been acknowledged on all sides as a great fact. It had now become a greater fact than ever. The promptitude of its action on this occasion, the liberality with which its members again and again contributed to its funds, produced a profound sensation through the country. The protectionists, disheartened, divided, and fearing treachery everywhere, made no sign, or exhaled their ill-temper in vehement abuse of Peel and his colleagues. The liberal party was now thoroughly united. Mr. Bright could truly boast, at a great meeting held at this time in Covent-garden Theatre, that employers of labour and operatives were united as one man in favour of free trade, in spite of all the efforts that had been made to sow discord between them, and that the government of England, on protectionist principles, had become impossible. All felt that there must be something in a cause which awakened such strong convictions, which was supported with such unprecedented liberality. It was evident that the quarter of a million of money which the league now asked for would be raised as promptly as the smaller amounts which had been previously subscribed, if circumstances should still require the agitation to be continued.

We must not conclude our narrative of the events of the year 1845 without referring to the death of Sydney Smith, which occurred on the 22nd of February in this year. Though most of his works relate to subjects the interest of which has to a great extent passed away, they will probably be read with admiration and delight as long as the English language endures. The great characteristic of his mind was masculine common-sense, possessed in a most uncommon degree. Unrivalled among his contemporaries in wit and humour, he was equally unapproachable by them in sound wisdom. Indeed, his wit consisted in the clearness with which he saw and held up to ridicule the weak points of the arguments which he opposed, and the laugh he raised was chiefly the utterance of the joy that was felt at the discovery, by a sudden stroke, of a truth that had never been so clearly exhibited before. No man ever made a better use of his talents, or was more successful in bringing public opinion to bear with force and effect on the manifold abuses that prevailed in his time; and thus his works present a valuable and interesting picture of the evils of his day, the removal of which was in a great measure due to his efforts. He has been accused of treating religious subjects with levity; but the manner in which he handled them belongs rather to his own joyous temperament, and to the age in which he lived. It is true that he delighted in holding up fanaticism, superstition, and empty pomposity to derision and ridicule, and it sometimes perhaps happened that in doing so he was not sufficiently careful to separate the outward profession from the inward reality which it aped. But he was a sincerely religious man, and never intentionally dropped from his pen, in his lightest moments, an expression calculated to bring genuine religion into contempt. He felt, and justly felt, that he had not received the recognition of his services that he was entitled to claim. Had he prostituted his genius to be the apologist of the abuses which he so vigorously attacked, he would probably have climbed to the highest places of the church of which he was the greatest ornament in his day. As it was, the ecclesiastical giant saw ecclesiastical pigmies raised above him, and that too by governments whose principles he had so effectively propagated in the days of their seemingly hopeless adversity. As he somewhat bitterly complained, after having been assailed with all the Billingsgate of the French Revolution, of which Jacobite, leveller, incendiary, regicide were the gentlest appellations used, he had to bear the chuckling grin of noodles, the sarcastic leer of the genuine political rogue, probendaries, deans, bishops made over his head, reverend renegades advanced to the highest dignities in the church, for helping to rivet the fetters of Catholic and Protestant dissenters. It was only in his old age that a tardy and inadequate recognition of the great services he had rendered to his country was bestowed on him. The year of his death witnessed the mitigation of one of the abuses against which he had generously striven. In that year Mr. Bright succeeded in ameliorating those game-laws—fruitful of murder, of ruin to the farmer, of demoralisation to the peasantry, of bitter hatred towards the peerage and the magistracy—by whose influence the iniquitous system that

Sydney Smith disinterestedly denounced was upheld and defended.

The pressing nature of the emergency that had arisen imposed on ministers the duty of summoning Parliament at a much earlier period than usual. The session of 1846 commenced on the 14th of January, and was opened by the Queen in person. The speech from the throne dwelt on the success which had attended the removal of restrictive duties, and suggested that the same policy should be carried farther, but did not directly touch on the vexed question of the corn-laws. Ministers were anxious to avoid all premature discussion of that important question, and to bring forward the measures by which they proposed to deal with it with the least possibly delay. But Lord F. Egerton and Mr. Beckett Denison, the mover and the seconder of the address, could hardly pass by in silence a topic which was uppermost in the thoughts of all those in whose presence they spoke. Both candidly admitted that their opinions on this question had undergone a very considerable change. Then came the turn of Sir R. Peel. His conversion was already known, but the greatest anxiety was felt to learn in what manner he would treat the subject, and by what arguments he would justify a change of opinion and action so complete, and especially how he would explain his conduct to those who had carried him triumphantly into office and sustained him in the position to which they had raised him, but the cardinal principle of whose policy he was now about to assail, and whose party-organisation he was evidently destined to destroy. He rose, amidst the mournful silence of his own supporters and the triumphant cheers of the opposition, to announce that his opinions in reference to the corn-laws had undergone an entire change, and that the force of events had brought him to the conviction that the protection he had so long supported, and up to a very recent period had expected still to support, must be speedily relinquished. He had now to employ the arguments which had been so often put forward by the free-traders, and which he himself had so often risen to combat, but of which he now acknowledged the force and soundness, and to which he was now determined to give effect. The house was of course quite prepared for the avowal of a change of opinion, which was already a matter of notoriety. Nevertheless, when it came, it was received by both sides as if it had been altogether unexpected. It is impossible adequately to depict the rage and indignation of the majority of those who had put their trust in him as their champion against all comers, or the triumph of the free-traders when they heard their own arguments ably reproduced and admirably put to the house by him who had hitherto been the most formidable opponent of their views, and the last possible defender of the system they had combined to overthrow. It must be confessed that the old supporters of Sir Robert had some ground for their complaints. He had been too reticent with them; he had not taken them sufficiently into his confidence; he had expected them to follow him in his changes of opinion without sufficiently acquainting them with the reasons by which he had himself been brought to feel the necessity of these changes. But this was not the fault of the man, but rather of his character and temperament. Though so copious, fluent, and unabashed a public speaker, he was naturally taciturn and shy; and these constitutional defects prevented him from taking council with his supporters, and giving them the explanations they were perhaps entitled to expect from their leader.

Sir R. Peel immediately followed the seconder of the address.

'My opinions he said have been modified by the experience of the last three years. I have had the means and the opportunity of comparing the results of periods of abundance and low prices with periods of scarcity and high prices, and of marking from day to day the effect upon great social interests of freedom of trade and comparative abundance. I have not failed to note the results of preceding years, and to contrast them with the results of the last three years; and I am led to the conclusion, that the main grounds of public policy on which protection has been defended are not tenable. I do not believe, after the experience of the last three years, that the rate of wages varies with the price of food, or that with high prices wages will necessarily vary in the same ratio. I do not believe that a low price of food necessarily implies a low rate of wages. Neither can I, after seeing the results of the change in the tariff during the last four years, maintain that protection to domestic industry is necessarily good. Then, as to the other argument which, I confess, made a great impression on me in the first instance, and which is sanctioned by great authority—that because we have a heavy debt, and a high rate of taxation, we must be protected from competition with foreign industry. That argument has been submitted to the test of the last three years, and so far as the experience of that period can teach us, we find that a large debt and heavy taxation are best encountered by abundance and cheapness of provisions, which rather alleviate than add to the weight of the burden. Let us take the result of that experience of constantly diminished protection on wages, on trade, and on revenue. First, as to wages: who can deny the fact that during the three years that had preceded the month of October last, prices were comparatively low? There was comparative cheapness and plenty, and yet at no period were the wages of labour higher. If you take the three preceding years, you will find high prices and low wages coexistent with them. I cannot, therefore, resist the conclusion that wages do not vary with the price of provisions. They do vary with the increase of capital, with the prosperity of the country, with the increased power to employ labour; but there is no immediate relation between wages and provisions; or if there be a relation, it is in an inverse ratio. Now as to the tariff: during the last four or five years we have been acting on the admitted principle of removing prohibitions, reducing duties, or abating, and in some cases destroying, protection to native industry. Now what has been the result? The total value of British produce and manufactures exported from the United Kingdom was, in 1839, 53,000,000*l.*; in 1840, 51,000,000*l.*; in 1841, 51,000,000*l.*; in 1842, 47,000,000*l.*; in 1843, 52,000,000*l.*; in 1844, 58,000,000*l.* But it may be said the China trade made all the difference. Now let us deduct the whole of that trade. In 1842 our exports to all the countries except China amounted to 46,411,000*l.*; and in 1844 they increased 10,000,000*l.*, amounting to 56,000,000*l.* Such is the state of our foreign exports under this system of continued removal of protection. Now let us take the returns of the revenue as bearing on this question: ought there to be a high protection in a country encumbered with an immense public debt and heavy taxation? In 1842 I proposed a reduction in the customs to an estimated amount of 1,438,000*l.*; in 1844 I proposed a farther reduction in the customs duties to the amount of 273,000*l.*; in 1845 to the large amount of 2,418,000*l.* I estimated the total loss from these several reductions at 4,129,000*l.*; and let it be remembered that I discarded altogether the revenue from corn. How have these calculations been verified? Have 4,000,000*l.* been lost? No; the total amount of the loss has been 1,500,000*l.* I dealt with the excise last year: the whole of the glass duties, the whole of the auction duties, were taken off. The loss on that occasion was estimated at 1,000,000*l.*; but I felt confident that other branches of industry would be vivified, and the revenue would derive some compensation. And I believe that, notwithstanding this great reduction, this absolute loss of 1,000,000*l.*, the revenue from the excise will this year be greater than ever. Well, then, with this evidence before me, could I contend that on account of high taxation or great debt you must necessarily continue high protective duties? But I will now refer to more important considerations than those either of trade or of revenue. I will take the state of crime in the country. In the year 1842 there was an increase of crime and commitments; in 1843 there was a turn, and a decrease began, and continued to 1845, and this in an increasing population. With respect to crimes connected with sedition, discontent, and disaffection to the government, there has been only a single prosecution for an offence of this nature during the whole of the last year, because the crime of sedition did not exist. In 1840-1-2-3—listen to this, and seriously consider it—there were 1257 persons committed on charges of seditious and riotous offences. In 1843-4-5 only 124 persons were admitted so charged, instead of 1257; while in the last year I believe there was not one. In 1845 there were 422 persons sentenced to transportation less than in 1842. In the last three years there were 1701 persons sentenced to transportation less than in the three preceding years. This has been during a period of comparative abundance and low prices. Is it possible to resist the inference that employment, low prices, comparative abundance, contribute to the diminution of crime? Have these great social advantages been purchased by any serious detriment to that great interest whose welfare ought to be one of the first objects of our concern—the agricultural interest? Let us take the four great articles in respect of which there has been a diminution of protection. Foreign flax has for many years been admitted at a very low duty into this country. What duty remained was remitted last year. In 1824 the duty on flax was 10*l.* 14*s.* 6*d.* per ton. It is now absolutely nothing. What has been the effect on the price of flax? The price of fine flax in Belfast market in 1843 was 65*s.* to 70*s.*; in 1844, it was 63*s.* to 68*s.*; in 1845, from 65*s.* to 68*s.*; and in January 1846—the present month—the price of fine Irish flax in the Belfast market is from 70*s.* to 80*s.* There was no reduction which caused so much alarm, or was prophesied to do so much injury, as the removal of the absolute prohibition on the importation of foreign cattle, and their admission at a very low rate. Now has serious injury been sustained by that reduction? There has been a gradual increase in the importation, and concurrently with that increase there has been an increase in the price of the article. One prophecy, if I recollect rightly, was that there would be an importation into this country of 3,500,000 pigs, and that the price of salt pork would be immensely reduced. But look at the price of salt pork rising from 3*l.* 15*s.* 10*d.* to 6*l.* 12*s.* 4*d.*; and I think about 4,000 swine have been imported. There was no article last year that caused so much alarm as lard. The duty was then taken off. In 1840 there was 97 cwt. of foreign lard imported into this country. In 1842 the duty was reduced from 8*s.* to 2*s.* a cwt., and there were then imported 48,312 cwt.'; in 1844, 76,000 cwt. were imported; and in 1845 the importation had reached above 80,000 cwt. And what has been the price of domestic lard at Belfast during that period? In 1844 it was 48*s.* a cwt.; in 1845 it was 67*s.*; and in January of the present year, notwithstanding the increase caused by this importation, the price has risen from 48*s.* in 1844 to 62*s.* In wool there has been an enormous increase in the imports, in consequence of the reduction of the duty; and yet in December the price was higher than before that reduction and importation took place. I have now shown that by the removal of protection domestic industry and the great social interest of the country have been promoted, crime has diminished, and morality has improved. I can bring the most conclusive proof that the public health has been improved; yet the national trade has been extending, our exports have increased, and this—I rejoice in it—has been effected not only without serious injury to those interests from which protection has been withdrawn, but I think I have shown that it has been concurrent with an increase in the prices of those articles.'

After avowing that, considering the change which had taken place in his opinions with regard to this question, he was not the man to propose an alteration of the present corn-law, he went into a detailed account of the considerations that had induced him and his colleagues to tender their resignation, and showed how, owing to the inability of Lord John Russell to form a government, they had been constrained, by the force of circumstances, to propose the abolition of that protection which they had so long maintained. After reading various communications, showing the extent to which the potato disease prevailed, and the necessity of providing at once against the imminent danger of famine, Sir R. Peel sat down. Then Lord J. Russell rose and gave a full explanation of the course he had adopted during the late ministerial crisis, and of the cause of his failure to form a ministry. He was followed by Mr. Disraeli, the fittest man in the House to give utterance to the feelings of rage and indignation that were boiling in the hearts of that large party which still clung to protection, and who not unnaturally considered that they had been basely and unworthily betrayed by the man whom they had chosen to be their champion. Hitherto he had borne a name not wholly unknown in the walks of literature. He was the writer of novels remarkable for the wild exuberance of fancy they displayed, and for the eccentric character of the political doctrines they aimed at inculcating; he had delivered speeches sparkling with wit, and edged with trenchant sarcasm; yet up to this moment he had not obtained any commanding position in the House and in the country. But his time was now come. In the whole of the great body of protectionists, which, after all the defection it had suffered, was still the strongest party in the House, not one was to be found who could give voice like him to the fierce passion by which his party was agitated, or inflict such fierce vengeance on the man whom they regarded as their betrayer. This he did effectually; and from that moment he stood forth in the eyes of Parliament, and of the country, as the real standard-bearer, about whom,' not without some repugnance and reluctance, the protectionists rallied, whoever might be their nominal leader. At the moment when the protectionists were disheartened, disorganised, scattered, but still a mighty host if properly rallied, Mr. Disraeli stepped forward, and thus addressed the House:

'I should have abstained from obtruding myself on the House at the present moment, had it not been for the peculiar tone of the right hon. gentleman. I think that tone ought not to pass unnoticed. At the same time I do not want to conceal my opinions on the general subject. I am not one of the converts. I am perhaps a member of a fallen party. To the opinions which I have expressed in this House in favour of protection I still adhere. They sent me to this house; and if I had relinquished them, I should have relinquished my seat also. I must say that the tone of the right hon. gentleman is hardly fair towards the House, while he stops discussion upon a subject on which he himself has entered with a fervency unusual to him. Sir, I admire a minister who says that he holds power to give effect to his own convictions. I have no doubt that the right hon. gentleman has arrived at a conscientious conclusion on this great subject. The right hon. gentleman says it is not so much by force of argument as by the cogency of observation that he has arrived at this conclusion. But, sir, surely the observation which the right hon. gentleman has made might have been made when he filled a post scarcely less considerable than that which he now occupies. What, sir, are we to think of the eminent statesman, who, having served under four sovereigns, who having been called to steer the ship on so many occasions and under such perilous circumstances, has only during the last three or four years found it necessary entirely to change his convictions on that important topic which must have presented itself for more than a quarter of a century to his consideration? Sir, I must say that such a minister may be conscientious, but he is unfortunate. I must say also that he ought to be the last man in the world to turn round and upbraid his party in a tone of menace. Sir, there is a difficulty in finding a parallel to the position of the right hon. gentleman in any part of history. The only parallel I can find is an incident in the late war in the Levant, which was terminated by the policy of the noble lord opposite. I remember when that great struggle was taking place, when the existence of the Turkish empire was at stake, the late sultan, a man of great energy and fertile in resources, was determined to fit out an immense fleet to maintain his empire. Accordingly a vast armament was collected. It consisted of many of the finest ships ever built. The crews were picked men, the officers were the ablest that could be found, and both officers and men were rewarded before they fought. There never was an armament which left the Dardanelles similarly appointed since the days of Solyman the Great. The sultan personally witnessed the departure of the fleet; all the muftis prayed for the success of the expedition, as all the muftis here prayed for the success of the last general election. Away went the fleet; but what was the consternation of the sultan when the lord high admiral steered at once for the enemy's port! Now, sir, the lord high admiral on that occasion was very much misrepresented. He too was called a traitor; and he too vindicated himself. "True it is," said he, "I did place myself at the head of this valiant armada; true it is that my sovereign embraced me; true it is that all the muftis in the empire offered up prayers for my success. But I have an objection to war; I see no use in prolonging the struggle; and the only reason I had for accepting the command was that I might terminate the contest by betraying my master." It is all very well for the right hon. gentleman to come forward to this table and say, "I am thinking of posterity; although, certainly, I am doing on this side of the table the contrary to that which I counselled when I stood upon the other; but my sentiments are magnanimous, my aim is heroic, and appealing to posterity, I care neither for your cheers nor for your taunts." But we must ask ourselves what were the means, what the machinery, by which the right hon. gentleman acquired his position, how he obtained power to turn round on his supporters, and treat them with contempt and disdain? Well do we remember, perhaps not without a blush, the efforts we made to raise him to the bench on which he now sits. Who does not remember "the sacred cause of protection," for which sovereigns were thwarted, Parliament dissolved, and a nation taken in! Delightful, indeed, to have the right hon. gentleman entering into all his confidential details, when, to use his courtly language, he "called" upon his sovereign. Would his sovereign have called on him, if, in 1841, he had not placed himself, as he said, at the head of the gentlemen of England? It is all very well for the right hon gentleman to take this high-flying course, but I think myself—I say it with great respect for gentlemen on this side of the House and the other; I say it without any wish to achieve a party triumph; for I believe I belong to a party which can triumph no more—for we have nothing left on our side except the constituencies which we have not betrayed;—but I do say that my conception of a great statesman is of one who represents a great idea; an idea which may lead him to power; an idea with which he may identify himself; an idea which he may develop; an idea which he may and can impress on the mind and conscience of a nation: that, sir, is my idea of what makes a man a great statesman. I do not care whether he is a manufacturer or a manufacturer's son. That is a grand, that is indeed an heroic position. But I care not what may be the position of a man who never originates an idea— a watcher of the atmosphere—a man who, as he says, takes his observations, and when he finds the wind in a certain quarter, trims his sails to suit it. Such a man may be a powerful minister, but he is no more a great statesman than a man who gets up behind a carriage is a great whip.'

This specimen is sufficient. In this strain he went on at great length, giving vent to the bitterness which rankled in the hearts of the protectionists against their late leader; sneering at his 'mouldy potatoes;' reminding him of the cry of 'Register, register, register!' with which he had plied the conservative party; describing him as 'making protectionist speeches, a great orator before a green table beating a red box.' All this, and much more than this, amidst the loud and ringing cheers in which the protectionists gave utterance to their indignation and disappointment. After some smaller explosions of rage from a few other protectionists, the address was quietly agreed to, and the House adjourned.

On the 27th of January, in accordance with notice previously given, the prime minister came forward to explain his financial plan for the year, which, as was already known, was to include those alterations that he proposed to make in the duties on corn, as well as a measure for their ultimate and not very distant repeal. Never perhaps, since the introduction of the Reform Bill, had so anxious a curiosity been exhibited to learn the exact nature and extent of the proposed change. The approaches to the House were thronged; the house itself crowded with members, and strangers who had been fortunate enough to obtain places. In the seats allotted to peers were Prince Albert and the Duke of Cambridge. After explaining some reductions which he proposed to make in the duties on Russian tallow and French and Genevan brandy and sugar, he came to that part of his plans which his auditors were burning with impatience to hear. He announced his intention to abandon the sliding scale entirely; to impose a fixed duty of ten shillings the quarter on corn; when the price of it was forty-eight shillings per quarter to reduce that duty by one shilling for every shilling of rise in price till it reached fifty-three shillings a quarter, when the duty should be four shillings. This was to continue for three years, at the expiration of which period the duty was to be finally abolished. In order to compensate the agriculturists for the immediate loss that these changes would occasion to them, Sir Robert proposed to lighten some of the burdens with which they were at present loaded. This plan was not likely to satisfy the league,—indeed it could hardly have satisfied Sir Robert himself; but he probably felt that while he was bound by his convictions to carry out the principles of free trade, he was also bound to maintain the revenue, and to use his best endeavours to obtain the most favourable terms possible for the agricultural interest, which had brought him into power under expectations which he now felt himself compelled to disappoint.

He entered on this part of his speech by announcing that he intended to propose the gradual removal of protective duties not only on agriculture, but also on manufactures, and on every description of produce; and he appealed to the patriotism of those engaged in the manufacture of linen, woollen, and cotton fabrics to set an example of cheerful relinquishment of the protection they at present enjoyed. We will not weary our readers with the details of the reductions which the minister proposed to make. It is sufficient to say that the principle of free trade was applied to almost every species of produce and manufacture, so far as the necessity of providing for the expenditure of the country, and avoiding the hardships that might arise from a too sudden withdrawal of protection in certain cases, would allow. The differential duties on sugar, by which it was designed that the owners of free-grown sugars should be 'protected' against the producers of slave-grown sugars, were to be diminished, but not abolished. In approaching the question of agricultural protection, Sir R. Peel reminded the House of the necessity of maintaining the revenue, especially at a moment when the government had found it necessary to propose to the House considerable augmentations of our land and sea forces. He announced that the government proposed to remove at once all duties on the importation of cattle. He urged the agriculturists to submit to the withdrawal of the protection that had hitherto been enjoyed with the same cheerfulness that he had asked the manufacturers to display. He announced to them that he did not intend to propose an immediate repeal of the corn-laws, but that there should be a continuance of that protection till the year 1849, when it was to be altogether withdrawn. But in the mean time he deemed it of the highest importance that proper precautions should be taken against the contingencies that might arise out of the present scarcity of food. He proposed to provide against these dangers as far as possible by an immediate reduction of the duties on all kinds of grain;—that grain imported from any of the British colonies should be admitted on a merely nominal duty;—that the duties on the export of meal from the colonies should be taken off, as well as that on maize brought in from the United States of America.

The provisions for the removal of protection were to be accompanied by other measures intended to compensate the agriculturist. In the first place, Sir Robert proposed to deal with the highway rate, which had been so much insisted on being one of those peculiar burdens on agriculture that gave the agriculturists a right to demand that it should be countervailed by a peculiar protection. It was therefore proposed to render compulsory an act, now only permissive, which empowered parishes to combine for the more effectual and economical management of their highways. In the next place Sir Robert proposed to relieve the land from a great burden, and the labourer from a cruel injustice, by improving the law of settlement, which up to that time allowed a man to spend his best years in a manufacturing district, and then to be sent back in sickness and old age to be supported at the expense of the ratepayers in the place of his birth, which had derived no benefit from his labour. It was now proposed that a residence of five years in any place should confer a right of settlement in that place on the man who so resided, and that neither he, nor his wife, nor his children, whether legitimate or illegitimate, nor his widow, should be in any way chargeable on the parish from which he came. In addition to this boon, provision was made for the advance of public money for the improvement of land, under certain restrictions. It was likewise proposed that the cost of prosecutions and the expense of supporting prisoners should be transferred from the county rate to the treasury. These demands were to met by an annual grant, in order that the expenditure thus incurred might be brought more directly under the control and supervision of the House of Commons, and abuses connected with its administration corrected. Provision was likewise made for the appointment of school-masters, school-mistresses, and auditors, with salaries paid by the treasury. Arrangements were also to be made for medical attendance in a manner which would be advantageous to the agriculturists. Having explained at great length the main features of the plan which, with the concurrence of his colleagues, he had determined to bring forward, the prime minister went on to make the following observations on the question of reciprocity, which at that time, as before and since, was strongly insisted on by the protectionists as a condition which should be exacted from foreigners before we consented to admit their produce.

'I fairly avow to you that, in making this great reduction on the import of articles the produce and manufacture of foreign countries, I have no guarantee to give you that other countries will immediately follow our example. Wearied with our long and unavailing efforts to enter into satisfactory commercial treaties with other nations, we have resolved at length to consult our own interests, and not to punish those other countries for the wrong they do us in continuing their high duties upon the importation of our products and manufacture. We have had no communication with any foreign government upon the subject of these reductions. We cannot promise that France will immediately make a corresponding reduction in her tariff. We cannot promise that Russia will prove her gratitude to us for our reduction of duty on her tallow by any diminution of her duties. You may therefore ask, why this superfluous liberality, that you are going to do away with all these duties, and yet you expect nothing in return? I may perhaps be told, and truly, that many foreign countries which have benefited by our relaxations have actually applied to the importation of British goods higher rates of duties than formerly. I give you the benefit of that argument, and I rely upon that fact as a conclusive proof of the policy of the course we are pursuing. It is a fact that other countries have not followed our example, and have in some cases levied higher duties on our goods. But what has been the result upon the amount of your export trade? It has greatly increased. Now why is that so? Partly because of your acting without wishing to avail yourself of their assistance, partly because of the smuggler, not engaged by you, in so many continental countries, whom the strict regulations and the triple duties, which are to prevent any ingress of foreign' goods, have raised up; and partly, perhaps, because those very precautions against the ingress of your commodities are a burden, and the taxation increasing the cost of production, have disqualified the foreigner from competing with you. But your exports—whatever be the tariff of other countries, or however apparent the ingratitude with which they have treated you—your export trade has been constantly increasing. By the remission of your duties upon the raw material, by inciting your skill and industry, by competition with foreign goods, you have defied your competitors in foreign markets, and you have even been enabled to exclude them. Notwithstanding their hostile tariffs, the declared value of British exports has increased above 10,000,000*l.* during the period which has elapsed since the relaxation of duties on your part. I say, therefore, to you that these hostile tariffs, so far from being an objection to continuing your policy, are an argument in its favour. When your example could be quoted in favour of restriction, it was quoted largely; when your example can be quoted in favour of relaxation, as conducive to your interests, it may perhaps excite at first in foreign governments or foreign boards of trade but little interest or feeling; but the sense of the people, of the great body of consumers, will prevail; and in spite of the desire of governments and boards of trade to raise revenue by restrictive duties, reason and common sense will induce relaxation of high duties. Our last accounts from the United States give indications of the decline of a hostile spirit in this respect. In Naples liberal views are beginning to prevail. In Norway exertions to obtain a relaxation of duties are increasing. In Sweden and many other countries there is a disposition to follow the same course. Austria, too, shows some disposition at least not to follow other countries in their restrictive policy. Hanover has also taken her own course; and I do not despair of the early arrival of the period when your example will tell upon the conduct of other countries, and when they shall quote our relaxations as a lesson to their governments in commercial affairs. I trust that this improved intercourse with foreign countries will constitute a new bond of peace, and that the lovers of peace between nations will derive material strength from the example which I have advised, by remitting the impediments to commercial intercourse.'

A long and desultory discussion—it can hardly be called a debate—took place on the proposal placed before the House, and continued till midnight, when it was arranged that the committee should sit again on the 9th of February, with the understanding that the question placed before the House by the hon. baronet at the head of the ministry would then be fully debated. Mr. Miles, in accordance with notice previously given, proposed that the House should resolve itself into a committee on this day six months, thus fairly engaging the conflict between the protectionists and the free-traders.

The issue which the amendment raised was unfortunate and ill-chosen. It was in effect to say that the House would not comply with those recommendations of the Queen's speech, which in the address it had promised to carry out, and that it would refuse so much as even to entertain, not only the proposed alteration of the corn-laws, but the relaxations and reductions of duties which by general consent had proved to be attended with great advantage to the country. However, for twelve long nights was the debate carried on. At length, on the 27th of February, the division took place, and ministers triumphed over their opponents by a majority of ninety-seven. We do not propose to give any account of this monster debate, the merits of which were by no means equal to its duration; for it was chiefly made up of attacks on and apologies for the conduct of the government; a very small portion indeed of it being devoted to the narrow issue which the amendment raised.

On the 2nd of March the ministerial plan had to go through the ordeal of a free-trade attack. Mr. Villiers proposed an amendment, the object of which was to dispense with the three years' interval between the condemnation of the corn laws and their final repeal. In the previous discussion the government had been enabled to defend the protectionists through the assistance they had received from the free-traders, and now they had to fight the free-traders with the assistance of the protectionists. Mr. Villiers had very strong reasons to urge in favour of his motion. It was known that as early as the 1st of November, 1845, in view of the distress then impending over this country, and still more threateningly over Ireland, the premier himself had proposed a temporary suspension of the corn-laws, which on his own admission would have been a virtual abolition of them. He could not deny that since he brought forward that proposal, the distress which prompted him to make it had not abated, nor had the prospects of the country at all improved. Why, then, should he resist an amendment so much in accordance with his own views and opinions? The protectionists themselves had over and over again said that they preferred immediate repeal, which would let them know the worst, to the state of suspense and uncertainty in which they had so long been kept. On the other hand, the leader of the opposition had distinctly expressed his opinion in favour of immediate repeal. Delay would aggravate instead of removing the difficulties of the proposed change; for delay would keep up among the agriculturists a hope that protection might after all be retained, and thus prevent them from making the preparations for meeting the altered circumstances in which repeal would place them until that repeal actually came into operation. For the sake of the people immediate repeal was greatly and manifestly desirable. There had been a deficient harvest in most countries, and there was therefore almost everywhere a disposition to import rather than to export. Already had corn destined for this country been turned from that destination to Antwerp, and found a ready market there. It was quite possible that there might be a series of deficient harvests both here and on the Continent, in which case the proposed duty of four shillings, might prevent a great quantity of corn needed for the relief of this country from being imported. Lastly, he referred to a solemn pledge, by which Mr. Cobden and the other leaders of the league had bound themselves to dissolve that body the moment that the abolition of the corn-laws was secured, but to keep it in activity until success had finally crowned their efforts. He therefore strongly urged the desirableness of totally repealing the corn-laws at once, and thus putting an end to the existence of a body so formidable as the league, which, though established for the attainment of great and beneficial ends, was nevertheless pregnant with danger to the state. On this question Lord J. Russell, Mr. Hume, Mr. Wakley, and several other free-traders, declared that, though they would have preferred total and immediate repeal, they nevertheless thought it their duty to give their support to the government; which, after a debate extending over two nights, triumphed on division by a majority of 187.

The whole interest of Parliament and the nation throughout this session was concentrated on this great question so completely, that it was difficult to obtain due attention to questions of great but less pressing importance. The policy of obstruction, which had been carried to such lengths in the debates on the Reform Bill, was resorted to in opposition to the measure now before the House, and every artifice of delay was employed by the more violent opponents of free trade. Sir Robert now underwent a not undeserved retribution for the encouragement he had given to the factious opposition offered to the Reform Bill, when that measure was under discussion. But while thus suffering the punishment due to past political errors, he nobly redeemed them by the patience he exhibited in carrying through this measure, and the wonderful command of temper and courtesy he displayed under the most galling provocations. He so frankly and cheerfully admitted his own errors; he showed such a mastery of every principle and every detail of the measure under discussion; he displayed so strong a desire to put the best possible construction on the motives of his adversaries; he was so anxious to seize every opportunity of giving the honour of the great reform he was engaged in carrying out to those to whom it was due—and especially to Mr. Cobden; he manifested such evident indifference to power and office; that his change of opinion served to raise him immeasurably in the eyes of all candid and unprejudiced men throughout the country, and nowhere more so than in the House of Commons. At length the measure passed the Commons by a majority of 98 votes.

The bill was then carried up to the House of Lords. It was certain to meet with a strong opposition in an assembly which probably did not number among its members more than five or six really convinced free-traders. No fewer than fifty-three lords took part in the discussion of the question. Lords Stanley and Ashburton led the opposition to the bill; Lords Brougham, Grey, Clarendon, and Lansdowne were foremost among its supporters; but the immense influence which the Duke of Wellington enjoyed in the House, and the earnest support he gave to the bill, were the inducements which weighed with the greater number of their lordships in either giving it their vote, or abstaining from opposing it. He grounded the support he gave to it on the duty and gratitude he owed to the crown; on the recommendation of the measure in the Queen's speech; on the impolicy of putting the House of Lords in opposition to the two other branches of the legislature; on the danger of forcing a dissolution of Parliament at the present moment and under existing circumstances. Into the merits of the bill itself he did not enter. Probaby he regarded it as an inevitable evil, and as such accepted it with reluctance. He and the lords with him had learnt a lesson from the Reform Bill that they were not likely to forget or disregard. The prudent counsels he gave were followed; and the second reading of the bill, which practically settled the question, was carried by a majority of 47.

The financial measures of the government included, as we have seen, many farther reductions of customs duties. To some of these strong opposition was offered, and especially to the lowering of the duties on hops and timber; but the government succeeded in carrying all its proposals.

The increasing distress of Ireland was attended by an increase of those crimes of violence with which almost every page in the history of that country is more or less stained. The number of these offences in 1844 was 1495; in 1845 it had risen to 3642, and was still increasing. In five counties especially, Tipperary, Clare, Roscommon, Limerick, and Leitrim, all personal security had disappeared. Under such circumstances it was the clear duty of the government to ask Parliament for additional repressive powers. A bill for this object was introduced into the House of Lords, and passed there without difficulty. In the House of Commons it encountered a strenuous opposition. Even the first reading, which by ordinary courtesy and almost invariable custom is accorded as a matter of course to all bills coming down from the House of Lords, was contested, but carried by a majority of 49 votes, the protectionists, faithful in this respect to their party traditions, supporting the government. A long interval was allowed to elapse before anything farther was done in the matter, and the motion for the second reading was not brought forward till the 9th of June. Lord G. Bentinck, speaking not for himself only, but for the protectionist party, of which, if not the leader, he was on this and on many other occasions the mouthpiece, declared that he was an advocate for protection to the British farmer, but not to the Irish murderer; and therefore that, though he regarded the measure as unconstitutional in many of its provisions, he would have supported it if he had not considered himself as released from all obligation to do so by the conduct of the ministers, whom he bitterly reproached for having allowed a measure which they professed to regard as highly necessary, and which, he said, could be justified only on the ground of its imperious necessity, to be delayed for weeks and months together. He pronounced that it was a mockery and an insult both to England and Ireland for ministers to brandish before their eyes a measure never intended to be carried; and that, feeling it to be a mockery and an insult, he would oppose it to the uttermost, and do his best to kick it and the ministry out together. He then launched forth into a vehement invective against Sir R. Peel, denounced the 'forty paid janisaries, and the seventy other members, who, in supporting him, blazoned forth their own shame.' He reproached the premier with having separated himself in 1827 from the government of Mr. Canning, on the ground that he could not support a minister who supported Catholic emancipation, though two years before he had declared to Lord Liverpool (as he had since confessed in Parliament), that the concession could not safely be resisted much longer. 'It is time now,' exclaimed Lord George—'it is time that atonement should be made to the betrayed honour of Parliament and the betrayed constituencies of the empire. It is time that Europe and the world should know that treachery has been committed by the ministers in power, but that they do not represent the honour of England. The agricultural interest may be betrayed and ruined; but let not the world think that England is a partaker in the guilt of those who now sit on the treasury benches. The time has now come when they who love the treason that has recently been committed, though they hate the traitor, should join with those who sit on the protectionist benches in showing that they do not approve the recent conduct of the ministers.'

This philippic, which so faithfully reflected the passions by which at the moment the minds of the protectionists were agitated, produced a profound impression on the House. They who viewed the conduct of Sir R. Peel in its true light were indignant at what they regarded as the injustice of the attacks made on him. The protectionists, on the other hand, who considered that they had been betrayed by one in whom they had put confidence, applauded to the echo. Mr. Sidney Herbert replied on the part of the government to the invectives of the champion of the protectionists. He charged Lord George himself with being responsible for the delay that had occurred in carrying forward the bill. He reminded the House that the noble lord had firmly declared, that if the House delayed for a single day to press that bill forward, the blood of every man that was murdered in Ireland would be on the heads of ministers and of those who supported them; and he asked, ' On whose head will it be now ? ' Lord J. Russell announced and justified his intention to vote against the second reading. Sir R. Inglis, on the other hand, and Mr. Spooner, with that calm and high-principled consistency and absence of party spirit which distinguished their legislative career, declared, that though members of the party on behalf of which Lord George Bentick had spoken, they should vote in favour of a bill which they believed to be imperatively required under the circumstances in which Ireland was then placed. The charges that had been made by Lord G. Bentinck in the early part of the debate were reiterated and reinforced by Mr. Disraeli towards the close of it, and were ably answered by Sir R. Peel. A few calm words from Mr. Cobden, announcing that he would vote with the protectionists, but that he entirely disapproved of, and separated himself from, all participation in the charges they made against Sir R. Peel, closed the debate on the evening of the 26th of June. On the division the numbers were—

| | |
|---|---|
| For the second reading . . . . . . . | 219 |
| Against . . . . . . . . . | 292 |
| Majority against the government . . . | 73 |

Thus, five years after the vote of want of confidence which in 1841 had overthrown the Whig government and brought Sir R. Peel into power, another vote was given which necessarily involved the overthrow of his government. There can be no doubt that he must have been rejoiced to be released from the situation he occupied. The labours he had undergone, the bitter reproaches with which he had been loaded by his former supporters, had told on his constitution. His eye had lost its brightness, and his step its accustomed firmness; a ring of melancholy was distinguishable in the tones of his voice. He was weary of the strife; his feeling of personal dignity was cruelly hurt by the invectives that were heaped on him. Of the emoluments of office he had always been independent and careless. In fact, the expenditure that his office caused him probably exceeded the amount of his salary. He was conscious too of having rendered to his country a great service; and he knew that the enthusiastic cheers with which he was greeted as he quitted the House of Commons after his defeat would find an echo in the hearts of the great majority of his countrymen in every part of the empire. Above all, he was a man whose tastes and character led him to find his chief happiness in the bosom of his family, and he rejoiced in an event which enabled him to enjoy these private and domestic joys, of which the all-engrossing duties of his office had to a great extent deprived him. He was fortunate in the opportuneness of his political demise. On the very evening of his defeat the corn bill passed the House of Lords. About the same time he received the gratifying intelligence that the Oregon dispute with the United States of America had been satisfactorily settled. It now only remained to announce formally to the two Houses the resignation which, as a matter of course, must follow such a defeat as the government had undergone. This announcement was made on the 29th of June, three days after the rejection of the bill for the repression of crime in Ireland. The Duke of Wellington in the House of Lords, and Sir R. Peel in the House of Commons, stated that the resignation of the cabinet had been accepted by the Queen, and that Lord J. Russell had been commanded by her Majesty to form a new administration. The Duke of Wellington confined himself to a simple statement of the fact of the retirement from office of himself and his colleagues in the ministry, and with proposing that the lords should continue to sit, but only for the transaction of pressing and necessary business, until the new cabinet had entered upon its duties. Sir R. Peel, on the other hand, spoke at some length in abdicating his position not only as prime minister, but as the leader of a great party. In doing so, he briefly reviewed the important questions which he had been called on to deal with. He congratulated himself and the House on the results he had been enabled to achieve, and thanked those who had so strongly opposed him for having loyally accepted the decision of Parliament on measures which they were fully entitled to censure and combat; explained his reasons for not having recourse to a dissolution of Parliament; and gave a detailed account of the settlement of the Oregon affair, warmly praising the manner in which the negotiations on our side had been conducted by Lord Aberdeen, and on the other hand by the government of the United States. He dwelt with regret on the loss of the confidence of honourable men, whose support he had previously enjoyed, and declared that his government had been actuated by no other motive than a desire to promote the interests of the country by passing a measure which they felt must necessarily draw after it the fall of the government; an event which was perhaps not to be regretted, but rather regarded as a just chastisement of the mistake they had committed in supporting, or appearing to support, principles they were now compelled to abandon. Of the punishment he did not complain. It was infinitely better to lose power than to keep it without a complete certainty of enjoying the confidence of the House. He stated, that whatever merit might attach to the measures he had introduced, did not belong to him, but ought to be attached to the name of the man whose pure motives, indefatigable energy, unpretending and unadorned eloquence, had forced them all to listen to him—the name of RICHARD COBDEN.

He thus concluded his address: 'In quitting power I shall leave behind a name severely blamed, I fear, by many men, who, without any personal interest, but only with a view to the public good, will bitterly deplore the rupture of party ties, from a belief that fidelity to party engagements and the maintenance of great parties are powerful and essential means of government; that I shall also be blamed by others, who, without personal interest, adhere to the principle of protection, which they regard as necessary to the prosperity of the country; that I shall leave a name detested by all monopolists, who, from less honourable motives, claim a protection by which they largely profit; but I shall, perhaps, leave a name which will sometimes be pronounced with expressions of good-will by those whose lot in this world is to labour, who in the sweat of their brow eat their daily bread, and who may remember me when they renew their strength by food at once abundant and untaxed, and which will be the better relished because no longer embittered by any feeling of injustice.'

He resumed his seat amidst the loudest applause from all sides of the House, which was again and again repeated. It was a long time before the assembly had sufficiently recovered its ordinary condition to listen to any other speaker. When at length silence was obtained, Lord Palmerston and Mr. Hume successively stood up to express the esteem and admiration which they felt in common with the great majority of those present. The House adjourned to the 3rd of July. When Sir R. Peel left Westminster Hall, leaning on the arm of Sir G. Clerk, member for Stamford, a vast multitude filled the street. Every head was bared, the crowd made way for him, and many accompanied him in respectful silence to the door of his house. There were at that moment two men who occupied a higher place in the esteem and affection of their countrymen than had ever been accorded to any statesmen before them. These two men were ROBERT PEEL and RICHARD COBDEN. If anything could increase the feeling of respect with which the former of these two great men was regarded, it was the announcement that he had refused for himself and his family any title or other public acknowledgment of his great services.

The formation of the new administration, which had been confided to Lord J. Russell, was accomplished before the 3rd of July, the day on which the House of Commons resumed its sittings. The following were the chief members of the new government, and formed the cabinet:—

| | |
|---|---|
| Lord Cottenham | Lord-chancellor. |
| Marquis of Lansdowne | President of the Council. |
| Earl of Minto | Lord Privy-seal. |
| Sir G. Grey | Home Secretary. |
| Viscount Palmerston | Foreign Secretary. |
| Earl Grey | Colonial Secretary. |
| Lord J. Russell | First Lord of the Treasury. |
| Mr. C. Wood | Chancellor of the Exchequer. |
| Lord Campbell | Chancellor of the Duchy of Lancaster. |
| Mr. Macaulay | Paymaster-general. |
| Viscount Morpeth | Woods and Forests. |
| Marquis of Clanricarde | Postmaster-general. |
| Earl of Clarendon | Board of Trade. |
| Sir J. Hobhouse | Board of Control. |
| Lord Auckland | First Lord of the Admiralty. |

As the course which had been followed by Sir R. Peel had completely broken up the conservative party, no regularly organised opposition existed either in Parliament or in the country. The members of the House of Commons who had accepted office under the new administration were reëlected without opposition, and appeared in their places when Parliament reassembled on the 16th of July.

Many questions urgently demanded the attention of the new ministers. Of these the first and the most imperative was that of the sugar duties, which had hitherto been dealt with on protectionist principles, and to which even Sir R. Peel had proposed to extend an exceptional protection, at least for a time, in order to afford the planters an opportunity of effecting under favourable conditions the transition from slavery to free labour, but which the present government were pledged to deal with on free-trade principles. The late ministers before their retirement from office had given notice of a provisional measure to extend the duties, which ought to expire on the 5th of July, to the 5th of August. But the delay caused by the change of ministry had rendered necessary a farther extension of the duties to the 5th of September, and a bill for this purpose was brought in and carried by the new government. On the 20th of July Lord J. Russell brought forward the bill which he and his colleagues had devised for the final settlement of the question. He proposed to make the duties permanent, to reduce the differential duties now in force year by year till the year 1851, when they were to disappear entirely, and all sugars were to come in at the same rate of duty. In order to compensate in some degree the West-Indian proprietors for the loss they would sustain in consequence of the withdrawal of the protection that had hitherto been afforded to them, Lord J. Russell proposed to provide certain encouragements and facilities for the introduction and employment of free negro labourers from Sierra Leone and other parts of Africa, and to reduce the differential duty on West-Indian rum from one shilling and sixpence to one shilling. By these changes he expected that the revenue derived from the sugar duties would be considerably improved, and that even in the present year it would yield an increase of 625,529*l.*, which would at once convert the deficiency into a surplus, and would probably in future years yield a much larger amount, besides conferring on the people of this country the benefit of a larger and cheaper supply. These proposals gave rise to long debates. Sir Robert Peel, though still of opinion that the protection hitherto given to free-grown sugar ought to be continued for a longer period than was proposed in the bill, nevertheless felt it his duty to support the government rather than take the responsibility of giving a vote which might have the effect of throwing it out of office. Lord G. Bentinck, however, was not deterred by this possibility from proposing an amendment to the resolutions brought forward by the government. At the conclusion of the debate, Lord J. Russell distinctly announced that a defeat on this question would draw after it his resignation; and on a division the second reading was carried by a majority of 130. In the House of Lords the government plan was strenuously opposed by Lords Stanley and Brougham and the Bishops of Oxford and London, chiefly on anti-slavery grounds; but notwithstanding this opposition, the second reading was carried by a majority of 18, and the bill afterwards passed.

Meanwhile the distress and crime in Ireland were increasing with frightful rapidity. Fifty-eight districts were proclaimed by the lord-lieutenant to be in a state of distress; and distress was a word that was far from adequately expressing the frightful reality. In the district of Skibereen alone, out of 62,000 inhabitants, 5,000 died in three months, and 15,000 could not tell in the morning where to look for the food required for the day. At Bantry there were forty verdicts of 'died from starvation' given at inquests held at the same time. In some cases the wretched peasants wounded the cattle they met, and sucked their blood to assuage their hunger. Under such circumstances, no minister could escape from the necessity of providing extraordinary means for the repression of the crimes of lawless violence which this state of things engendered, and which fearfully aggravated the calamities of Ireland. Therefore, though the members of the present government had thrown the late government out of office by voting against them on the Irish Arms Bill, they found themselves, now that they were in office, obliged to reproduce that measure. At the same time they earnestly entreated the House not to judge the policy they intended to pursue towards Ireland by this bill. Finding the objection entertained to it very strong, Lord J. Russell agreed to strike out of it three or four of the clauses which he had himself condemned when the measure was brought forward by his predecessors in office; and the bill was ultimately withdrawn in deference to the strong feeling that prevailed against it in the House, and especially among the supporters of the government.

A discovery that tends greatly and extensively to diminish human suffering and preserve human life is not undeserving of the attention of the student of history, and therefore we ought not to pass unnoticed the discovery in this year of the property of sulphuric ether in virtue of which it renders the person inhaling it temporarily insensible to pain, and enables him to undergo terrible surgical operations without enduring the agony that would otherwise attend them. This beneficent discovery was speedily used for the purpose of carrying out operations which would without it have been impossible, and by which many lives have been saved. One instance will serve to show the value and the efficacy of this anæsthetic. The person on whom it was employed was a man of sixty-eight years of age, and was afflicted with stone and with a diseased bladder. The attempts made to sound the bladder occasioned so much pain, owing to the state of irritation that prevailed in it, that lithotrity was out of the question; and lithotomy would have been equally impossible, if the man had not been put under the influence of the new anæsthetic. The catheter was first introduced, and some water injected through it; but not more than two or three ounces could be injected; and this, which was only retained by pressure, was expelled the moment that the staff was introduced, which, owing to the diseased state of the parts, was not effected without difficulty and delay. The bladder was then cut into. The stone was grasped, but it at once crumbled under the forceps of the operator, necessitating repeated re-introductions of that instrument, and the employment of a scoop to remove the crushed calculus matter. After all this had been done, the bladder had to be injected four or five times in order to cleanse it thoroughly. During the whole of this dreadful operation, which under other circumstances could not have been effected, the man remained quite insensible to pain; and when consciousness was to some extent restored, by the administration of brandy and ammonia, he complained of nothing but soreness, which however did not prevent him from remaining in a dreamy and, to use his own words, 'very comfortable state.' He said that he had suffered no pain; that he was aware indeed that something was being done to him, but recollected nothing after the blowing of the horn. This and other similar cases proved that this anæsthetic was not only a means of preventing pain, but also of saving life, by allowing the performance of operations which would otherwise have been altogether impossible. The use of this means of preventing pain was not, however, unattended by danger, as in some cases death was caused by the administration of the sulphuric ether. But the discovery at once turned the attention of chemists and medical men to the important question of anæsthetics; and in the following year the sulphuric ether was to a great extent superseded by the discovery of the similar properties of perchloride of formyle, or chloroform; an agent more efficacious, more easily applied, less disagreeable, and less costly, than the ether; and this seems likely in its turn to be superseded by the more recent discovery of the anæsthetic properties of ether spray.

In the course of this year a 'system of ethics,' to which its author gave the name of Secularism, was widely propagated by Mr. G. J. Holyoake, a London bookseller. We place before the reader the description of the system as given by its founder:

'Secularism is the study of promoting human welfare by material means; measuring human welfare by the utilitarian rule, and making the service of others a duty of life. Secularism relates to the present existence of man, and to action the issues of which can be tested by the experience of this life; having for its object the development of the physical, moral, and intellectual nature of man to the highest perceivable point, as the immediate duty of society; inculcating the practical sufficiency of natural morality apart from Atheism, Theism, or Christianity; engaging its adherents in the promotion of human improvement by material means, and making these agreements the ground of common unity for all who would regulate life by reason, and ennoble it by service. The secular is sacred in its influence on life; for by purity of material conditions the loftiest natures are best sustained, and the lower the most surely elevated. Secularism is a series of principles intended for the guidance of those who find theology indefinite, or inadequate, or deem it unreliable. It replaces theology, which mainly regards life as a sinful necessity, as a scene of tribulation through which we pass to a better world. Secularism rejoices in this life, and regards it as the sphere of those duties which educate men to fitness for any future and better life, should such transpire.'

Secularism is, in fact, the religion of doubt. It does not necessarily clash with other religions; it does not deny the existence of a God, or even the truth of Christianity; but it does not profess to believe in either the one or the other. Nay, most of its advocates have often and strongly assailed both. It differs little, if at all, in substance from the opinions of the free-thinkers of the last century, but it differs widely from them in the manner of its propagation, and the persons by whom it was embraced. The old free-thinkers made few converts, and these chiefly, if not exclusively, among the upper classes; but Secularism was embraced by thousands and tens of thousands of the working classes. The success which attended the attempts made to propagate it was due partly to the fact that great masses of the working classes, especially in the large manufacturing towns, were already lost to Christianity, and had, in many cases, almost unconsciously adopted the ideas which Mr. Holyoake fixed, and shaped into distinct doctrines, but which are, in fact, the views that naturally replace Christianity in the minds of those who have practically renounced it; partly to the zeal, activity, ability, and boldness with which Secularism was propagated and defended; and in no small degree also to the qualities of Mr. Holyoake, who had assiduously cultivated great natural gifts, who delivered his opinions with a calm, quiet, and persuasive earnestness, and had won the favourable attention of the working classes by the enlightened interest he had on many occasions taken in their welfare, and the thorough mastery he displayed of many social problems in the solution of which they were deeply interested. Like many other systems, Secularism made its chief advances at the time of its first propagation, since which it seems to have remained stationary, if it has not actually retrograded.

At the opening of the session of 1847 great changes had taken place in the aspect of the House of Commons. The Whigs of course occupied the ministerial benches. Sir R. Peel appeared as an independent member, giving a general support to ministers, criticising their measures in a friendly spirit, with a view to their improvement. On the right hand of the speaker sat the new opposition, formed under the nominal leadership of Lord G. Bentinck, but chiefly guided by Mr. Disraeli, at once the ablest councillor and the most eloquent exponent of the views of his party, but who acted as his faithful lieutenant.

Parliament assembled on the 19th of January, and on the 25th of that month Lord J. Russell explained at great length the plans proposed by the government for meeting the terrible distress that prevailed in Ireland. Large sums were to be expended in giving employment and wages to the suffering Irish; and a poor-law was brought forward, based on the same general principles as the English law, but having some new features introduced into it, which the experience of the working of the poor-law in England had suggested, or the peculiar circumstances and condition of Ireland rendered necessary. All parties displayed a humane and patriotic eagerness to relieve the sufferings of the Irish. A bill was introduced by Lord G. Bentinck for a grant of 16,000,000*l.*, to be expended in the construction of Irish railways. This gigantic scheme was opposed by the government, and rejected by the House; but the government introduced another bill, by which it was to be empowered to make advances to Irish railway companies; though strongly opposed by Sir R. Peel, Mr. Goulburn, and Sir W. Molesworth, it was read a second time by 175 to 62, and accepted by both Houses. Measures were also adopted for the purpose of facilitating emigration from Ireland to the colonies: and the government proposed to meet the Irish distress by a temporary suspension of the corn-laws, and the navigation-laws, so far as they affected the importation of corn. Before they decided on this course, they had very anxiously considered whether it would not be better at once to abolish these laws, instead of merely suspending them; and had adopted the latter course in order to disarm as much as possible the opposition which the abolition would have excited, and to procure the adoption with the least possible delay of a measure that was urgently required for the relief of the starving Irish. These proposals, which, under other circumstances, would no doubt have encountered a strong and obstinate opposition, were agreed to unanimously; and the bills which embodied them passed rapidly through the legislature, and were speedily brought into operation.

These measures of relief for Ireland were closely followed by the government plan for the modification of the duties on sugar and rum, with a view to compensate in some degree the West-India proprietors for the immediate loss which was likely to follow from the abolition of the differential duties on sugars. The proposal, after some discussion in the Commons, and still more in the Lords, was finally adopted without any change.

The government followed the example which their predecessors had set them, of bringing forward the annual financial statement at an early period of the session. It was made on the 22nd of February by the chancellor of the exchequer, who observed that many years had elapsed since any person holding the office he now filled had been obliged to make so heavy a demand on the exchequer as it would be his duty to make for the services of the ensuing year. The extraordinary expenditure which necessitated this extraordinary demand was caused by the failure of the potato crops, not in this country only, but throughout the west of Europe, and especially in Ireland. But while these unusual demands were made on the treasury, the revenue of the country was higher than it had ever been before. The balances now in the exchequer amounted to more than 9,000,000*l*. The revenue yielded by the customs and excise had greatly exceeded the expectations of Mr. Goulburn. Still it was necessary to proceed with caution, and not to reckon on a continuance of this state of things; because the high price of food on the one hand, and of cotton on the other, would probably bring on a commercial crisis like those of 1825 and 1836; and though it might not be so disastrous as on these two occasions, yet it was necessary to be prepared for it, and not to act as if the present prosperous condition of the revenue was likely to be perpetuated. After going through the various items of the revenue, the chancellor of the exchequer calculated that it would amount for the year to 52,065,000*l*. On the other hand, the estimated expenditure would be augmented by the increase of the navy and the money that must be spent on our naval stations in consequence of the changes made in modern warfare by the employment of steam power, amounting to 51,570,000*l*.; but this, he said, did not include the extraordinary expenditure caused by the famine in Ireland, and which he estimated at the enormous sum of 8,000,000*l*. sterling in addition to a sum of 2,000,000*l*. that had to be advanced, making a total expenditure on Irish distress of 10,000,000*l*. The chancellor of the exchequer was of opinion that the deficiency thus caused could not be made up by any increase of the income and property tax, or by any fresh taxation. It was therefore necessary that he should go into the market as a borrower; and the only question was whether the whole of the 8,000,000*l*. should be raised by loan or only a portion of that sum; and the conclusion at which he arrived was, that the safest and best course was, considering all the circumstances of the case, to borrow the whole of this amount. The surplus he had in hand was 489,000*l*. The interest on the amount which he thought it necessary to borrow, and which he believed he could borrow at $3\frac{1}{2}$ per cent., would be 280,000*l*. After referring to the addition which would be made to his surplus by the amount of 450,000*l*. which he expected to come from China, and various deductions which, on the other hand, he expected would be subtracted from it, he calculated that the surplus would not be large enough to allow him to make any reduction on tea, tobacco, malt, copper, windows, &c. He concluded by congratulating the House, and especially Sir R. Peel, on the success of the financial operations of the previous government. He then moved a formal vote for a grant of 8,000,000*l*. out of the consolidated fund for the relief of Ireland.

This sum was borrowed at 3*l*. 7*s*. 6*d*. per cent. In order to hasten its payment into the treasury, which had been nearly emptied by the demands made on it, the chancellor of the exchequer proposed and carried motions for giving a discount of 5 per cent. to those contributors who should pay their contributions into the Bank of England before the 18th of June, and 4 per cent. to those who should pay them before the 10th of September.

A motion made by Mr. Ricardo on the 9th of February for the appointment of a committee to inquire into the navigation laws, was supported by Mr. M. Gibson and Lord J. Russell on behalf of the government and by Sir R. Peel, and, notwithstanding the opposition of the protectionists, was carried by a majority of 94.

Among the more important bills introduced in the course of this session was one for the shortening of the hours of labour in factories, proposed by Mr. Fielden, member for Oldham, and a very large manufacturer. In asking leave to bring in the bill, he stated that his object was to limit the labour of young people between the ages of thirteen and eighteen to twelve hours a day, allowing two hours out of the twelve for meals; that is, to ten hours of actual work per day for five days in the week, and eight hours on Saturdays. He proposed to carry out this alteration by restricting the hours of actual labour to sixty-three hours in the week until the 1st of May, 1848, and after that date to fifty-eight hours in the week; and he farther proposed that the same restriction should apply to females above eighteen years of age.

Mr. Fielden, in bringing forward this proposition, argued that the time of working in factories was too long, had been very mischievous, and if persevered in would produce great national evils. He asserted that the people employed in factories wished for it, and had petitioned the legislature to concede it to them; he pointed to the fact that ministers of religion, medical practitioners, and persons of all classes who had opportunities of observing the present system, deprecated it as destructive of the moral and physical condition of a vast and most important class of the community; and he affirmed that the question involved the very existence of thousands, who, as he feared, were sacrificed annually for the want of these due and sufficient regulations, without which the late Sir R. Peel had asserted that our improved machinery would become our bitterest curse.

In support of these assertions Mr. Fielden read the following quotations from the quarterly return of the registrar-general for September, 1846: 'The population of the extra-metropolitan districts of Surrey was, in 1841, 187,868, and the population of the town of Manchester was 163,856; yet in Manchester, with this lower population, the deaths registered in seven years (1838-1844) were 39,922, and those in Surrey only 23,777.' It is added, 'the population of Surrey exceeded that of Manchester, yet in seven years 16,000 persons died in Manchester over and above the deaths in Surrey, the mortality in which, from the poverty of the labourer and the slighter degrees of the influences so fatal in Manchester, is higher than it should be. There were 23,523 children under five years of age in Surrey, and the deaths of the children of that age were 7,364; the children in Manchester were 21,152, the deaths 10,726. In the seven years 13,362 children in Manchester alone fell a sacrifice to known causes, which, it is believed, may be removed to a great extent; and the victims in Liverpool were not less numerous. . . . The returns of the past quarter prove that nothing effectual has been done to put a stop to the disease, suffering, and death, by which so many thousands perish. The improvements, chiefly of a showy, superficial, outside character, have not reached the homes and habits of the people. The house and children of a labouring man can only be kept clean and healthy by the assiduous labour of a well-trained industrious wife, as any one who has paid the least attention to the subject is aware. This is overlooked in Lancashire, where the woman is often engaged in labour from home. The consequence is, that thousands, not only of the children, but of the men and women themselves, perish of the diseases formerly so fatal, for the same reasons, in barracks, camps, gaols, and ships.'

Other extracts from the same document, also read by Mr. Fielden, showed that while the mother was working in the factory, the children suffered from every kind of neglect, and were drenched with opiates which undermined their health. He farther contended that the measure was not opposed to the principles of political economy rightly understood, and asserted that the feeling of the working classes in favour of it, so far from having been weakened, as Mr. Cobden and others had predicted it would be when the question was last discussed, was, on the contrary, strengthened and confirmed. The motion was seconded by Mr. Ferrand, whose advocacy of it was not calculated to diminish the jealousy with which the manufacturers generally regarded the proposed legislative interferences.

The government decided to make this bill an open question. Lord J. Russell observed, in the course of the debate on the second reading, that the propriety of parliamentary interference had already been decided, for Parliament had interfered. It was, therefore, now only a question of the degree and extent to which Parliament should carry its interference. Mr. Roebuck and others contended that the shortening of the duration of the hours of labour must be attended by a diminution of wages; but it was at once replied, that the operatives were quite ready to run that risk in order to obtain the desired relaxation. Eventually the bill was read a second time by a majority of 195 to 87. When it came into committee, Mr. Bickham Escott attempted to defeat it by moving that the house should go into committee that day six months, thus renewing the discussion which had already taken place on the second reading. Mr. Brotherton, the member for Salford, carried the sympathies of almost every member of the house with him, when, in simple but forcible language, he described the weariness of toil he had endured when a boy working in a factory, and the resolution he then formed, and to which he still adhered, to endeavour to obtain shorter time for the boys who should come after him. Sir J. Graham urged that the question was not whether women should be forced to work twelve hours a day, but whether industrious men should be restrained from working twelve hours a day if they desired to do so.

Sir Robert Peel argued against the bill on the ground that it was not for the interest of the working classes themselves that the restrictions it proposed should be adopted.

'If,' he said, 'you could convince me that the present measure would tend to the moral and intellectual improvement and the social welfare of the great labouring class, I confess I should be almost tempted to make the experiment, because I feel that the point at which we should all strive is to improve the condition and elevate the feelings of that class of society. I tell you it is not safe unless you do it. You are giving these classes intellectual improvement; and unless you remove every law inconsistent with that intelligence, the institutions of the country will be in danger, especially in the event of a calamity occurring in this country such as that which is now desolating Ireland. I tell you that, if your legislation is found to restrict, to diminish, or to interfere with the comforts of the working classes, then their intellectual improvement will become a source of danger. I feel that we should all work at this point; and whether it be by the improvement of the sanitary condition of the people, or in any other way, that we should do all in our power to increase the enjoyments and improve the character of the working classes. I firmly believe, as you do, that the source of the future peace, happiness, and prosperity of this country lies in the improvement, religious as well as moral, of the different classes of society. But it is in thus advocating the elevation of the people that I oppose these restrictions. Sir, I do not deny the advantage of leisure; but I am perfectly convinced that the real way to improve the condition of the labourer, and to elevate the character of the working classes of this country, is to give them a command over the necessaries of life.'

Notwithstanding the high authority and forcible arguments of many of those who opposed the bill, its advocates triumphed on a division by 190 to 100. It was a case in which the feelings and sympathies of the house triumphed over the cold principles of political economy, and caused them to listen to the promptings of their hearts rather than to the dictates of their understandings.

Still the progress of the measure was resisted step by step, but it was carried through all its stages unimpaired in its efficiency. The ten-hours provision was sustained in spite of the opinion expressed by Lord J. Russell, and others who, like him, were friendly to the principle of shortening the time of factory labour, that eleven hours would be a preferable arrangement. In the House of Lords the bill was brought forward by Lord Ellesmere, who urged that it was better to have 'a well-fed easy-to-do class of poor, though noisy and turbulent, than the want and squalor often seen in Salford.'

Never, perhaps, did Lord Brougham throw into his opposition to any measure more of that vehemence of voice, gesticulation, and language, which belonged to his ardent temperament, and which he was accustomed to put forth in his denunciation of any measure to which he entertained a strong objection.

'I shall do my endeavour, by divine assistance, to lay before the House such views of this question, in its relation to the real good of the working classes, as to show that the bill is not a measure that merits support. There is no connection between this bill and the doctrines of political economy, excepting that those doctrines are founded on plain common sense and daily experience, and this bill is an outrage on common sense and that experience.

'The amount of cotton, silk, flax, and woollen manufacture now exported is 37,000,000$l$. or 38,000,000$l$. To abridge the time by one-sixth will be to diminish the exports by a proportionate amount, namely 6,000,000$l$. There must also be a proportionate diminution of wages, and a proportionate stoppage of employment and of engines, to the great detriment of the manufacturer. It has been accepted as a fact, that working a mill ten hours a days, that is five days in the week, is just sufficient to pay the expenses of the establishment, the wages of the workmen, and the cost of the goods manufactured. The entire profit made by working a mill is consequently derived in the other two hours, or the sixth day; and the whole of that profit would be completely swept away by this enactment. . . . A year ago this bill was rejected by 297 to 159, being a majority of 138. In May 1846 the majority against the bill dwindled down from 138 to 10. What was the cause of this sudden change? The same cruelty, the same hardships, the same want of instruction, existed in 1844 as in 1846; but it did happen that in the interval the corn-laws had been repealed. In the course of the severe contest that preceded that repeal the landed men were ranged against the cotton and wool men. The repeal was supported chiefly by the cotton men, and the spinners and mill-owners were constantly assailed by the landed aristocracy. The manufacturers having beaten the land on the corn question, the land said, "We will retaliate a little on the subject of mills;" and so the majority came down from 138 to 10. This year there has been a continuation of the same events, and the same conversions; the movement downwards has been accelerated; and the bill now comes up to your lordships backed by a large majority in its favour, though two years only have elapsed, and all the circumstances of the case remain precisely the same—no, I beg pardon, the circumstances are infinitely stronger against the bill than ever they were before. This is a crisis, of all conceivable periods in the history of the country, when a prudent conscientious regard for the safety of the people and the best interests of the country, above all for the best interests of the working people, make it an imperative duty that we should show the utmost reluctance to change our commercial policy. While we are menaced with dangers like these; when the poor-rates of 6,000,000*l.* a year are likely to increase to one-half more; when Ireland is suffering and bleeding from every pore; when we are obliged to send over supplies of food and money to prevent starvation from thinning the land; when the public peace is disturbed, and in one county within the last three days two hundred special constables have been sworn in, and the yeomanry called out, on account of food riots,—this is the time when we are called on, without experience, on speculation, on assertion, on assumption, on fantasy, to pass a measure which must affect every working man in the country in the four great branches of its manufacture.

'Why interfere specially on behalf of the manufacturing operatives? The people in other occupations, in agricultural labour, for instance, actually endure as much fatigue and misery as the factory operative. The peasant grows old before his time, and scarcely ever reaches the natural term of human existence. Why, then, stop at cotton factories? Why not legislate for the peasant, for the brass-filer, and thousands of others who are engaged in the endless variety of other unhealthy employments?'

Lord Brougham concluded by moving that the bill should be read that day six months. In the course of the discussion which ensued, Lord Clarendon thus argued against the proposed reduction of the hours of labour:

'The loss in wages will not be the only loss. The act will reduce the amount of fixed and floating capital, and will affect other trades. There will be less coal consumed, less oil, less tallow, less leather, less flour, less cotton, wool, flax, hemp, silk, indigo, madder, dyes; there will be less shipping, less labour for the shipping; indeed, all classes will suffer from this apparently humane effort to lessen the hours of labour. The leases of factories are framed on the basis that the machinery is to run twelve hours; the leaseholders will suffer proportionately. Foreign competition already presses on this country. Russia imported 15,000,000 pounds of cotton yarn, and, for the first time, last year she imported 55,000 bales of raw cotton.'

When the House divided, there were found to be 53 in favour of the second reading, and 11 against it. The measure then passed without farther obstruction.

A bill for limiting the time of service in the army was introduced into the House of Commons on the 22nd of March, by Mr. Fox Maule, and was warmly supported by the Duke of Wellington, who now filled the office of commander-in-chief. The protectionists generally opposed it; but it was carried with some amendments, introduced into it with the consent of the government.

When the annual educational vote, the amount of which had been gradually raised to 100,000*l*., came before the House of Commons, great dissatisfaction was expressed, because, while Wesleyans and other dissenters were allowed to claim a share of the grant, the Roman Catholics were still excluded from all participation in it by a regulation which directed that the authorised version of the Scriptures should be used in all the schools to which the aid of the government was extended. The regulation was not only condemned by men of all parties, and by none more strongly than by Sir R. Peel, but was chiefly attacked by an amendment, which was moved by Sir W. Molesworth. Lord J. Russell, however, and several of his colleagues gave such full and satisfactory assurances of their anxious desire to admit the Catholics to a share of the vote, and pledged themselves so distinctly to a speedy change of system in regard to it, that Sir W. Molesworth wished to withdraw his amendment, but was prevented from doing so by some of his supporters, who insisted on going to a division on it; when only 22 members voted for it, while 203 supported the government.

A bill was rapidly passed through Parliament towards the end of the session to give effect to the recommendations of the Ecclesiastical Commissioners for the foundation of a bishopric at Manchester. It provided that, in consequence of the addition thus made to the number of bishops, the junior member of the episcopal bench for the time being should not have a seat in the House of Lords. Some efforts were made to resist this innovation; but it was supported by the Archbishop of Canterbury and the Bishop of London, and sustained by a majority in both Houses.

A motion made by Mr. Hume on the annexation of Cracow to the Austrian empire, which he complained of as being an infraction of the treaty of Vienna by Austria, Russia, and Prussia, releasing us, as he contended, from the obligation to pay to Russia 3,947,187*l.* in accordance with the terms of that treaty, was withdrawn, after a long discussion. The health of towns and the encumbered estates bills were also withdrawn on account of the approaching dissolution of Parliament, which prevented members from paying due attention to the measures before the House. Towards the close of the session a review of it was made by Lord Brougham, who severely blamed the government on account of the small number of measures they had succeeded in carrying.

The remodelling of the new poor-law commission, long demanded, often promised, and as often postponed, was at length undertaken in good earnest towards the end of this session, and carried out.

This year witnessed the departure of one whose vices, no less than his virtues, the defects of whose character, no less than its excellent qualities, had contributed to render him greatly powerful both for evil and for good in England, and still more in Ireland. On the 8th of February, Daniel O'Connell addressed the House of Commons for the last time. The question on which he spoke was the destitute persons (Ireland) bill. That buoyant health and vigour, which once forced a hostile and angry senate to listen to unwelcome truths, was now gone for ever; the voice which formerly shook the hall was now sunk almost to a whisper. But the members from all sides of the House gathered round the weary and fainting athlete, and the last words he delivered in the House of Commons formed a not unfitting close to his career there.

'I am afraid,' he said, in the course of this address, 'that the House is not sufficiently aware of the extent of the misery; I do not think that its members are sufficiently impressed with the horrors of the situation of the people of Ireland; I do not think they understand the miseries, the accumulated miseries, under which the people are at present suffering. It has been estimated that 5000 adults and 10,000 children have already perished from famine, and that twenty-five per cent. of the whole population will perish, unless the House will afford effective relief. They will perish of famine and disease, unless the House does something speedy and efficacious; not doled out in small sums, not in private and individual subscriptions, but by some great act of national generosity, calculated on a broad and liberal scale. If this course is not pursued, Parliament is responsible for the loss of twenty-five per cent. of the population of Ireland. I assure the House most solemnly that I am not exaggerating. I can establish all I have said by many and many painful proofs, and the necessary result must be typhus fever, which in fact has broken out, and is desolating whole districts. It leaves alive only one in ten of those whom it attacks.'

It was still hoped that a visit to a warmer climate, and to new and interesting scenes, might restore the enfeebled health of the great Irish agitator, and reinvigorate his shattered constitution. With that object he determined to visit the metropolis of that church of which he had been so loyal and devoted a champion. A reception, such as policy and gratitude alike dictated, was prepared for him at Rome. Already arches of triumph were being erected; already Pius IX., then in the zenith of his fame and popularity, was preparing to testify his affection and esteem for the liberator; when death interposed to prevent Rome from conferring and O'Connell from receiving the honours that were being prepared for him. At Genoa his illness suddenly increased, and soon terminated fatally. His heart was embalmed, and carried on to that great and venerable city towards which he was hastening as fast as his infirmities would permit. The body was conveyed back to Ireland, where, in spite of rivals, in spite of his failing health, in spite of the disappointment of the hopes he had held out to his countrymen, he was regarded with unimpaired affection and veneration to the very hour of his departure. In Dublin the intelligence of the event was posted up at all the public offices immediately after its arrival. Crowds collected round the announcements. In silence each read, and in silence he walked away. The bells of the Roman Catholic chapels throughout the country tolled out the sad and solemn tidings; and masses were everywhere celebrated for the repose of the soul of the illustrious deceased. Every mark of respect for his memory that could be shown was shown. On this side of the Channel the feeling excited by the intelligence was very different. Here his pertinacious demands of 'justice for Ireland' had been listened to almost with derision. His strong zeal for Romanism made him hateful to zealous Protestants. He had been ridiculed as the 'big beggar-man;' he was despised as a blustering demagogue and the mercenary agitator for a repeal which he did not really desire. But though the people of England had been somewhat severe in their estimate of him during his life, they did not forget the services he had rendered to the cause of progress and reform, especially by the part he had taken in forcing forward the great measure of Catholic emancipation. Few of them, however, appreciated at their real value the services he had rendered to his own country, and thus indirectly to ours. But while Englishmen generally were disposed to render less than justice to his memory, foreigners, and especially his co-religionists abroad, were disposed to do more. To them his virtues and his services were immensely magnified, while the defects and blemishes of his character were lost in the distance. We cannot give a better idea of the feelings entertained for him abroad than by quoting a few lines from the eulogium pronounced on his memory by the most enlightened and eloquent preacher that the church of Bossuet, Fénelon, Massillon, and Bourdaloue has produced in this century.

'Honour, glory, and eternal gratitude,' exclaimed Lacordaire, 'to the man who collected in his powerful hand the scattered elements of justice and deliverance, and who, pushing them to their logical conclusions with a vigorous patience which thirty years could not exhaust, at last poured on his country the unhoped-for delight of liberty of conscience, and thus deserved not only the title of Liberator of his country, but the œcumenical title of Liberator of the church. For it is not Ireland only that has profited by the emancipation. Where is the man in the church since the time of Constantine who has at one stroke enfranchised six millions of souls? Recall your remembrances, search through history, from the first and famous edict which granted liberty of conscience to Christians, and see if you can discover an act fit to be compared for the extent of its effects to the act of emancipation. Behold seven million souls free to serve and love God to the end of the world; and every time that this people, going forward in its life and in its liberty, shall carry back the view of the man who shall study the secret of its ways, it will meet the name of O'Connell at the end of its servitude and at the commencement of its regeneration (*renaissance*).'

The body of O'Connell was interred in the cemetery of Glasnevin. It was followed to the grave by a procession of at least 50,000 persons, in which Orangemen and Ribbon men walked side by side, while a far larger number assembled to see the remains of the great agitator borne to their last resting-place. The halt, the maimed, and the blind gathered around the coffin, in the hope that a miraculous virtue would go forth from it to heal their infirmities. At the head of the sorrowing crowd that followed the corpse were the lord chancellor of Ireland, the lord mayor of Dublin, and a crowd of archbishops, bishops, and other dignitaries of the Roman Catholic church.

The protectionists had repeatedly asserted that the league would be continued for the agitation of ulterior objects after the great question for which it professed to agitate exclusively, and from which it derived its name, had been set at rest. The Duke of Richmond, in particular, had declared in his place in the House of Lords, that the league never would be dissolved till it had destroyed the church and every institution of the country. The falsity of these predictions was speedily manifested. On the 25th of June the bill which repealed the duties on corn passed the House of Lords. On the 2d of July, in the same year, the league was dissolved, with the necessary precaution of appointing a committee to call it again into existence in case any serious attempt should be made to reverse the policy of which it had secured the triumph. The good faith of the league was farther manifested by the disposition it made of its remaining funds. On the day of its dissolution 10,000*l*. were voted to Mr. Wilson, its chairman, as an acknowledgment of the great services he had rendered in that capacity, and of the sacrifices of time and attention to his private affairs that he had made. It was well known that Mr. Cobden had lost at least 20,000*l.* through the manner in which his time and attention had been engrossed by the share he had taken in promoting the free-trade cause. Steps were therefore taken not only to reimburse him, but to raise such a sum as would enable him for the future to devote his great abilities to the service of his country.

The year that was marked by the great economical events that have been narrated was also illustrated by the accomplishment of a great scientific feat—the discovery of the planet Neptune. It had some time before been observed that the planet to which the names of Uranus, Herschel, and Georgium Sidus had been given, and which up to this time had been supposed to be the outermost planet of our system, deviated at a certain part of its orbit from the curve in which it previously moved, in a manner that led the German astronomer Bessel to conjecture, and to state in a lecture delivered at Königsberg in 1840, that these perturbations were due to the existence of a planet outside Uranus. A long series of most difficult and laborious calculations were carried on simultaneously by two young astronomers, M. Leverrier of Paris and Mr. Adams of the University of Cambridge; and they both arrived at conclusions nearly identical with regard to the position occupied by the supposed planet. Guided by the information afforded by Leverrier, M. Galle of Berlin succeeded in pointing his telescope on the planet on the night of the 23d of September; and on the 1st of October Professor Challis announced that, proceeding on the calculations that had been communicated to him by Mr. Adams, he had discerned it on the night of the 12th of August. Thus priority of discovery seems to have belonged to the English astronomer, but priority of publication to his French confrère. There can be no doubt that their merits were equal, and that each had conducted his own investigation independently of the other.

# CHAPTER V.

### THE PEOPLE'S CHARTER.

WHILE the body of O'Connell was being conveyed from Genoa to its final resting-place in Ireland, the general election was taking place. The circumstances under which it occurred caused it to be carried on with unprecedented order and tranquillity. There was 'no appeal to the people,' on any great question of national polity. The adoption of free trade had taken away the great bone of contention; and though a more vigorous policy was anticipated from Lord J. Russell than from Lord Melbourne, it was not expected that the present government would undertake any of those great organic changes which were demanded by a considerable portion of the community, and the announcement of which would have roused the partisans of the ministry to greater enthusiasm, and prompted them to make greater exertions. On the other hand, the remnant of the conservative party, which had ranged itself under the leadership of Lord Stanley, Lord G. Bentinck, and Mr. Disraeli, had nothing to hold out to its supporters beyond vague and general professions of attachment to our ancient institutions. Thus, if there was little enthusiasm for the Whigs, there was less for their opponents; so that on the whole the government gained by the election. The city of London sent three liberals, first among whom was the prime minister, and one conservative, who, however, headed his liberal opponent, Sir G. Larpent, by only three votes. The metropolitan boroughs, almost without exception, sent radical representatives to the new Parliament. Bath rejected Roebuck; Edinburgh lost the honour of being represented by Macaulay, and sent a wealthy paper manufacturer to replace the great historian;* Mr. Gladstone's seat for

---

* It ought to be added, in justice to the electors of the Scottish capital, that they reëlected Mr. Macaulay about five years after.

Oxford was strongly but unsuccessfully contested by Mr. Round, a champion of the no-popery party. Though the government could boast that it had a few more nominal supporters in the new Parliament, it was doubtful whether it had gained in real strength by the dissolution, on account of the great number of independent members returned, who, though willing to give the government a general support, were in no way pledged or disposed to go with them if they disapproved of the measures they brought forward.

The new Parliament was summoned to meet on the 18th of November for two reasons. First, because great commercial distress prevailed throughout the United Kingdom to an extent that required the intervention of the legislature; and next, because the murders, robberies, and other outrages perpetrated in Ireland had become so numerous and so atrocious, that the government was compelled to go to Parliament at once for additional repressive powers. The session was opened by commission; and the Queen's speech indicated an intention on the part of the government to bring before the House the question of the navigation laws; a question nearly allied to that of protection, and which might therefore be expected to be decided in accordance with those free-trade principles, that were now completely in the ascendant.

The commercial distress was the most pressing and the most important subject, and chiefly obtained the earliest attention of the House. On the 2d of December the chancellor of the exchequer proposed the appointment of a committee to investigate its causes, and to endeavour to ascertain how far it had been affected by the laws regulating the issue of bank-notes payable on demand. The consideration of this question had been in some degree anticipated in the debates on the address. Nevertheless it was long and eagerly discussed; for though there was no doubt at all as to the reality of the distress, there was much difference of opinion as to the causes to which it was to be attributed, and consequently as to the manner in which it should be dealt with. The motion of the chancellor of the exchequer was ultimately adopted, and another committee for the same object was appointed by the Lords.

This subject having been thus disposed of for the present, the attention of the legislature was next directed to the question of the repression of crime in Ireland, in reference to which the government was placed in a very embarrassing position. Little more than a year had elapsed since they had obtained office by opposing the Arms bill of their predecessors. They had then themselves taken up that bill, and had been obliged to abandon it, on account of the strong objections that were entertained against it by many of their own supporters; and now they found themselves once more compelled to come to Parliament, and to ask it to grant them powers at least as great as those which at their instigation had been refused to their predecessors. Indeed, the state of Ireland was such that no government could possibly abstain from asking for extraordinary powers, or could honourably continue to hold office if those powers were refused. Sir G. Grey, in introducing a measure on the subject, referred to four classes of crimes, the increase of which justified the demand which the government made for extraordinary powers: the number of homicides, which in the six months ending October 1846 was 68, in the six months ending October 1847 was 96; the number of attempts on life by firing at the person, which in six months of 1846 was 55, was in the same six months of 1847, 126; the number of robberies of arms, which was in six months of 1846, 207, in the same six months of 1847 was 530; and the number of firings of dwellings, which in six months of 1846 was 51, was in the same six months of 1847, 116. These facts, however, were far from giving an adequate idea of the increase of those offences in districts which were now particularly infested by crime. The total number of the offences he had just mentioned amounted in the last month to 195 in the whole of Ireland; but the counties of Clare, Limerick, and Tipperary furnished 139 of them. Sir R. Peel, casting aside all personal considerations, avowed that he could not resist the appeal which Sir G. Grey had made to him and to the House in favour of the bill; and as an Irish member had urged that reparation was due to him for having been turned out of office on a coercion bill, he generously replied, 'The best reparation that can be made to the last government will be to assist the present government in passing this law.' This noble conduct, calculated to raise not only the estimation in which Sir R. Peel was deservedly held, but the character of British statesmanship in the eyes of both Englishmen and foreigners, no doubt influenced considerably the result of the division on the question of the introduction of the bill, which was carried by a majority of 213.

The general election had the result of bringing a very important question a stage nearer to its final settlement. One of the members who had been returned with Lord J. Russell for the city of London was Baron Rothschild, a Jew both by extraction and by religion. It was natural, therefore, that a premier whose name was identified with the cause of civil and religious liberty, and who had already exerted himself to obtain emancipation for the Jews, should be stimulated to make a fresh effort now that he was thus specially urged to it by the great constituency which he represented, and which had returned him at the head of the poll. His duty, his interest, and his convictions, all combined to lead him to support in the strongest manner the claim of his colleague to take his seat in the assembly to which the suffrages of the metropolis had sent them both. He accordingly submitted to the House the following resolution: 'That it is expedient to remove all civil disabilities at present affecting her majesty's subjects of the Jewish religion, with the like exceptions as are provided for her majesty's subjects professing the Roman Catholic religion.' This resolution was supported not only by most of the Whig members of the House, but also by three personages whose party connections led men to expect from them an adverse vote, Lord G. Bentinck, Mr. Gladstone, and Mr. Disraeli, the last himself belonging to the proscribed nation, and proud of his lineage. It was adopted by a majority of 67. A bill founded on the resolution was carried through the House of Commons; but, like many succeeding measures having the same object in view, knocked in vain at the door of the House of Lords. On the 20th of December, the special business for which Parliament had been assembled at this unusual season of the year having been transacted, the two Houses adjourned to the 3d of February.

Towards the close of this year two struggles took place in relation to the appointment of bishops, which at the time excited a deep interest, and served to bring into great prominence the unsatisfactory condition of the relation that existed between the church and the state in regard to this matter. In the course of this year two bishoprics were vacant—the newly-constituted see of Manchester and that of Hereford. The persons appointed to fill them were the Rev. J. P. Lee, head master of King Edward's School at Birmingham, and the Rev. Dr. Hampden, regius professor of divinity in the University of Oxford. To both these appointments very strong objections were entertained. Mr. Gutteridge, a surgeon in Birmingham, had openly and distinctly charged Mr. Lee with having been intoxicated while performing divine service, as well as on other occasions. This charge, publicly made, had never been publicly met. When, therefore, the gentleman who was the subject of it was appointed to be the first bishop of Manchester, a general feeling prevailed that the grave accusation thus made against him ought to be investigated. This feeling was strongly entertained and very forcibly urged in several public journals, and representations on the subject were made to the prime minister through the archbishop of Canterbury. He, however, persisted in the appointment, though it is probable from the event that he stipulated that Mr. Lee should, before consecration to the office of bishop, take some steps to vindicate his character from the aspersions that had been cast on it; for, between his election to the see and the consecration, Mr. Lee brought an action against Mr. Gutteridge, which terminated most completely in his favour, Lord Chief-Justice Denman declaring that, so far from being tarnished, his character shone the brighter for the charges that had been brought against him, and at the same time remarking with great severity on the conduct of his accuser in refusing to make an affidavit of his own belief of the truth of the charges which he had brought against the bishop elect. Mr. Gutteridge was subsequently tried for libel at the Warwick assizes, and convicted.

The case of Dr. Hampden, though perhaps involving less important issues, attracted much greater attention, and excited stronger feelings. He had been accused of publishing heretical doctrines; and on his appointment by Lord Melbourne to the office of regius professor of divinity in the University of Oxford, the work which was said to contain them had been censured by a formal vote of the majority of the convocation of the University of Oxford; a body not likely to deal with such charges as had been made against Dr. Hampden in a calm and judicial spirit, and whose censure therefore, in the eyes of dispassionate men, carried with it little weight. However, this decision had been so far respected by the university authorities, acting in concert with several bishops, that Dr. Hampden had been deprived of the privilege which had belonged to his predecessors in the regius professorship of divinity, of granting certificates of attendance at his lectures to students of the sacred profession as a necessary preliminary to their being admitted to holy orders. In spite of these censures, Lord J. Russell advised the crown to appoint Dr. Hampden to the bishopric of Hereford. This recommendation was not unnaturally regarded by the opponents of the designated bishop as an insult to the church. If they regarded his appointment to the regius professorship as highly objectionable, they must of course regard his nomination to the episcopal bench as still more censurable. The consequence was, that a far louder outcry was raised against his appointment than against that of the new bishop of Manchester, though the former was only accused of doctrinal error, while the latter was accused of gross and indecent immorality. The bishop of London, the leading high churchman, and the bishop of Winchester, the leading low churchman, on the episcopal bench, signed a remonstrance to Lord J. Russell, which was also subscribed by several other bishops. Dr. Merryweather, the dean of Hereford, and the head of the chapter by which Dr. Hampden was to be elected, wrote to Lord J. Russell letters, in which he strongly protested against the appointment, and announced that, if it were persisted in, he should disregard all consequences, and give his vote against the election of Dr. Hampden to the bishopric.

These two cases of Dr. Lee and Dr. Hampden were probably the two first in which any opposition had been offered to the nominee of the crown, and they served to show how completely all the precautions that had once existed against an improper appointment had been nullified in practice, and had become a solemn and almost blasphemous farce. The empty form of an election by the dean and chapter is gone through. A *congé d'élire* (permission to elect) is sent down, requiring and commanding the electors, by their faith and allegiance by which they stand bound to her majesty, that they elect such a person as may be devoted to God, &c. This license is, however, accompanied by a recommendation of the nominee of the crown. The members of the chapter then assemble in the choir of the cathedral. There they solemnly invoke the aid of the Holy Spirit to assist them in choosing well. They then proceed to the chapter-house to make the election; but if their choice should fall on any other person than the one recommended to them by the crown, they incur the pains and penalties of præmunire, which involve deprivation of their benefices, confiscation of their property, imprisonment for life or during pleasure, being put out of the pale of the law, and any proctors or lawyers who may defend them are liable to similar penalties. Such were the stringent regulations with which Henry VIII. had intrenched and defended his prerogative, and to which general attention was now drawn in consequence of the two appointments to which we have referred. In the case of Dr. Lee the election was carried out without opposition; but in that of Dr. Hampden the dean fulfilled his threat of giving his vote against the election; but as he was only supported by one other member of the chapter, he neither prevented the election from taking place, nor incurred the penalties which would have attended a successful opposition to it. Still, however, another farce remained to be gone through,—the confirmation of the election of the two bishops elect. This takes place for the northern province in the church of St. James's and for the province of Canterbury in Bow church. In both cases objections were offered; but in that of Dr. Hampden they were made with a great array of lawyers, who had been retained by the opponents of the bishop elect. The judge took his place, opponents were called on to appear, proclamation was made that their objections would be heard, and that if they should withhold them, they would be regarded as 'contumacious.' The opponents accordingly came forward, and were told that they were contumacious for making the objections, and that the court would incur the penalties of præmunire unless it proceeded to confirm the nomination without regard to the objections that had been urged. After this opposers were once more called on to appear, and pronounced to be contumacious because they did not appear. Thus a legal mockery was added to an ecclesiastical mockery. In the case of Dr. Hampden an appeal was made to the court of Queen's Bench, but without success.

Parliament resumed its sittings on the 3rd of February, 1848, the day to which it had been adjourned over the Christmas vacation. The first question that occupied the attention of the House of Commons on the resumption of its sittings was that of the condition of our West-India sugar-producing colonies, in which great distress prevailed. This distress the protectionists naturally attributed to the gradual removal of the protection which had been afforded to those colonies, and Lord G. Bentinck moved for and obtained the appointment of a select committee to inquire into their present condition and prospects. The next attempt to afford them relief came from the ministerial side of the House. The chancellor of the exchequer proposed a loan of 200,000*l.*, subsequently reduced to 170,000*l.*, to be employed in promoting the immigration of free labourers into the colonies. The debate on this motion gave rise to a violent explosion of angry personalities, Lord G. Bentinck accusing Mr. Hawes, the under colonial secretary, of having suppressed an important despatch, in order to keep the House and the public in the dark with regard to the real condition of the colonies. This insinuation was repelled by Mr. Hawes with great warmth; and Lord J. Russell, who followed him, expressed himself still more indignantly.

'In general,' said the noble lord, 'with regard to these matters, it is quite evident that these mean frauds, these extremely disgraceful tricks, which the noble lord imputes to my noble friend, are not the faults and the characteristics of men high in office in this country. They are the characteristics of men who are engaged in pursuits which the noble lord long followed. (*Loud cries of* " Oh, Oh ! " *and great uproar.*) Some time ago the noble lord very greatly distinguished himself by detecting a fraud of this nature (*loud cheers and counter cheers*) with respect to the name and age of a horse, a transaction in which he showed very great quickness of apprehension.' (*Great confusion.*)

Lord J. Russell proceeded in a similar strain and with like interruptions for some time longer. Then Mr. Disraeli rose to avenge his noble friend, and no one could render that service with greater force and effect. He said:

'Sir, charges of this nature are not to be disposed of by appeals to high station and pedigree. Lord George Bentinck's indefatigable spirit of investigation and courage are not to be cowed by any bravo, whatever his position, nor to be bullied either in the ring or on the treasury bench. In the matter of the horse, Lord George has been thanked by a meeting at Newmarket, the chairman of which meeting was the Duke of Bedford. This is not the first time that despatches have been treated unsatisfactorily by an administration. The House may remember the suppression of the despatches of Sir Alexander Burnes.'

Strong personalities were bandied backwards and forwards, until at length Mr. Hawes indulged in language which drew on him the rebuke of the speaker, which put an end for the present to the dispute. On a division, the votes were—

| | |
|---|---|
| For the government proposal . . . . . . . . | 260 |
| Against it . . . . . . . . . . | 245 |
| Majority for the government . . . . . | 15 |

This division showed pretty plainly, what indeed was already well known to be the case, that the government was far from commanding such a majority as would enable it to carry in their integrity the measures it deemed to be necessary. This division, however, decided the question in favour of ministers; but the discussion was still carried on at considerable length in both Houses.

Following the good example of their predecessors in office, ministers brought their financial statement before the House at the earliest possible period. But here the resemblance ended. They did not exhibit that skill and steadiness in dealing with financial questions, that complete mastery over all the details of taxation, which inspired such confidence in the guidance of Sir R. Peel. Their difficulties and embarrassments were no doubt great, and they had increased them not a little by lending too ready an ear to the outcry that had been raised for the increase of the army and navy through suspicion of the designs of France against our country. As this was the first of the invasion-panic budgets, it is desirable that we should place before our readers the grounds on which it was defended by the prime minister. After going through the estimates of the revenue and expenditure of the country, and showing that the expenditure would probably exceed the income by about 2,141,209*l.*, he remarked that this deficiency must be met either by increased taxation or by great reductions in the army and navy. In reference to the latter alternative he thus expressed his opinions and those of his colleagues:

'No one can dispute that this country *may* be involved in a war. Since the peace of 1815, disputes between this country, the United States, Russia, and France have only been allayed by great forbearance on both sides. However tranquil, therefore, the atmosphere may be at present, there may at any time be an unforeseen storm; and I am the more convinced of that circumstance, when I recollect that Mr. Pitt in 1792 anticipated a long continuance of peace. It must be borne in mind that in the last three hundred years the elements on various occasions have been our friends, and expeditions against us, prepared with most zealous care, have been defeated only by adverse winds. The science and skill of late years have enabled seamen to traverse the sea against winds and tides, and that circumstance may induce hostile powers to consider this country more open to invasion. Under a king who is a sincere lover of peace, since 1833 the active preparations and increase of the naval force of France have been very extensive. The number of seamen has been increased from 18,000 to 20,000; vessels at sea, from 153 to 216; steamers, from 66 to 120; the expenditure from 2,280,000*l.* to 3,902,000*l.* The whole expense of the French army and navy in 1847 was 23,817,000*l.* Preparations have not been wanting on our side. Since 1835 we have increased the number of our seamen from 26,000 to 43,000 men; of our soldiers from 100,991 to 138,769; and our ordnance corps from 8,252 to 14,294, making an increase of 60,321 on our military force in the whole. Besides, the late government has organised 15,000 soldiers of the line as pensioners. The present government has formed a force of 9,800 men out of the workmen in the dockyards, who as infantry and artillery are in possession of and capable of working 1,080 guns. A plan has also been carried into effect for drilling and organising the coastguard, and for keeping a supplemental force ready in case the services of the coastguard should be wanted elsewhere, which would supply a force of 6,000 men. The charge of the army, navy, and ordnance has increased from 11,730,073*l.* in 1835 to 17,340,096*l.* in 1847. I propose to make an increase of 164,000*l.* on the naval estimates; but of that sum only 70,000*l.* will go to the real increase of our naval expenditure, 94,000*l.* being for expenditure not naval. The deficiencies of the defences of our ports and dockyards attracted the attention of the late government, which gave orders for their examination. That subject had been too long neglected; but since the year 1844, 262,000*l.* has been expended on works for the defence of Portsmouth, Plymouth, Devonport, Pembroke, Sheerness, and the Thames; and they are now, in the opinion of the Duke of Wellington and the master of the ordnance, in a satisfactory state. Ministers do not intend to increase the force of the army by a single man, yet the number of soldiers in the United Kingdom will be augmented by the return this year of 5,000 men, if not more, from India; so that in the course of the summer I expect we shall have a force of 60,000 men in the British Isles. As compared with the year 1835, this will be an increase of 20,000 men. The whole increase on the military, naval, and ordnance estimates will be 358,000*l.*; but, in addition to this, I propose to take a vote of 150,000*l.*, to lay the foundation of a militia force for the defence of the country in case of an invasion; a contingency which, however remote, it is necessary to take into our calculations.'

Lord J. Russell stated that the expenditure he contemplated for the year ending 1849 was 54,596,500*l.* To meet the deficiency which this expenditure would occasion, he proposed, amidst loud murmurs, to continue the income tax, which would expire in April next, for five years longer, and increase its amount from 7*d.* to 1*s.* in the pound. He proposed to remit the highly-injurious duties imposed in 1842 on copper ore, and which produced 41,000*l.*; and he calculated that he would then have a surplus of income over expenditure amounting to 113,000*l.* In another year he hoped that the surplus would be largely increased by the cessation of the war which was now being carried on against the Caffres, and that then he should be enabled to remit some of those duties which pressed most heavily on the elastic springs of industry.

Never, perhaps, did any budget call forth a greater amount of adverse criticism. The free-trade party, represented by Messrs. Hume, Cobden, and Bright, regarded it with dismay, and loudly demanded that our expenditure should be brought down to the level of our income, instead of our income being brought up to the level of so extravagant an expenditure by increased taxation at a time when the distressed state of our commerce and manufactures seemed to require considerable reductions. The protectionists exulted over the testimony to the correctness of their opinions and predictions of the disastrous results of free trade which seemed to be afforded by the statement of the prime minister. Independent members reminded Lord J. Russell of his speeches against the income tax when brought forward by Sir R. Peel, and demanded that now, when it was reimposed, it should at least be more justly distributed. One or two only faintly praised the ministerial proposal.

But if the dissatisfaction which the proposal to increase the income tax excited in the House was great, it was still greater in the country. In vain did the chancellor of the exchequer attempt to mollify public feeling by farther explanations. Petitions and remonstrances against the government plan poured in from all sides, and it soon became evident that the country would not endure the proposed increase of the income tax, and that neither this nor any other administration could carry it. Under these circumstances, ministers wisely resolved to yield without delay; and on the 28th of February the chancellor of the exchequer announced that the government had resolved to abandon their intention of proposing an increase of the income tax, and submitted to the House the changes in the budget which this concession rendered necessary.

A long debate took place on the question raised by an amendment proposed by Mr. Hume, that the income tax should be renewed for a single year. The discussion turned not only on the serious question at issue, but on the income tax, and the financial system introduced by Sir R. Peel, and the relative merits of direct and indirect taxation. Of course the government resisted Mr. Hume's proposal, and urged as an additional cause for maintaining the credit of the country at this moment, the revolution which had taken place in France, and had compelled King Louis Philippe to seek a refuge on our shores. In the course of the debate Sir R. Peel announced his intention to support ministers on this question, and declared his unabated confidence in the system of finance which the income tax had enabled him to inaugurate, and which the present ministers were carrying out to the best of their ability under the great difficulties in which they were placed by the present distress. Their commercial and financial policy was also ably vindicated by Messrs. Wilson and Gladstone, and was assailed by Lord G. Bentinck and Mr. Disraeli. Mr. Cobden put the argument for direct taxation with that admirable clearness and perspicuity that were characteristics of his mind. 'While the House frets over its sevenpence in the pound, the poor are paying twice that number of shillings in the pound on the great staples of their consumption. For every 20s. the working classes expend on tea, they pay 10s. of duty; for every 20s. they expend on sugar, they pay 6s. of duty; for every 20s. they expend on coffee, they pay 8s. duty; on soap, 5s.; on beer, 4s.; on tobacco, 16s.; on spirits, 14s. When you bear in mind that the working classes expend much more income on these articles than people of our class, you cannot but see that this amounts to an income tax not of 7d. per pound, but sometimes of 12s., 15s., or 16s. in the pound; while men of some thousands a year expend a vast deal more in buying furniture, horses, carriages, books, and other things which pay comparatively little tax. And hence it is that in this country, where we derive so much revenue from articles which enter largely into the consumption of the working classes, you find, when trade is bad in Lancashire or throughout the country, the chancellor of the exchequer reminding you that the state of the revenue has been affected by the state of trade. Both for the sake of trade, and for the sake of the people, you must diminish your expenditure, or increase the amount of your direct taxation.'

Mr. Cobden next proceeded to deal in the same perspicuous manner with the subject of the inequalities of the income tax, and the necessity that existed for their removal.

'Make your tax *just*,' he exclaimed, 'in order that it may be permanent. It is ridiculous to deny the broad distinction that exists between incomes derived from trades and professions, and those drawn from land. Take the case of a tradesman with 10,000*l.* of capital; he gets 500*l.* a year interest, and 500*l.* more for his skill and industry. Is this man's 1,000*l.* a year to be mulcted in the same amount with 1,000*l.* a year derived from a real property capital of 25,000*l.*? So with the cases of professional men, who literally live by the waste of their brains. The plain fair dealing of the country revolts at an equal levy on such different sorts of property. Professional men, and men in business, put in motion the wheels of the social system. It is their industry and enterprise that mainly give to realised property the value that it bears; to them therefore the state first owes sympathy and support. Every leading member has admitted the injustice of the tax, yet government has neither taken any means, nor shown any disposition, to apply a remedy. It is not too late even now to have an inquiry into this matter. Appoint a committee, and let there be upon it—what there is not in the cabinet—an equal proportion of merchants, manufacturers, professional men, and landed proprietors or other possessors of realised property; and I engage that in less time than it would take to fix the tariff of a railway company, to determine whether coal should pay a penny a ton, lime threehalfpence, and corn twopence, they will find a mode of adjusting the tax on equitable principles. But no attempt of that kind has been made, and no promise is held out that such an attempt will be made. It is the dry pedantic adhesion to the letter of the law, which has roused the indignation of the country. If a distinction were made between permanent and precarious incomes, if a gradation of duty were established, I undertake to say that you would have no remonstrance from the great manufacturing seats of the north.'

Lord J. Russell admitted the inequality of the tax, but declared that it was impossible to remedy it; and maintained that the attempt to do so would render the tax far less productive and far more vexatious than it had ever been before. With regard to the proposal that the estimates should be reduced, he said that they had been framed at a time when everything appeared tranquil, but even then he felt the necessity of being prepared for any emergency that might arise; and this was much more necessary now after the extraordinary events that had occurred on the Continent. Mr. Hume's amendment was supported by 138 and opposed by 363 members.

Then came the discussion of the proposal for the extension of the income tax to the sister country. It appeared that the great majority of the Irish members had voted for the imposition of an income tax on England, and it was urged that the English members might fairly return the favour. The proposal was, however, resisted by the government on the ground of the distress still prevailing in Ireland, and was negatived by 218 to 138.

We have seen that the government had proposed to meet an anticipated deficiency in the revenue amounting to about 3,000,000*l.* by an increase in the income tax, which, however, the force of public opinion had compelled them reluctantly to abandon. It was therefore necessary that they should resort to some other means of equalising the revenue of the country with its expenditure. Something was hoped for from the labours of a select committee which had been appointed to consider what reductions could be made in the army, navy, and ordnance estimates; but as it was evident that their recommendations were not likely to produce a saving which would be equal, or nearly equal, to the amount of the deficiency, it was anticipated that ministers would bring forward some scheme of taxation calculated to fill up the void in the revenue. The chancellor of the exchequer, however, steadily resisted all efforts that were made to induce him to state the intentions of the government till the report of the select committee had enabled them to measure the amount of the deficiency which they would have to deal with; and it was not until the 25th of August that the amended financial statement of the government was brought forward by the chancellor of the exchequer in a committee of the whole House. He then announced that, on the one hand, by reductions to the amount of 828,000*l.* that had been effected in the military, naval, and miscellaneous expenditure, and, on the other, by an increase that had taken place in various items of the ordinary revenue amounting to not less than 340,000*l.* above what Lord J. Russell had calculated on, to which he added 80,000*l.*, the last remnant of the China money, the deficiency of the revenue that had to be made up had been reduced to 292,305*l.*, and he expressed a confident expectation that at the end of the financial year this deficiency would have disappeared. But the extraordinary expenses that had been incurred in the Caffre war and in other ways had raised the amount of the total deficiency to be provided for to 2,500,000*l*. The demands on the consolidated fund were already so great, that it was undesirable to supply this deficiency from that source, and he therefore proposed to borrow the 2,000,000*l*. needed to supply the deficit. Lord G. Bentinck suggested that the difficulty should be met by a reimposition of the customs duties taken off, as he maintained, to the very serious injury of the revenue, and by the removal of which the foreigner was the only gainer; in fact, by a return to the policy which Parliament had so deliberately discarded. Of course, this suggestion was not entertained by the government.

The speech from the throne had indicated that it was the intention of ministers to bring forward in the course of this session a bill for the alteration of the navigation laws, and the measure that had thus been announced was looked forward to by both parties as the great battle-field of the session. It was not, however, introduced till the 15th of May, when it was discussed at great length; but as it was ultimately withdrawn, in order to be reintroduced in the following session, we reserve our account of the arguments that were employed for and against the measure, for the period when Parliament was finally called upon to pronounce its decision on the question.

While these events were occurring a revolution had been effected in Paris, which had swept away the throne of Louis Philippe, and substituted for it a provisional government. The best of all republics, as Lafayette had denominated the rule of the citizen king, when he was called to assume the chief power in France, had made way for a really republican government. This revolution had the effect almost everywhere of raising the hopes and expectations of those who desired to witness the overthrow of the existing governments, but nowhere more so than in Ireland, where the chronic discontent had been increased by suffering, and by the operation of those repressive laws to which the English government and legislature had been compelled to resort. The place which had been occupied by Mr. O'Connell was filled by Mr. Smith O'Brien, who led the discontented party with more violence, but far less tact, ability, and caution. He avowedly aimed, not only at a repeal of the legislative union between the two kingdoms, but an entire separation of them; and it was quite evident that the great body of his countrymen were prepared to support his projects, and that nothing but a favourable opportunity was wanting to bring on a civil war, in which, though the mother country was sure to triumph in the end, much blood would be shed, and multitudes of the loyal people of Ireland would probably be massacred. It was necessary that steps should be taken to prevent these disastrous consequences; and the government, acting under the advice of the lord lieutenant of Ireland, determined to propose to Parliament the suspension of the habeas-corpus act in that country. The serious character of the emergency silenced for the moment the strife of party. Lord J. Russell introduced the proposed measure to an assembly evidently prepared to give it a very favourable reception. Sir R. Peel generously supported it, without indulging in one syllable of reproach against ministers for the opposition they made to the repressive measures he had proposed, and the rejection of which, through their assistance, had brought about the dissolution of his administration. Mr. Disraeli, and the protectionists generally, vied with him in giving their warm support to the measure of the government. Only Mr. Feargus O'Connor, Mr. Sharman Crawford, and a few Irish members objected. Even Sir Lucius O'Brien, the brother of Mr. Smith O'Brien, but a man of very different political opinions, announced that he had felt it his duty to support the proposition of the government. The bill was passed without a division, and the standing orders in both Houses were suspended in order that it might be passed more rapidly. It was generally felt—felt even by the majority of the repealers in the House of Commons—that Ireland was in danger of being pushed into a wicked and disastrous insurrection by men, who, if against all human probability they should achieve a momentary success, were incapable of constituting a government, and were certain to bring on their unhappy country evils compared with which even the sufferings she was now enduring might well be regarded as light and unimportant.

But while most of the Irish members readily acquiesced in the expediency of this precautionary measure, they demanded that it should be accompanied or closely followed by remedial measures really calculated to remove the sufferings under which their country laboured. These demands were strongly put forward by Mr. Sharman Crawford, who proposed a resolution to the effect that it was the duty of Parliament, in the present disturbed condition of Ireland, to bring forward such measures 'as may be necessary to improve the condition, redress the grievances, and establish the just rights of the Irish people.' At the same time he announced that if this motion should be carried, he intended to follow it up by proposing the resolution moved by Lord J. Russell in 1844, namely, that the whole subject of Irish grievances should be referred to a committee of the whole House. The reply of Lord J. Russell to these proposals was a cry of regretful helplessness. He deplored the rejection of an eviction of tenants bill by the House of Lords, pleaded for gradual improvements, deprecated hasty legislation, gave his opinion that the Protestants of Ireland had a right to insist on the maintenance of an established church, and dilated on the obstacles that stood in the way of the establishment of the Roman Catholic church in Ireland. Mr. Osborne reminded the House that on that very day, forty-five years ago, the House was engaged in suspending the habeas-corpus act; and he bitterly complained that nothing, absolutely nothing, had been done in the interval for the pacification of Ireland.* Mr. Crawford's motion was rejected by a majority of 70.

One remedial measure, however, was adopted in the course of this session. One cause of the distress under which Ireland almost continually laboured, and under which at this time she was suffering most intensely, was that many estates were so loaded with mortgages and other charges, that the proprietors received little or nothing from them, and were destitute of the means, even if they had the will, of spending money on the improvement of their property. The government therefore brought in a

---

* This was hardly the fact. The Catholic-emancipation bill, and a great many other acts, had been carried for the benefit of Ireland, which, though they had not altogether attained the desired end, had removed many of the grievances of which Irishmen generally and justly complained.

bill called the 'encumbered-estates bill,' intended to facilitate the sale of properties placed in such circumstances; in other words, to facilitate the transfer of these estates from those who were without capital to those who were able and willing to make such improvements in the land of Ireland as would make it more productive. The bill was introduced in the first instance into the House of Lords, and went through it without any important changes, but was considerably altered in the House of Commons. On its return to the upper House, Lord Stanley moved that the amendments of the Commons should be referred to a select committee; but the majority decided to accept them without farther consideration, and this important bill was adopted.

The French revolution of 1848 had sent through Europe a shock as of a republican earthquake, shaking every throne, and spreading consternation far and wide. In England alone the news of that event produced no commotion, but nevertheless excited much uneasiness. There was, indeed, some ground for alarm. We have seen that Ireland was ready for an outbreak; and in England the Chartists, who were very numerous among the working classes, would have been only too glad of an opportunity of following the example which had been set them by the French nation, by establishing a republic in England, or at all events by carrying out those changes in the constitution which were embodied in the document which was styled the 'People's Charter.' The majority of the English people had confidence in the stability of our institutions, and entertained no fear that the example which had been set by the French people would be followed in England; but they were apprehensive of a very serious outbreak, and feared that much injury might be done to life and property. Before we proceed to relate the extent to which these fears were realised, we must sketch the history of the movement that gave birth to them. The agitation we are now to record is one altogether different from that for the repeal of the corn-laws, but is one which was no less characteristic of our country, and no less deserving of serious attention. The long, patient, though not always wise, and temperate pursuit, chiefly by the poorest of the working classes, of objects which were once scouted by all parties, but have now been to a great extent attained, and that too partly by the help of the party which, when they were first proposed, recoiled from them most strongly, is a spectacle which deserves the serious attention of those who would fully understand the working of a constitution under which every demand that is founded on truth and justice is sure at length to obtain a respectful hearing, and an ultimate triumph.*

Before the introduction of the Reform Bill, a strong and highly popular party advocated universal, or at least household suffrage, vote by ballot, and the shortening of the duration of Parliaments. But these proposals were so distasteful to the king and to Earl Grey, that though strongly urged at the opening of the year 1831, the attempt to bring them forward in connection with that measure was abandoned, and its liberal character reconciled the advocates of these changes to their postponement, and induced them to join in the cry that was raised in favour of ' the bill, the whole bill, and *nothing but the bill;*' and the feeling which this cry expressed continued to prevail for some time after that measure had become law. But though the radical party were satisfied for the moment, they had no intention to allow the ulterior changes, on which they had all along insisted as being the necessary complements of the reform bill, to be indefinitely postponed, or altogether put aside; and therefore, though well aware that they could not effect anything in the legislature, they began to agitate for those changes. They proposed to confer the franchise on every adult man, though they were not yet prepared to adopt the suggestion of Coleridge, and bestow it also on unmarried women. But even if this point should be gained, there were other difficulties to be removed before their principle could have its full realisation. The voter might be bribed, influenced, or intimidated into giving a vote contrary to his conviction, or not voting at all. To meet this difficulty, it was proposed that all votes should be given secretly. The voter should therefore be protected by the ballot. Again, the vote of a man who lived in a town with a popu-

---

\* The substance of the following history of English chartism was published by the author in the *Fortnightly Review* of April 1, 1867. It has since been carefully revised, entirely rewritten, amplified in some parts, abridged in others, and submitted to the correction of some who laboured and suffered in the cause of which it relates the vicissitudes.

lation of more than 300,000 persons had evidently much less influence in the result of a contest than that of a man who inhabited a borough of only 300 or 400 inhabitants. The remedy for this anomaly was to divide the country into electoral districts nearly equal in population. It might happen also that the man in whom the majority of the electors deemed best fitted to represent their views in the House of Commons, might be too poor to bear the cost of an election, or the loss and expense of a residence in London. It was therefore suggested that all members of the lower House should receive a salary for the performance of their legislative duties. Lastly, the member sent to represent a district in the House of Commons might prove recreant to the pledges he had given his constituents, and might totally *mis*represent those who sent him thither. This difficulty it was proposed to meet by making elections annual, so that the unfaithful representative might know that his treachery would be speedily avenged, and the constituency would be able very soon to replace him by another member, who would more truly represent their opinions. Considerations such as these led the members of what was called the extreme radical party to advocate universal or rather manhood suffrage, vote by ballot, equal electoral districts, annual parliaments, and the payment of members of the House of Commons. To the argument that the people were not sufficiently educated to make a wise and proper use of the privileges which the adoption of this plan would bestow on them, it was answered that the people never would be educated until they obtained the power of voting for representatives in Parliament, and that then, and only then, the ruling classes would feel the necessity of giving the people such an education as would lead them to exercise rightly a power they ought to possess, and which they would acquire by force, if it should be much longer withholden.

No sooner was the Reform struggle concluded than these views became prominent, and almost all men hoped or feared, according to the character of their political views, that they would soon be carried out. Several representatives of these opinions were elected members of the first reformed Parliament; but their numbers in that assembly were by no means in proportion to the numbers of those by whom these views were supported in the country. They were, however, advocated by many persons of great intelligence and natural eloquence, and by the *élite* of the working classes, especially in the manufacturing districts. These were the leaders of the movement; while the rank and file was chiefly composed of those who were disappointed in the extravagant expectations they had formed of the benefits which would flow from the Reform Bill, and especially of those whose incurable habits of indolence had been severely but vainly disciplined by the operation of the new poor-law. Out of these heterogeneous elements two classes of Chartists, as we may now begin to call them, were gradually formed: the first composed of the more educated, who hoped to attain their ends by legal and constitutional means; the second, which was prepared to have recourse to insurrection and revolution. The former came afterwards to be styled moral-force Chartists, and the latter were known as physical-force Chartists; and as in every great movement of this kind the most violent language and the strongest measures are sure to be the most popular, the advocates of physical force were the most loudly applauded, and could boast of having at least the most numerous, if not the most intelligent and influential, following.

We have already seen that proposals for the purpose of realising some portions of the Chartist programme had been brought before Parliament, and rejected by majorities so large as to render success hopeless; and we have not thought it necessary to mention how, year after year, various motions were made on the subject, with no other result than that of occupying to very little purpose the attention of the House of Commons. There was, however, one motion of which we deem it necessary to make especial mention on account of its connection with the Chartist agitation.

At the meeting of Parliament in the commencement of the year 1838, the question of the adoption of the ballot and the shortening of the duration of Parliaments, was raised by an amendment to the address on the Queen's speech, proposed by Mr. Duncombe, member for Finsbury, and seconded by Sir W. Molesworth. In the course of the debate on this motion, the following declaration was made by Lord J. Russell:

'The opinion of the majority of the people is, I do believe, against progressive reforms in the representation, of which the effect would be only to introduce endless uncertainty, and incessantly to revive all those agitating circumstances which, it may be recollected, impeded all the operations of commerce in the years 1831 and 1832. And I farther believe that, having gone through the struggles of the Reform Bill, they do not think it would be for their interest to go on adopting fresh changes, to be made in their turn the foundation of still farther alterations, and to end in a plan for universal suffrage. We, as a government, think it right to stand by the declarations of Lord Grey and Lord Althorp; we are not ashamed to be the followers of such men, and by their principles we are contented to abide.'

When the House divided, twenty members voted for Mr. Duncombe's amendment, and this of course settled the question so far as the House of Commons was concerned. But the matter was not allowed to stop there. Six of these members were invited to confer with a deputation of six working men from a society which had been formed a short time before, and had taken the name of the 'Working Men's Association.' The result of this consultation was a document drawn up in the shape of a parliamentary bill, to which was given the title of the 'People's Charter.' It contained the six points already mentioned: 1. universal—or, as it is now more correctly designated, manhood—suffrage; 2. annual parliaments; 3. vote by ballot; 4. abolition of the property qualification then required for members of the House of Commons; 5. the payment of members; 6. equal electoral districts. The obvious effect of this plan, if carried, would be to give every man a vote; to make the representative constantly responsible to his constituents; to protect the voter from intimidation or corruption; to give to the inhabitants of each electoral district the freest and most unconstrained choice of a representative by removing all obstacles likely to prevent the object of their choice from accepting the task confided to him; and lastly, to make the votes of all men throughout the kingdom as nearly equipollent as possible. The charter certainly possessed the merit of embodying in a perfect logical and coherent manner the wishes and ideas of the most numerous and extreme portion of the radical party. At the conclusion of the deliberations which had led to its adoption, O'Connell, on behalf of his fellow-members, handed it to the secretary of the Working Men's Association, saying, 'There, Lovett, is your charter. Agitate for it, and never be content with anything less.' The charter was subsequently submitted to a public meeting, by which it was enthusiastically approved.

During the months of August and September 1838 two large and important meetings were held, one at Birmingham, the other in the New Palace-yard, at which the six points we have mentioned were advocated, and much strong language used in reference to them. At the latter of these meetings an incident occurred which at the time attracted much attention. Mr. Vincent, the chief Chartist orator, said in the course of a speech he delivered at it, 'We are kept down by knaves. Lord J. Russell is a knave, Henry Brougham is a knave, Peel is a knave, the Duke of Wellington is a knave.' At this apostrophe Colonel Sir William Napier, who was present, rushed to the front of the hustings, and exclaimed in a most excited manner, 'I contradict that: the Duke of Wellington is no knave. He fought for his country, nobly, bravely, and successfully; and he is no knave.'

Armed with the document which these meetings had sanctioned, the Working Men's Association lost no time in acting on the advice which O'Connell had given to their secretary. The principal agent in this work was Henry Hetherington. He was a man of solid rather than showy abilities, more logical than eloquent, but gifted with indomitable energy, courage, and perseverance. With him were associated Henry Vincent—the Demosthenes of the new movement—Lovett, the secretary of the association, and several other men of considerable natural parts, though generally ill-educated. These men have often been represented as mere mercenary traders in agitation, who aimed at leading the working classes to seek their elevation rather from political changes than from honest labour. Nothing can be more false or unjust than these imputations. That there were among the Chartists men who were actuated by low and sordid motives, there can be no doubt; but the leaders whose names we have mentioned, and most of those who were associated with them, were thoroughly honest enthusiasts, who earnestly at least, if not wisely, advocated the social elevation of the working classes. The spirit which pervaded both the leaders and the great mass of their followers in this agitation was well expressed by the following sentence printed at the bottom of the cards of membership of the association: 'The man who evades his share of useful labour diminishes the public stock of wealth, and throws his own burden on his neighbour.'

The lead in the new agitation, however, speedily devolved on Feargus O'Connor, who became at once the soul and the bane of it. He was originally an Irish barrister, and claimed descent from the ancient kings of Ireland. In 1831 he was employed as an agent to promote the return to the House of Commons of followers of O'Connell. His frame was herculean, his bearing aristocratic and commanding; he was endowed with great natural eloquence, and had an earnest and enthuiastic zeal for the cause, which he served to the very best of his ability with tongue, pen, and fist. His legal knowledge, though not very profound, was of considerable service to a party very destitute of it, and therefore gave him credit for more of it than he really possessed. He quickly became a prominent man, was warmly patronised by O'Connell, to whom he rendered very important services; and in 1833 successfully contested the county of Cork, but lost his seat for want of a qualification. He then quarrelled with O'Connell, and finding his political career in Ireland closed, he threw himself into the Chartist agitation, and speedily took the lead in it. There can be no doubt that he was thoroughly honest, and animated with a hearty desire to benefit the working classes; but he was intensely fond of power and popularity, and could bear no rival near his throne. The consequence was, that the interests of the agitation were often sacrificed to his petty jealousies, and that he alternately praised and abused, caressed and attacked, encouraged and thwarted, almost every man who took a prominent part in the Chartist agitation. Thus though his adhesion to it was the means of imparting to it a certain degree of respectability, and though at first he rendered it valuable services, it cannot be denied that one chief reason of its ultimate and signal failure was, that he sacrificed the cause to his desire to retain the leadership of the movement.

The promulgation of the Charter soon brought under one banner the scattered hosts who were before agitating in a desultory and isolated manner in support of the views of the radical party. That document so happily and exactly embodied the ideas which were floating in the minds of a large portion of the population of this country, that it became a daystar of hope to them, and enlisted the sympathies of thousands. Nothing showed this more clearly than the number of periodicals which the publication of the Charter brought into existence, and the large circulation they enjoyed during the prosperous days of the Chartist agitation. London produced its *Dispatch*, Edinburgh its *True Scotsman*, Newcastle its *Northern Liberator*, Birmingham its *Journal*. To these may be added the *Operative*, edited by Bronterre O'Brien, who afterwards became the rival of O'Connor; the *Charter* and the *Champion*, which represented the opinions of Cobbett. Many other periodicals came into existence afterwards, among which we need only specify the *Chartist Circular*, price one halfpenny, which had a very extended circulation. But they were all far surpassed in popularity, if not in the ability with which they were conducted, by the *Northern Star*, the property and the organ of Feargus O'Connor. It attained to a circulation of 50,000 copies; an enormous number, considering the price at which it was sold and the poverty of most of the Chartists. The feeling in favour of the Charter was farther manifested by the number and enthusiasm of those who attended the public meetings. The vast multitudes that were present at them, the excitement and ardour that attended them, often caused the military to be ordered out when they were held, though their active intervention was rarely needed. It would be an endless and wearysome task to attempt to enumerate these assemblages. It is sufficient to say that they were held in all parts of the kingdom, and often repeatedly in the same town or neighbourhood; sometimes in rooms, sometimes in the open air, sometimes on moors, to which people flocked from considerable distances. We shall have occasion hereafter to speak of some of them which presented peculiar and noteworthy features. This agitation gradually brought out into greater and greater prominence the difference that existed between the moral and physical force parties. These two divisions of the

Chartist body were soon openly at variance, and, as the agitation proceeded, the breach gradually widened, producing first estrangement, then hostility; the most violent party gradually assuming the direction of the whole movement, in spite of the protests of the ablest and most moderate of the Chartists. As for O'Connor, he oscillated between them. He was by no means deficient in courage, and would probably have had no objection to attain his ends by a successful insurrection; but he must have been well aware of the responsibility that would have devolved on himself if such a movement had taken place, and the small chance, or rather the absolute impossibility, of success. He knew too that if physical force should be resorted to, he must either take the lead in the matter, or abdicate in favour of those who were prepared to do so. His opinions were, no doubt, those of the moral-force Chartists, and he endeavoured to maintain his authority over them by the frequent use of language such as he knew that they would approve; but, seeing that by casting his lot with them he would alienate the physical-force majority, he also gave them some encouragement, without absolutely committing himself to their views, and thus he was occasionally led to employ violent language and to encourage hopes that he must have well known could not be fulfilled.

Meanwhile meetings were multiplied, and as the Chartists could not assemble in the day, could not afford to pay for rooms, and often were too numerous for any room that could be procured, open-air torchlight meetings were resorted to. The circumstances attending these meetings naturally increased the alarm which the progress of the movement and the violence of its advocates had already excited. At one of them the Rev. J. R. Stephens, a Methodist minister of Ashton-under-Lyne, at the close of a long and furious harangue, demanded of those who were present whether they had come armed. The question was at once answered by a discharge of a few firearms. This did not satisfy him; and in reply to a second question a more general discharge took place, whereupon he concluded by saying, 'I see it's all right; good-night.' The government had thus far abstained from all interference with these meeting; but when the speakers openly incited those whom they addressed to rebellion, such forbearance was no longer possible. On the 12th of December a proclamation was issued, declaring the torchlight meetings to be illegal, and warning persons that those who attended them rendered themselves liable to punishment. O'Connor at once advised that they should be discontinued, but soon found how much easier it is to excite the feelings of a multitude than to restrain them. The incitements to insurrection which had been sounded forth from a thousand platforms, and which, if O'Connor himself had not sanctioned, he had certainly not condemned, had made a deep impression on the minds of those to whom they had been addressed, and they were now ready to carry out in action the sentiments they had so often and so frantically applauded. If their leaders would but give the word, they would not flinch. O'Connor, it is true, hung back, but Stephens was still undaunted. He denounced the proclamation as an insult to the oppressed people, a violation of the constitution, and declared it to be destitute of legal authority. A warrant was at once issued for his apprehension, and he was taken into custody. When he was brought before the Manchester magistrates, an immense crowd lined the streets, and received their champion with thunderous applause. O'Connor, though he must have disapproved the conduct of Stephens, did not desert him in the hour of danger. Probably he felt that he could not discountenance him without risking the loss of his power over the Chartists. Stephens is said not to have displayed on this occasion the resolution which his previous conduct seemed to promise. His defence was weak and undignified. But the menacing shouts of the multitude outside penetrated the room in which the magistrates were sitting, and so alarmed them, that they requested O'Connor to endeavour to appease his followers. He readily complied, and his appearance at the window at once put an end to the tumult. After professing in very warm terms great affection and reverence for his accused associate, he added, 'Mr. Oastler has predicted that he will be transported. That is impossible, for it is not a transportable offence. But if tyrants should so far strain their authority as to sentence him to transportation, his manacled limbs shall never pass to the transport ship but over my lifeless body.' Stephens was committed for trial, but liberated on bail. The Chartists collected 2,000*l.* to defray the cost of his defence, and he employed his interval of liberty in exciting still farther the ardour of his admirers by speeches, and by the delivery of a series of 'political sermons,' afterwards published under that title. These sermons were listened to by great multitudes, had an enormous sale, and were read by some of the better-educated Chartists to large crowds who congregated to hear them. The trial of Stephens came on at Chester, before Justice Patteson, on the 15th of August, 1839. He had, however, in the mean time, not only very much moderated his language, but had begun to preach doctrines the very reverse of those which had brought him into this trouble. He defended himself in a speech, the delivery of which occupied five hours. He neglected to explain how he had been led to employ the language of which he was accused; he declared himself an advocate for submission to every law that was not contrary to the law of God; but he contended that the new poor-law only left him the choice of disobeying man or God. He was condemned to be imprisoned for eighteen months, but was treated with great lenity.

In the mean time a convention of Chartist delegates had been holding its sittings in London. In this assembly, as in the stormier meetings outside, the physical-force men decidedly preponderated. The more moderate and judicious delegates, finding themselves unable to stem the torrent, withdrew from the assembly, and left it almost completely in the hands of the extreme men, who became every day more absurd and violent. At length, on the suggestion of Mr. Attwood, its sittings were removed to Birmingham, where several large meetings were held, to give the delegates an opportunity of explaining their views to the citizens. But the authorities of Birmingham suppressed the meeting, and violent riotings followed, in which several houses were burnt. The mob armed themselves with iron railings, which they had torn down, and were with difficulty dissuaded by their leaders from attacking the police with these formidable weapons. The appearance of the military at this moment put a stop to a disturbance which otherwise might have produced very serious consequences. As it was, the mischief done was so great, that the Duke of Wellington stated in his place in the House of Lords, that in all his military experience, he had never known a town taken by storm to be worse treated by the troops than Birmingham had been by the mob. The municipal authorities prevented the delegates from obtaining rooms suitable for their assemblies, and thus compelled them to return to London, and to resume their sittings there.

Among the other expedients that had been suggested in this convention, was that of observing what was called 'a sacred month,' during which the working classes throughout the whole kingdom were to abstain from every kind of labour, in the hope of compelling the governing classes to concede the charter. This wild and mischievous proposal, made at a moment when trade was generally unremunerative, and when the cessation of labour would be rather a benefit than a disadvantage to the capitalist, seems to have been too much even for the physical-force Chartists of the convention; but it was popular with the violent and unreflecting majority out of doors; and its opponents, finding themselves unable to stem the torrent of feeling in its favour, proposed that, before resorting to it, the Chartists should make another effort to obtain from the legislature a redress of the grievances of which they complained. A petition in favour of the charter was accordingly drawn up, and signed, as was alleged, by 1,286,000 persons, and presented to the House by Mr. Attwood, in the form of a large cylinder of parchment about four feet in diameter. The ponderous document, borne by twelve men, was rolled to the table before the speaker on which petitions are laid. The House wisely showed every disposition to treat the petitioners with consideration and respect. The standing orders which forbid speeches to be made on the presentation of petitions were suspended, to allow Mr. Attwood an opportunity of stating at length the case of his clients, and his motion made on the 12th of July that the petition should be printed was adopted without opposition; but when, on the same evening, he moved that the House should resolve itself into a committee for the purpose of considering its prayer, the motion, after a long debate, was rejected by 237 against 148. This decision showed that the Chartists had nothing to expect from the House of Commons, and threw them back on the idea of the 'sacred month.' Accordingly, when the convention met on the

13th of July, Mr. Lowery, one of the most violent of the physical-force party, thus recurred to the subject:

'It is useless to expect anything more from the House of Commons. Belgium and America did not obtain their liberty till they took it, nor will the people of this country. I have been in Scotland, Cumberland, and Westmoreland, and the people are of opinion that the best time for commencing the sacred month will be when the potatoes are in the ground. I agree with that opinion, and therefore I move, That the House of Commons having refused to go into Committee on the prayer of the national petition, it is vain to expect redress from that House. It is therefore the opinion of the National Convention that the people should work no longer after the 12th of August, unless the power of voting for members of Parliament to protect their labour is guaranteed to them.'

In vain did Messrs. Attwood and Fielden endeavour to pursuade the convention to try the effect of petitions from all parts of England. The language which had been employed by some of the speakers in the discussion of Mr. Attwood's motion had irritated the convention; and after a debate, first adjourned to Monday, and then again to Tuesday, Mr. Lowery's motion was adopted by the convention. It was, however, subsequently resolved, on the motion of Mr. O'Brien, that a committee of five should be appointed to submit to the people on the 5th of August the question of the commencement of the 'sacred month.' The persons named on this committee were O'Connor, O'Brien, Fletcher, Lowery, and Meeson. On their recommendation, the convention decided to abandon the 'sacred month' for the present. But many of their followers were dissatisfied at this reversal of the resolution of the convention, and on the 12th of August disturbances more or less serious occurred at Bolton, Wigan, Chorley, Hindley, and other places, but without any important result. The abandonment of this foolish scheme was due to the unwearied personal exertions of O'Brien, who, much to his credit, strenuously opposed an attempt which must have been attended with much unavailing misery and bloodshed. The complete failure of this cherished scheme was fatal to the convention. Thinned by the desertion of its ablest and the imprisonment of its boldest members, it was fast sinking into contempt. A motion having been made for its dissolution, the members for and against were equal, but Mr. Frost, a linendraper and magistrate of Newport, who presided on the occasion, gave his casting vote in favour of the resolution.

The proposal of the 'sacred month,' and the violence with which it was advocated, alarmed the government, and determined them to resort to strong measures for the suppression of the agitation. Many of those who had used the most violent language were apprehended, tried at the assizes, and sentenced to varying periods of imprisonment; others traversed to the following assizes. Some of the prisoners were treated with great severity, for the purpose of deterring others from following their example. The consequence was the suppression of larger demonstrations, but meetings of a less ostentatious character were still holden. The severe treatment to which the prisoners were subjected greatly exasperated the Chartists, who regarded them as martyrs in the cause of liberty. This feeling produced an outbreak which threatened to have very serious consequences. There was none of the prisoners whose sufferings excited a deeper or more wide-spread sympathy than Vincent. He was the most eloquent and the most popular of the Chartist orators. He was imprisoned at Newport in Wales, and it was reported that he had been treated with great cruelty. It was determined to make an attempt to release him by force. The neighbourhood of the town abounded with miners—men of great strength and determination, rude and ill-educated, most of them strongly attached to the physical-force party, which was indeed the only kind of force they understood. On the evening of November 3rd, 1839, they congregated in large bodies by previous appointment on the hills about Newport. They assembled in three large divisions, which were to meet at a certain place, and march together on the town. One division assembled at Bleakwood under the command of Frost, whom we have already seen presiding over the convention at Birmingham; another at Nant-y-Glo was led by Zephaniah Williams, a beerhouse-keeper, and the third, at Pont-y-Pool, was under the direction of a watchmaker of the name of William Jones. These three divisions were to meet at midnight at the Welsh Oak public-house, near Risca, and to march upon Newport, where they might be expected to arrive about two o'clock in the morning, under the command of Frost. Most of them were armed with guns, swords, pikes, bludgeons, or mandrils, a kind of pickaxe used by the coal-miners. It was afterwards alleged that the object of their leaders was not so much to obtain the liberation of Vincent as to give the signal for a rising throughout the country. It appeared that they had intended to have broken down the bridge over the river Usk, in order to prevent the mail from going to Birmingham. It was stated that its detention for more than an hour and a half beyond its usual time of arrival in that town was the preconcerted signal for a rising there, and it was hoped that the example thus given would be followed in every town in the country. The number of persons who assembled on this occasion, and the care with which they were organised, give probability to this supposition. Frost's division arrived at the place of rendezvous at the appointed hour; Williams and his party, being delayed by heavy rain, did not reach it till morning had already dawned; and the division from Pont-y-Pool arrived still later. The consequence was, that Frost, after waiting a long time, started for Newport ten minutes before Williams came; and instead of entering the town at two in the morning, he appeared there at nine with his own division, only, though followed at a little distance by that of Williams. This delay was fatal to the enterprise. The magistrates, having received notice of the approach of the rioters, had made preparations to resist them. They met at the Westgate Hotel, in front of which a party of police were stationed, while a company of the 45th regiment were placed within, out of sight, but ready to act in case their assistance should be required. A number of special constables had also been sworn in, and were posted in various parts of the town. Frost and his party arrived in front of the hotel, and demanded the release of the prisoners; but as their demand was not complied with, they attacked the police and special constables who were drawn up in front of the hotel, and drove them into the house, into which they endeavoured to follow them. They also fired into the room occupied by the soldiers, who were concealed from view, and prevented from acting by the closed shutters, which were at once opened, at the risk of their lives, by Mr. Phillips, the mayor of Newport, and Lieutenant Grey, the commander of the soldiers, the former of whom received two gunshot wounds. The soldiers now commenced firing; and after a conflict which lasted about ten minutes, and during which the rioters vainly attempted to force their way into the building, they were repulsed with a loss of ten killed and about fifty wounded, and retreated out of the town. Not one of the soldiers was injured. Some of the fugitives met the divisions led by Williams and Jones, which at once dispersed and fled. The three leaders were apprehended, as well as a large number of their followers. The trial of Frost, which took place on the 6th of June, 1840, was watched with great interest throughout the country. He was prosecuted by the attorney- and solicitor-generals for high treason, and defended by Sir F. Pollock, and Mr. Fitzroy Kelly. The jury, after deliberating for half an hour, returned a verdict of guilty, accompanied by a recommendation to mercy. Williams and Jones were also convicted of high treason. All three received sentence of death. A technical objection to the indictment taken by Sir F. Pollock, was argued before the fifteen judges, and decided by them to be valid, but not sustainable, because it had not been made at the proper time. However, the sentence on the prisoners was commuted to transportation for life, and they were subsequently released on condition that they should not return to England. The mayor of Newport, Mr. Phillips, was afterwards knighted as an acknowledgment of his courageous and judicious conduct. About the same time, some three hundred and eighty persons were apprehended on charges connected with the Chartist agitation. A few were acquitted; some who were accused of trifling offences pleaded guilty, and were dismissed; but by far the larger number were imprisoned during periods which varied from one month to two years. Among these were O'Connor, M'Doual, O'Brien, Collins, Lovett, and several other Chartists of less note. These vigorous measures produced the desired effect. The meetings were less frequent and less formidable, the language of the orators more measured, and a large number of Chartist periodicals, which had hitherto enjoyed a considerable circulation, languished or disappeared. Dissensions too, the natural fruit of adversity, became rife, and the agitation which had lately appeared so alarming seemed now to be on the point of expiring.

It was not dead, however. The blaze was over, but the fire still smouldered, and was ready to burst forth with renewed violence whenever circumstances should favour its revival. A wide-spread spirit of discontent still prevailed amongst the working classes. It was true that most of the leading Chartist orators and editors were in prison;.but the masses to whom they had spoken and written were still at liberty, animated by their old sentiments, retaining their old opinions, and ready for renewed agitation. Scarcely had the government prosecutions terminated than efforts were made to re-organise the Chartists. On the 29th of July 1840 a number of delegates assembled in Manchester, and determined to merge all local societies in one great confederation, which was to be called the National Charter Association, and to agitate the country in favour of the charter. The Chartist leaders, as the periods of their imprisonment expired, came forth one after another, and the release of each gave a fresh impetus to the reviving excitement. Some awakened pity and indignation by their emaciated appearance; others excited admiration by their declaration of readiness to undergo again all their sufferings in the cause of the charter. All related, and some probably exaggerated, the hardships they had endured. Thus the Chartists, who a little before appeared to have been completely put down, now seemed likely to become as formidable as ever, and were all animated with a violent irritation against the Melbourne government, at a moment when that government, defeated, as we have already seen, on a vote of want of confidence, appealed to the country.

O'Connor urged them to do all they could against a government which had treated them with such severity; but O'Brien, in spite of all he had suffered at the hands of the Whigs, dissuaded them from so suicidal a policy. The angry Chartists listened to the former, threw themselves into the arms of the Conservatives, and by, giving them their support, contributed to the downfall of the Melbourne administration. They also put forward several candidates of their own, none of whom were successful, but who, by dividing the liberal party, promoted several conservative triumphs. But though O'Connor succeeded on this occasion in dictating the policy of the Chartist body, he thereby roused a spirit of opposition, which gradually became more and more formidable to him. The Manchester association, which was devoted to him, and to which in turn he gave the whole weight of his influence, was the centre of the Chartist organisation. Attempts were made to form associations that should be independent of it; but though supported by O'Brien and other Chartist leaders, they only served to increase the dissensions that already prevailed. This, however, was a result for which O'Connor was much more to blame than those who refused to submit to his reckless and vainglorious leadership. To put an end to these divisions, as well as to promote the Chartist cause, another convention was assembled on the 12th of July 1842, of which only six of those who had belonged to the previous convention were members. To give increased force to this movement, great efforts were made to effect a combination of English Chartists and Irish Repealers; and by their joint efforts a petition for the charter and the repeal of the union between England and Ireland obtained, as was asserted, about 3,300,000 signatures. It was brought up to the House of Commons on the 2nd of May by a large and orderly procession. It was carried along the streets by sixteen men; but when it was brought to the door, it was found to be too large to pass it. It was therefore divided into several portions, and in that way was deposited on the floor of the house. Mr. Duncombe, who presented it, afterwards moved that the petitioners should be heard at the bar of the house by their counsel or agents. A long debate ensued, in the course of which Mr. Macaulay the historian opposed the motion with great vehemence; and Mr. Roebuck, although he supported it, denounced the writer of the petition as a fierce, malignant, cowardly demagogue. Some of the speakers who followed not unfairly argued, that persons who allowed themselves to be guided by such a man as Mr. Roebuck described did not deserve a hearing. Mr. Duncombe's motion was rejected by 287 to 49.

The National Chartist Association was now at the flood-tide of its prosperity. It could boast 400 affiliated societies, and 40,000 members. But O'Connor, finding that it was not as subservient to his authority as he wished it to be, determined to dissolve it. Thomas Cooper of Leicester, who up to this time had been a devoted follower of O'Connor, brought forward a series of resolutions strongly condemnatory of his proceedings. But the association itself was soon drawn into measures much more fatal to its authority than any direct assault on it could have been. The exasperation which had been caused by the rejection of Mr. Duncombe's motion, and the severe treatment of so large a number of Chartists, was greatly increased by successive reductions of wages. The idea of the sacred month was revived; and though discountenanced by the Chartist leaders, who had a painful recollection of the consequences of the last attempt of that kind, it found favour with the multitude. At a meeting near Ashton several speakers advocated a cessation of labour as a means of obtaining higher wages. These exhortations soon bore their natural fruits. On the 5th of August 1842 the factory operatives at Ashton turned out; and at a meeting held at Mottram Moor on the 7th, it was resolved that they would not resume work again till the charter should have become the law of the land. This resolution was followed by attempts to compel those who were still at work to join the turn-outs, which most of them did very willingly. Next day a large body of them marched on Manchester. They were met in Pollard-street by the mayor, Mr. Nield, and a troop of cavalry under the command of Colonel Wemyss. After a short parley, in the course of which they promised not to commit any breach of the law, they were allowed to enter the town, where they at once turned out the hands employed at the various factories and other works. It was easy to see that most of them only wanted the appearance of constraint to excuse their conduct. The ease with which the factories at Manchester were stopped encouraged similar proceedings in other manufacturing towns. They were visited by large bodies of turn-outs; the plugs were withdrawn from the steam-engine boilers, so that work could not be resumed for some time; and in the course of a few days the Chartists could boast that for fifty miles round Manchester every loom was still, and every industry arrested save those connected with the supply of food. An exception was also considerately made in favour of some products, which would have been spoiled if they had not been allowed to be finished. A committee sat daily for the purpose of granting leave in such cases, and seeing that the liberty they accorded was not carried farther than was absolutely necessary.

The conduct of the working classes on this occasion was highly creditable to them. Though the whole of the north of England was absolutely at their mercy, and though many of them at the time were sunk in deep poverty and destitution, little violence was done to person or property. It is true there were some exceptions. At Preston, for instance, the people stoned the soldiers, who at length fired and killed several persons. It now seemed that the dream of a sacred month was at last really on the point of being realised. Attempts were made in Staffordshire, Yorkshire, Ireland, and Wales, to extend the movement to those parts of the kingdom. On Monday, August 22nd, meetings were held at Paddington and Kennington-common to incite the working men of London to follow the example set them by the working men of the north, and it was sanguinely hoped that the sacred month would be kept throughout the United Kingdom. But the ardour of the orators was considerably damped by the arrest of no fewer than twenty of the leading Chartists at these two meetings. Discouraging tidings too arrived from the north. A strong appeal had been made to the working classes throughout the kingdom in a placard issued by the Manchester Chartist convention; but it was unsuccessful. The turn-outs were already giving way. On the very day on which the meetings were held at London many of them returned to their work; and in a very short time this great strike came to an end. At the Lancashire assizes for 1843 O'Connor and fifty-eight of his associates were tried for the part they had taken in it and all found guilty. They sued for a writ of error on the ground that the indictment had not mentioned the place in which the alleged offences had been committed. The objection was probably regarded as fatal by the legal advisers of the crown. At all events, sentence was never passed. Other Chartist leaders were not so fortunate. Cooper was sentenced to two years' imprisonment; John Richards and Jeremiah Yates were imprisoned for one year; a man named Ellis, residing in the midland counties, was transported for life; and several others were convicted and punished.

Towards the end of 1842 an effort was made to combine the middle-class radical Reformers and the Chartists in what was called a complete-suffrage union. Mr. Sturge of Birmingham was placed at the head of this movement, and elected president of a conference assembled in that borough on the 27th of December. Delegates from the principal towns of the kingdom attended at it, and as the Chartists almost everywhere outnumbered the Radicals, they had a very large majority in the conference. The Radicals were willing to admit the six points of the charter, which they embodied in a 'bill of rights.' But the Chartists would not give up a name endeared to them by the memories of a long and arduous struggle. The same Lovett who had received the charter from the hands of Mr. O'Connell proposed that it should be retained, and its retention was affirmed by a large majority. Mr. Sturge and his friends at once withdrew, with the exception of one or two, who deemed it right to bow to the decision of the majority. But their departure did not produce unity in the assembly. Lovett himself seceded soon after. Between three and four hundred delegates had presented themselves at the commencement of the conference, but their numbers had dwindled down to thirty-seven before its close. The remnant decided to hold another conference in London in April, 1843; but it was afterwards postponed to September, and then held in Birmingham. In the interval O'Connor, feeling that the direction of the movement was fast escaping him, proposed sundry plans of reorganisation, and at last issued his famous land-scheme, which had been concocted under his direction by the Rev. William Hall, the editor of the *Northern Star*, and some other friends, and which embodied ideas he had long been endeavouring to diffuse. He proposed to create a capital of 5000*l*. in shares of 2*l*. 10*s*. each. Of this amount 4125*l*. was to be devoted to the purchase of an estate, on which fifty of the members were to reside, and by whose labour he reckoned that the value of the property would be greatly enhanced. Four thousand pounds was to be borrowed on this property, with which, and the balance of 875*l*., he would purchase a second estate, to be occupied and mortgaged in the same manner as the first; and so on till eight estates had been purchased, which, according to his calculations, would give labour and support to 400 men. He expected in this way that the estates would not cost more than 33,000*l.*, and that at the end of four years they would be worth 60,000*l.* through the improvements made in them; thus yielding a balance of 27,000*l.* to the members of the association. An estate was accordingly purchased at Flemingsgate, and inaugurated with great ceremony. But the scheme was denounced by O'Brien, Cooper, and other Chartist notabilities, who did not spare O'Connor himself. They stated that he was deeply in debt; they pointed out that, as Mr. Tidd Pratt had refused to enrol the society on account of its political character, its members had no legal security; they accused him of appropriating a portion of the funds to the support of the *Northern Star*, and challenged him to meet them publicly and try to disprove their charges. But though O'Connor met these accusations in a way which showed that they were not altogether groundless, such was the confidence and affection with which he was regarded by the great body of the Chartists, and such their gratitude for the real or supposed sacrifices he had made for them, and for his unquestionable desire to benefit them, that they continued to put confidence in him, and to hope that he had found in his land-scheme the means of realising a social millennium for the working classes. There can be no doubt of O'Connor's honesty and sincerity; but his calculations were erroneous, and the men to whom he had confided the working of the scheme were incapable. However, for the present all seemed to promise well; and though many of his old friends had now become his bitterest enemies, their loss was in some degree compensated by the adhesion of Ernest Jones, a rising young barrister, who in eloquence and capacity far surpassed all the other Chartist leaders.

O'Connor made another great mistake about this time by putting himself in violent opposition to the anti-cornlaw agitation. Whether it was that his jealousy was awakened by the extraordinary popularity of Cobden and Bright; whether he felt that the free-trade agitation was drawing away the thoughts and hopes of the working classes from the Chartist agitation; or whether he hoped to force them to unite with him in agitating at once for free trade and for the charter; it is certain that, though he condemned the corn-laws in the strongest terms, he used language no less strong against the agitation which was being carried on for the repeal of them, and went so far as to challenge Cobden and Bright to a public discussion. It was clearly their policy to avoid a contest with the Chartists, whose assistance they hoped and desired to obtain. But O'Connor was bent on an encounter, in which he expected to obtain a signal victory. Messrs. Cobden and Bright had been invited to a meeting at Northampton on the 4th of August, 1844. O'Connor procured a requisition from his followers asking him to confront them on this occasion. The great majority of those present at the meeting were Chartists, and received their leader on his appearance with shouts of anticipative triumph. Cobden spoke with his usual eloquence and complete mastery of the subject, adducing facts and figures in support of his arguments. O'Connor, whose frothy declamation presented a most unfavourable contrast to the lucid speech of Mr. Cobden, followed. Then came M'Grath, another Chartist leader, who surpassed his chief in his treatment of the questions at issue, but whose voice was too weak to reach the majority of those who were present. Mr. Bright concluded the discussion with one of those trenchant and effective replies which no man knew better to make than he did. There could be no doubt to which of the two sides the victory in argument belonged; many of the Chartists were gained over; and when the show of hands took place, the chairman decided that the majority was in favour of the corn-law repealers, though the correctness of his decision was denied by O'Connor and his friends. At all events, it was certain that the numbers were nearly equal, and that the Chartist leader had greatly damaged himself by the course he took on this occasion. At Southampton the Chartists were more successful: they broke up a free-trade meeting held in that town, and compelled Lord Radnor, who presided, to quit the chair.

There were various other attempts, some successful, some unsuccessful, on the part of the Chartists acting under the guidance of O'Connor, to cripple the free-trade agitation; but as the anti-corn-law struggle approached its crisis, his star paled before that of Cobden and Bright. The working men quitted the party which seemed to be breaking up, to join that which was evidently about to be successful, and if successful to be productive of great advantage to them.

At length Sir R. Peel himself had become convinced of the soundness of those principles of free trade which Mr. Cobden had so strongly upheld, and which Mr. O'Connor, while professing to support them, had done all he could to resist. These principles Sir Robert had already applied to many other articles of commerce besides corn with remarkable success; and feeling that the duty which, as prime minister of this country, he owed to his sovereign and his country must prevail over the ties of party, himself proposed and carried through the repeal of the corn-laws in the year 1846. The result of his conduct was the alienation of the majority of his supporters, and the breaking up of the great and strong party which he had hitherto led. As has already been mentioned, an adverse vote on the Irish Arms bill, produced by a combination of a large number of his former supporters with the Whig opposition, brought about the downfall of his administration, which was replaced by a Whig ministry under Lord J. Russell. This event led to a general election, at which a larger number of Chartist candidates appeared on the hustings than on any former occasion; and though many of them did not proceed to the poll, the Chartists had, on the whole, good reason to congratulate themselves on the evidence afforded of the progress their principles had made in the country. Duncombe and Wakley, who had given them valuable parliamentary support, were returned for Finsbury. Fielden and Halliday unsuccessfully contested Oldham. George Thompson, who, though not himself a Chartist, was regarded as friendly to their cause, was returned for the Tower Hamlets by a majority of more than 2000 over his opponent Mr. Miall. James went to the poll at Halifax; M'Grath at Derby, Thomas Clark at Sheffield, Hardy at Worcester, Muntz at Birmingham, and Dr. Epps at Bolton. At Tiverton Julian Harney gained the show of hands against Lord Palmerston, though he did not proceed to the poll. But the great triumph of all the Chartists in this general election was the return of O'Connor for Nottingham by a majority of 1257 votes, against 893 given to his opponent Sir J. Cam Hobhouse, a member of the new administration. This victory brought the Chartist leader to the zenith of his popularity. The land-scheme still seemed to be prospering; a second estate had been purchased, and the land fund was said to amount to nearly 50,000*l.* A new paper had been projected, which was to be called the *Democrat*, and for which it was expected that the name of O'Connor would insure a very extensive and remunerative circulation. A petition against his return for Nottingham was met by a subscription of 400*l.* for the defence of his seat, and was speedily abandoned. His land-scheme was indeed strongly assailed, and the old accusation of having taken large sums from the land fund to support the *Northern Star* was revived. To meet these charges he went to Manchester, addressed a crowded meeting at Carpenter's Hall, and elicited the warmest expressions of the most unbounded confidence.

The revolution of February 24th, 1848, in France—followed by a momentary triumph of republican principles in that country—gave an immediate and enormous impulse to the Chartist agitation in England, and the more so because it occurred at a time when the working classes here were in a state of great suffering. The Chartist leaders did their utmost to increase the excitement produced by that event. Numerous meetings were held in all parts of the country, and the most intemperate language and the strongest incitements to insurrection were received with enthusiastic shouts, while the speakers who counselled prudence and moderation could not obtain a hearing. The establishment of a republic in France was continually referred to, accompanied by declarations that the people would have either the charter or a republic in England. A new convention, assembled on the 6th of April, resolved on the preparation of another petition for presentation to the House of Commons, which it was hoped would greatly surpass all previous petitions in the number of signatures attached to it; and a monster meeting was held at Kennington-common, whence the petition should be carried to the House of Commons, followed by a procession in which it was calculated that half a million of persons would take part. This project excited general alarm, and there was no doubt the execution of it would be fraught with danger to the public peace. In fact, many Chartists dreamed of effecting a revolution like that which had been made in the neighbouring country. The procession was decided to be illegal, and a proclamation was issued warning all persons not to take part in it. The convention therefore determined to hold the meeting, but were silent with regard to the procession, which many of their body still wished to carry out in spite of the prohibition of the government. London waited the issue in anxious suspense. The preparations made to meet the danger showed the alarm that was felt. The police force was greatly strengthened. A large number of special constables—amounting, as was said, to 170,000—were sworn in. Among them was Louis Napoleon Bonaparte, who soon after became President of the French Republic, and then Emperor of the French. Two thousand stands of arms were supplied to the officials of the General Post-office, to enable them to defend that establishment in case of an attack. The Admiralty was garrisoned by a body of marines. The Tower guns were mounted, and its defences strengthened and repaired. The Bank was supplied with artillery and filled with soldiers; its windows were defended by strong timbers, and sand-bag parapets were raised on its roof. The ships on the river were placed under the surveillance of the police, in case any of the sailors should manifest a disposition to join in the anticipated insurrection. No public vehicles were allowed to pass along the streets, lest they should be employed in the construction of barricades. The military arrangements were intrusted to the Duke of Wellington, who concealed his troops in places at which an attack might be expected, but especially in the neighbourhood of the different bridges, in case the threatened procession should attempt to cross any of them. In this state of defence and preparation the citizens of London waited calmly, though not without anxiety, the result of the meeting. It took place, as was announced, on Kennington-common. But instead of the promised half million, only about thirty thousand appeared on the ground. Mr. Mayne, the head of the police, told Mr. O'Connor that the meeting might be held, but that the procession would be stopped, and that if any conflict took place between the multitude and the authorities, they would hold him responsible for the consequences. Accordingly O'Connor, in addressing the meeting, put forth all his powers of persuasion to induce those who attended it to abstain from any procession. This advice was followed. No disturbance took place which the police were not easily able to quell, and the tranquillity of the metropolis was not in any way disturbed. The petition was presented by Mr. O'Connor, who asserted that it had received 5,700,000 signatures. It was, however, subjected to an ordeal which neither he nor his associates had anticipated. It was referred to the committee on public petitions, who employed thirteen law-stationers' clerks to make a careful examination of it. The result of their inquiry was reported to the House by Mr. Thorneley, the chairman of the committee. He stated that the whole number of signatures attached to the petition was 1,975,469. Of these, many were evidently fictitious, such as Victoria Rex, Prince Albert, the Duke of Wellington, Sir R. Peel, Lord J. Russell, Colonel Sibthorp, Nocheese, Pugnose, Flatnose, Punch, &c. &c. He added that whole sheets of signatures were in the same handwriting. Another member of the committee informed the House that eight per cent. of the signatures were those of women.

These failures and these revelations were fatal to Chartism. From being an object of terror, it suddenly became an object of contempt. Henceforward all was discontent, dissension, crimination, and recrimination. The new assembly did indeed meet—not on the 24th of April, the day originally fixed, but on the 1st of May. After much violent and threatening talk, it dissolved itself, without having effected anything. Attempts made by O'Brien, Vincent, and others to resuscitate the movement were utterly unsuccessful. Many of the leaders emigrated; others found employment as editors of newspapers, agents for insurance companies, &c. O'Connor, after having vehemently denounced all attempts to unite with middle-class reformers, joined and supported with all his power the household-suffrage association. But his support was now of little value to any cause. He was the wreck of what he had been. His land-scheme had proved an entire failure; and soon after he became an inmate of a lunatic asylum. Chartism was dying; or rather let us say, the soul that once animated it and rendered it so formidable was transmigrating into a fresh body. We shall meet it again in a new shape and under very changed conditions. The miserable termination of the great Kennington-common meeting, the ridicule with which the revelations of the petition committee had covered the monster petition, the signal failure of O'Connor's land-scheme—these were the most noticeable, but by no means the only causes of the wreck of Chartism. The alleviation of distress which followed the adoption of free trade relaxed the sinews of agitation. The operation of the new poor-law was now telling on that great incubus of pauperism which had pressed and weighed down the industry of the country. The rapid spread and amazing success of the coöperative movement turned the attention of the working classes to a surer means of moral, intellectual, and social elevation than could be looked for from political agitation, and promised soon to give them a power that would enable them to assert their rights with irresistible force,—to all these causes must be added the impulse given to the progress and prosperity of the nation by the wiser legislation which the great bill of 1832 had inaugurated.

We have said that Chartism was not dead; and we find that no long time elapsed after the events we have related before it reappeared in a shape better calculated to secure general attention. A large instalment of the charter was proposed to the House of Commons by Mr. Hume, in the following resolution, which was supported by the presentation of a large number of numerously-signed petitions:

'That this House as at present constituted does not fairly represent the population, the property, or the industry of the country, whence has arisen great and increasing discontent in the minds of a large portion of the people; and it is therefore expedient, with a view to amend the national representation, that the elective franchise shall be so extended as to include all* householders; that votes shall be taken by ballot; that the duration of Parliament should not exceed three years; and that the apportionment of members to population should be made more equal.'

The following were the chief arguments urged by Mr. Hume in support of his resolution:

* This word was omitted in the first instance by mistake, but was afterwards inserted by Mr. Hume.

'Taxation and representation should go together. Every man should have his share in sanctioning the laws by which he is to be governed, the sole difference between a freeman and a slave. The crown, lords, and commons, form the best method of giving effect to that constitutional government. The House of Commons ought to be invested with the highest authority and influence in this country; no act of the crown ought to be valid without its sanction; and the large classes of the community ought to be represented. But what is the fact? Five out of every six male adults in this country are without any voice in the election of representatives of this House. The rest are placed in an inferior situation, and deprived of the *right* which by the constitution they are entitled to enjoy.'

After quoting a number of documents intended to prove that every Englishman is entitled to be present in Parliament either in person or by deputy, and to show how partially and unequally the franchise was distributed, he thus proceeded: 'Another evil is the great diversity of the franchise. Although the ten-pound rental is the standard for boroughs, and the forty-shilling freehold is the standard for counties, there are in truth no fewer than eighty-five different kinds of franchise. It is scarcely possible to appreciate the confusion, the delay, and the expense such a system produces. What the House ought to do is to render the suffrage as simple, as general, as easily obtained, and as easily defended as possible. Not desiring change for the sake of change, I will not cut up the country into electoral districts, and I will not disturb the distribution of members for England, Ireland, and Scotland. I think that the duration of Parliament for three years will afford sufficient control over members. There is no property qualification in Scotland; and I see no reason why England and Scotland should not be put on the same footing.'

Lord John Russell rose nearly at the commencement of the debate thinking that the House was entitled to an early declaration of his views. After giving some preliminary explanation, he thus proceeded to deal with the argument by which Mr. Hume had supported the resolution:

'If Mr. Hume's assertion is correct, that every man who has contributed to the taxes has a right to a vote, there is no occasion for those restrictions and qualifications with which he is now going to encumber that pretended right. Even under his definition of household suffrage, some two or three millions of adult males will be excluded from the representation, and the universal content which he wishes to introduce will not be obtained. I differ from him as to the basis of the proposed representation. That which every man of full age has a right to is the best possible government, and the best representative system which the legislature could form. If universal suffrage would give the best representative system, the best laws, and the best government, the people have a right to it. A Parliament elected by householders and lodgers would not be a better Parliament than that which we now have. Such a representative system would render it necessary to adopt the division of the country into electoral districts, as was contemplated in the so-called People's Charter. Such a division would not be conducive to the interests of the people, and would lead to collisions of opinion between the representatives of the town and country districts that would be very injurious to their future tranquillity. As for the vote by ballot, I am of opinion that it would be no remedy against intimidation. I am satisfied with the present duration of Parliament, and shall give my vote against any change in it. Since the Reform act has passed, this House has not been the servant of the aristocracy, or the bigoted opponent of all plans of amelioration. No one who has considered the changes that have been made since 1832 can say that the House of Commons has not responded quickly and readily to public opinion. Look at the great measures it has passed in that period: as, for instance, the abolition of slavery, the opening of the China trade, the commutation of tithes, the remedy of the grievances of dissenters as to births and marriages; the reform of the municipal corporations in England, Scotland, and Ireland; the alterations in the tariff, the alterations in the postage system; and lastly, the total repeal of the corn-laws, which proves that the House is not under the rule and dominion of the landed aristocracy. But thinking, as I do, that the Reform act was an improvement of our old representative system, still I have always been of opinion that it will admit of amendment from time to time. It appears to me that the public mind is now turned to the subject, and that the time is at hand, if it has not already come, when some reform must be made in our representative system. The inquiries that the House is now making into the proceedings of some corrupt boroughs will give it farther information, and we shall then know whether it should disfranchise these boroughs or only the freemen in them. The great defect in the Reform act appears to me to be, that it reduced too much the varieties of the right of voting under the old constitution, and I think that some variety of suffrage might be made without injuring the basis of our representation. I am therefore not disposed to say that you cannot beneficially alter the Reform act; but I am not prepared at present to introduce bills to carry into effect the amendments I have mentioned. This is not the moment, when such dangerous opinions respecting capital, wages, and labour are afloat, to make great and extensive changes in the construction of the House of Commons, which I believe represents the nation fairly. The advantages of our constitution are to ourselves invaluable. The stability of our institutions amid the existing convulsions of the world has excited the admiration of every lover of peace and order in every nation; and therefore I hope that this House will do nothing to diminish that admiration, or forfeit that respect. I trust that the House will not choose the present as the time for making an alteration which stops indeed short of the charter, but which must ultimately terminate in it, but that it will think it due to other branches of the legislature, and to that great people of which it is the representative, to give a decided negative to this resolution.'

*Mr. W. J. Fox:* 'Sir, the question at present before Parliament is this: Are the working classes of this country represented as they ought to be? and if not, can they be so represented without danger to our institutions? I declare that they are not represented; that they are like helots in the land, serfs on the soil that bred them, having no concern with the laws except to obey them. This state of things is unjust to the unenfranchised, and injurious to the whole community. The reasons which Lord J. Russell urged first in 1822, and afterwards in 1832, exist in still greater force at the present time. I therefore implore the House to emancipate its serfs, and so to make of Englishmen a united nation. If it does so, it may arm the whole population, in the full confidence that if war should betide us, it would be rolled back to the terror and confusion of our enemies.'

*Mr. Cobden:* 'Sir, the division in favour of this motion may not be large, but the list will show that all those members who represent large 10*l.* constituencies, where the people have the free power of giving their votes, will be in the number of those who support it. I appeal to that fact as a proof that the middle classes are anxious to open the portals of the constitution to those who are anxious to come within them. There has as yet been no organisation in favour of this movement; but it has already made great way. One hundred and thirty meetings in its favour have been held within the last week, and it has already excited as much feeling in its support as had been acquired by the Anti-corn-law League after five years' agitation. The present representative system is a sham; but if it were amended, as Mr. Hume proposes, it would be a reality. Mr. Hume's scheme of household suffrage would not create a change in the government, but would only bring the legislature into harmony with the wants of the people. It would also produce economy and retrenchment, and a fair and equitable appropriation and imposition of the public taxation. I strongly recommend a new division of electoral districts. The constituencies of London are as much too large as the constituencies of the country are too small. I think it would be better to divide such constituencies into wards, and to give each of them the power of electing a member, instead of giving all of them the power of electing a great number.\* I am convinced that this country cannot be governed peaceably while the bulk of the people are excluded from the representation. I do not want to increase the number of representatives in this House; but if this motion is assented to, we must increase the number of representatives in some districts, and diminish it in others. I will not say much on the ballot, for it is a question which has great strength in this House and among the middle classes. The farmers, to a man, are in favour of it.'

---

\* This was a very favourite scheme of Mr. Cobden's, and one to which he frequently reverted both in his public addresses and his private conversation. It appears to me to be worthy of much more consideration than has hitherto been given to it.

*Mr. O'Connor:* 'Sir, I deny that the principle of Mr. Hume's motion has ever been adopted by a majority of the working classes. They are in favour of the principles of the people's charter, and will not be content with less. For my own part I am strongly in favour of annual parliaments, and would rather have household suffrage with annual than household suffrage with septennial parliaments. I am glad to find that Lord J. Russell prefers the people's charter to Mr. Hume's nostrum of reform. However, I will vote for that nostrum as the least of two evils. But if this motion is passed, it will not be a settlement of the question; for I should argue as energetically and enthusiastically for the people's charter as I have done before.'

At the close of a tolerably long debate a division took place, when the numbers were—

| | |
|---|---|
| For Mr. Hume' motion . . . . . . . . | 84 |
| Against . . . . . . . . . . . | 351 |
| Majority against . . . . . . . . | 267 |

This division was, however, far from representing the real state of public opinion in reference to this question. The majority in favour of a farther extension of parliamentary reform was as great in the country as the majority against it was in the House of Commons. But owing to the imperfection of the representation, the popular voice on this question was not distinctly heard. Meanwhile the finality policy of the Whigs, and their continual delays in carrying out reforms which they admitted to be highly desirable, damaged them with the country.

The state of Ireland at this period excited great and not unfounded alarm. Mr. Smith O'Brien and his principal associates openly avowed that they aimed at the establishment of a republic in Ireland, under the protection of the new French government, and they were evidently preparing to avail themselves of the first favourable opportunity of taking up arms to effect this object. Ministers therefore brought into the House of Commons a bill for the purpose of effectually repressing the seditious and treasonable objects of the discontented party, some of the leaders of which had accompanied Mr. Smith O'Brien to Paris, and boasted that they would be assisted in the accomplishment of their designs by a French army of 50,000 men. The chief proviso of the ministerial measure was embodied in a clause which punished with transportation persons 'conspiring, imagining, or levying war against her Majesty, and inciting and stirring up foreigners to invade these realms by publishing or printing any writings, or by open and advised speaking.' Strong objections were urged against this provision of the bill, and especially against those words of it which referred to open and advised speaking. In the course of the debate Mr. S. O'Brien, having now returned from his visit to Paris, spoke for the last time in the House of Commons, and met with a reception from that assembly which can only be compared to that given to Catiline by the Roman senate after his designs against the city had been unmasked by Cicero. The bill went through the House of Commons by overwhelming majorities, and was speedily passed by the Lords without change or opposition.

Another precautionary measure adopted in the course of this session was a bill for the registration of aliens. It did not pass the House of Commons without some opposition, especially from Sir W. Molesworth, who strenuously protested against it; reminding the House that Lord John Russell delivered his maiden speech against a bill which agreed almost word for word with that which was now being introduced by the government of which he was the head; that in 1824 he had again opposed it, being teller with Lord Denman against it; and that (alas for human sagacity and forethought!) he had on the last occasion on which it was brought forward expressed a hope that he should never again be obliged to raise his voice against it. Sir William added that he would not, because he had confidence in the ministry now in office, consent to give them powers which every person on their side of the House would have refused to Sir R. Peel. The opposition to the measure did not, however, prevent it from passing.

A bill for the establishment of diplomatic relations with the court of Rome received an amount of attention and discussion out of all proportion to its real importance. The country which had so long kept up diplomatic relations with the Sultan was convulsed at the idea of entering into diplomatic relations with the Pope, or rather of carrying on openly the negotiations with the head of the Roman Catholic religion that were now carried on in an indirect and irregular manner. The subject was accordingly approached with much caution and apprehension. Ministers pointed out to the House that by the treaty of Vienna we had guaranteed to the Pope the possession of his dominions, and that at this very moment the English government was called on to fulfil its treaty obligations, by giving naval and military support to a potentate to whom the law did not allow it to offer either advice or remonstrance. They announced that the Pope was contemplating the division of England into Roman Catholic sees in a manner which her Majesty's advisers regarded as an invasion of the rights of the crown, but against which, as matters now stood, they could not make any official representation. These considerations, however, were disregarded. The party which had opposed Catholic emancipation, which had opposed every subsequent attempt of the government to extend to Roman Catholics the rights they justly claimed, —the party which still resisted inch by inch every concession of religious liberty to the Roman Catholics, offered a persistent opposition to this proposal. A majority in the House of Lords, though warned that what they were proposing to do would in all probability defeat the object which the ministers had in view in bringing in the bill, insisted on inserting a clause to prevent the government from receiving an ecclesiastic as the representative of the Pope in this country. In the lower House the opposing party succeeded in substituting the words 'Sovereign of the Roman state' for the words 'Sovereign Pontiff,' which had originally been placed in the bill. Not content with having introduced these changes into the measure, the ultra-protestant party endeavoured, by a factious and vexatious opposition, to prevent it from passing. The opponents of the measure could not indeed by these means prevent it from being carried; but they succeeded in rendering it inoperative through the amendments they had introduced into it. The Pope refused to avail himself of the permission, so grudgingly and offensively accorded him, of sending a representative to this country; and thus an opportunity of treating with one who was regarded as their spiritual head by many millions of British subjects was unfortunately thrown away, with results that we shall soon have occasion to narrate.

One great improvement in the government of this country, which, though not quite peculiar to the period embraced by our History, had been employed during it with a frequency previously unknown, was the selection of thoroughly competent commissioners to prepare the way for legislation on difficult and complicated questions by careful preliminary investigations. The repeated issue of these commissions since the passing of the Reform Bill had afforded ground for a very loud and plausible outcry against Whig jobbery; and had even led Sydney Smith—who, after a long life spent in the vigorous denunciation of abuses, had in his old age become playfully obstructive—to say with jocose exaggeration that the barrister of seven years' standing—the usual condition of serving on one of these commissions—had become the *primum mobile* of human affairs; and that if a man could discover an institution to be destroyed, he was at once put on a commission, and his fortune was made. However, in spite of the denunciations of the wise and witty canon, and in spite of popular outcries, there can be no doubt that the inquiries of these commissions, conducted as they generally were by men selected on account of their peculiar qualifications for conducting the investigations intrusted to them thoroughly and completely, did most usefully pave the way for legislation, and enabled the government to put before Parliament more information on the questions submitted to it, and measures better framed and more carefully prepared than they could have done without the assistance which the labours of these much-abused commissions afforded them. The consequence of the experience of the value of investigations conducted in this manner was, that scarcely any legislation of importance requiring previous inquiries to be made was undertaken by any government, whether liberal or conservative, until the ground had been prepared for it by the investigations of a commission. Indeed the Conservatives, although when out of office they had raised loud outcries against the Whig commissions, yet when in office made even more frequent use of them than the Whigs had done. Sir R. Peel not only profited by the inquiries which had been carried on by the commissions appointed by his predecessors in office, but issued other commissions himself.

Perhaps there was none of these commissions—not even the poor-law commission itself—that had rendered such important services to the community by its investigations as the sanitary commission; the reason of which was, that the prosecution of the inquiries which that commission was appointed to carry on had been chiefly intrusted to two most competent investigators—Mr. Edwin Chadwick and Dr. Southwood Smith. By far the larger share of the inquiry and of the recommendations founded on it belonged to the former of these two gentlemen, though the latter also contributed many valuable and important suggestions.

The frequent returns of cholera, typhus, and other forms of zymotic disease, which had hitherto been ascribed to the 'visitation of God,' were now beginning to be seen to be more or less traceable to exposure to a vitiated and polluted atmosphere; and the general attention of enlightened men began to be drawn to the necessity that existed for preventive measures in the shape of sanitary reforms. But the nation was not yet sufficiently awakened to the pressing importance of providing against the recurrence of those terrible pestilences by which many parts of the country had from time to time been ravaged. However, a commission was appointed in the first instance to inquire into the sanitary state of the metropolis, where the condensation of a vast population produced all kinds of nuisances injurious to health, and conditions of the water and the atmosphere pregnant with danger to those who inhabited its more crowded districts. The investigations of the commission thus appointed were soon extended to the general sanitary condition of the labouring classes of the community in all parts of the kingdom; and led to the preparation and presentation of a report drawn up by Mr. Chadwick, and which entered very fully into the whole question. This report, which was published in 1842, attracted perhaps more attention and produced a greater effect than any other document of the same nature. Nearly 10,000 copies were sold or officially circulated.

The following are the conclusions which the investigations of Mr. Chadwick and Dr. Smith led them to adopt, the grounds of which were given in the report itself.

'That high prosperity in respect to employment and wages, and various and abundant food, have afforded to the labouring class no exemption from attacks of epidemic disease, which have been as frequent and as fatal in periods of manufacturing and commercial prosperity as in any others.

'That the formation of all habits of cleanliness is obstructed by defective supplies of water.

'That the annual loss of life from filth and bad ventilation is greater than the loss from death or wounds in any war in which this country has been engaged in modern times.

'That of the 43,000 cases of widowhood and 112,000 cases of destitute orphanage relieved from the poor-rates in England and Wales alone, it appears that the greatest proportion of deaths of heads of families occurred from the above-specified and other removable causes; that their ages were under forty-five years—that is to say, thirteen years below the natural probabilities of life as shown by the experience of the whole population of Sweden.

'The experience of the effect of sanitary measures proves the possibility of the reduction of sickness in the worst districts to at least one-third the existing amount. Amidst classes somewhat better situated, it is possible to reduce the sickness to less than one-third; it was an under estimate to take the probable reduction at one-half.'

The report then goes on to show how large a saving might be effected for the labourer in medical attendance and insurance against sickness and death by the adoption of proper sanitary measures.

The fierce contest carried on between the two great parties in the state, ending in the repeal of the corn-laws by Sir R. Peel, and the consequent dissolution of his ministry, prevented farther action in this matter until the year 1847, when another commission was appointed. It issued two reports. Several very useful acts were suggested by the commission, the most important of which were the towns-improvement act of 1847, the public-health, the nuisances removal, and the metropolitan-sewers acts of 1848, the metropolitan-interment act of 1850, and the extension of that act to the whole of the kingdom in 1852; and this has been followed by a host of sanitary acts down to the present time, the most noteworthy of which, because it embodied the principles on which all those that followed it have been based, was the public-health act, passed in 1848, and founded on the recommendations of Mr. E. Chadwick and Dr. S. Smith. Under this act a general board of health was appointed, the members of which were Lord Carlisle, Lord Ashley, Mr. E. Chadwick, and Dr. Southwood Smith. This measure, one of the most important for the great mass of the labouring population of this country that was ever adopted by the legislature, passed almost without notice, the popular indifference with regard to it contrasting in a very striking manner with the eagerness with which debates involving a change of the *personnel* of the government were devoured.

The year 1848 closed with somewhat brighter prospects. The revolutionary tornado which had swept over the Continent was subsiding. Ireland, though not pacified, was strongly held down. O'Brien, McManus, O'Donoghue, and Meagher, the leaders of the malecontents in that country, were lying under sentence of death; and though it was not the intention of the government to carry that sentence into effect, they were destined to be banished for life, and thus disabled from doing farther mischief. The potato-disease still raged; but the new Irish poor-law, the wholesale emigration which had taken place, the relief afforded by private benevolence and public liberality, were gradually alleviating the distress that it caused, and there was now reason to hope that this terrible visitation would ultimately prove the means of regenerating that unhappy country by substituting a more nutritious food for the vegetable that had hitherto been the staff of life to the Irish peasant, and which, insufficient as it always had been, was now shown to be also quite unreliable. Meanwhile England was slowly recovering from the crisis of distress through which she too had passed, and there seemed to be good ground for hoping that she would at length realise the advantages of those free-trade measures which up to this time had never had fair play.

In the course of the autumn of this year occurred the sudden and melancholy death of a man who had rapidly risen to a very conspicuous position. Up to the time when Sir R. Peel broke up the conservative party by avowing himself convinced of the necessity of a repeal of the corn-laws, Lord G. Bentinck had been chiefly known as a great patron of the turf, one who spent his days in fox-hunting, and his nights at the House of Commons, where he sat on the back benches, his scarlet hunting-coat covered by a light paletot, silent but attentive. He was the nephew of Mr. Canning, and had acted as his secretary, in which capacity he had rendered very valuable services. He gave to the Whigs a very independent support while the Reform Bill was under discussion, but withdrew it after the passing of that measure. He then joined the conservative party, and was offered a post in Sir R. Peel's ministry, which he declined from a disinclination to undertake the labours and responsibilities of office. At length, when the protectionists, abandoned by their old leaders, found themselves left alone, he was put at the head of the newly-formed party; and though a very hesitating and embarrassed speaker, he accepted the position, and discharged its duties to the satisfaction of his followers. He now devoted himself to politics, sold off his stud, and withdrew himself almost entirely from all participation in those amusements to which he had hitherto been so much devoted. It is probable that this sudden adoption of sedentary habits by one who had long been accustomed to violent exercise and to spending the greater part of the day in the open air, had seriously though imperceptibly injured his constitution. However the mischief seems not to have shown itself in any way until the 21st of September in this year. On that day he appeared at the breakfast-table in more than usual spirits, and occupied himself with writing letters till about twenty minutes past four in the afternoon, when he set out with the intention of walking to Thoresby, the seat of Lord Manvers, where he had arranged to spend two days. He never reached the house. A search was made for him, and he was found lying on his face, quite dead, with one arm under his body. His death, which had been instantaneous, was found on examination to have been caused by a spasm of the heart, probably brought on by over-exertion and the want of sufficient food, as he had taken nothing since breakfast. His frank and open bearing, his honourable character, his undoubted sincerity, the generous warmth of his disposition, had made him a favourite with men of all parties, and caused the tidings of his death to be received with general regret. To his political friends the loss was very serious; for though there were among them men of more shining abilities and of equal application, yet his long parliamentary experience and his aristocratic connections gave him an authority among them which would not have been readily accorded to any other leader. Only a few days before his death he had shown his superiority to party considerations by bearing testimony to the conduct of Lord John Russell's ministry with regard to the sister country, in which he declared that in his opinion 'the brightest page in the history of the present government is that which records the firmness and determination with which it put down rebellion, maintained peace, and brought criminals to justice in Ireland.' The body of Lord George was interred privately in the old church of St. Marylebone, in a remote corner of which his friend and political associate, Mr. Disraeli, watched the service.

The death of Lord G. Bentinck left the Conservative party in the House of Commons without a head, and it seemed for some time doubtful whether the chief place in it would be assigned to the Marquis of Granby, whose rank recommended him to many, and who was by no means deficient in the necessary qualifications of a parliamentary leader, or to Mr. Disraeli, who was beyond all question the ablest man and the most eloquent speaker, and who had been the most trusted associate and the most active coadjutor of Lord G. Bentinck. Meanwhile the evident weakness of the Whig ministry encouraged the hope that the time would soon arrive when the newly-formed conservative party would be called on to undertake the government of the country.

The session of 1849 was opened by the Queen in person on the 2nd of February. The address in reply to the speech from the throne was discussed in both houses at far greater length than had been usual of late years. In the upper House an amendment moved by Lord Stanley was opposed by the Duke of Wellington, and rejected by a majority of only two. The debates in the House of Commons, which were long and animated, turned chiefly on foreign affairs; but the amendments proposed were ultimately withdrawn.

The question of the navigation laws, was again brought forward at the commencement of this session, with a fair prospect of being settled.

The system with which the government proposed to deal dated from the year 1651, when the Protector's Parliament, in order to restrain the growing competition of the Dutch, passed an act which prohibited the importation into the United Kingdom and its dependencies of any goods the produce of Asia, Africa, or America, except from the places of their production, and in ships 'of which British subjects should be the proprietors and right owners, and whereof the master and three-fourths at least of the mariners should be English subjects.' The act also prohibited the introduction of goods the growth, production, or manufacture of Europe, except in British ships, or ships that belonged to the country where the goods were produced, or from which they could only be, or usually had been, imported. The stringency of this law was slightly mitigated by another act passed in the reign of Charles II.; but the modifications thus introduced were of slight importance. A farther relaxation made at the conclusion of the war of independence, allowed the produce of the United States to be imported in ships belonging to citizens of those states. The last amendment of the original law was obtained in the year 1825 by Mr. Huskisson, who made some important changes in it. The law, then, which the legislature had to reconsider in the year 1849 stood thus: the produce of Asia, Africa, and America might be imported from places out of Europe into the United Kingdom, if to be used therein, in foreign as well as in British ships, provided that such ships were the ships of the country of which the goods were the produce, and from which they were imported. Goods which were the produce of Europe, and which were not enumerated in the act, might be brought thence in the ships of any country. Goods sent to or from the United Kingdom to any of its possessions, or from one colony to another, must be carried in British ships, or in ships of the country in which they were produced and from which they were imported. Then followed some stringent definitions of the conditions which constituted a vessel a British ship in the sense of the act. These restrictions were not without their defenders. Even the great founder of economic science, Adam Smith, while admitting that the navigation laws were inconsistent with that perfect freedom of trade which he contended for, sanctioned their continuance on the ground that defence is much more important than opulence. But as it was more and more strongly felt that these laws were part and parcel of that baneful system of monopoly which, under the name of protection, had so long been maintained and was now so completely exploded, it began also to be seriously doubted whether they were necessary to the defence of the nation, and whether its security would not rather be increased than diminished by the entire abolition of laws which shackled in so artificial and inconvenient a manner the natural freedom of trade. These views had already, as we have seen, been pressed on the legislature, and the government had taken the matter up, and brought forward a measure on the subject which had been withdrawn in the last session. Therefore, on the 14th of February in this year, Mr. Labouchere, as president of the board of trade, proposed a resolution on the subject couched in the following terms:

'That it is expedient to remove the restrictions which prevent the free carriage of goods by sea to and from the United Kingdom and the British possessions abroad, and to amend the laws regulating the coasting trade of the United Kingdom, subject nevertheless to such control by her Majesty in council as may be necessary; and also to amend the laws for the registration of ships and seamen.'

A long debate took place on the question of the second reading of the government measure, which was strenuously supported by Sir J. Graham, and opposed by the protectionists.

214 members followed Mr. Disraeli into the lobby, while 275 voted with the government, which therefore had a majority of 61.

In the upper house Lord Brougham astonished friend and foe by coming forward as the strenuous and uncompromising opponent of the ministerial measure, vehemently affirming, and endeavouring to show, that the question of the navigation laws had nothing to do with the question of free trade. However, the second reading was carried by a majority of 10. The smallness of this majority caused some anxiety to the supporters of the measure with regard to its ultimate fate; but this anxiety was relieved by the withdrawal of the most conspicuous opponents of the bill, which consequently passed without farther opposition. A rider proposed by the Bishop of Oxford, and which was designed to withhold the benefit of the act from Spain and Brazil until the governments of those countries had given full assurances that they would carry out the treaties into which they had entered for the suppression of the slave-trade, was rejected.

It was now the turn of the new Conservative party to bring forward their policy, which was announced to the house in a resolution proposed by Mr. Disraeli on the 8th of March. Although he and his friends had frequently declared that the free-trade measures had completely failed, and must soon be abandoned, they did not venture to bring forward any proposal for a return to the system of protection, but endeavoured to make out, on behalf of the landed interest, a plausible claim for relief from some of the burdens which during the late distress had pressed on it with more than ordinary severity. The resolution stated the case of the agriculturists so well and so fully, that it well deserves perusal.

'That the whole of the local taxation of the country for national purposes falls mainly, if not exclusively, on real property, and bears with undue severity on the occupiers of land, in a manner injurious to the agricultural interests of the country, and otherwise highly impolitic and unjust. That the hardship of this apportionment is greatly aggravated by the fact that more than one-third of the whole revenue derived from the excise is levied upon agricultural produce, exposed by the recent changes of the law to direct competition with the untaxed produce of foreign countries; the home producer being thus subject to a burden of taxation which, by greatly enhancing the price, limits the demand for British produce, and to restrictions which injuriously interfere with the conduct of his trade and industry. That this House will resolve itself into a committee to take into its serious consideration such measures as may remove the grievances of which the owners and occupiers of real property thus justly complain, and which may establish a more equitable apportionment of the public burdens.'

In supporting this resolution Mr. Disraeli adduced the

evidence of Mr. Cobden to prove the reality and severity of the distress, and to show that the farmers had not been fairly treated. He supported his assertion that the agricultural interest bore more than its fair share of taxation, by showing that the county, highway, church, and poor rates amounted to 12,000,000*l*., levied on a rental of 67,000,000*l*. a year, while the income from other property amounted to 249,000,000*l*. a year. And he asked why this direct taxation of ten or twelve millions a year should be levied exclusively on a portion of the income of the country which was only a little more than a fourth part of the whole amount of that income? He farther argued that this taxation, though nominally levied for local objects, was in reality expended for the general advantage of the nation. He therefore asked that one half of the objects on which these rates were now expended should be provided for out of the consolidated fund. Mr. Hume proposed an amendment to Mr. Disraeli's resolution, to the effect that the public expenditure ought to be reduced to such an extent as to permit the repeal of the duties on malt and hops; thus outbidding the farmers' friends themselves. Other speakers showed pretty conclusively that the plan proposed by Mr. Disraeli was better calculated to benefit the landlord than the tenant farmer, who, instead of gaining by it, would be loaded with his share of the additional income tax, which must necessarily be imposed in order to enable the country to meet the additional expenditure which this plan would throw on it. The motion and the amendment were both rejected.

Meanwhile Ireland and its affairs were still pressing themselves on the attention of Parliament with an urgency that would not be overlooked. The scarcity still continued. The potato disease, which had at one time seemed to be abating, now raged with renewed virulence. Crime, too, as might be expected, was as rife as ever. Open insurrection had indeed been put down, but secret disaffection still prevailed very widely. It therefore became the imperative duty of the government to propose that the suspension of the Habeas-Corpus Act should be renewed; and their recommendation was backed in both Houses by large majorities, though it did not escape the strenuous opposition of a small but determined band of repealers. This act of repression was properly accompanied by acts of grace and liberality. A grant of 50,000*l*. was voted for the relief of those who were suffering from the famine. A select committee was appointed by each House of Parliament to inquire into the working of the new Irish poor-law. This was followed by a proposal, emanating from the government, for a rate in aid of the suffering districts, to be levied throughout Ireland; and after long debates and close divisions the plan was adopted by the legislature. It was succeeded by another government proposal for a loan of 100,000*l*. on the security of the rate. This was also adopted, though it gave rise to considerable discussion, and encountered strong opposition. Another encumbered-estates bill was brought in and passed. At one time it seemed likely that the measure would be lost, owing to the lords having introduced into it amendments which raised a question of privilege between the two Houses; but the amendments were ultimately accepted, and the bill passed. Measures allowing advances of public money for drainage and other improvements, and for the encouragement of emigration, were also passed.

While the affairs of Ireland were occupying so large a share of the attention of the British legislature and people, the colonies were obtaining an almost equal portion of it. The ignorance and consequent indifference that prevailed respecting them were being rapidly dispelled by the spread of education, and by the diffusion of information relating to them. The interest in them thus awakened was increased by the large amount of emigration to them from all parts of the United Kingdom, but especially from Ireland, and from the discussions which had from time to time been raised in Parliament on the advantages of emigration as a means of relieving English and Irish distress. We may therefore date from this year the serious commencement of an agitation carried on in and out of Parliament with the object of improving the system of colonial government. In furtherance of this subject three colonial questions were formally brought under the notice of the legislature during this session, and gave rise to long and important debates.

Heavy charges of improper appointments, extravagant expenditure, and needless and excessive cruelty in suppressing insurrections, were brought against the authorities in British Guiana and Ceylon. In respect to the latter colony a deep impression was made on the House by the statement that Lord Torrington, the governor, had carried through the council of the island by his own casting vote a bill to indemnify himself from the consequences of his illegal conduct; that a Cingalese priest had been shot in his pontifical robes; and that the pretender to the throne of Candy had been ignominiously flogged before being transported: acts respecting which Lord J. Russell declared in his place in the House that he declined giving any opinion.

A question still more important was raised, or rather was forced on the attention of the House, relative to Lower Canada. The Legislature of that province had passed a bill granting indemnities to those whose property had been injured during the insurrection which had taken place there. It was strongly opposed by the British party in the province, on the ground that it would have the effect of compensating many of those who had taken part in the insurrection, and that thus rebels would be indemnified out of the taxation levied on the loyal part of the community. Notwithstanding these objections, the bill was carried by a large majority, and received the assent of Lord Elgin, the governor. But the passing of the measure was the signal for an outbreak of the British party, in which the Parliament-house of the colony was destroyed. The matter of course came before the House of Commons, and Lord Elgin was strongly attacked for having given his assent to such a measure; but his conduct was defended on the ground that no person could properly be treated as a rebel unless legal proof was afforded of his having taken part in the insurrection, and that a person claiming an indemnity for the destruction of his property could not equitably be required to prove that he was not a rebel. In the course of these discussions, bitter complaints were made by some of the radical party in the House that the colonial secretary, Earl Grey, had done nothing to remedy abuses in the administration of his department, which, when out of office, he had strongly condemned. There do not, however, seem to have been just grounds for these complaints. Lord Grey was trammelled by a system, for the vices of which Parliament was really responsible. That system needed a thorough and searching reform, and there were men in the House of Commons who very distinctly saw what changes were needed in the administration of the colonies, and were prepared to deal with the question in a vigorous and enlightened spirit. Chief among these were Sir W. Molesworth, Mr. Gladstone, and Mr. Roebuck. The first-mentioned of these gentlemen brought forward a motion for the appointment of a royal commission to inquire into our colonial policy, and to report on it. As the question was one which concerned the mother country as well as her colonies, it is desirable that we should examine the statements and arguments of a gentleman who had perhaps devoted more time and attention to the subject than any other person in the kingdom, had succeeded in thoroughly mastering it, and could distinctly see and clearly point out the principles on which the government of the colonies by the mother country ought to be conducted.

He contended that our system of colonial government ought to be revised; a broad distinction being drawn between those colonies which have or ought to have representative institutions and those of the crown colonies which are unfit for free institutions, and that it would be necessary also to consider what would be the best form of local government for these latter colonies.

Turning next to the colonial expenditure, he urged that if the commission which he proposed should be appointed, it should inquire to what extent it was necessary for us to keep troops or build fortifications in our colonies; whether we ought to do so in any colonies except such as are strictly military stations; what colonies should be considered to be military stations; and what would be the best mode of checking the present excessive and uncontrolled ordnance expenditure. He remarked that the salaries paid to British colonial governors exceed those paid to the state governors in the United States by nearly nine times. The proposed commission would deal with the questions both of the salaries and appointment of governors, would determine in what cases the payment should be made from colonial and imperial funds, and would devise checks where required on lavish expenditure.

He also proposed that the commission should inquire

into colonisation and emigration. It would determine whether or not convict emigration is to continue; whether, on the whole, the empire is the gainer by it. It should also investigate the obstacles which impede emigration to our colonies, and the cause that emigrants from this country generally prefer the United States. He alleged that the misgovernment of the colonial office, convict emigration, and other causes, which a commission might be able to probe and investigate, now turned the tide of colonisation from our own settlements. The commission would likewise assist in determining what powers ought to be reserved for the imperial government, and what intrusted to the local legislatures. His reason for proposing a commission was the fear that the subject would be too large for a parliamentary committee. It might consist of four persons, one representing each of the four sections of the House of Commons, and to these he proposed to add one distinguished political economist, as, for instance, Mr. John Stuart Mill.

This proposal, seconded by Mr. Hume, was met by the under colonial secretary Mr. Hawes with the usual official plea for being let alone. He ridiculed the 'happy family' that Sir W. Molesworth proposed to assemble. He eulogised the principles and the administrative ability of his chief, Earl Grey. He affirmed, which was no doubt true, that the success of our free-trade policy was beginning to show itself, and deprecated an inquiry which in his opinion, would raise hopes and expectations that were sure not to be realised. Mr. Gladstone supported the motion of Sir W. Molesworth in a speech which showed how far he was in advance of the men with whom he usually acted, and gave unmistakeable promise of those liberal principles which he has since more fully avowed. Lord J. Russell urged that the question was one which ought to be left in the first instance to the ministers of the crown, to be brought forward by them on their own responsibility, under the control and supervision of Parliament; a course which, he urged, was in accordance with the principles of the constitution. Sir W. Molesworth's motion was negatived by 163 against 89.

The subject of the grant of Vancouver's Island to the Hudson's Bay Company, brought forward by Lord Lincoln, was got rid of by a count-out; but a bill for the administration of justice in that colony was read a second time in the House of Lords, in spite of the strongly-expressed opinion of Lord Brougham and several other high legal authorities that the charter under which the island had been ceded to the Hudson's Bay Company was invalid.

We have already referred to the distracted state of the Continent, produced by the revolution that had so suddenly precipitated Louis Philippe from the throne of France. The condition of affairs to which that event had given birth still prevailed. Under the influence of the passions it had produced, Charles Albert, king of Sardinia, had put himself at the head of the party of Italian independence, had attempted to liberate Italy from the control of the Austrians, had been defeated in a succession of battles by Marshal Radetzky, and had been compelled to abdicate. The Pope, whose capital was in the hands of the republican party, had escaped in disguise to Naples, but was restored by a French army commanded by General Oudinot, which had besieged and taken Rome, and placed there a large French garrison to repress any farther movement of the revolutionary party against the pontifical Government. Sicily had revolted from the king of Naples, and the insurrectionary government which was established in that island had been supplied with arms manufactured for our army, with the consent of the ordnance and the foreign office. Hungary, in revolt against Austria, was demanding the restitution of its ancient privileges. In all these cases our government was, or at least thought itself, bound to interfere with advice—which generally was not heeded—and sometimes, as we have just seen in regard to the Sicilian revolt, with something more than advice. These things, though occupying a large share of the attention of the legislature, only awakened a very languid interest in England, where the excitement produced by the first tidings of the French revolution had entirely subsided.

The disturbed state of the Continent might seem to afford a reason for making reductions in our naval and military expenditure. Our nearest neighbour, France, was evidently far too much engaged with her internal troubles to think of attacking this country; and so too were the other great powers of Europe, all of which had been more or less shaken by the wave of the revolutionary earthquake which had overturned the throne of Louis Philippe. In England the prevailing feeling of contentment with the national institutions had hardly been ruffled. These circumstances seemed to many to afford a favourable opportunity for reducing the military and naval expenditure of the country. Accordingly that party which had compelled the leader of the protectionists to concede free trade, which had supported the multitudinous improvements that had been made in our fiscal and financial arrangements, now came forward, under the leadership of Mr. Cobden, to ask for a reduction of our military and naval establishments, and a corresponding diminution of that load of taxation, the weight of which was doubly oppressive at a moment when the effects of the potato-rot were still felt, and when the long-continued commercial distress was still unremoved. On the 26th of February, when the House was about to go into a committee of supply, Mr. Cobden proposed that the expenditure of the country should be reduced as soon as possible to that which in 1835 had been found sufficient to maintain the security, honour, and dignity of the nation; in other words, that a reduction should be made in the expenditure to the extent of nearly ten millions sterling. The chancellor of the exchequer met this motion by arguing that the expenditure of 1835 fell short of the requirements of the country, and that many changes had occurred, especially in the colonies, which necessitated an increased expenditure. At the same time he admitted that our prospects of internal and external peace in this year were much more promising than they had been in 1848; and therefore he contemplated a reduction of forces to the extent of 10,000 men, and of expenditure to the amount of about a million and a half of money, and, as a result of these reductions, a diminution of the deficiency to 370,000*l*. The government was supported by the protectionist party in its resistance of Mr. Cobden's motion, which was consequently rejected by the large majority of 197.

The plan of which Sir R. Peel had set an example, of making the financial statement at a very early period of the session, and which had hitherto been adopted by his successors in office, was this year departed from, and the budget, though frequently asked for, was not brought forward till the 29th of June. The chancellor of the exchequer announced that, though there was an actual deficiency of

269,378*l*., this arose from some items of expenditure which he had not anticipated—for Irish distress, emigration to Canada, excess of naval expenditure in preceding years. These extraordinary demands had converted what would otherwise have been a surplus into a deficiency. The chancellor of the exchequer turned to the consideration of the prospects of the year 1849-50, in which he calculated that, deducting the excess of previous years from the current expenditure, the surplus of receipt over expenditure would amount to 739,936*l*.

Mr. Hume complained of the steady rise of taxation, and of the amount of the burdens which had been imposed on the country since 1824. He reminded the House that an annual charge of 836,000*l*. had been imposed on the country in perpetuity through the increase of the debt. He called for farther savings in order that the excise might be abolished; and, to show the possibility of such reductions as he advocated, he instanced the salary of the governor of Sierra Leone, amounting to 7,000*l*., by the reduction of which the House would be enabled to repeal the tax on books. They might also transfer the duties of the ordnance to the war department, and thus save 250,000*l*. a year. He held up to the present government the example afforded them by Sir J. Graham, who had reduced the expenses of the Admiralty by 1,200,000*l*. Mr. Milner Gibson recommended the remission of the penny-stamp duty on newspapers, of the excise duty on paper, and the advertisement duty; and he enforced his argument against them by referring to a petition lately presented to the House of Commons by the Messrs. Chambers of Edinburgh, in which they stated that the tax on paper had caused them to discontinue the publication of a work intended for the humbler classes, of which 80,000 copies had been circulated. The Whigs, he said, and truly, had always deserved credit for their repudiation of the taxes on knowledge; and the course he proposed was therefore thoroughly in accordance with the principles and professions of the Whig party, and well calculated to establish them in the confidence of the country. Mr. Gibson gave a very satisfactory account of the condition of the working classes in the north of England, alleging that they had never commanded a larger share of the necessaries and comforts of life. The claims of hops, malt, bricks, soap, tea, timber, to remission of the duties imposed on them, were urged by speakers who took part in the discussion that followed the introduction of the budget. On the 20th of July Mr. Herries proposed the imposition of a small fixed duty on corn, for revenue only, which, as he tried to show, would yield a considerable income to the country, without enhancing the price of corn. The assertion of Mr. Herries, that the tax would really be paid by the foreigner, was briefly but most completely disposed of by Mr. Bright, who showed that our supplies of corn came from all parts of the world ; but that if the range were to be circumscribed, if corn could only be brought at a certain price from China or the Black Sea, and could be brought at a lower price from the Baltic, the contraction of the circle would diminish the source of supply, and raise the price of corn in the ratio of the duty.

In the course of the session Mr. Hume made another effort in favour of parliamentary reform. He moved, on the 4th of June, for leave to bring in a bill to amend the national representation by extending the elective franchise to all householders, by secret voting, by triennial parliaments, and by rendering the proportion that representation bore to population more equal. As the bill was introduced without the slightest expectation that it would pass, and chiefly for the sake of agitating the country in favour of such a reform as was proposed, and as we shall meet with the question again and again in the course of this History, it would be superfluous to give any account of the debate on the motion. Suffice it to say that it was rejected by a majority of 186.

In June Mr. Cobden brought forward his celebrated plan for settling international disputes by arbitration instead of by war. Lord Palmerston, the foreign secretary, speaking on behalf of the government, met the proposition with a respectful negative, by moving the previous question, which, after an important debate, was carried by a majority of 57. A new bill for the admission of Jews to Parliament was carried through all its stages in the lower House, and was again negatived by the Lords, the majority against it being 25. Another bill, destined to be often proposed and often rejected, was brought this year into the House of Commons by Mr. Stuart Wortley—a bill for the removal of the legal prohibition of marriage with a deceased wife's sister. This prohibition, founded on a doubtful interpretation of a passage in Leviticus, had been established in the reign of Henry VIII., at the time when he was seeking to invalidate his marriage with Catherine of Arragon. However, it had become nearly obsolete, and the alliances prohibited by it had been in many instances contracted. For this reason a bill had been introduced by Lord Lyndhurst in 1835, and carried through both Houses, legalising the marriages that had already taken place in spite or in ignorance of the law, but making all such marriages illegal for the future, and declaring that henceforth they would be null and void. However, notwithstanding this act, the marriages it prohibited continued to be contracted, and it was affirmed that the legitimacy of no fewer than forty thousand persons was in consequence affected. There was, nevertheless, a strong opposition to Mr. Wortley's bill, founded partly on the supposed scriptural condemnation of such marriages, and partly on the law of the church of England, which distinctly prohibited them. The opposition to the measure was much strengthened by a statement very widely diffused, that it was brought forward for the relief of one wealthy and influential individual, who, having violated the law himself, was willing to spend a large sum of money to procure the repeal of it. However, if the bill was strongly opposed, it was also powerfully supported, and its second reading was carried by a majority of 34; but the delay caused by the opposition offered to the bill, and by repeated adjournments of the debates on it, compelled Mr. Wortley to withdraw it. A bankruptcy bill proposed by Lord Brougham, and some other legal reforms of less importance introduced by the attorney-general, completed the public legislative work of the session. Before it closed, Mr. Disraeli, who had now become the recognized leader of the opposition in the House of Commons, made a final trial of the strength of his party. On the 2nd of July he moved for a select committee to inquire into the state of the nation. In bringing forward this motion he arraigned the whole policy of the government, but he more especially assailed its free-trade principles. His speech was in fact intended to prove that free trade was a failure, and that the commercial and financial embarrassment in which the country was now involved was chiefly attributable to the adoption of that system. He alleged that European tranquillity and English influence had disappeared together; that many of our colonies were ruined, others discontented, and some in insurrection; that our exports had declined 7,000,000*l.*; our once prosperous agriculture was prostrate; Ireland was in a state of social decomposition; and, instead of a surplus revenue of 3,000,000*l.* there had been a deficiency to that amount, terminated not by any act of the cabinet, but by the interference of this House.

He quoted official documents, which showed that a great depression of wages and a great increase of pauperism had taken place among the labouring classes. After reading these papers, he proceeded to explain the reasons to which he referred the distress of the population, and the general deterioration of their condition. A principal reason was the decline in value of our foreign commerce. Notwithstanding continental convulsions, the quantity of goods exported from the United Kingdom in 1848 was equal to that of the great years 1845-1846; but the declared value of the imports in the two latter years averaged 59,500,000*l.*, while in 1848 it was only 53,000,000*l.*; so that our working classes, for the same quantity of goods, had received 6,500,000*l.* less in 1848 than in 1845 and 1846. He insisted that these and other facts showed that the principles of interchange with foreign nations adopted in our new commercial theory were erroneous, rendering British labour of less exchangeable value. Other reasons were to be found in the state of the home market and the fall of prices, which diminished the means of employment; and in the increase of emigration from Ireland, the result, not of famine, but of the policy of the government.

Sir Robert Peel again came to the assistance of the government, defending the policy which had been so strongly impugned by the leader of the opposition, and showing that free trade not only had not caused any of the evils complained of, but had greatly mitigated them. He maintained that by the policy adopted in 1842 the legislature had gained the confidence and the good-will of powerful classes, and this country had been enabled to pass through a storm which convulsed other nations.

The House divided on Mr. Disraeli's motion, which was rejected by the large majority of 140; a very distinct manifestation of the continued confidence of the House in those free-trade measures which Sir R. Peel had induced it to adopt, and which the present government was gradually applying and farther developing.

The business of the session being disposed of on the 1st of August, Parliament was prorogued by commission.

On the 2nd of December the Queen-dowager breathed her last, in the 57th year of her age. From the moment that her husband showed reactionary tendencies she was suspected of having exerted an influence over his opinions and conduct which had produced this result, and a double share of the unpopularity which befell him descended on her, and attached to her throughout the rest of his reign. When Lord Melbourne was dismissed in 1834, the *Times* came out with the announcement, 'The Queen has done it;' and these ominous words, placarded in large letters in the streets of London, produced a very strong feeling against her through the nation. How far these suspicions were just is doubtful. She certainly regarded the Reform Bill, and the measures of the Whig ministry in general, with alarm. That she should have communicated her fears to her husband was natural and pardonable; but that she exerted any improper influence over the exercise of his prerogative has never been proved, and from her modest and retiring character is highly improbable. She spent the years of her widowhood in unostentatious retirement, doing all the good she could with the large sum which the liberality of Parliament had settled on her after her husband's decease, and enjoying, and by her amiable qualities deserving, the respect of men of all parties. In accordance with her own earnest request her body was not opened or embalmed; there was no lying in state after her decease; and the interment took place with as little as possible of the pomp and ceremony that are usually observed on such occasions. Her memory obtained that respect which purity, goodness, and unpretending piety in a high station are sure sooner or later to command; and the justice which had been denied her during a large portion of her husband's reign was fully accorded to her after his death.

## CHAPTER VI.

#### THE GREAT EXHIBITION.

Thus far the free-trade measures which Sir R. Peel and his colleagues had carried had hardly enjoyed a fair trial. The badness of the harvest; the failure of the potato-crop; the consequent derangement and stagnation of business; the distress which affected every class and every trade, prevented the beneficial working of the recently inaugurated system from being perceived. Its advocates were forced to admit their disappointment, but they alleged that the distress which prevailed so widely would have been ten times greater, and the famine that had ravaged Ireland ten times more desolating, if the system of protection had been maintained. On the other hand, the upholders of that policy warmly contended that the distress was due to the abandonment of it; that it was precisely what they predicted would follow that abandonment; and that it would continue and increase until the old system was restored. Meanwhile most of the farmers, without weighing the arguments of the two parties, or being able to discover the causes of their suffering, felt that they were worse off than before, and saw in the calamities that had come upon them a fufilment of the predictions with which they had been so plentifully plied during the period of the anti-corn-law agitation by the self-styled farmers' friends. They were therefore more than ever attached to that protective policy, to the withdrawal of which they imputed their present condition. Such was the state of feeling and opinion in the country when Parliament assembled on the 31st of January 1850. The session was opened by commission. Amendments to the address were moved; but were negatived in the upper House by a majority of 49, and in the lower House by a majority of 119.

Mr. Disraeli, ascribing the distress that prevailed in the agricultural districts to the withdrawal of the duties on foreign corn, but acknowledging that, in the present Parliament at least, it was impossible to obtain their reimposition, now pleaded, not for protection, but for compensation. He asked for a committee of inquiry, which he hoped would recommend the transfer of a portion of the expenses, which had hitherto been defrayed out of the rates, to the general taxation of the country. His motion was opposed by Sir G. Grey and Sir J. Graham; but was supported by Mr. Gladstone, on the ground that the concession of Mr. Disraeli's demands would tend to weaken the argument in favour of a return to protection, which had all along been claimed on the ground that the agriculturists were subjected to peculiar burdens; an argument which would be altogether taken away by the removal of any excess of taxation under which it might be found on investigation that the agriculturist laboured, and many moderate protectionists would thus be detached from the party that demanded a return to the abandoned policy. Sir J. Graham had argued against the proposals of Mr. Disraeli, on the ground of justice to the other classes of the community, and Mr. Gladstone supported them on the ground of justice to the agriculturist. Sir J. Graham maintained that the proposed measure would only benefit landowners; Mr. Gladstone, on the contrary, contended that the farmer and the yeoman would reap the chief advantage from the change. After some other speakers had delivered their opinions on the question, Sir R. Peel addressed the House in a speech of considerable interest, because it contained his latest convictions on a question which he surveyed from so many different points of view, and on which he now for the last time delivered his deliberate opinions. The argument that the landowners were entitled to peculiar protection because they were subject to peculiar burdens had been his favourite argument, and that he had based on it his justification of the monopoly which they enjoyed, and which he at one period had so strenuously defended.

After speaking of the ability and moderation that Mr. Disraeli had displayed in bringing forward this motion in a manner which, considering the terms in which that gentleman had denounced and opposed him on former occasions, was honourable to both parties, he condemned the proposal to transfer 2,000,000*l.* of taxation to the consolidated fund, as the first of a series of measures which would appropriate the surplus of this and succeeding years. 'What,' he asked, 'will be the effect of this scheme on the finances of the country? It will preclude the legislation for the remission of taxes affecting the industry and the comforts of the people; it will either compel the continuance of the income tax, or the imposition of a duty on every foreign product in order to maintain public credit. And is the measure really for the benefit af the agricultural class itself? The proposed transfer of 2,000,000*l.* of rates to the exchequer would relieve the land only of 900,000*l.*, the remaining 1,100,000*l.* being now borne by other descriptions of real property. Yet all must be made up by the occupying tenant (in common with other classes), who would not gain a greater remission than threepence or fourpence in the pound.'

He then went on to object to the motion, on the ground that it endangered a reversal of the successful commercial policy which had been carried out during the last six years.

When the division took place the numbers were—

| | |
|---|---|
| For Mr. Disraeli's motion | 252 |
| Against it | 273 |
| Majority against the motion | 21 |

The smallness of the majority by which the motion was defeated was a matter of great triumph to the protectionists, who had never before mustered so large a number on any division, and who, from being a concourse of isolated individualities, were now becoming a great, organised, and formidable power in the state.

Mr. Hume renewed his efforts to obtain a large measure of parliamentary reform; but as the plan which he brought forward embodied the principles contained in the motion he made before, it met with the same fate, and it is not necessary or desirable that we should go into any details respecting it, or the discussion which took place on it in the House of Commons. We shall meet with this question again and again as we advance.

The great change that had been made in the navigation laws had necessarily been followed by a great change in the relations between the mother country and her colonies, and had even caused the question to be raised, whether it was for her advantage to retain them at all. There were not wanting those who contended that it would be better for us to part with them on friendly terms, and leave them to govern themselves, only stipulating for the admission of our goods into their ports on favourable terms. The government, though not prepared to go to these lengths, had come to the conclusion that it had become absolutely necessary that many of them should be allowed a more complete control of their own affairs, and a more popular form of government than they had hitherto enjoyed. A colonial reform association had been formed—had diffused much information, which had considerably influenced public opinion in favour of the changes it advocated. A bill, introduced by the government for the purpose of giving a more popular government to our Australian colonies, raised the whole question of colonial reform. Sir W. Molesworth and Mr. Gladstone made great but ineffectual efforts to introduce their principles of colonial reform into the government bill, and the latter gentleman moved a clause giving to the church of England in the colonies the same privileges with regard to synodical action that were enjoyed by other religious communities. The bill passed through both Houses, but not without being amended in the lower House with the consent of the government, and in the upper in spite of its remonstrances. An attempt made by Sir F. Buxton to restore protection to free-grown as against slave-grown sugar was defeated in a full House by a majority of 41.

In this session Ireland was neither forgotten nor neglected; but the Irish legislation was not of such a nature as to affect appreciably the course of events in England. The distress that continued to prevail in that country once more occupied the attention of the legislature. A measure for the extension of the franchise there, passed with some amendments introduced into it by the lords. A bill was brought in by Lord J. Russell for the abolition of the office of lord lieutenant, the second reading of which was carried by the large majority of 225, but which the pressure of other business caused to be deferred.

The budget of this year was introduced on the 15th of

March, and it showed that the fiscal policy which Sir R. Peel had inaugurated when he came into office was now beginning to manifest the effects which its authors had predicted that it would produce, but which the potato disease, the failure of the crops, and the consequent commercial, manufacturing, and agricultural distress had countervailed. The chancellor of the exchequer, in making his statement, calculated that the income of the country for the financial year 1851-2 would amount to 52,285,000*l*., and that the expenditure would be 50,763,000*l*., leaving in round numbers a surplus of 1,500,000*l*. His first object would be to reduce the debt. During the last twenty years the government had borrowed no less than 35,000,000*l*., whereas the surplus income applied to the reduction of the debt had been only 8,000,000*l*. So that during twenty years of profound peace they had increased the principal of the debt by no less than 27,000,000*l*. He thought that half of the surplus should be applied towards the extinction of this obligation. He next proposed measures of relief from taxation. First he proposed to benefit small owners of land by considerable reductions of the stamp duties on the transfer of landed property and upon mortgages under 1000*l*., and that within the same limit the stamp duty on leases should be a uniform half per cent. His next proposal was to increase the comfort of the labouring classes by improving their dwellings, and to facilitate agricultural improvement by repealing the duty on bricks. The loss of revenue by these two remissions would be 750,000*l*., half the expected surplus. At the same time he proposed another measure calculated to promote the outlay of capital on drainage and land improvements, the benefits of which had been sensibly felt, and to advance for these purposes 2,000,000*l*. for England and Scotland, and 1,000,000*l*. for Ireland, 800,000*l*. of the latter sum being applicable to arterial drainage. These advances could be made in the present state of the exchequer without any addition to the public debt, and the repayments would be available for its reduction.

In the course of the subsequent debate on the various parts of the budget, a motion proposed by Sir Henry Willoughby, reducing the proposed duty on a loan of 50*l*. from 2*s*. 6*d*. to 1*s*., was carried in spite of the declaration of the chancellor of the exchequer that it would add a loss of 70,000*l.* to the reduction of the 300,000*l.* which he had originally proposed. After a good deal of chaffering, after the withdrawal of the bill in order to the introduction of another more in accordance with the wishes of the majority of the House, and a long delay, the chancellor of the exchequer announced towards the end of the session that, as the revenue had increased more than he expected at the time when he made his financial statement, as he believed that the loss from the reduction of the stamps would not be so great as he then estimated, and as the commencement of the act was postponed to October, so that it would only be in operation during half of that year, he would reduce the duty on conveyances altogether to one-half per cent., and the duty on mortgages to a uniform eight per cent. He calculated that the loss to the revenue by the whole of the proposed remissions would be about 500,000*l.*; but the result showed that he had greatly over-estimated its amount.

At this time the feeling in favour of economy was quite as strong among the Conservatives as among the Radicals. The distress that pervaded the agricultural districts had converted their representatives into earnest advocates of retrenchment. While both sides of the house were thus vying with each other in promoting reductions of expenditure, ministers felt that they must do something. They intended to begin with a reduction of official salaries, which was the plan chiefly insisted on by the advocates of retrenchment; and Lord J. Russell proposed to refer this important question to a select committee. This proposal was resisted by Mr. Disraeli, Mr. Hume, Mr. Henley, and several others, on the ground that a select committee would not be able to obtain any information on the subject which was not already within the reach of the government; and they contended that it was the duty of ministers to deal with the matter on their own responsibility. In behalf of the proposal made by the government, it was argued that it was in accordance with precedent, and that persons whose interests might be touched by the alterations which the committee suggested would probably submit to the reduction of their incomes with a better grace if recommended by a body so constituted as to command the confidence of all parties, and after due and impartial investigation. The government plan was adopted by a majority of 208 to 95. The feeling in favour of economy that prevailed both in the House of Commons and in the country gave birth to several measures originated by independent members. Thus, on the 8th of March Mr. Cobden again brought forward his proposal for the gradual reduction of the expenditure of the country to the point at which it stood in the year 1835. He showed that, by allowing pensions to lapse, by suppressing or reducing the appointments of such embassies as those to Hanover and Bavaria, by lowering judicial salaries, cutting-down excessive consular expenditure, and diminishing the amount devoted to the maintenance of the army and navy, it would be quite possible to reduce the total expenditure of the country by 10,000,000*l.*; a sum equal to the whole expenditure of the United States before the Mexican war, and more than the whole expenditure of Prussia. In answer to a pamphlet which had been published by a gentleman named Norman, for the purpose of proving that the country was very lightly taxed, Mr. Cobden remarked that it might be true, as this gentleman asserted, that the wealth of the country had increased, but the wealth of the country did not pay the increased taxation. Mr. Labouchere, on the part of the government, attempted to show that the increase of the expenditure since the year 1835 on which Mr. Cobden based his motion was more apparent than real, and was due to accumulated expenditure left from previous years, to accumulated charges which had been forced on the government by the House itself under the pressure of demands from different constituencies, such as those for harbours of refuge, payments in aid of rates, and expenses arising out of unforeseen calamities, as, for instance, the destruction of the two Houses of Parliament. At the close of the debate the motion was rejected by a majority of 185.

On the 13th of March Mr. Henry Drummond brought forward a motion for the diminution of the salaries of all servants of the crown, and for the removal of every impediment that checked the growth of raw produce. This motion was got rid of by the common expedient of moving the previous question.

Lord Duncan introduced a motion, which he had already

moved unsuccessfully more than once before, for the total repeal of the window tax. This impost was perhaps the most unpopular tax that existed, and not without reason; for, in order to evade it as much as possible, houses were so constructed as to diminish the quantity both of light and fresh air admitted into them. The motion was resisted by the government, and rejected, but by a majority of three only, in a house of 157 members; and the smallness of this majority was regarded both by the friends and opponents of the tax as a proof that it would not be long maintained. A renewed attempt to repeal the malt tax was met by the argument that the exchequer could not afford the loss of a revenue of five millions, and was defeated by a majority of 124.

In the course of this year one of the most remarkable cases that has ever occurred was litigated with a degree of obstinacy and perseverance seldom equalled.

The Rev. George Cornelius Gorham had been appointed by the lord chancellor to the vicarage of St. Just in the diocese of Exeter, in the year 1846, and had been duly instituted to that living by Dr. Phillpotts, the bishop. In the following year he was appointed by the same patron to the living of Bamford Speke, and in due course applied to the bishop for institution to his new benefice. The bishop then took the strictly legal but very unusual course of subjecting Mr. Gorham to an examination in reference to certain points on which he supposed him to be unsound. The examination was carried on at great length, no fewer than 140 questions having been put by the bishop, and answered by Mr. Gorham. It extended over the 17th, 18th, 20th, 21st, and 22d of December, and the 8th, 9th, and 10th of the following March; and at the conclusion of it the bishop declined to give Mr. Gorham institution. The matter was then carried to the Court of Arches. There it appeared that the ground of his rejection was a denial of the doctrine of baptismal regeneration as laid down in the baptismal services of the church of England. It was argued on his behalf that the opinions he held on this subject were in accordance with those of Cranmer, Ridley, Latimer, and other leading reformers. To this argument the court replied that, if this was the case, they decidedly had not so declared their opinions in any of the services of the church, in the articles, or in any part of the book of Common Prayer; and gave a decision in favour of the bishop. From this court the case was carried by Mr. Gorham to the judicial committee of the privy council, on which a final appeal from the ecclesiastical tribunal had been recently conferred. Before this court the question was argued on both sides at great length; and the unusual nature of the dispute, and the strong feeling with which it was regarded by the two great parties in the church, caused the sentence to be expected, not only by the clergy, but by the public generally, with great interest and impatience. The gist of the judgment given by the court of appeal is contained in the following sentences:

'These being, as we collect them, the opinions of Mr. Gorham, the question which we have to decide is not, whether they are theologically sound or unsound, not whether in some of the doctrines comprised in the opinions other opinions opposite to them may not be held with equal or even with greater reason, by other learned and pious ministers of the church; but whether these opinions now under our consideration are contrary or repugnant to the doctrines which the church of England by its articles, formularies, and rubrics requires to be held by its ministers, so that, upon the ground of these opinions, the appellant can lawfully be excluded from the benefice to which he has been presented.'

After examining at great length the various passages of the articles, rubrics, and formularies of the church of England that bore upon the question at issue before the court, the judgment thus concluded:

'It appears that opinions, which cannot in any important particular be distinguished from those entertained by Mr. Gorham, have been propounded and maintained by persons so eminent and so much respected, as well as by very many others; which appears to us sufficiently to prove that the liberty which was left by the articles and formularies has been actually enjoyed and exercised by the members and ministers of the church of England.'

The decision of the judicial committee therefore was, that Mr. Gorham ought not, by reason of the doctrine held by him to have been refused admission to the vicarage of Bampton Speke; and the sentence pronounced in the Court of Arches was reversed.

This decision raised a ferment in the church. The evangelical party, most of the members of which held opinions very similar to those which had been maintained by Mr. Gorham, had been filled with alarm. They dreaded that, if his appeal should prove unsuccessful, they might be ejected from their benefices, or at all events prevented from obtaining farther preferment. They were therefore delighted at a decision which seemed to justify them in holding opinions which had been denounced by the orthodox party as plainly inconsistent with the articles and formularies of the church, and which it was certainly very difficult to reconcile with the plain language of her baptismal services. On the other hand, there was a not inconsiderable body of old high-church men, and of men who belonged to neither of the two great parties into which the church was then divided, who, though they disliked Mr. Gorham's opinions, were nevertheless unwilling to intrust to the bishops that power which the prelate of Exeter claimed for his order, and dreaded that bishops holding opinions different from those of the present incumbent of that see might subject their theological opponents to an examination as rigorous as that which Mr. Gorham had undergone, and might end with refusing to institute them to livings to which they might be appointed. These, therefore, though regretting the sanction given by the court of final appeal to the doctrines of Mr. Gorham, were not sorry to see this attempt to increase the power of the bishops defeated; and the patrons of livings throughout the kingdom, whose rights were seriously compromised by the claim put forward by Dr. Phillpotts, sympathised with this feeling almost to a man. But the Oxford tracts, which had now run their course, had produced a new high-church party, the members of which did not indeed all of them accept the whole of the teaching of those tracts, but were to a man zealous for the doctrine of baptismal regeneration, and warmly contended that the right of stating and determining her own doctrine was inherent in the church, and one with which no lay tribunal ought to intermeddle. They contended that any question involving doctrine ought to be referred to the spirituality, meaning by that term either the bishops alone, or the bishops and clergy in convocation assembled. They were therefore unanimous and indignant in their condemnation of the judgment, and attempt after attempt was made to procure a reversal of it, the question being carried first into the court of Queen's Bench, then into the court of Common Pleas, and finally into the court of Exchequer, in the vain hope of upsetting the judgment which the judicial committee had given.

Apart from this feeling, there were strong and well-grounded objections to the constitution of a court which had now for the first time been called on to decide an important theological question. It was not only composed of laymen, but it might be composed of persons dissenting from the church, who would thus decide on her doctrines, and on the manner in which her services might be conducted. It might indeed be urged that it was the business of the tribunal not to make laws, but to interpret them, and that a dissenting lawyer might be, and probably would be, a better and a more dispassionate interpreter of the law of the church than an orthodox divine; but it was contended on the other hand, that, when the doctrines of the church or the meaning of her formularies were in question, she possessed the right, and ought to be permitted the opportunity, of declaring what they were. Besides, the manner in which the judges who were to sit on each case were named was alleged to be very unsatisfactory, and to open the door to the selection of men whose leanings were known to be in favour of a particular decision, and whose judgment on a given case might be anticipated beforehand. It was also objected, that the judges of this court were supposed to claim and exercise a certain discretionary power, and to be guided by considerations of expediency, to decide in such a manner as they deemed best adapted to advance the interests of the state as well as of the church. For these reasons this court did not enjoy that confidence which has been accorded to the great civil tribunals of the country, and its decisions have never commanded the respect and acquiescence which are almost invariably yielded to the decisions of the Queen's Bench, the Exchequer, and the Common Pleas.

But in the Gorham case there was a circumstance which

increased the dissatisfaction with which the decision was received. The archbishops of Canterbury and York, and the bishop of London sat as assessors to the judges. The two first-mentioned prelates had been recently appointed by the government, whose patronage was in question, and which was exceedingly unpopular with the clergy. It was understood that they had given their opinions in favour of Mr. Gorham; but that the bishop of London, acknowledged on all hands to be a far abler man than either of them, and possessing in a far higher degree than either the confidence of churchmen generally, had given his opinion decidedly in favour of the bishop of Exeter. And so strongly did he object to the character of the court in which he had sat and by which this question had been decided, that he introduced a bill into the House of Lords on the 3d of June for the establishment of a new tribunal for ecclesiastical appeals in the place of the judicial committee of the privy council. Had he attempted to remodel that court in such a manner as to inspire greater confidence in its competence and impartiality, he would probably have succeeded; but instead of doing this, he proposed to substitute for that body a court of bishops. This proposal was open to objection on many grounds; but the chief argument employed against it was founded on its supposed interference with the royal supremacy. But, whatever force there may have been in the other objections to the bill, this does not appear to carry much weight with it. In either case the supremacy would be exercised through a regularly-constituted tribunal; and whether it should be a court of laymen or a court of bishops seems to be immaterial so far as the question of the supremacy is concerned. But a tribunal composed of bishops would certainly have commanded even less confidence than the existing tribunal. However, a long debate ensued, which was carried on with a degree of animation and emotion seldom displayed in the upper house. On the question of the second reading of the measure the numbers were—

| | |
|---|---|
| For the second reading .. .. .. .. .. .. | 51 |
| Against .. .. .. .. .. .. .. .. | 84 |
| Majority against the bill .. .. .. .. | 33 |

This decision settled the question for a long time; and

though every subsequent judgment of the court has been attended by an amount of dissatisfaction that the judgment of no other English court excites, all attempts at obtaining a change in its constitution were long regarded as hopeless, partly on account of the difficulty experienced in obtaining the attention of the legislature to such subjects, but still more from the difficulty of devising a substitute for it which would command general confidence.

A debate which excited a lively interest in the House of Commons was raised on the motion of Mr. James Heywood, member for North Lancashire, for an inquiry with a view to a reform of the universities of Oxford, Cambridge, and Dublin. It required no small amount of moral courage to introduce such a proposal into an assembly like the House of Commons, filled as it was with men who had received their education at these venerable institutions. The question had indeed been already brought before the House by Mr. G. W. Wood, Mr. Christie, and others; but the manner in which their proposals had been dealt with was not calculated to encourage others to follow their example. Mr. Heywood had himself been educated at Trinity College, Cambridge; but being a Unitarian he had been prevented from taking his degree by a regulation of the university requiring all persons who wish to graduate to sign a declaration that they were *bonâ-fide* members of the church of England. In this respect Cambridge was more liberal or more fortunate than the sister university; for while she only required a declaration of church membership before taking the degree, the other university made it a condition of matriculation. Thus the nonconformists, repelled at Oxford at the very entrance, found an asylum at Cambridge, received there the best education the university could afford, might attain to the highest honours she conferred on her successful students, and was only stopped at the point of taking the degree which should crown and complete a university career. Mr. Heywood was well known to be enthusiastically attached to his *alma mater;* he had devoted much time and labour to the examination of its statutes and the study of its constitution; he had thoroughly mastered the question in all its bearings; he had ascertained how much the resources of the universities were wasted; and how much need there was of some means of reforming the abuses that had grown up in the course of ages, and of adapting the curriculum of university teaching to the circumstances of the times. He was also anxious to redress the grievances of which the dissenters complained. In order to effect these objects he moved, on the 23d of April, 'That an humble address should be presented to her Majesty, praying her to issue a royal commission of inquiry into the state of the universities and colleges of Oxford, Cambridge, and Dublin, with a view to assist in the adaptation of these important institutions to the requirements of modern times.' The subject was not new to the prime minister, for his attention had been drawn to it by the unsuccessful motions of Messrs. Wood, Christie, &c., and still more directly by the presentation in 1848 of a very able memorial in favour of a royal commission of inquiry drawn up by the Rev. Mr. Stanley, now Dean of Westminster, and signed by some of the most eminent members of the universities which it was proposed to reform. When Mr. Heywood brought forward his motion, the House of Commons presented an unwonted appearance. The six university members were ranged on the bench usually occupied by the leaders of the opposition, thus announcing their uncompromising hostility to the proposal which was to be submitted to the House. Behind them were ranged a large body of men who had received their education at one or other of those universities into whose affairs Mr. Heywood proposed to inquire. But the House was taken by surprise when Lord J. Russell rose and announced that if Mr. Heywood would withdraw his motion, the government would advise the crown to issue a royal commission to inquire into the state of the universities. On the 18th of the following July he made a fuller explanation of the intentions of the government. 'We propose,' he said, 'to make such inquiries as were made with respect to the municipal corporations and the ecclesiastical bodies ; and if it should on inquiry be thought necessary that any alteration should be made, it will afterwards be the time to inquire what was the authority by which these alterations should be effected.' The commission appointed in pursuance of this pledge encountered great difficulties in the prosecution of the investigations it was directed to make. It did not possess the power of compelling the attendance of witnesses, or of administering oaths to those who gave evidence. This would have been a matter of little consequence, if the university authorities had been willing to give information on the subjects to which the researches of the commission were directed. But this was not the case. The vice-chancellor of Oxford positively refused to give evidence; and the example thus set was followed by many other office-bearers of the universities and colleges; so that in several instances the revenues of the colleges could not be even approximately calculated. In order to avoid the necessity of again recurring to this subject we may further state that the report of the commission was published in 1852, during the short-lived administration of Lord Derby, who contented himself with distributing copies of it to those whom it chiefly concerned. In 1854, when the Earl of Aberdeen was in power, the question was again brought forward. A memorial, signed by 100 members of the House of Commons, was presented to Lord J. Russell, requesting the introduction into the bill of clauses abolishing religious tests at matriculation and graduation in the University of Oxford. As Lord J. Russell declined to accede to this suggestion, Mr. Heywood proposed clauses having that effect, which were carried by overwhelming majorities in the House of Commons.

This result was in a great measure due to the efforts of dissenters in the constituencies under the guidance of the Liberation or Anti-state-church Society. Still it remained to overcome the resistance of the House of Lords, in which an overwhelming majority was strongly indisposed to admit the proposed changes. The unmistakable tendency of public opinion disposed the peers to yield a point for which a large majority of the commons had voted. But much depended on the course taken by the late Earl of Derby as leader of the opposition in that assembly. In this, as in some other instances, that eminent nobleman showed that the liberal spirit of his earlier days had not altogether departed from him. He supported the opening of matriculation and of the degree of bachelor of arts at Oxford, with a rider attached to the clause, in the House of Lords, that such degrees should not qualify their possessors to hold offices which had hitherto been held by members of the church of England; and in this form the bill became law.

In conformity with the provisions of this measure, commissioners were sent to Oxford in 1854 to carry out its enactments; and in 1856 similar arrangements were adopted with regard to Cambridge. More recent legislation has opened the fellowships and scholarships of the various colleges, and removed the disabilities under which the nonconformists previously laboured. But the revision of the studies of these ancient seats of learning still remains to be carried out, and probably will not be delayed much longer. The practical result of the parliamentary commission of 1854 has been to raise considerably the value of the college estates, and the income of the universities. The chief result of the act adopted during the Aberdeen administration was the transfer of the government of the universities from a board composed of the heads of houses to the resident masters of arts, a younger and more liberal body. The work, commenced in the manner and under the circumstances we have described, has been carried forward since, till, at the present time, almost all university offices, and, as far as the statutes of the colleges allow, all college offices also, have been thrown open to nonconformists.

The session of 1850 witnessed a reintroduction of the deceased-wife's-sister bill, which, after a protracted and more than ordinarily able debate, after an opposition that might almost be termed vexatious, passed the commons, but only to be quietly and respectfully shelved by the lords.

Few events have ever roused a stronger feeling, or produced greater manifestations of discontent, than a very simple motion adopted by the House of Commons. Lord Ashley moved a resolution for an address to her Majesty, praying that she would be graciously pleased to direct that the collection and delivery of letters should in future entirely cease on the Lord's-day in all parts of the kingdom. This motion was carried by 93 votes against 68 The government therefore, partly from deference to the will of the majority, partly from annoyance at the defection or absence of their usual supporters, which had allowed the vote to be carried against them, but with a full foresight of the inconveniences which would arise from the carrying-out of this vote, and the discontent it would produce in all parts of the kingdom, determined to give effect to it as promptly as possible. When their intention became known, protests and representations poured in from all parts of the kingdom. The matter was brought before Parliament by Mr. Fox, the member for Oldham, who stated that the newspaper agents were placed under great difficulties by the shortness of the notice afforded them, and asked that more time should be allowed them to make the necessary changes in their arrangements. The chancellor of the exchequer elicited loud laughter by stating in his reply to Mr. Fox, that the instructions which had been given were in strict accordance with the vote of the house; that he had not a doubt of their inconvenience; and that he hoped that in due time honourable gentlemen would receive representations which would induce them to rescind their vote. In the mean time, however, that vote was faithfully carried out, and for several weeks there was an entire cessation of the Sunday delivery of letters and newspapers throughout the kingdom. If the complaints had been loud when the intentions of the government were first announced, they waxed louder still when they were thus put in force, and the inconveniences attendant on the new arrangement began to be felt. The press, which not only reflected the opinion of the public on the subject, but had grievances of its own to complain of, and whose interests were most seriously affected by the change, agitated strongly for a return to the old practice. Lord Ashley for a time was the most unpopular man in the kingdom. On the 29th of July Mr. Locke moved another address to her Majesty, praying her to institute an inquiry in order to ascertain whether the Sunday labour might not be reduced without putting an end to the collection and delivery of letters on that day. The motion was intended to procure a reversal of Lord Ashley's resolution. Mr. Locke argued that the change which had been made, so far from diminishing the amount of Sunday labour employed in the delivery of letters and newspapers, had rather increased it by causing that delivery to take place to a large extent through indirect channels. Mr. Roebuck, in seconding the motion, said that the evils of the change fell most heavily on the poor man, to whom the pot-house was open, though the newspaper was shut. Lord Ashley, on the other hand, demanded for his measure a fair, full, and sufficient trial, which it could not have in twenty-one days. He appealed to the case of the metropolis, which had long been without any Sunday delivery, and bore the privation without complaint. However, the result of the debate was a return, after a brief interval, to the old practice, which has ever since been continued, without any serious attempt having been made to change it again.

Lord Ashley was more successful in another measure which he introduced. The last factory bill was so worded, that in the opinion of the law-courts it did not carry out the known intentions of its proposers or of the legislature which passed it. Lord Ashley therefore brought in a bill to amend it; and, with the consent of its mover and several of his supporters, a compromise was effected, establishing the short-time system as it is now in force almost in its entirety; whereupon the government took the measure into its own hands, and carried it through both Houses of Parliament.

On the 26th of July Baron Rothschild made another attempt to take his seat in the House of Commons, and thereby gave occasion to another debate on the Jew question. On the motion of Mr. Hume he was allowed to take the oath on the Old Testament; but as in taking it he omitted to recite the words 'on the true faith of a Christian,' which were contained in the oath, it was decided that he could not be permitted to take his seat.

But of all the debates of this session, the most remarkable was one occasioned by the foreign policy of Lord Palmerston, who had asserted, in a very high-handed manner, the rights of English citizens against the government of Greece. A vote of censure on that policy had been adopted by the lords, and, if maintained, would have necessitated the retirement of that minister, and probably the resignation of the government. To prevent this result Mr. Roebuck brought forward a motion couched in terms which not only conveyed an approval of the foreign policy of Lord Palmerston, but also implied an oblique censure on the somewhat different policy of Lord Aberdeen, who had held the seals of the foreign office under Sir Robert Peel. Never had Sir Robert displayed greater moderation or kindliness. He warmly and ably defended his late colleague; spoke of Lord Palmerston in the highest terms; gave him wise and sound advice, but pointed out the dangers that attended his policy, and announced his intention to vote against the motion; which, however, was carried by 310 to 264. It was early on Saturday morning when Sir Robert Peel quitted the House, and the sun had risen before he lay down to rest. But he could not give many hours to sleep, for at twelve o'clock he was to be present at a meeting of the commissioners of the great industrial exhibition, that was to take place next year, and at that meeting the place in which the exhibition should be held, was to be decided. After his return from it, he passed the afternoon in his study until five o'clock, when he went out to take a ride in the park. After calling at Buckingham Palace, and writing his name in the Queen's visiting-book, he went on to Constitution Hill, where he met Miss Ellis, a daughter of Lady Dover, who was also on horseback, and stopped for a moment to chat with her. His horse, which was young and fresh, suddenly shied and threw him off, but as he still clung to the bridle, he caused it to fall with its knees on his shoulders. A medical man, Dr. Foucart of Glasgow, happened to be on the spot, and, with the assistance of another gentleman, lifted Sir Robert into a carriage which was passing at the time. Before it reached his home Sir James Clark, one of the physicians of the Queen, who had heard of the accident, came to offer his assistance, and with Dr. Foucart accompanied him to his house. The sight of Lady Peel, and the distress that she showed, caused Sir Robert to faint on his arrival. Sir Benjamin Brodie and all the first surgeons of London were sent for; but their aid was of little avail. Sir Robert's nervous system was peculiarly sensitive to pain, and this sensitiveness had increased by age and labour. Every attempt which his medical attendants made to ascertain the nature of the injuries he had received was frustrated owing to the frightful anguish it caused. It was only after his decease that it was ascertained that one of his ribs had been fractured, and that the broken end penetrating the left lobe of the lungs had caused the fatal result.

Meanwhile he was sinking rapidly. The presence of his wife and children produced such a dangerous irritation, that it was necessary to remove them from his chamber. At one moment, under a violent access of delirium, he tried to spring out of bed ; in the next he sank into such a state of prostration that he seemed to be at the point of death. He was visited by his old friend Dr. Tomlinson, bishop of Gibraltar, and his family were readmitted to his chamber while the bishop offered up at his bedside the prayers for the sick. The dying man's consciousness for a moment returned. He extended his hand over the mournful and kneeling group, and said in slow and half-articulate accents, 'God bless you! God bless you!' His intimate friends and political associates, Lord Hardinge and Sir James Graham, whose names had been frequently on his lips in the incoherent utterances of his delirium, were admitted to his bedside, and in their presence, and that of his medical attendants and several of his relations, he sank quietly into his last sleep on Tuesday the 2d of July, at nine minutes past eleven in the evening.

While these things were passing in the dying man's chamber, all London was agitated with sorrow and anxiety. The multitudes of inquiries were so great that policemen were stationed at diffcrent places near his house with bulletins, which they were ordered to read to the crowds of all ages, sexes, and conditions that flocked to Whitehall, anxiously inquiring after the chances of recovery of the suffering statesman. Never perhaps did the intelligence of any event cause more genuine grief in the country than the news of his death. Since his retirement from office he had withdrawn from the arena of party conflict. The enmity caused by the course he had pursued in reference to the corn-laws had disappeared, while the gratitude and admiration which his conduct had excited in the breasts of those who approved it were still fresh and lively. When he rose to speak on any question before the House of Commons, the words that dropped from his lips were listened to on both sides of the House as the utterances of an oracle. The House of Lords was sitting at the moment when it was announced. One who was present described the scene to me. Lord Stanley was addressing the House with his usual force and eloquence. A slip of paper with the sad news written on it was passed from hand to hand. No work was spoken, no look exchanged ; Lord Stanley, who alone was uninformed of the sad event, continued his speech, but a solemn sadness stole over the faces of the peers, and they sat as men who had been suddenly converted into statues.

In both houses of Parliament such allusions were made to the event, and such tributes offered to the memory of the illustrious departed, as might have been anticipated; but from all that was said on the occasion I would only select the short but feeling speech of Lord Stanley, separated from the deceased statesman by deep-rooted convictions, but united to him by the tie of a warm friendship and sincere respect. These are the words in which he delivered his feelings on the sad event:

'It has been my deep regret, that during the last four years of his life I have been separated from him by a conscientious difference of opinion on an important matter of public policy. It is with deep regret that I know that that difference prevailed between us up to the last period of his valuable life; but it is a satisfaction to me personally, my lords, to know that whatever political difference there was between us, there was no personal hostility on either side. I am confident that there has been none on my side—quite as confident that there has been none on his. I never was one of those who attached unworthy motives to a course of conduct which I cannot but deeply lament. I believe that, in that step which led me to differ from him, he was actuated by a sincere and conscientious desire to obtain that which he believed to be a public good. Mistaken as he was in that view, I am satisfied that on that occasion, as on all others, the public good was the leading principle of his life, and that to promote the welfare of his country he was prepared to make, and did actually make, every sacrifice. In some cases those sacrifices were so extensive, that I hardly know whether the great and paramount object of his country's good was a sufficient reason to exact them from any public man. However, this is not a time to speak of differences, but to speak of agreements, when a great man and a great statesman has passed away from us by a sudden and inscrutable dispensation of Providence.'

The Duke of Wellington, so long and so intimately associated with him both in public and private, said of him, with tears running down his aged cheeks:

'In all the course of my acquaintance with Sir R. Peel, I never knew a man in whose truth and justice I had a more lively confidence, or in whom I saw a more invariable desire to promote the public service. In the whole course of my communications with him I never saw an instance in which he did not show the strongest attachment to truth ; and I never saw, in the whole course of my life, the smallest reason for suspecting that he stated anything which he did not firmly believe to be the fact.'

A noble-minded opponent—one who had constantly differed from him, who had driven him from office, and had been driven from office by him, and now, mainly through his generous support and generous forbearance, occupied the position of first minister of the crown—gave his testimony to the great qualities of Sir Robert Peel, and offered, that if the family of the deceased baronet thought it desirable that the course should be taken which was adopted on the death of Mr. Pitt or that of Mr. Grattan, he would be ready to concur, and could promise the sanction of the crown. A peerage was also offered to his widow; but both these offers were declined by the family, in compliance with the desire of the deceased statesman. A monument to his memory was erected in Westminster Abbey ; but, in accordance with his own wish, he was buried without pomp or ostentation by the side of his father and his mother, in the family vault beneath the little village church of Drayton Bassett.

But the tributes paid to the memory of this great man were not confined to his own country. In the legislative assembly of France, M. Dupin, who presided there, took the extraordinary and unprecedented course of delivering a short but well-expressed encomium on his character, and especially on the policy he had all along pursued in his dealings with the French nation. But a still more honourable tribute was afterwards paid to his memory by a French statesman of the highest eminence—whose services were somewhat similar to his own, and who, after the death of Sir R. Peel, gave a testimony in his favour, which we quote because it places his character in a light in which it has not often been regarded, and attributes to him a desire to do good in a manner for which he has not often received credit.

'What struck me most,' says Guizot, 'in the conversation of Sir Robert Peel, was his constant and impassioned anxiety with regard to the condition of the working classes in England; an anxiety which was as much moral as it was political, and beneath which, under a certain coldness and formality of expression, the feelings of the man as well as the foresight of the statesman were clearly visible. "There is there," he was continually accustomed to say, "too much suffering and too much perplexity. It is a disgrace and a danger to our civilization. It is absolutely necessary that we should render the condition of the manual labourer less hard and less precarious. We cannot do everything; but something may be effected, and something ought to be done." In the active thought of his leisure, this was evidently for him the dominant idea of the future.'

Another event that occurred in the course of this year, was the laying down of the first submarine electric telegraph connecting France with this country. It was commenced on the English side at the foot of Shakspeare's Cliff, near to the town of Dover, and was landed on the French side of the Channel at Cape Grisnez. Though this achievement has been altogether eclipsed by far greater feats of the same kind which have since been accomplished, it is worthy of notice as the first successful attempt made to effect instantaneous communication between countries separated from one another by wide and stormy seas.

Nothing perhaps more strongly illustrates the greatness of the loss which the country had sustained through the accident that so tragically closed the mortal career of Sir Robert Peel than the excitement which was caused, towards the close of the year, by what was generally described as the 'Papal aggression '—an excitement which his judicious and tolerant counsels and high authority would probably have calmed. We have seen how in 1848 the attempt to establish diplomatic relations with the Roman Pontiff with a special view to an intended introduction of a Roman hierarchy in England had been frustrated. It had therefore been determined by the heads of the Roman Catholic church without communication with our government that the English branch of their communion, hitherto governed by vicars-apostolic, who were bishops taking their titles from places situated *in partibus infidelium*, should have a new division of dioceses, and should be ruled by bishops taking their titles from English towns, and having an Archbishop of Westminster at their head. Dr. Wiseman, who was at that time the most conspicuous ecclesiastic of the Roman church in England, and who had hitherto exercised a kind of primacy over the English Roman Catholics, under the title of Bishop of Melipotamus, was now created a cardinal, appointed to be the first Archbishop of Westminster, and sent to England as the head of the new Romish hierarchy, to superintend the carrying out of the arrangements which had been made at the Vatican, and to act as the primate of the English Roman Catholics. These plans and intentions were announced, and the boundaries of the new sees defined, in a document couched in the grandiloquent style which had been employed by the bishops of Rome in the high days of their power during the middle ages, and which the Roman chancery still used. The appearance of this manifesto was followed by the publication of a pastoral from the new cardinal, which surpassed it in pretentious absurdity, though probably not intended or expected to give offence, being meant chiefly for the Roman Catholics of England, to whom it was addressed. But whatever may have been the intentions of those by whom these documents were issued, they roused the anti-popery feeling, which, notwithstanding the many blows and heavy discouragements it had received from recent legislation, was still strong, and had been not a little exasperated by the proceedings of the Tractarians. The excitement would soon have passed away, if the prime minister had not taken up the matter in a way that raised a tempest, from the effects of which his own government soon after suffered shipwreck.

Lord J. Russell's whig principles and presbyterian tendencies caused him to regard with strong and peculiar jealousy the progress that the Tractarians were making, which was sharpened by the opposition offered by them to the appointments he had made to the episcopal bench, the language they used with regard to the royal supremacy, and the unconcealed dislike with which they regarded the whig party. Therefore, without consulting any of his colleagues, he gave vent to his feelings in the following letter addressed to the Bishop of Durham, and which was long celebrated under the name of the Durham Letter:

'My dear Lord,—I agree with you in considering the late aggression of the Pope upon our protestantism as insolent and insidious, and I therefore feel as indignant as you can on the subject. I not only promoted to the utmost of my power the claims of Roman Catholics to all civil rights, but I thought it right, and even desirable, that the ecclesiastical system of the Roman Catholics should be the means of giving instruction to the numerous Irish immigrants in London and elsewhere, who, without such help, would have been left in heathen ignorance. This might have been done, however, without any such innovation as we have now seen.

'It is impossible to confound the recent measures of the Pope with the division of Scotland into dioceses by the episcopal church, or the arrangement of districts in England by the Wesleyan Conference. There is an assumption of power in all the documents which have come from Rome, a pretension to supremacy over the realm of England, and a claim to sole and undivided sway, which is inconsistent with the Queen's supremacy, with the rights of our bishops and clergy, and with the spiritual independence of the nation as asserted even in Roman Catholic times.

'I confess, however, that my alarm is not equal to my indignation. Even if it should appear that the ministers and servants of the Pope have not transgressed the law, I feel persuaded that we are strong enough to repel any outward attacks. The liberty of protestantism has been enjoyed too long in England to allow of any successful attempt to impose a foreign yoke on our minds and consciences. No foreign prince or potentate will be permitted to fasten his fetters upon a nation which has so long and so nobly vindicated its right to freedom of opinion, civil, political, and religious.

'Upon this subject, then, I will only say that the present state of the law shall be carefully examined, and the propriety of adopting any proceedings with reference to the recent assumptions of power deliberately considered.

'There is a danger, however, which alarms me much

more than the aggression of a foreign sovereign. Clergymen of our own church, who have subscribed the thirty-nine articles and acknowledged in explicit terms the Queen's supremacy, have been the most forward in leading their flocks step by step to the verge of the precipice. The honour paid to saints, the claim of infallibility for the church, the superstitious use of the sign of the cross, the muttering of the liturgy so as to disguise the language in which it was written, the recommendation of auricular confession, and the administration of penance and absolution,—all these things are pointed out by clergymen as worthy of adoption, and are now openly reprehended by the bishop of London in his charge to the clergy of his diocese. What, then, is the danger to be apprehended from a foreign prince, of no great power, compared to the danger within the gates from the unworthy sons of the church of England herself?

'I have but little hope that the propounders and framers of these innovations will desist from their insidious course; but I rely with confidence on the people of England; and I will not bate a jot of heart or life so long as the glorious principles and the immortal martyrs of the Reformation shall be held in reverence by the great mass of a nation which looks with contempt on the mummeries of superstition, and and with scorn at the laborious endeavours which are now making to confine the intellect and enslave the soul.—I remain, with great respect, &c.,

'J. RUSSELL.

'Downing Street, Nov. 4.'

This letter, which appeared in the papers on the day on which it was dated, strongly stimulated the agitation which the 'aggression' had already raised. Many of the bishops induced their clergy, through their archdeacons and rural deans to sign remonstrances echoing the sentiments conveyed in the prime minister's letter. The bishop of London in particular, who was supposed to regard with too indulgent an eye some of the practices which the premier denounced so strongly, delivered a charge to his clergy, in which he condemned in the most decided manner the papal rescript. Laymen of all classes and of all Christian denominations came forward to resist by addresses to the crown, and in other ways to oppose papal pretentions. Even Jews took part in the meetings that were held to defend 'our common protestantism.' As Lord J. Russell's letter appeared on the 4th of November, the ferment was naturally at its height on the 5th, and consequently effigies of the Pope and the Cardinal throughout. the kingdom took the place of those of Guy Fawkes, and were committed to the flames with all the honours of squibs, crackers, and rockets which were usually bestowed on that worthy. Meanwhile Cardinal Wiseman treated the noisy and riotous demonstrations of which he was the object with calm disregard. He wrote a quiet and sensible letter, in which he explained that the substitution of bishops for vicars-apostolic, and the changes which had been made in the boundaries of the Roman Catholic dioceses, were purely ecclesiastical arrangements, which ought not to have awakened alarm or given offence. But Lord J. Russell, and the party that had taken up the cry he had raised, were too excited to listen to reason. There were nevertheless many among his ablest and most valued supporters who strongly disapproved of the Durham letter, and felt that the violent anti-popery storm it had raised was sure to be followed by a reaction, by which the Roman Catholic church would largely profit. The excitement, however, was industriously fomented; many addresses in the sense of the Durham letter were numerously signed; and when Parliament assembled on the 4th of February 1851, the Queen's speech contained an allusion to the aggression, and announced that a measure would be laid before Parliament calculated to 'maintain the rights of the crown and the independence of the nation against all encroachments.'

It was a regrettable circumstance that this pitiful squabble should be engrossing the attention of the government, the legislature, and the country, at the commencement of the year which had been fixed for the Great Exhibition of the Industry of all Nations, suggested by Prince Albert, and which was hoped and expected to collect the products and natives of almost every nation under heaven. It was probably the desire to get rid of the embarrassing question before the inauguration of the great cosmopolitan fête that was to assemble strangers of all countries and all religions, that led Lord J. Russell to bring in his measure relating to the papal aggression only three days after the meeting of Parliament. It prohibited the assumption of territorial titles by Roman Catholic bishops; but it could not prevent other persons from giving them those titles, and had the effect of causing those titles to be more ostentatiously and offensively employed than they would have been if the aggression had been passed by in dignified silence. Lord J. Russell publicly recommended the new cardinal to adopt the title of Archbishop *in* Westminster instead of Archbishop *of* Westminster, and to remain at Rome instead of coming to England. But with both these suggestions the cardinal quietly declined to comply. He showed no undue haste to enter on his new functions; but he assumed them after some little delay with a calm dignity that contrasted most advantageously with the blustering violence of the attacks that had been made on him. The ill-advised clamour raised against him recoiled on his assailants, and increased immeasurably the zeal and enthusiasm of his adherents. The bill, however, was read a first time by a majority of 332; a majority that seemed to hold out a prospect that it would speedily be carried; but that prospect was somewhat changed by events we shall presently have occasion to relate.

In the mean time the distress which had so long prevailed and had so often forced itself on the attention of the legislature was still unabated, and had even increased in its severity. It was acknowledged and lamented in the Queen's speech at the opening of the session. Mr. Disraeli therefore moved a resolution to the effect, that it was the duty of the government to introduce measures for its alleviation without delay. To this resolution the government and their friends replied by alleging, that though it was true that the landlords and farmers were suffering, yet that the condition of the labouring classes had greatly improved; and, in proof of the truth of this assertion, it was shown that a decrease in pauperism had taken place in England to the extent of fourteen in every hundred, and in Ireland to the extent of one-half, while in Scotland there had also been a considerable reduction in the number of paupers. The revenue, in spite of all the remissions of taxation which had been made, had reached the unexampled amount of 70,000,000*l*. Notwithstanding the repeal of the navigation laws, the outward tonnage of British merchant ships was 180,000 in excess of that of 1849, and an enormous and unprecedented quantity of wheat had been imported, consumed, and paid for by millions who, without this supply, would have been destitute of food. Sir James Graham, by whom these arguments were forcibly urged, thus concluded his speech against the motion:

'I come to the conclusion, that the real object of this motion is to turn out the present administration, dissolve Parliament, return to protection, and reimpose a duty on corn. I see therefore that we are on the eve of a serious struggle, and we must gird up our loins, and prepare to offer a firm, manly, and uncompromising resistance. I appeal,' he added, 'to the latest declaration of the author and champion of our present policy, the late Sir R. Peel. Though dead, he still speaks, and from the tomb I hear the echo of his voice. I earnestly hope that I may never live to see the day when the House of Commons shall retrace its steps.'

Notwithstanding these arguments the division was close, and showed that the protectionist party was rapidly gaining strength, and would probably be able before long to defeat ministers, and take possession of the government of the country. The numbers were—

| | |
|---|---|
| For Mr. Disraeli's motion | 267 |
| Against it | 281 |
| Majority | 14 |

Thus ministers triumphed—triumphed, indeed, by a small majority, but still were victorious. On the next question on which their strength was tried they underwent a very damaging defeat.

Mr. Locke King, the member for East Surrey, asked leave to introduce a bill for assimilating the county franchise to that of the boroughs. His motion was resisted by Lord J. Russell; but, being supported by many of the liberal party, was carried by a majority of 100 against 52. The defeat of the government took place on the 20th of February. On the 17th of that month the chancellor of the exchequer made his financial statement, which was received with expressions of dissatisfaction from various quarters, so strong that ministers, feeling that they no longer commanded the confidence of the House, determined to retire; and that determination was announced in the *Times* and other newspapers on the morning of the 21st. The House was therefore crowded in all parts on the evening of that day, in the expectation that some explanation would be made of the views and intentions of the government: it was announced, however, that no statement would be made till the 24th. It was then deferred till the 28th, when it was announced that Lord Stanley had found it impossible to construct a protectionist ministry; that the Earl of Aberdeen, summoned to assist in the reconstitution of Lord J. Russell's administration, had been prevented from lending his assistance by the insuperable repugnance with which he and other members of the Peel party regarded the penal measures against Roman Catholics with which Lord J. Russell had encountered the papal aggression, and which had been accepted by a large majority in the House of Commons. Under these circumstances, Lord J. Russell and his colleagues had consented, at the request of the Queen, to retain their offices. The ecclesiastical-titles bill was once more brought forward, shorn of all its efficiency, and toned down into a mere *brutum fulmen*, insulting to the Catholics, but little in accordance with the expectations that the Durham letter had raised, and not even satisfactory to the Inglises, the Spooners, the Newdegates, and the Plumptres; while it encountered the strong opposition of almost every man who had assisted in removing those restrictions on the religious liberties of Englishmen, which Lord J. Russell had done more perhaps than any living man to take away. Seven nights were spent in debate on the second reading of the bill; and when the House divided on it, the numbers were—

| | |
|---|---|
| For the second reading | 438 |
| Against | 95 |
| Majority for the government | 343 |

But the minority, small as it was when compared with the number of those who voted in favour of the second reading, comprised all the ablest advocates of civil and religious liberty in the House: Graham, Gladstone, Roundell Palmer, Cobden, Bright, Roebuck, Milner Gibson, Hume. Sir J. Graham argued against the bill with great force; and it was remarked that his speech elicited loud cheers from the ministerial benches; while Lord J. Russell spoke amidst the chilling silence of his own supporters and the loud applause of the opposition, and especially of those members of it who had all along offered the most uncompromising resistance to every effort for the promotion of civil and religious liberty.

The farther progress of the measure was doggedly contested at every step by the Roman Catholic members; repeated divisions took place, in all of which ministers triumphed, but which delayed the progress of the bill; and when Sir F. Thesiger moved a string of resolutions embodying the views of those who were dissatisfied with the ministerial measure, because they considered that it did not go far enough, the Irish Roman Catholic members rose in a body and walked out of the House, leaving the ministers to contend as they could against the more violent supporters of their own measure. The consequence was, that three of the resolutions proposed by Sir F. Thesiger, all of which the government opposed, and the last of which it opposed strenuously, were carried; and an attempt made by Lord J. Russell to get rid of them on the third reading of the bill was defeated by large majorities. When the question was put, That this bill do now pass, there was no debate; and the numbers on the division were—

| | |
|---|---:|
| For the motion | 263 |
| Against | 46 |
| Majority for government | 217 |

In the House of Lords the measure was dealt with, if not more satisfactorily, at least more shortly. The debate on the second reading extended over two nights; in one night more the bill went through committee without alteration, and soon after received the royal assent.

The chief cause of the resignation of the government was the dissatisfaction with which the budget was regarded; and now that they had decided to remain in office, it was necessary that they should modify their financial measures in such a way as to meet the objections urged against them. Accordingly, on the 5th of April, the chancellor of the exchequer made a second statement. Following out the policy, which had been now adopted for some years, of reducing the taxes which pressed most heavily on the labouring classes, and which had been carried out last year by the reduction of the duty on bricks, he now proposed to reduce the duty on timber. Admitting the force of the objections which were urged against the window tax as being a tax on air and light, he pleaded that to give it up without a substitute would be to relinquish almost the whole of the surplus. He therefore proposed to substitute for it a uniform house tax of ninepence in the pound, with a lower duty on houses containing shops and on public-houses. As great complaints were made of the adulteration of coffee, he proposed to reduce the duty on that article, and thus remove to a great extent the temptation to adulterate it. In conclusion, he deprecated an attack on the income tax, which he knew to be in contemplation, urging that, though it was originally imposed for the purpose of meeting a deficiency, it was continued to enable an improvement to be made in our financial legislation by the removal of impolitic restrictions on industry and commerce, many of which still existed. This statement met with a much more favourable reception than that which had been made before the resignation of the government.

The attempt to put an end to the income tax, which the finance minister had foreseen and deprecated, was not long delayed.

On the 5th of April Mr. Herries moved the following resolution: ' That the income and property tax, and the stamp duties in Ireland, were granted for limited periods, and to meet temporary exigencies; and that it is expedient to adhere to the declared intentions of Parliament, and, in order to secure their speedy cessation, to limit the renewal of any portion of those taxes to such an amount as may suffice to provide for the expenditure sanctioned by Parliament, and for the maintenance of the public credit.'

Mr. Herries, in moving this resolution, contended that the surplus, which the chancellor of the exchequer had estimated at 1,892,000*l.*, would really turn out to be 2,200,000*l.* or 2,300,000*l.* The tax had originally been proposed by Sir R. Peel for special and temporary purposes, arising out of the financial maladministration of the six years prior to 1840, and had been strongly condemned by the present prime minister, on account of the 'inequality, the vexations, and the frauds,' that were inseparable from it. In 1848 the government of Lord J. Russell had asked for its continuance solely on the ground of the almost unparalleled difficulties of the crisis. Mr. Herries quoted strong denunciations of it by Mr. Labouchere, Lord Howick, Sir F. Baring, and Sir C. Wood, and called on the government to state the grounds on which, without necessity, with a surplus revenue, they proposed the continuance of a tax admitted to be full of inequality, and which, if it were not now stopped, would no doubt be made permanent, in violation of the pledges which the House had given to the country. He urged that at least two-sevenths of the tax might be remitted, which would give relief to the extent of 550,000*l.*; a far greater boon than the removal of the window tax, and one that would afford a prospect of the ultimate extinction of an impost denounced and stigmatised by the very men who now recommended its continuance.

The resolution was resisted by Sir C. Wood, who declared that he still retained the unfavourable opinion of the tax which he had formerly expressed, but that he advocated its retention to allow of the repeal of taxes which were even more mischievous. He declared that the proposal of Mr. Herries was in reality the first step in the policy which Lord Stanley had shadowed forth, that of the reimposition of a duty on corn. After some farther discussion, the motion was negatived by 278 against 230. Mr. Herries had proposed a diminution in the amount of the income tax, with a view to its ultimate extinction. Mr. Spooner, notwithstanding the rejection of this more moderate proposal, sought to get rid of the tax entirely; and therefore moved as an amendment on the second reading that the bill should be read a second time that day six months; but this amendment was not pressed to a division.

Mr. Hume was more fortunate in a motion he made that the grant of the income tax should be limited to one year, in order that the whole question of the tax might be deliberately considered in a select committee. This amendment was carried. The numbers were—

| For Mr. Hume's amendment | . | . | . | . | . | . | 244 |
| Against | . | . | . | . | . | . | . | 230 |
| Majority against the government | . | . | . | 14 |

A difficulty, however, arose with regard to the appointment of the select committee, in consequence of the discordant views of the two parties that had combined to carry Mr. Hume's motion. That gentleman wished to inquire with a view to the improvement of the tax. As the matter was well put by Mr. Herries, 'My proposition is either to amend the tax or abolish it. Mr. Hume's proposition is, Amend it if you can; but if not, keep it as it is.' This difference of view in the two parties that had combined to carry Mr. Hume's amendment made it very difficult to find members who were willing to sit on the committee that was to carry out the proposed investigation. However, after making many applications, and experiencing many rebuffs, Mr. Hume at last succeeded.

A long debate took place on resolutions submitted to the House by Mr. Disraeli, the object of which was to prevent the repeal of the window and timber taxes, on the ground that the possible discontinuance of the income tax next year rendered it desirable that they should be retained; but the resolutions were rejected by a majority of 113. Persistent attempts made by Mr. Baring to prevent the adulteration of coffee with chicory were also defeated by large majorities. Motions made by Mr. Cayley for the entire repeal of the malt tax, and by Mr. Bass for the repeal of half of it, were likewise rejected. In the last session Lord Naas had succeeded in carrying against the government a motion for making an allowance for evaporation and leakage in raising the revenue on spirits, and the government had with some difficulty succeeded in reversing the decision on the question to which the House had come. This year Lord Naas renewed his motion, and on a division the numbers on both sides were 150; whereupon the speaker, in accordance with custom, gave his casting vote for going into committee on the question, and thus allowing the House an opportunity for farther consideration of the matter. On another division, which took place on the 6th of June, government was in a minority of seventeen; but by great efforts this decision was at length reversed, and the bill proposed by Lord Naas rejected by a majority of 28. Ministers suffered yet another defeat on a bill introduced by Lord Robert Grosvenor to repeal the duty on attorneys' certificates; but they were more fortunate at a later stage, when they succeeded in rejecting the measure.

The bill of Mr. Locke King, which, if not the chief, was certainly the immediate cause of the resignation of the government, was again brought forward on the 2nd of April by that gentleman, who moved that it should be read a second time. This motion drew from Lord J. Russell a distinct pledge that the government would bring forward a measure of parliamentary reform early in the following session, and induced Mr. Disraeli to make a statement of his views on the subject, which possesses a permanent interest in consequence of the course he adopted in reference to this question many years afterwards.

'I repudiate the description of the opposition which has been given by Mr. Fox Maule, in the course of his almost convulsive effort to reconstruct a reform party, as being banded together against every species of parliamentary reform. And while in a broad view I accept the act of 1832 as a great settlement, I yet entirely protest against what is popularly understood in a political sense as the principle of "finality." But I do pledge myself to oppose any measure of parliamentary reform flagrantly having for its object the returning and confirming in power of some political section, or the displacement of the proper territorial influence and power, which, as I believe, constitutes the best security for our liberties, and the best means of retaining the stable and confirmed character which the institutions of the country have preserved.'

The pledge given by ministers that they would introduce a reform bill at the commencement of the following session had the desired effect, and the bill of Mr. Locke King, which had been accepted in the first instance by so large a majority, was now rejected by a still larger majority, the numbers being—

| | |
|---|---|
| For the second reading . . . . . . . | 83 |
| Against . . . . . . . . . . | 299 |
| Majority against the second reading . . . | 216 |

Mr. Henry Berkeley, who had succeeded Mr. Grote as the annual mover of a resolution in favour of the ballot, carried his motion this year, in spite of the opposition of Lord J. Russell and the government, by a majority of 37.

A debate of more than ordinary interest and importance took place on the proposal made by Mr. Cobden for the adjustment of international disputes by arbitration instead of by war. After having extracted from Lord Palmerston a very strong assurance of the desire entertained by himself and his colleagues to do everything in their power to preserve peace and a good understanding with France, Mr. Cobden withdrew the motion. A bill for the admission of Jews into Parliament was introduced into the House of Commons, and read a second time by a majority of 25, and a third time without a division; but was rejected in the upper House by a majority of 36. This, however, did not altogether settle the question, even for this session. Alderman Salomons, a member of the Jewish community, had been elected for Greenwich. Before his election he had pledged himself to the constituency that, if he should be the object of their choice, he would take his seat in the House of Commons. Accordingly, on the 18th of July he presented himself before the speaker, and demanded to be allowed to take the oath. Like Baron Rothschild, he omitted the words, ' on the true faith of a Christian.' He was then ordered to withdraw: instead, however, of complying with the order, he took his seat on a bench at the right hand of the speaker; but on receiving a second order he retired below the bar. On the evening of the 21st, however, he walked up the House amidst tremendous cries of ' Order!' and took his seat below the gangway on the ministerial side of the House. The speaker again desired him to withdraw; but in spite of the loud and angry outcries of a large number of members, he kept his seat. The speaker then appealed to the House to support him in the discharge of his duty, and Lord J. Russell moved that Mr. Salomons should be ordered to withdraw. To this motion Mr. B. Osborne moved an amendment, to the effect that as Mr. Salomons had taken the oaths in the manner that was most binding on his conscience, he was entitled to a seat in the House. Mr. Anstey then rose, amidst an uproar that made it impossible for a single word that he uttered to be heard. He at length, however, succeeded in moving an adjournment of the debate; but the motion was negatived by a majority of 275 to 65, Mr. Salomons himself voting in the minority. After some farther discussion, the amendment proposed by Mr. Osborne was put to the vote, and rejected by a majority of 218. But Mr. Salomons, who, as the question was one which affected him personally, had abstained from taking part in the division, reëntered the House and took his seat in it, notwithstanding the decision which had been come to, another uproar ensued, and Mr. Hobhouse called on Mr. Salomons to state to the House the course he intended to adopt. Thus challenged, Mr. Salomons stood up, and gave the following explanation of his conduct:

'I should not have presumed to address you, sir, and this House, in the peculiar position in which I am placed, had it not been that I have been so forcibly appealed to by the honourable gentleman who has just sat down. I hope some allowance will be made for the novelty of my position, and for the responsibility that I feel in the unusual course I have judged it right to adopt; but I beg to assure you, sir, and this House, that it is far from my desire to do anything that may appear contumacious or presumptuous. Returned as I have been by a large constituency, and under no disability, and believing that I have fulfilled all the requirements of the law, I thought I should not be doing justice to my own position as an Englishman and a gentleman, did I not adopt that course which I believed to be right and proper, and appear on this floor; not meaning any disrespect to you, sir, or to this House, but in defence of my own rights and privileges, and of the rights and privileges of the constituents who have sent me here. Having said this, I beg to state to you, sir, that whatever be the decision of this House, I shall abide by it, provided that there be just sufficient force used to make me feel that I am acting under coercion. I shall not now further intrude myself on the House, except to say that I trust and hope that, in the doubtful state of the law, such as has been described to us by the eminent lawyers who have addressed you, no severe measures will be adopted towards me and my constituents without giving me the fairest opportunity of addressing the House, and stating before the House and before the country what I believe to be my rights and the rights of my constituents.'

The discussion was still continued, and two farther divisions were taken, in both of which Mr. Salomons again voted; and having been once more ineffectually directed by the speaker to withdraw, he was at length led out of the House by the sergeant-at-arms. His departure, however, did not put an end to the discussion to which his entrance had given rise. It was carried on still at great length, adjourned, and afterwards resumed, with no other result than the deliverance of a great number of conflicting legal opinions, and a decision that Mr. Salomons was not entitled to a seat in the House.

A bill was passed in the course of this session which empowered the Court of Chancery, by the creation of new judicial offices, to perform its functions with more dispatch. But the session as a whole was remarkably barren of legislative results; a circumstance partly owing to the time consumed by the debates on the ecclesiastical-titles-assumption bill, but still more to the manner in which the attention both of Parliament and the country was drawn away from many of those political questions which had been for some time pressing for a solution, to the Great Exhibition of the Industry of all Nations.

The idea on which this Exhibition was founded was not altogether new. Exhibitions of a somewhat similar nature, though on a far smaller scale, had been held in Paris in 1801, 1806, 1836, and 1849. They had also been held in Belgium, Germany, Spain, and other European countries. But the one that approached most nearly to it in character, and might be regarded as in some sort its true precursor, was the great free-trade bazaar, held in Covent-garden Theatre in 1846, which we have already had occasion to mention in our account of the Anti-corn-law League. But the exhibition which was now to take place completely eclipsed all that had gone before it, not only in the quantity, quality, and variety of the articles exhibited, but in the national, or rather cosmopolitan, character which belonged to it. The holding of it was, in fact, the commencement of a new era in the history of industrial progress. It was a solemn glorification of industry; a world-wide recognition of the position which it had won for itself; a proclamation to the uttermost parts of the earth that it was no longer its destiny to be the despised drudge of the Nimrods and mighty hunters of the world, but that it had made good its claim to a place of full equality with them. Such was the significance of this great event. To Prince Albert belongs the honour of having brought it about. As president of the Society of Arts, and then as president of the royal commission issued mainly through his influence, he had promoted it with all the active earnestness of his character, and with all the power that belonged to his high position. Indeed, it would have been impossible for any person possessing less influence, or occupying an inferior place, to have carried out the grand idea which the great exhibition embodied on a scale so magnificent, and with such signal success. Under his earnest and energetic lead, 64,000$l$. was subscribed, and a guarantee fund of 200,000$l$. promised. The first difficulty with which he and the other promoters of the design had to contend was the selection of a site for the building which was to contain the objects sent for exhibition. The southern part of Hyde-park was, after careful consideration, pitched on. But no sooner was the choice publicly known, than a loud outcry was raised against what was ridiculously termed 'the profanation of the park,' and all kinds of exaggerated statements were made of the extent to which the enjoyment of the park by the public would be interfered with by the construction of the building. Answers were made to these complaints, which, if they did not satisfy the grumblers, satisfied all reasonable men. The next difficulty was the selection of a plan. It was announced in June, 1850, that one had been selected, out of some 140, by the building committee, and accepted by the commissioners. It was an immensely long and wide but low structure, like an enormous railway shed, with a huge and disproportionate cupola considerably larger than that of St. Peter's at Rome in its centre. However, this choice was not made without many doubts and misgivings. The cost of its erection would be enormous. Then there was the consideration of the prodigious mass of bricks and other materials which must be employed in its construction, and which would have to be taken away after the close of the exhibition. It was just at this moment that a lucky thought struck Mr. Paxton, the head-gardener of the Duke of Devonshire. He had superintended the great conservatory at Chatsworth. He had been engaged on the construction of many other buildings of a similar character, though on a smaller scale. He was thoroughly acquainted with all the advantages of such buildings, and he had overcome many of the practical difficulties which had hitherto attended their construction. The thought occurred to his mind, 'Why not erect a palace of glass and iron large enough to contain all the articles that are likely to be sent for exhibition?' No sooner did the thought occur to him than he proceeded to plan such a building as he had imagined in his mind. He drew the first rough sketch of it on a piece of blotting-paper which happened to be lying before him in the board-room in which he was sitting. He then inquired if there was yet time to admit a new proposal. After some hesitation the question was answered in the affirmative, and a fortnight was allowed him for the preparation of his plans and drawings. Before the end of that time all was ready, and the building committee was furnished with all requisite information it required.

The chief advantages of the plan thus submitted at the eleventh or rather at the twelfth hour were, the quantity of light admitted, the extraordinary simplicity of the construction of the building—which was to consist of nothing else but glass and the iron supports of the glass—the facility with which it could be prepared, erected, removed, and reërected on some other site if needful, the gracefulness of its appearance, and the advantages it afforded for ventilation. The following concise description of the plan was from the mouth of Mr. Paxton himself:

'The building will be 2100 feet long by 400 broad. The centre aisle will be 120 feet broad, or 10 feet wider than the conservatory at Chatsworth. The glass and the iron supports comprise the whole structure. The columns are precisely the same throughout the whole building, and would fit every part; the same may be said of each of the bars; and every piece of glass will be of the same size, namely, 4 feet long. The whole will be put together like a perfect piece of machinery. The building is entirely divided into 24 places—in short, everything runs to 24;

so that the work is made to square and fit without any small detail being left to carry out. The number of columns 15 feet long is 6024. There are 3000 gallery-bearers, 1245 wrought-iron girders, 45 miles of sash-bars, and 1,073,760 feet of glass to cover the whole. The building will stand on upwards of 20 acres of ground; but the available space which may be afforded by the galleries can be extended to about 30 acres if necessary. The whole will be covered in by the 1st of January, 1851. Now if, after the purposes of the exhibition are answered, it is thought desirable to let the building remain—and I sincerely hope it will not be pulled down, nor sent to America—there might be an excellent carriage-drive round the interior, as well as a road for equestrians, with the centre tastefully laid out and planted; and then there will be nearly six miles of room in the galleries as a promenade for the public.'

An engraving and brief description of the proposed palace of glass appeared in the *Illustrated News* of July 6, 1850; and though this representation hardly did justice to the design, and did not contain the transepts and other improvements, which added greatly to the elegance of the actual structure, yet, imperfect as it was, it produced a strong public opinion in its favour, which helped to remove many obstacles that stood in the way of the adoption of Mr. Paxton's ideas. His plan triumphed. The contract for the carrying out of the work was undertaken by Messrs. Fox and Henderson. They employed an army of labourers numbering nearly two thousand men. They had to contend with many difficulties—with a singularly wet and unfavourable season, with the shortness of the time allowed them for the completion of the building, with combinations of the workmen employed in its construction. But with all these obstacles they manfully and successfully grappled; and in spite of every hindrance, the work was not only done, but well done, and quite within the time stipulated. Then the commissioners met with fresh embarrassments in the apportionment of the space to the various countries which had announced their intention of sending specimens of their productions or of the results of their industry to the great world-bazaar. This difficult point was to some extent settled by the happy idea of a geographical arrangement. It was decided that the transept should represent the equator, and that the various contributing nations should be arranged in the building according to Mercator's projection. This device appeased many disputes; but even with the help of a plan so manifestly equitable, the utmost possible tact and discretion were needed to arbitrate in the differences, often of the most absurd character, to which national jealousies and susceptibilities gave rise. Thus, for one instance illustrative of the absurd punctilios with which the executive committee had to contend, we may mention that Spain refused to be represented at the Exhibition unless she was provided with an entrance distinct from that assigned to Portugal. Another difficulty, which at any other time would have been almost insurmountable, was that of finding interpreters to carry on the communications between the English authorities and the exhibitors, that came from all parts of the world and spoke almost every language under heaven. This difficulty was overcome by the employment of refugees, who during the political troubles of the Continent had fled to England. These men, being for the most part in a destitute condition, were glad to give their services for a very moderate remuneration.

The contents of this vast building were arranged under the four classes of—1, natural productions; 2, machinery; 3, manufactures; and 4, works of art. It would be superfluous and wearying to the reader to attempt to give any detailed account of the multitudinous articles exhibited under these different heads, and it is the less necessary, because many subsequent exhibitions of the same nature have followed, which, though they have been inferior to this first one in the interest excited, the results produced, and the bold originality of the building, have nevertheless surpassed it in the quantity and variety and the orderly classification and arrangement of their contents. The opening ceremony took place on the 1st of May. The day was all that could be wished. A countless multitude of spectators of all nations and languages had gathered outside, and covered the park in every direction. At mid-day precisely the Queen and Prince Albert drove up to the building amidst the enthusiastic shouts of the vast assemblage. The moment they entered it the royal standard rose majestically high above the hundred and one flags of various nations which decorated the building and contributed in no small degree to enhance its beauty. A grander spectacle or more striking pageant than that which took place within was perhaps never exhibited, when, amidst all the pomp and splendour that the court of England could display, amidst the sound of many trumpets, the solemn and jubilant strains of loud-pealing organs, amidst a crowd of eminent Englishmen and illustrious foreigners, the Queen of England, then in the prime of her youth and beauty, opened this unrivalled collection of the triumphs of human genius in the most striking and original building that any age has produced, and the largest that human skill and perseverance has ever erected. After the Queen, surrounded by the ladies of her suite, the ministers of state, ambassadors from all parts of the world, and the archbishops and bishops of the church, had seated herself on a throne that had been set for her, while the organ pealed forth the well-known notes of the national anthem, and a multitude of voices, like the sound of mighty waters, poured forth the grand old hymn, Prince Albert descended from the daïs, and putting himself at the head of those eminent men who were appointed to carry out the preparatory arrangements, read the report of the commission in a clear and sonorous voice, and then handed the Queen a copy of it, accompanied by a splendidly bound catalogue of the articles to be exhibited. Then a suitable prayer was offered up by the archbishop of Canterbury. The Hallelujah chorus appropriately closed the inaugural proceedings. From this time the Exhibition continued open, and was visited by multitudes from all parts of England, and by foreigners of all nations. In order to insure as far as possible the pecuniary success of the enterprise, the prices of admission were gradually reduced. Five-shilling days were succeeded by half-crown days, and these in turn by shilling and even sixpenny days. Twice the public were admitted without any charge. This went on till the 15th of October, when the Exhibition was finally closed with another solemn ceremony, over which Prince Albert presided. It had been in every respect highly successful. Not the least among the many advantages that attended this great gathering of the natives and assemblage of the productions of almost every country of the world was the tendency it had to promote peace and good-will, and to cause the institutions of England to be better understood and more highly appreciated. Foreigners were particularly struck by the orderly conduct of the vast multitudes who were congregated about the building to witness the opening ceremony, and by the almost entire absence of police to control them. The holding of the Exhibition also gave occasion to the exchange of many international civilities. England and France regarded with interest the splendid hospitalities exchanged between the municipalities of London and Paris. Thus the Crystal Palace was at once a temple of industry and a temple of peace. It made the productions of the various nations of the world to be better known. It taught manufacturers where best to seek the raw materials they required, and how to improve their manufacturing processes. It fostered a healthy and industrial emulation, it gave rise to other exhibitions having like objects and producing similar results. And all this it effected at a moment when the ties that bound the great nations of Europe together were being subjected to a strong strain, and when it was particularly desirable that they should not be torn asunder. For all these advantages it should be remembered that England and Europe were chiefly indebted to the enlightened guidance and zealous patronage of Prince Albert. If all the visions of peace, prosperity, and of the advent of a new golden age which the Exhibition raised were afterwards rudely dispelled, the fault was not his. The palace having been purchased by a company, the first pillar of it was erected at Sydenham on the 6th of August in the following year.

Side by side with our account of the opening of the Crystal Palace we may not unfitly place the foundation of Owens College in Manchester; an event which, though of more limited importance, may in its nature be classed with that great and successful effort to benefit mankind.

Mr. John Owens, a merchant of Manchester, died on the 29th of July 1846, leaving behind him a large property. Having no near relatives, he proposed to bequeath the bulk of it to his intimate friend Mr. George Faulkner. This gentleman, however, refused the legacy for himself, and suggested the application that was actually made of it. In compliance with his recommendation, Mr. Owens left by will the sum of 100,000*l.* to found within the borough of Manchester 'an institution for providing or aiding the means of instructing and improving young persons of the male sex, and being of an age of not less than fourteen years, in such branches of learning and science as are now or may be hereafter usually taught in the English universities.' He farther directed that neither the students nor the teachers should be subject to any religious test, and that the institution should be open to all applicants without distinction of rank or place of birth, preference being given first to natives of Manchester, and next to natives of South Lancashire. The college, which was established in accordance with these provisions, was opened on the 12th of March 1851 with a principal, and professors of logic, mental philosophy, languages and literature of Greece and Rome, English language and literature, history, mathematics, and natural philosophy,\* chemistry, and natural history, and was affiliated to the University of London. It is hardly necessary to add that an institution of this nature, planted in a city so remarkable for the liberality and public spirit of its citizens, and strongly disposed to welcome the ideas on which its founder had based it, was not likely to languish for want of support. Accordingly, it has been enriched with benefactions which rival in their amount those which have been bestowed on the colleges of the two great English universities. In the year following the opening of the college upwards of 10,000*l.* were contributed. In 1854 Mr. George Faulkner, whose share in the first institution of the college has already been mentioned, in addition to several other donations previously made, gave the land and buildings it at present occupies, with the exception of the chemical laboratory, which was erected subsequently. The first Bishop of Manchester on his death bequeathed to the college a library of 7000 volumes, rich in biblical and patristic literature, and especially in materials for Greek Testament criticism. Lastly, not to mention many smaller contributions, upwards of 100,000*l.* has been raised for the purpose of erecting a new and more suitable building on a better site, in order to make the institution more generally available, and in the hope of ultimately rendering it the university of the manufacturing districts, in furtherance of which object

\* Several other professorships have since been established.

a legal and a medical school have been recently added, and an act of parliament obtained.

The interest taken in politics, which had been momentarily eclipsed by the interest taken in the great Exhibition, revived in full force at the approach of the session of 1852. Two circumstances contributed to give it greater intensity—the dismissal of Lord Palmerston, and the promise of a new reform bill. The first of these events excited considerable attention, not only on account of the boldness and ability which had characterized Lord Palmerston's administration of foreign affairs, but also because it was generally expected that his removal would speedily draw after it the dissolution of the ministry. The Queen's speech showed that the premier had not forgotten the pledges he had given on the subject of parliamentary reform, for it intimated an intention on the part of the government to propose 'such amendments in the act of the late reign relating to the representation of the commons in Parliament as may be deemed calculated to carry into more complete effect the principles upon which that law is founded;' and Lord J. Russell lost no time in producing the promised measure. He asked leave to bring in his bill on the 9th of February, thus showing a sincere desire to carry it through the house in the course of the session. It is needless to enter into an examination of the details of a scheme, the provisions of which were never discussed. It will suffice to say that Lord J. Russell proposed to enfranchise some large towns, disfranchise some small boroughs, to lower the borough and county qualifications, to strike out the words 'on the true faith of a Christian' from the oath taken by members of Parliament, and thus get rid of the obstacle to the admission of Jews to the legislature, and to abolish the practice in virtue of which members of the government transferred from one office to another under the crown vacated their seats.

This measure was not very favourably received either by the house or the country. It did not satisfy the hopes and expectations of ardent reformers, and it alarmed those who thought that the electoral qualification was already too low. However, leave was given for its introduction without opposition.

Meanwhile the public curiosity with regard to Lord

Palmerston's dismissal was gratified by very full statements made by the prime minister, and by Lord Palmerston himself. And as these explanations throw some light on a constitutional question which is generally shrouded in a good deal of mystery, namely, the relations between the sovereign and the prime minister on the one hand, and the prime minister and his colleagues on the other, it has an historical interest and importance that does not generally attach to personal explanations, and therefore may be given with more fulness than would otherwise be desirable.

The grounds of Lord Palmerston's dismissal were thus stated by Lord J. Russell in reply to a question from Sir B. Hall:

'It will be right that I should state to the house what I conceive to be the position which a secretary of state holds as regards the crown in the administration of foreign affairs, and as regards the prime minister of this country. With respect to the first, I should state that when the crown, in consequence of a vote of the House of Commons, places its constitutional confidence in a minister, that minister is, on the other hand, bound to afford to the crown the most frank and full detail of every measure that is taken, or to leave to the crown its full liberty, a liberty which the crown must possess, of saying that the minister no longer possesses its confidence. Such I hold to be the general doctrine. But as regards the noble lord, it did so happen that in August 1850 the precise terms were laid down in a communication on the part of her Majesty with respect to the transaction of business between the crown and the secretary of state. I became the organ of making that communication to my noble friend, and thus became responsible for the document I am about to read.'

Lord J. Russell then read the following extract from a letter addressed by the Queen to Lord Palmerston: 'The Queen requires first, that Lord Palmerston should distinctly state what he proposes in a given case, in order that the Queen may know as distinctly to what she is giving her royal sanction. Secondly, that having once given her sanction to a measure, that it be not arbitrarily altered or modified by the minister. Such an act she must consider as failing in sincerity towards the crown, and justly to be visited by the exercise of her constitutional right of dismissing that minister. She expects to be kept informed of what passes between him and the foreign ministers, before important decisions are taken based upon that intercourse; to receive the foreign despatches in good time; and to have the drafts for her approval sent to her in sufficient time to make herself acquainted with their contents before they must be sent off. The Queen thinks it proper that Lord John Russell should show this letter to Lord Palmerston.'

'I sent that accordingly, and received a letter in which the noble lord said, "I have taken a copy of this memorandum of the Queen, and will not fail to attend to the directions which it contains."

'The first important transaction in which Lord Palmerston took a part since the end of the last session of Parliament was his reception of a deputation of delegates from certain metropolitan parishes respecting the treatment of the Hungarian refugees by the Turkish government. On this occasion I thought that my noble friend exhibited some want of due caution, but I gave him the credit of supposing that this was through an oversight. The next occasion to which I think it necessary to refer relates to the events which took place on the 2d of December in France. The instructions conveyed to our ambassador by the Queen's government were to abstain from all interference in the internal affairs of that country. Being informed of an alleged conversation between Lord Palmerston and the French ambassador repugnant to these instructions, I wrote to that noble lord; but my inquiries for some days met with a disdainful silence, Lord Palmerston having in the meanwhile, without the knowledge of his colleagues, written a despatch containing instructions to Lord Normanby, in which, however, he evaded the question whether he had approved the act of the President. I consider the noble lord's course of proceeding in this matter to be a putting himself in the place of the crown, and passing by the crown, while he gave the moral approbation of England to the acts of the President of the republic of France, in direct opposition to the policy which the government had hitherto pursued. Under these circumstances I had no alternative but to declare that while I was prime minister, Lord Palmerston could not hold the seals of office; and I have assumed the sole and entire responsibility of advising the crown to require the resignation of my noble friend, who, though he has forgotten and neglected what was due to the crown and his colleagues, has not, I am convinced, intended any personal disrespect.'

To these charges Lord Palmerston thus replied:

'I should be sorry if the house and the country were to run away with the notion that Lord J. Russell seems to entertain that I have abandoned principles. I concur in Lord J. Russell's definition of the relations between the foreign minister and the crown, and I have done nothing inconsistent with those relations. With reference to the deputation on the subject of the release of the Hungarian refugees, I thought it my duty to receive it; but I repudiated certain expressions contained in the address, and I said nothing on that occasion which I had not uttered in this house and elsewhere. With reference to the *coup d'état* in France, which has been represented by Lord J. Russell as forming the ground of my removal from office, that event happened on the 2d of December: on the 3d the French ambassador, with whom I was in the habit of almost daily communication, called on me at my house to inform me of what news he had received, and to talk over the events of the preceding day; and I stated conversationally the opinion I entertained of the events that had taken place, and the French ambassador, as I am informed, in a private letter communicated the result of that conversation to his minister. On that day, the 3d of December, her Majesty's ambassador at Paris wrote a despatch to ask what instructions he should receive for his guidance in France during the interval before the vote of the French people on the question that was to be proposed to them, and whether in that interval he should infuse into the relations with the French government any greater degree of reserve than usual. I took the opinion of the cabinet on that question, and a draft of that opinion was prepared, and sent for her Majesty's approbation. Her Majesty's ambassador was instructed to make no change in his relations with the French government, and to do nothing that should wear the appearance of any interference with the internal affairs of France. There was no instruction to communicate that document to the French government; it simply contained instructions, not, in fact, what the English ambassador was to do, but what he was to abstain from doing. The ambassador, however, thought it right to communicate to the French minister for foreign affairs the substance of that document, accompanying the communication with certain excuses for the delay, which, however, did not rest with that noble marquis, as his despatch to the English government was dated the 3d of December. The French minister stated that he had nothing to complain of with respect to that delay, and the less, indeed, because the day before he had received from the French ambassador in London a statement that I had entirely approved of what had been done, and thought the President of the French fully justified. Those particular words I never used, and probably the French ambassador would not have conceived it consistent with the dignity of his country to ask the approval of a foreign secretary of state. Consequently, the approval was not asked, and was not given. When the Marquis of Normanby's despatch reached Lord J. Russell, he wrote to say that he trusted I could contradict the report. There was, as he has stated, an interval between the receipt of the noble lord's letter and my answer. The noble lord's letter was dated the 14th, and my answer the 16th. I was at the time labouring under a heavy pressure of business; and wishing fully to explain the opinion I expressed, it was not until the evening of the 16th that I was able to write my answer. The noble lord got it early next morning, on the 17th. My answer was, that the words quoted by Lord Normanby gave a high colouring to anything I could have said in the conversation with the French ambassador; but my opinion was, and that opinion no doubt I expressed, that such was the antagonism arising from time to time between the French Assembly and the President, that their long coexistence became impossible, and that in my opinion, if one or other of them were to prevail, it would be better for France and for Europe that the President should prevail than the Assembly; and my reason was, that the Assembly had nothing to offer as a substitute for the President unless an alternative of civil war or anarchy; whereas the President, on the other hand, had to offer unity of purpose and unity of authority; and, if he were inclined to do so, he might give to France internal tranquillity, with good and permanent government.

My noble friend replied to that letter, that he had come to the reluctant conclusion that it would not be consistent with the interests of the country to allow the management of its foreign affairs to remain any longer in my hands. He said that the question between us was not whether the President was justified or not, but whether I was justified or not in having expressed any opinion on the subject. To that I replied, that there was in diplomatic intercourse a well-known and perfectly understood distinction between conversations official by which governments were bound, and those unofficial conversations by which governments were not bound, and in which the speakers only expressed the opinions they might themselves for the moment entertain.'

The noble lord expatiated at some length on this topic. He stated that the prime minister himself and two other members of the cabinet had given an opinion on the question in conversation with the French ambassador. It must, however, be admitted that filling as he did an official position which gave great importance to his lightest communications with foreign governments, his colleagues had just right to complain of his having uttered an opinion, whether in conversation or otherwise, which would convey the impression that the English government approved of a policy which they had not deliberately adopted, and had taken a side in the conflict which was being carried on between two sections of the French people. There is, however, good reason to believe that the chief, though unavowed, cause of Lord Palmerston's dismissal was a difference of opinion between him and Lord J. Russell on the desirableness of bringing forward a measure of reform. It had the effect of converting one of the ablest members of the administration into one of its ablest opponents; and no long time elapsed before he showed the government how formidable an adversary they had raised up.

The change which had taken place in France caused much alarm in England. It was feared that Napoleon might seek to strengthen his position by yielding to the popular feeling in favour of a war with England to avenge the disaster of Waterloo; and there was consequently a very general demand for some measures of defence and precaution. The government was so far influenced by the popular outcry as to make an effort to strengthen the force of the country in such a manner as would involve the least possible expenditure consistent with efficiency; and with this view they determined to recommend such an organization of the militia as would in their opinion suffice to enable them to meet any attack that might be contemplated. The ministerial plan was brought forward and explained to the House of Commons by Lord J. Russell on the 16th of February. Though some members of the house, such as Mr. Hume and Mr. Cobden, opposed the scheme on economical grounds, and others, like Messrs. Reynolds and O'Connell, objected to the omission of Ireland from the bill, yet on the whole it met with a favourable reception; and Lord Palmerston in particular distinguished himself by the heartiness of the approbation he gave to it, only objecting to its being made a local militia, and suggesting that the word 'local' should be omitted in the bill. Subsequently he moved the insertion of the words 'and consolidate,' and the substitution of 'regular' for 'local.' The consequences of this amendment gave it an importance which would not otherwise have belonged to it. It was carried by a majority of eleven; and Lord J. Russell at once declared that he was stopped on the threshold, and told that the government did not possess the confidence of the house. This was, of course, understood as an intimation that he intended to resign; and it is probable that he was glad to seize the opportunity afforded him of escaping from a position which he felt that he could no longer usefully or honourably occupy. It was generally, and naturally, expected that the leader of the opposition would take his place, and therefore it excited neither surprise nor emotion when it was announced that Lord Stanley, who, in consequence of the death of his father in 1851, had now become Earl of Derby, had been sent for by the Queen, and had accepted the task of endeavouring to form an administration. In the upper house Lord Lansdowne, who, as Lord Henry Petty, had been one of the ablest and firmest of the band of great men who in a hopeless minority resisted the war policy of Pitt, and who now in his old age had represented the government in the House of Peers with remarkable dignity, ability, moderation, and eloquence, announced his own resignation and that of his colleagues in terms which drew forth the plaudits of all sides of the house, and the regrets even of his opponents. His merits were acknowledged in terms no less dignified and honourable by Lord Malmesbury, who, in the necessary absence of Lord Derby, represented the new government.

Lord J. Russell made in the lower house the same announcement that had been made with so much tact and dignity by Lord Lansdowne in the upper chamber. He stated that his colleagues had unanimously thought it their duty to resign their offices into her Majesty's hands without advising her to have recourse to a dissolution; and he declared that he should feel it his duty to oppose out of office, as he had opposed in office, any restoration of the duty on corn, whether under the name of protection or of revenue, and to support an extension of the suffrage, believing that it would add strength and solidity to our parliamentary system.

On the 27th February the new first lord of the treasury stated to his peers the principles on which the administration he had formed was to be conducted. They were, with regard to foreign nations, absolute non-intervention; with regard to defence, the maintenance of the present military and naval force, which he believed to be sufficient for the protection of the country and its numerous colonies; and the organization of the militia as a precaution against the danger of invasion. He promised to protect political refugees, but warned them against abusing the hospitality of this country by organizing against their own governments measures known to be in violation of the laws of England. On financial questions he spoke with a vagueness necessitated by the position occupied by his cabinet in face of a hostile majority in the popular branch of the legislature. But he made this very significant remark: 'When the entire supply of an article comes from abroad the whole increase of the price falls on the consumer, but that is not the case when the article is partly of foreign and partly of home supply, and I will not shrink from declaring my opinion that there is no reason why corn should be the solitary exception to the rule.' The new premier stated that he did not intend to take up the measure of franchise reform, which had been proposed by the late government: a measure which, in his opinion, unsettled everything and settled nothing; and declared that he was favourable to the extension of a system of religious education based on the study of the Scriptures. He said that to uphold the established church in its integrity was the interest and duty of the government. Relying on the assistance of God, he would endeavour to promote the social, moral, and religious improvement of the country.

The only part of this programme which called forth any animadversion was that which touched on the question of raising a revenue on corn. This elicited a protest from Earl Grey, and a declaration from Lord Aberdeen that, as the intimate friend and colleague of the late Sir R. Peel, it was his determination to adhere to the free-trade policy of that lamented statesman by opposing any duty whatsoever on corn, whether for revenue or protection. These protests were not confined to the walls of Parliament. The members of the defunct Anti-corn-law League met in Manchester, and determined to resuscitate that body and to prepare for a vigorous renewal of the agitation in case a serious attempt should be made by the new government to reverse the free-trade policy which the legislature and the country had adopted. On the 15th of March Mr. C. Villiers interrogated Mr. Disraeli, as the leader of the ministerial party in the House of Commons, on the subject, and similar questions were put to the Earl of Derby in the House of Lords. The reply to these questions was to the effect, that the government did not intend to propose any return to the policy of protection during the present session, nor at any future time, unless a great majority of members favourable to that policy should be returned to Parliament. Another interrogation, made some days later, elicited an intimation that the government intended to dissolve in the course of the year, and not later than the autumn.

The following is a list of the new cabinet:

| | |
|---|---|
| The Earl of Derby | First Lord of the Treasury. |
| Lord St. Leonards | Lord-Chancellor. |
| Mr. Disraeli | Chancellor of the Exchequer. |
| Earl of Lonsdale | President of the Council. |
| Marquis of Salisbury | Privy Seal. |
| Mr. Walpole | Home Secretary. |
| Earl of Malmesbury | Foreign Secretary. |
| Sir J. Pakington | Colonial Secretary. |
| The Duke of Buckingham | First Lord of the Admiralty. |
| Mr. Herries | President of the Board of Control. |
| Lord J. Manners | First Commissioner of Works and Public Buildings. |

Of course the question which had proved fatal to the late administration demanded the prompt and careful consideration of the new government. A militia bill was therefore prepared, and introduced into the House of Commons on the 25th of March by the new secretary of state. On the motion for the second reading of it, which was made on the 23rd of April, an important debate took place, and was continued over two nights. Sir De Lacy Evans moved that it should be read a second time that day six months, and this motion was supported by Lord J. Russell and his adherents; but the bill was defended by Lord Palmerston, Mr. Sidney Herbert, as well as by the conservative party generally; and the second reading carried by 355 to 165. This majority, larger than even the most sanguine supporters of the government had ventured to hope for, greatly strengthened its position, and caused many who were wavering in their allegiance to the whig leader to give it their assistance. The division on the third reading, however, was much closer. It was carried by 187 votes to 142. In the upper house there was no serious opposition. This success was partly due to the authority of the Duke of Wellington, who, in a very able and interesting speech, urged the acceptance of the measure as necessary to the safety of the country and to the maintenance of what he declared the country had not possessed during the last ten years—a proper peace establishment.

As the government had so distinctly declined to deal with the question of parliamentary reform which their predecessors had raised, it was taken up by Mr. Hume, who proposed a considerable extension of the franchise; by Mr. Locke King, who proposed the assimilation of the franchise in the counties to that in the boroughs; by Lord Brougham, who proposed the shortening to thirty days of the interval between the dissolution of one Parliament and the meeting of the next. The two first of these propositions were rejected by large majorities, the other was carried. The new government brought in a bill for the disfranchisement of the borough of St. Albans, which had been proved to have been the scene of gross corruption; it also carried forward a measure which had been brought in by the late government, empowering the crown to send a commission of inquiry to any place at which it was reported by an election committee that bribery was extensively practised; and the bill passed with some amendments which the lords had introduced into it. A bill, giving a new constitution to the colony of New Zealand, was also passed, notwithstanding the energetic opposition of Sir W. Molesworth. Bills for the extension of the episcopal church in the colonies, and for the better management of bishops' estates and revenues, were brought in, but not carried. The Maynooth question, raised again by Mr. Spooner, was fully discussed, and quietly dropped. Motions by Mr. Gibson for the repeal of the paper, advertisement, and stamp duties were rejected; and Mr. Frewen suffered himself to be persuaded by the chancellor of the exchequer to withdraw a motion he had intended to bring forward relative to the duty on hops.

On the 30th of May Mr. Disraeli introduced his first budget. In the position in which he was placed, not having had time to examine fully the financial system of the country—a labour which, however, he professed himself ready to undertake if opportunity were afforded him—and being able to count only on the support of a minority in the present House of Commons, there was no other course open to him but that of provisionally proposing the continuance of the financial system which he and his colleagues on their recent entrance into office had found in operation. It was felt on all sides that it was desirable that the sense of the nation with regard to the policy of the new administration should be ascertained as speedily as possible. Lord J. Russell was of opinion that the state of public business was such as would not warrant him in resorting to a dissolution at the time when he found himself in a minority. Lord Derby was of the same opinion, and therefore resisted the importunities of many impatient partisans, who urged him to dissolve at once; but as soon as the necessary business of the session had been transacted, it was felt on all hands that the dissolution should not be much longer delayed. Parliament was therefore prorogued by the Queen in person after a session which, owing to the ministerial changes, had proved even more barren than that which preceded it, and which the great Exhibition had rendered so unfruitful of legislation; and the prorogation was followed by a dissolution.

The new Parliament assembled on the 4th of November, reëlected its speaker, and occupied itself with the swearing in of its members and other preliminaries till the 11th of that month, when the session was opened by the Queen in person. The result of the appeal made to the country had not answered the hopes of those by whom it was made. It had little altered the balance of parties in the House of Commons, and consequently left the government as they were before it took place, in a hopeless minority. A clever and elaborate system of finance brought forward by Mr. Disraeli, and recommended to the House by all the ability and eloquence of which he was master, was rudely handled by Mr. Gladstone, and rejected by a majority of 305 to 286. Ministers, who of course anticipated this defeat, at once resigned. The Earl of Aberdeen then formed a new cabinet, of which the following were members:

| | |
|---|---|
| Earl of Aberdeen | First Lord of the Treasury. |
| Lord Cranworth | Lord-chancellor. |
| Mr. Gladstone | Chancellor of the Exchequer. |
| Lord Palmerston | Home Secretary. |
| Lord J. Russell | Foreign Secretary. |
| The Duke of Newcastle | Colonial Secretary. |
| Sir J. Graham | First Lord of the Admiralty. |
| Earl Granville | President of the Council. |
| The Duke of Argyle | Lord Privy-seal. |
| Mr. Sidney Herbert | Secretary at War. |
| Sir Charles Wood | President of the Board of Control. |
| Sir W. Molesworth | First Commissioner of Public Works. |

The Marquis of Lansdowne occupied a seat in the cabinet without holding any office.

This government, formed by a coalition of the Whig and Peelite parties, underwent many changes and vicissitudes, and in the course of its existence led this country into one of the most formidable wars in which it ever embarked. It may not, therefore, be uninteresting to the reader of this History to be able to compare its early professions with its subsequent conduct, and therefore we give a condensed account of the principles on which the new premier announced to the House of Lords that government was to be conducted.

'With regard to foreign powers, the new ministry will adhere to the principles which have been pursued for the last thirty years, and which consist in respecting the rights of all independent states, in abstaining from interference in their internal affairs; in asserting her own rights and interests; and, above all, in our earnest desire to secure the general peace of Europe, without any relaxation of those defensive measures which have been lately undertaken and have perhaps been too long neglected. At home, the mission of the government will be to maintain and extend free-trade principles, and to pursue the commercial and financial system of the late Sir R. Peel. A crisis in our financial arrangements will speedily occur by the cessation of a large branch of the revenue, and it will tax the ingenuity of all concerned to readjust our finances according to the principles of justice and equity. The questions of education and legal reform will receive every attention at the hands of the government; and an amendment of the representative system, undertaken without haste or rashness, will not be excluded from its mature consideration. The measures of the government will be both conservative and liberal, for both are necessary.' As no farther business could be proceeded with at present, the two Houses adjourned to the 10th of February, 1853.

At the commencement of this year an accident brought to light an infamous fraud committed on the naval department of the government, which, if it had remained undiscovered, might have led to fearful consequences. The government had entered into a contract for a supply of preserved meats for the use of the navy. Suspicions having arisen with regard to its state of preservation, a board of examiners was appointed to inquire into the matter, and the canisters were opened in the presence of its members. It was found, not only that their contents were putrid, but that they were composed of the most horrible and loathsome materials,—pieces of heart, roots of tongues, palates, coagulated blood, ligaments of throats, intestines, filth, and indescribable garbage, all in such a state of putrefaction that the examiners could not support the stench they emitted. Out of about 10,000 that were inspected, only ten per cent. were found at all fit for use. The whole lot was taken out to sea and cast overboard. A similar inquiry carried on at the victualling yard at Deptford revealed even more worse results. This year was fertile in naval disasters; two of which, although they occurred out of England, were attended by circumstances which demand more than a passing notice. The first of these was the destruction by fire, in the month of January, of the splendid new West-India mail-steamer the Amazon, within two days' sail of the port, one hundred and two of her crew and passengers perishing in the flames, or being lost in attempting to escape. The other disaster produced a profound sensation throughout the country; a sensation of horror mingled with pride when it was announced that towards the end of February, the troop transport the Birkenhead, carrying a regiment of soldiers, had touched on a rock off the Cape of Good Hope, for which she was destined. While the women, the children, and a few invalids, were being carried ashore, the officers and soldiers ranged themselves on deck with as much tranquillity as if an inspection or review was taking place; and there they stood in their ranks as the vessel gradually filled and went down, not attempting to quit their places, or to enter the boats while the others were being saved: and so standing the regiment went down into the deep, no man making an effort to save himself until actually in the water; thus affording, perhaps, the most perfect example of cool heroism and military obedience that was ever exhibited.

At an early part of the same month the Bilbery reservoir burst during the night, and its contents, sweeping down the valley of the Holme, carried everything before them, causing the death of about one hundred persons, dashing down four factories, ten dye-houses, ten stoves, twenty-seven cottages, seven tradesmen's houses, seven shops, seven bridges, ten warehouses, eighteen barns and stables, and doing injury to a great quantity of property estimated at upwards of 600,000*l.*

During the interval between the dissolution and the re-assembly of Parliament, an event had occurred which deeply stirred the heart of the whole nation, from the Queen on the throne to the lowest and meanest of her subjects. The Duke of Wellington, who had attained to the 84th year of his age, had for some time past been becoming more and more infirm. On the 14th of September his feebleness had very perceptibly increased, and at about a quarter past three in the afternoon of that day he tranquilly breathed his last at Walmer Castle, where he was then residing. The qualities which caused him to be regarded with such deep reverence and admiration by the great majority of his fellow-countrymen, and made his decease, at the end of so long a life, to be deeply and sincerely regretted, were admirably described in words which Mr. Gladstone quoted from a former speech of Lord J. Russell, and which he eloquently complimented and applied to the present occasion.

'While many of the actions of his life, while many of the qualities he possessed, are unattainable by others, there are lessons which we may all derive from the life and actions of that illustrious man. It may never be given to another subject of the British crown to perform services so brilliant as he performed; it may never be given to another man to hold the sword which was to gain the independence of Europe, to rally the nations around it, and while England saved herself by her constancy, to save Europe by her example; it may never be given to another man, after having attained such eminence, after such an unexampled series of victories, to show equal moderation in peace as he has shown greatness in war, and to devote the remainder of his life to the cause of internal and external peace for that country which he has so served; it may never be given to another man to have equal authority both with the sovereign he served and with the senate of which he was to the end a venerated member; it may never be given to another man after such a career to preserve even to the last the full possession of those great faculties with which he was endowed, and to carry on the services of one of the most important departments of the state with unexampled regularity and success, even to the latest day of his life. These are circumstances, these are qualities, which may never again occur in the history of this country. But there are qualities which the Duke of Wellington displayed of which we may all act in humble imitation: that sincere and unceasing devotion to our country; that honest and upright determination to act for the benefit of the country on every occasion; that devoted loyalty, which, while it made him ever anxious to serve the crown, never induced him to conceal from the sovereign that which he believed to be the truth; that devotedness in the constant performance of duty; that temperance of his life, which enabled him at all times to give his mind and his faculties to the services which he was called on to perform; that regular, consistent, and unceasing piety by which he was distinguished at all times in his life: these are qualities that are attainable by others, and these are qualities which should not be lost as an example.'

A public funeral was of course decreed; and never in any country was such a solemnity celebrated. The procession was planned, marshalled, and carried out, with a discretion, a judgment, and a good taste, which reflected the highest honour on the civil and military authorities by whom it was directed. Men of every arm and of every regiment in the service, for the first and last time in the history of the British army, marched together on this occasion. But what was more admirable still was the conduct of the incredible mass of sympathetic spectators, who had congregated from all parts of the kingdom, and who formed no insignificant proportion of its population. From Grosvenor Gate to St. Paul's Cathedral there was not one foot of unoccupied ground; not a balcony, not a window, that was not filled; and, as far as could be observed, every face amidst that vast multitude wore an expression of respectful sorrow. An unbroken silence was maintained as the funeral cortège moved slowly and solemnly forward to the mausoleum prepared to receive the remains of England's greatest warrior in the centre of the stupendous masterpiece of Wren's architectural genius.

The recess continued till the 10th of February. Various questions occupied the attention of the legislature, without exciting much general interest, and without producing any very appreciable result: persecution of Protestants in Tuscany; the state of our relations with France; the consideration of an address which the city of London had sent to the French Emperor, and in which it was accused of trenching on the diplomatic functions which belonged to the government; a motion for inquiring into the education afforded to the students of Maynooth College. A bill dealing with the clergy reserves of Canada, in accordance with the wishes and recommendations of the colonial legislature, was fully discussed in both Houses, and adopted after a sharp struggle. The question of Jewish disabilities was again decided in favour of the Jews by the Commons, and against them by the Lords. An important bill on the subject of education was introduced by the government, but not proceeded with.

On the 8th of April Mr. Gladstone, as chancellor of the exchequer, brought forward a plan for the reduction of the national debt. This plan he submitted to the House in the form of fifteen resolutions. It consisted of three portions, which he fully and lucidly explained. By the first he proposed to liquidate certain minor stocks—the South-Sea stock, the old and new South-Sea annuities, Bank annuities of 1726, and three-per-cent. annuities of 1751—the total amount of which stocks was about 9,500,000*l.*, made up of stocks which differed only in denomination, and thus perpetuated a needless complication in the debt. He proposed that these stocks should either be converted into new securities or paid off, at the option of the holders; and he calculated that if by this operation the interest on these sums was reduced by a quarter per cent., the permanent annual saving to the country would be 25,000*l.* per ann., and that if the stocks were paid off, the saving would be still greater. His next proposal was to operate on exchequer bonds in such a way as would secure, if his anticipations should be fulfilled, a saving of one per cent. The third part of his plan was to effect the voluntary commutation of the three-per-cent. consols, and the three-per-cent. reduced, amounting altogether to 500,000,000*l.*, into one or other of two new stocks which he proposed to create, and which would be as like each other as possible in their conditions, so that the fundholders would probably be induced to take portions of both.

After this plan had been criticised favourably by Mr. Hume and several members of the radical party, and unfavourably by Mr. Disraeli and some of his principal followers, the resolutions were submitted to the House, and adopted by it.

On the 18th of April the chancellor of the exchequer made his financial statement in a speech of great ability, which, though occupying five hours in the delivery, was listened to from its commencement to its close with careful attention and unflagging interest.

The revenue of the financial year, which Mr. Disraeli had estimated at 51,625,000*l.* really amounted to 53,089,000*l.*; the expenditure, estimated at 51,163,000*l.*, had, in fact, only reached the sum of 50,782,000*l.*, thus leaving a surplus of 2,460,000*l.* But before considering how much of this amount would be available for the remission of taxation, it was necessary to announce the calculated expenditure for the year just commenced, which amounted to 52,183,000*l.*; so that three-fifths of the surplus was already disposed of. Mr. Gladstone estimated the amount of the revenue for the year 1853—4 at 52,990,000*l.*, giving an apparent surplus of 807,000*l.*; but he urged that, on account of the uncertainty of some of the items, it would be better to take it at 700,000*l.*, and of this sum about 220,000*l.* consisted of money which did not proceed from permanent or recurring sources. Mr. Gladstone next considered the question of the retention of the income tax. He pointed out what great things it had enabled the government and the legislature to effect, and how much loss, and how heavy an accumulation of debt, would have been avoided if it had been resorted to at an earlier period. Speaking no doubt with a mental reference to dangers which were impending, he exclaimed, 'It affords you the means, should unhappily hostilities again break out, of at once raising your army to 300,000, and your fleet to 100,000, with all your establishments in proportion: and much as may be said of the importance—in which I concur—of an army reserve and a navy reserve, I say this fiscal reserve is no less important; for if it be used aright, it is an engine to which you may resort, and with which, judiciously employed, you may again, if need be, defy the world.' This apostrophe elicited a tremendous cheer of approbation, which was not without a political significance. After thus dealing with the income-tax question, Mr. Gladstone next entered upon a very full and detailed examination of the proposal, so often urged, to draw a distinction between precarious and realised incomes, and between incomes derived from trades and professions; and he exhibited very clearly the almost absolute impossibility of drawing in practice the distinction which was contended for between these two classes of incomes. The government proposed to renew the tax for two years from April 1853 at the present rate of 7*d.* in the pound, and for two years more from April 1855 at 6*d*. in the pound, and from April 1857 for three years more at 5*d*. in the pound: so that it would expire altogether on the 5th of April 1860. But in order to enable ministers to accompany the present renewal of the tax with a farther relief from taxation, it was proposed to make it more productive by extending it down to a class of persons who were exempt from it. Hitherto the tax had only been paid by persons whose incomes amounted to 150*l*.; henceforth an income tax of 5*d*. in the pound was to be imposed on persons whose incomes were between 100*l*. and 150*l*. for the whole time that the tax was to be continued. Ireland had profited largely by the remission of taxation which the income tax had enabled the government to make; it was therefore very reasonably determined that Ireland should at length be made subject to the tax, and it was expected that this would yield an additional annual sum of 460,000*l*. By alterations he proposed to make in the legacy duties, Mr. Gladstone expected to realise 500,000*l*. for the year 1853—4, and no less than two millions for the year 1856—7, and this would probably become a part of the permanent revenue of the kingdom. He brought forward certain specified changes in the duties on Scotch and Irish spirits, and proposed to relieve Ireland from the consolidated annuities, amounting to 4,500,000*l*. After this enumeration of the taxes he intended to impose, Mr. Gladstone entered on the more agreeable task of announcing those he hoped to remit. In the first place, he stated that he contemplated the entire remission of the duties on soap, which would involve a net loss of revenue amounting to 1,111,000*l*., and for the current year of 771,000*l*. He would reduce the tax on life assurances from 2*s*. 6*d*. to 6*d*. He intended to substitute a uniform penny receipt stamp in the place of the stamps varying according to the sum received, which had hitherto been used. The duty on apprenticeship was lowered from 20*s*. to 2*s*. 6*d*. Reductions were also made in the taxes on solicitors' certificates and the articles of apprenticeship of solicitors, on hackney and other carriages, horses, dogs, post-horses, tea; in a word, 133 different taxes were to be reduced, and the total amount of the remissions of taxation which it was proposed to make was estimated at

5,384,000*l*. Four days before Mr. Gladstone made his statement, a motion made by Mr. Milner Gibson, one of the representatives of Manchester, for the abolition of the advertisement duty, had been carried against the government by a majority of 31. Mr. Gladstone announced that, before Mr. Gibson's motion was brought forward, the government had determined to reduce the advertisement duty from 1*s*. 6*d*. to 6*d*., and to repeal altogether the duty on newspaper supplements; and to this determination they adhered, in spite of the majority on Mr. Gibson's resolution. Mr. Gladstone entered into an elaborate statement of calculations leading to the conclusion that there was a reasonable prospect of really getting rid of the income tax in 1860. He then concluded the largest and certainly the ablest and most closely-reasoned financial statement which had ever been laid before the House with the following words:

'These are the proposals of the government. They may be approved, or they may be condemned, but I have this full confidence that it will be admitted that we have not sought to evade the difficulties of the position; that we have not concealed those difficulties either from ourselves or from others; that we have not attempted to counteract them by narrow or flimsy expedients: that we have prepared plans which, if you will adopt them, will go some way to close up many vexed financial questions, which, if not now settled, may be attended with public inconvenience, and even with public danger in future years, and under less favourable circumstances; that we have endeavoured in the plans we have now submitted to you to make the path of our successors in future years not more arduous; and I may be permitted to add that, while we have sought to do justice to the great labour community of England by furthering their relief from indirect taxation, we have not been guided by any desire to put one class against another; we have felt we should best maintain our own honour, that we should best meet the views of Parliament, and best promote the interests of the country, by declining to draw any invidious distinction between class and class, by adopting it to ourselves as a sacred aim to diffuse and distribute the burdens with equal and impartial hand; and we have the consolation of believing that by proposals such as these we contribute, as far as in us lies, not only to develope the material resources of the country, but to knit the various parts of this great nation yet more closely than ever to that throne and to those institutions under which it is our happiness to live.'

The various parts of the large and carefully-prepared plan of the chancellor of the exchequer were successively discussed, especially the income tax. The chief speakers in opposition to this feature of the budget were Messrs. Hume and Cobden, who argued for such a reduction in the expenditure of the country as would render the impost unnecessary; and Mr. Disraeli, who complained that the project of the chancellor of the exchequer was conceived in a spirit of injustice to the land. On a division the numbers were:

| | |
|---|---:|
| For the government plan | 323 |
| Against | 252 |
| Majority for ministers | 71 |

No sooner was this general question decided than Mr. Lawless raised another by moving that the words Great Britain should be substituted for United Kingdom; an alteration which would have had the effect of maintaining the exemption from the income tax which Ireland had hitherto enjoyed. In answer to the plea of continued distress, which was urged in favour of the maintenance of this exemption, it was justly replied, that those who were in distress would still be exempted, and only those who had incomes of more than 100*l.* would be liable to the tax. A long and almost riotous discussion followed; but the government plan was sustained. Several other amendments of less importance were proposed; but the recommendations of the chancellor of the exchequer, supported by a strong majority indoors, and wafted forward by a favourable breeze of popular confidence from without, were carried, with such modifications only as their author saw reason to admit. It was felt by all classes of persons throughout the country that its financial operations were directed by a master-hand: that the work which Peel had so ably commenced was being carried out by Gladstone, not in a spirit of servile imitation, but with a bold originality of conception and a happy force and eloquence of expression which placed him fully on a level with the lamented statesman whose work he was endeavouring to complete. The people therefore submitted cheerfully to the burden of a heavy and oppressive tax, in the full conviction that the continuance of it was necessary in order to enable the chancellor of the exchequer to place the national finances on a footing which would increase the wealth and promote the welfare of all classes of the community.

The session of 1853 was remarkable not only on account of the great and important financial reforms which it sanctioned, but also for its legislative activity, in which respect it contrasted strikingly with the two preceding sessions. Several important bills, among which we may mention a bill altering the law of transportation, and introducing the ticket-of-leave system, were carried. But the most important measure of the session was a bill for the future government of India, which was introduced and explained to the House of Commons by Sir C. Wood, in a speech which occupied five hours in its delivery. It is true that it was complained—and justly complained—by Mr. Bright, that the bill did not go far enough; that it only modified, and to some extent improved, a system of divided government, which ought to be altogether abolished. However, in spite of his arguments and those of other members, who took a similar view of the measure, it was felt that the alterations proposed were unquestionable improvements, and they were adopted by both Houses.

But if this session was marked by a considerable amount of legislative work, it was, like all other sessions, by no means free from legislative failures. A Jewish disabilities bill met with its accustomed fate; so too did a proposal for the improvement of the law of church rates; and in connection with this it may be mentioned that church rates virtually received their death-blow by the sentence of the House of Lords finally deciding the Braintree case in favour of those who appealed from the judgment of the court below, which decided that a minority might lay a rate against the will of the majority of the parishioners. A bill introduced by Mr. Chambers for the recovery of the liberty of persons confined in monastic and conventual establishments was opposed by the government on the ground that it proposed to interfere with those institutions in a manner calculated to give just offence to Roman Catholics. In the course of the debate on this measure Lord John Russell, speaking as the leader of the House, let fall some expressions which gave great offence to a large number of Roman Catholic members, and caused Messrs. Monsell, Keogh, and Sadleir, who held subordinate offices in the ministry to tender their resignation, on the ground that they could not honourably continue to serve under a government whose organ in the House of Commons had cast such offensive imputation on their church and religion. Thereupon Lord Aberdeen stated that he himself and many of his colleagues did not share the sentiments that Lord J. Russell had expressed in his speech, and begged the three gentlemen who had been offended by them to withdraw their resignations; which they accordingly consented to do.

Never, perhaps, had the condition and prospects of the nation been more satisfactory than they were during the later months of 1853. The parliamentary session had been fruitful of important measures. The ministry appeared to command general confidence, and to be likely to remain in office for a long time; the finances of the country, under the able management of Mr. Gladstone, were in a condition of progressive improvement; trade and manufactures were flourishing in almost all their departments. It was true that the harvest was not all that could be desired; but this was to a great extent compensated by the freeness with which corn could now be drawn from all parts of the world to supply the deficiencies of our own crops. The nation seemed to be entering on a period of unbounded prosperity and progress; but a dark cloud was slowly rising in the East, and casting its ominous shadows on the fair prospect.

It was from Russia more especially that it drew its blackness and its menacing character. During the period which had elapsed since the beginning of the fifteenth century, Russia had been running a career of eventful, but, on the whole, successful aggression and aggrandisement. At its commencement Russia consisted of the duchy of Moscow; but the sovereigns of that nucleus of future empire had pushed their conquests in every direction, until they had acquired a territory thirty times larger than that which had originally belonged to them. Immense tracts of country had been torn from Turkey, Persia, Sweden, and Poland; large nationalities had been incorporated into the dominions of the czar, who governed this prodigious empire with absolute and uncontrolled power.

In addition to this vast and continually extending temporal kingdom, the czar claimed to himself a still vaster spiritual dominion. He was the pontiff of the Russo-Greek church, exercising an authority like that claimed by the Pope, not only over his own subjects, but over numerous co-religionists in Greece, Turkey, and elsewhere; and he used his enormous political power to strengthen this spiritual authority. It was this claim that was the cause, or the pretext, of the events we are now about to relate as succinctly as possible.

The complications we have to trace had their source in a miserable squabble between Latin and Greek monks about what were called the holy sites; that is to say, the places which were traditionally regarded as the scenes of the Saviour's birth and sufferings; but the chief object of contention was the possession of the key of the great door of the church at Bethlehem, and the right to place a silver star in the cave or grotto in which it was alleged that the Saviour of the world was born, and which was covered by the sacred edifice. The Latins had already a key of a small door; but with this they were not satisfied, and desired to possess a key of the large door. Unfortunately the cause of the Greeks was supported by the Russian government, while that of the Latins was patronised by the new French government; each endeavouring by negotiations with the Porte to obtain the triumph of the party whose cause it espoused. The Russian government in all probability cared little about the squabble, and the French government nothing at all. But political considerations led both parties to press the matter with an earnestness out of all proportion to their real opinion of its importance. The Russian emperor was not disposed to yield an inch to the new French government, which he had reluctantly and ungraciously recognised; and the French emperor durst not allow himself to be humiliated by the czar. He knew that, in upholding the claims of the Latins he was maintaining a cause that was very dear to the majority of the French Catholics; and that nothing would be more likely to bring support to his government from the people of France, and especially from the liberal party of that country, now estranged from and hostile to him, than a firm attitude towards Russia. He knew that the French in general had not forgotten the disastrous retreat from Moscow, and that the French liberals in particular had neither forgotten nor forgiven the partition of Poland. However trifling, therefore, or unimportant the question between him and the Russian emperor might be, he could not venture to yield, and had the strongest possible motive for carrying his resistance even to the extremity of drawing the sword. There is, however, no reason to suppose that the French emperor was anxious for war. He seems, on the contrary, to have used every effort to bring the contest to a peaceful and honourable termination; but, having once entered on it, he could not draw back.

The sultan and his advisers, placed between these powerful antagonists, did their best to please both. They, of course, viewed the contest with Gallio-like indifference. They would gladly have given twenty keys, if by that means they could have satisfied the contending parties. But the polite contempt of the Mussulman was no match for the contentious obstinacy and wrong-headedness of the hostile Christians. The Turk wanted to keep out of the dispute; but the Latins and Greeks each pressed him to take their side. Unfortunately, in his anxiety to avoid offending either of the two parties he had recourse to artifices, which offended both. As the negotiations between the three parties were being carried on, the question of the holy sites unfortunately became complicated with another and still more dangerous question—that of the protectorate which the czar claimed over the Greek Christians in Turkey;—and this claim he pressed in the hope of obtaining at the expense of Turkey an extension of his already vast dominions, and an increase of his prodigious power; and, trusting in his proximity to Turkey, and the distance at which France was placed from it, he was disposed to carry matters with a high hand, and to set at defiance the remonstrances of the new French government.

But before taking this step he was anxious to secure the

neutrality of England, knowing that the English government considered itself bound by strong motives of interest and treaty obligations to uphold the integrity of the Turkish empire. Therefore, on the 9th of January, 1853, he began to sound Sir Hamilton Seymour, the British minister at St. Petersburg, on the subject, and he referred to it from time to time in a series of confidential conversations, in which he said that the sick man—meaning the Turkish empire—was dying, that it was, in fact, falling to pieces, and that some event was sure shortly to occur that would cause its dissolution. He did not desire that it should occur; but he could not prevent it, and he urged they ought to be prepared for the event. He did not want any agreement or treaty to be entered into on the subject, but such an understanding as would be binding among gentlemen. That if he could only have ten minutes' conversation with Lord Aberdeen, he was confident he could bring him over to his views. He said that he did not want Constantinople himself, and that he would not allow any other of the great powers to have it; but he was willing to allow England to take Egypt and the island of Candia; and he left it to be understood that we were to allow him to take some portion of the spoils of Turkey. Such were the chief topics of various conversations which he had with Sir Hamilton Seymour. To these overtures Sir Hamilton constantly replied in accordance with the uniform policy of the British government, that he must decline to enter into any consideration of an eventuality which had not yet occurred, and deprecated discussions which had a tendency to bring about the catastrophe to which they had reference.

Baffled in this attempt to bring over the British government to his views, the czar appeared for a time to have frankly abandoned his ambitious projects, and to be desirous of bringing the matter in dispute between himself and the sultan to an amicable settlement. Accordingly, he allowed a difference which had arisen with regard to the Christians of Montenegro to be arranged through the friendly intervention of the Austrian government, which was deeply interested in averting a war. However, the pacific intentions of the Russian potentate, if they really existed, did not last long. He determined to despatch an ambassador to Constantinople, and for this purpose he pitched on Prince Menschikoff. It would hardly have been possible for him to have made a more unfortunate choice. The prince was a soldier rather than a diplomatist; a man of violent temper and dictatorial demeanour, and who acted as if he had been sent rather to foment the existing quarrel than to assuage it. He came with a display of military and naval power which showed that he was intrusted with the means of supporting his negotiations, if needful, by force. His whole behaviour was that of a man who had come with the determination of picking a quarrel with the power to which he was sent. One of his first steps was to inflict an insult on Fuad Effendi, one of the sultan's ministers, which forced him to resign; and he was at once succeeded by Rifaat Pasha. His whole behaviour was of so haughty and menacing a character, that it produced a panic among the sultan's ministers, who, in their terror, appealed to Colonel Rose, then acting as *chargé d'affaires* in the absence of Sir Stratford Canning, the British ambassador. He took upon himself to order the Mediterranean fleet to come up to Vourlay, so as to be within reach, in case, as was dreaded, the Russian fleet should menace Constantinople. But Admiral Dundas, who commanded the British fleet, refused to obey the order, and it was disavowed by the English government. The knowledge that the order had been given encouraged the Porte in its resistance, and greatly provoked the czar; but the intelligence that it had been disavowed by the English government assuaged his anger; which, however, was again roused by the news that the French government had sent its fleet to Salamis. Meanwhile, Prince Menschikoff, having obtained a settlement of the question of the holy places, was still demanding the protectorate of the Greek church throughout the Turkish dominions. He offered the sultan the alliance of Russia, and promised a fleet and 400,000 men to support him against the western powers in case they should attempt to interfere with the proposed arrangement. He also insisted that these negotiations should be concealed from France and England. The Turk was far too jealous of his gigantic, powerful, and aggressive neighbour to put himself thus entirely into his hands; and though it would seem that some half promise of secresy had been given, the demands of Russia were divulged.

It was at this stage of the negotiations that Sir Stratford Canning, who had been absent from his post for nearly two years, was ordered to return to Constantinople. His long residence there had given him a more thorough acquaintance with all the questions at issue, and greater skill in treating them, than any other living man possessed; but this very circumstance enabled him to guide the policy of the government which he represented, even when he seemed to be most faithfully following out its intentions. The return of this able diplomatist to Constantinople was certainly unfortunate, because he was personally offensive to the Russian emperor, who had already inflicted on him the insult of refusing to receive him as ambassador. There is however no reason for supposing that the English ambassador allowed himself to be drawn aside from the path of his duty by a desire to mortify the man who had thus insulted him. It is certain that on many occasions he addressed to the government of the sultan counsels of moderation and prudence that they would have done well to follow. But though he appears to have conducted himself throughout the negotiations in a manner worthy of the representative of the British nation, this did not prevent the Russian emperor from suspecting that the adroit and skilful resistance which the Turkish government opposed to his demands was secretly inspired by the man whom he regarded as his mortal enemy, and by whom his diplomatic intrigues had been repeatedly foiled. Sir Stratford had been raised to the peerage by the title of Lord Stratford de Redcliffe, and thus came back invested with greater dignity than ever, an object of wondering awe and admiration to the Turks. He lost no time in entering into negotiations for the settlement of the question of the holy places with the French ambassador, who represented the Latin church, and the Russian ambassador, who represented the Greek church; and by his skilful management he brought about an arrangement which allowed each party to suppose that it had gained an advantage over the other, and wounded the susceptibilities of neither. Thus on the 22nd of April he had succeeded in removing altogether the original cause of the quarrel between the czar and the sultan.

But the former of these personages was deeply offended at the movement which the French fleet had been ordered to make, and which gave to the agreement about the holy places the appearance of a concession extorted by a menace. It was indeed too late to undo what had been already done; but the provocation made him more punctilious, more exacting, and less ready to listen to reason on the still unsettled question of the protectorate. On this point Prince Menschikoff was therefore instructed to insist very strongly; and in order to enforce the demand a large Russian force was gathering on the banks of the Pruth, and the Sebastopol fleet was prepared for sea. Prince Menschikoff, as might have been expected from his character, carried out his instructions in a very arrogant and dictatorial manner. The ministers of the sultan, advised by the English and French ambassadors, replied in language of studied courtesy and moderation; and thus with temperate firmness they resisted unreasonable demands offensively urged, making Turkey to appear to the world more completely in the right, and Russia more completely in the wrong, than they really were.

While these things were being done, the great powers of Europe were all seriously disquieted. Austria and Prussia especially had a much stronger interest in restraining the aggressive ambition of Russia than France or England; but they were less able to show their disposition to do so, because in the event of a war they were exposed to the attacks of that gigantic power, from which, owing to their naval superiority, France and England were altogether safe. Austria especially was deeply interested in preventing the Danubian provinces of the Turkish empire from being seized by Russia, because in that case a large portion of her own dominions would probably become an object of cupidity to that grasping power, and would be placed between two fires. For these reasons both Prussia and Austria, but Austria especially, were interested in counteracting the aggressive designs of the Russian emperor. Accordingly the representatives of the four great powers—England, France, Austria, and Prussia—held a congress at Vienna, and laboured to bring about an accommodation. They all agreed in the opinion that the Turkish government was right in the view it had taken of the question at issue; and they deputed the Austrian ambassador to make a last effort to avert the threatened attack on Turkey. The effort was unsuccesful; but it had the effect of placing the Russian ambassador more completely and conspicuously in the wrong. He broke off all negotiations, took down the Russian arms from the embassy, and quitted Constantinople. From this moment England was gradually drifting into war with Russia. The part that her ambassador had taken in encouraging the resistance offered by the Porte to the demands of Russia imposed on our government the duty of trying to shield Turkey from the consequences of conduct which we had to a certain extent counselled. It was hoped that Russia, finding how strongly her conduct was condemned by the public opinion of Europe, would draw back; and so, almost up to the last moment, those who enjoyed the best opportunities of insight into what was going on, incessantly repeated that there would be no war, nothing but an armed demonstration. However, to guard against the possible contingency of a sudden attack on Constantinople, the English and French governments, acting cordially together, ordered their combined fleets to enter the Dardanelles, and to be ready to obey any summons they might receive from their respective ambassadors at Constantinople. On the 3rd of May Count Nesselrode, on behalf of the czar, wrote a letter urging the Porte to accept without variation the note of Prince Menschikoff, and threatening that if this demand were not complied with within eight days, the Russian army would endeavour to obtain compliance with it by force. At the time when this demand was received the combined fleets were anchored in Besika Bay, at the mouth of the Dardanelles; and the government of the sultan, encouraged no doubt by its proximity, returned a firm but very courteous refusal to the Russian demands. Thereupon the emperor ordered his troops to enter the Danubian principalities; and on the 2nd of July they crossed the Pruth, their general assumed the government of the principalities, and enlisted a few soldiers in them. This was a very rash and ill-advised proceeding. In the first place, the invading army was thus put between the armies of Turkey on the south and those of Austria on the north and west, which might have been encouraged by promises of support from England and France to attack the Russians in the rear and flank, while the Turks assailed them in the front. In the second place, the czar, by occupying provinces of Turkey without actually declaring war, gave that power the opportunity of choosing her own time to attack the invading army. This step, as might have been anticipated, was strongly disapproved by the four great powers; nevertheless, they advised the sultan not to treat it for the present as a *casus belli*, but to hasten forward his preparations in such a way as to be able to meet the Russian army in case the outrage that had been committed should be persisted in. At the same time they addressed to Russia a collective protest against the occupation of the principalities; and hopes were still entertained that war would be averted. The English ambassador drew up a note having this object in view, to which he obtained the assent of the Turkish government. It was transmitted to Vienna, where the congress was sitting; but they, believing that it would not be accepted by the czar, substituted for it another note which it was ascertained that he would accept, and for which they endeavoured also to obtain the acceptance of the Turkish government. But the Porte was of opinion that this note contained expressions which virtually conceded the question of the protectorate, now the great bone of contention between them and the Russian emperor. They therefore proposed certain modifications of the note, which the czar would not accept.

Meanwhile, in Russia and Turkey the war-feeling was spreading, and was rapidly assuming that character which a dispute between two ignorant and fanatical populations might be expected to take. In the churches of Russia and the mosques of Turkey a crusade was preached with the most vehement enthusiasm. The two governments were pushed forward by the religious enthusiasm of the two nations; and it soon became evident that the continuance of the Russian troops in the principalities must lead to a war, and yet their withdrawal by the Russian government was daily becoming more difficult. Such steps once taken are not easily retraced. In a short time the popular feeling in Turkey had become such, that the Turkish government had to choose between war or a revolution certain to be followed by war. Under these circumstances it decided for war.

But it was not in Turkey only that the intelligence of the occupation of the principalities roused a strong popular feeling. It was condemned throughout Europe. Indignation against Russian insolence and Russian ambition prevailed everywhere, and nowhere more strongly than in England and France; so that at the moment when the Russian and Turkish governments were pushed forward by the populations they respectively governed, Lord Aberdeen and his colleagues had no other choice than that of either supporting Turkey against Russia, or resigning. But even this alternative was hardly open to them. The state of parties in the House of Commons was such as to render the formation of another ministry almost impossible; and Lord Aberdeen, after having presided over the negotiations which had been carried on up to the moment when war seemed imminent, could not honourably escape from the responsibility in which he was placed. Besides, his continuance in power seemed to be the best chance of peace; for of all the public men of the day he was the one,— with perhaps the exception of his colleague Mr. Gladstone, —who was most strongly opposed to war, and most resolutely determined to exhaust every means of conciliation before resorting to that last and greatest of evils. In the state in which the public opinion of England then was, his retirement from office must have at once led to the formation of a war ministry. He therefore sorrowfully and unwillingly remained at his post, drifting towards war, but struggling with all his force to avert that terrible calamity.

But if the position of the English government at this moment was delicate and difficult, that of the new French government was still more so. It did not possess the means of resisting the popular feeling against Russia that belonged to the older and more consolidated government of this country, and therefore it was carried towards war at a greater speed than our government, and the head of it was less disposed to stem the war torrent. It soon became evident to the people of this country that our government was lagging behind that of France, and was being dragged forward by her in a question which seemed to concern us much more nearly than our neighbours on the other side of the Channel. Yielding to the pressure thus brought on him from all sides, Lord Clarendon ordered the English fleet to proceed to Constantinople, in violation of the letter of a treaty made in 1841. It was indeed urged, that Russia had broken that treaty; but as Turkey had not at this moment declared war, it seemed that we had taken a step that was premature and unnecessary, even in the opinion of our own ambassador, who was certainly not disposed to lean to the side of Russia. Thus the *entraînement* of the French people and government acting on our government had led to another hostile step. We were drifting into war. In fact, it was very difficult for our government to know what course to take. It was impossible to tell whether a demonstration of force on our part would provoke the czar, or by alarming, dispose him to listen to reason. Too much backwardness on our part might do as much mischief as too much forwardness; for he evidently hoped that we would not go to war, and that hope had to a certain extent encouraged him in his arrogant proceedings.

While things were in this state, an event occurred which stimulated the war-feeling in England and France, almost to the pitch of frenzy. A squadron of Turkish ships was stationed at Sinope; a very superior Russian naval force had for some time been watching the harbour, to prevent the escape of this fleet, and had seized some Turkish vessels in the Black Sea. However, the emperor had hitherto abstained from striking a decisive blow; but news reached him that the Turks had captured the Russian fortress of St. Nicholas; that they were assailing Russia on her Armenian frontier; and that the combined fleets had reached Constantinople. He then determined to act while he could, and ordered an immediate attack on the Turkish fleet at Sinope. The admiral in vain appealed to his own government for assistance. The Sebastopol fleet advanced in order of battle; the Turkish ships made a gallant defence, but were soon destroyed; a great part of the town was also battered down, and it was reported that 4000 men had been killed. The tidings of this terrible vengeance produced a strong feeling in England; but Lord Aberdeen still stood out firmly against action which he feared would lead to war. Several of his colleagues, on the other hand, and especially Lord Palmerston, urged him to adopt a decisive course. A cabinet council was held as soon as the news of the disaster arrived; but the party of peace prevailed, and no resolution was adopted. Lord Palmerston then resigned, avowedly because the government intended to introduce a reform bill, really because he considered that a more vigorous policy ought now to be adopted towards Russia. But the public feeling would not bear this total inaction. The press strongly urged a more decided course; the government yielded, and it was determined that the British fleet should enter the Black Sea; not, however, for the purpose of attacking the Russians, but for the purpose of protecting the Turks, in order to do which they were to compel all armed Russian vessels to retire into the harbour of Sebastopol. The adoption of this measure satisfied Lord Palmerston, and he remained in office.

Thus England, under the influence of panic and passion, was being propelled and precipitated into a war which all parties desired to avoid, and which by judicious management might have been avoided still. And what was the reason of this? The chief cause, as it appears to me, is to be found in that secret and mysterious system of diplomacy, which did not prevent the English people from seeing much of what was going on, but which did not allow them to see the whole truth; which revealed to them the faults of the Russian emperor, but cast a mantle over the nearly equal faults of the Turkish government; which led the English to regard the czar as a monster of perfidy and ambition, when he really was a proud, indeed, but well-intentioned man, blinded by passion and fanaticism. If the whole truth had been clearly seen, the people of this country would probably have abstained from urging forward the government with that passionate vehemence which enabled the war party in the legislature and the cabinet to overcome the humane and prudent resistance offered by the prime minister. But the people saw the occupation of the provinces, the tragedy of Sinope, and other violent and foolish acts of the Russian government as through a lurid haze, and thus Lord Aberdeen was driven on towards a policy which he thoroughly abhorred. 'Here I am,' he exclaimed to his intimate friends, in the bitterness of his heart, 'with one foot in the grave, placed against my will at the head of the ministry, and forced on to that bloodshed against which, throughout the whole of my public career, I have hitherto successfully struggled;' and the old man wrung his hands in an agony of impotent despair. Like the doomed vessel which has entered the vortex of the Maelstrom, he was being drifted into WAR.

END OF VOL. II.

www.ingramcontent.com/pod-product-compliance
Lightning Source LLC
Chambersburg PA
CBHW022116290426
44112CB00008B/693